Techno-Social Systems for Modern Economical and Governmental Infrastructures

Alexander Troussov
The Russian Presidential Academy of National Economy and Public Administration, Russia

Sergey Maruev
The Russian Presidential Academy of National Economy and Public Administration, Russia

A volume in the Advances in Finance, Accounting, and Economics (AFAE) Book Series

IGI Global
DISSEMINATOR OF KNOWLEDGE

Published in the United States of America by
IGI Global
Business Science Reference (an imprint of IGI Global)
701 E. Chocolate Avenue
Hershey PA, USA 17033
Tel: 717-533-8845
Fax: 717-533-8661
E-mail: cust@igi-global.com
Web site: http://www.igi-global.com

Library of Congress Cataloging-in-Publication Data

Names: Troussov, Alexander, 1951- editor. | Maruev, Sergey, 1960- editor.
Title: Techno-social systems for modern economical and governmental infrastructures / Alexander Troussov and Sergey Maruev, editors.
Description: Hershey, PA : Business Science Reference, [2018]
Identifiers: LCCN 2017048750| ISBN 9781522555865 (hardcover) | ISBN 9781522555872 (ebook)
Subjects: LCSH: Data mining. | Big data--Social aspects.
Classification: LCC QA76.9.D343 T3643 2018 | DDC 006.3/12--dc23 LC record available at https://lccn.loc.gov/2017048750

This book is published in the IGI Global book series Advances in Finance, Accounting, and Economics (AFAE) (ISSN: 2327-5677; eISSN: 2327-5685)

British Cataloguing in Publication Data
A Cataloguing in Publication record for this book is available from the British Library.

Advances in Finance, Accounting, and Economics (AFAE) Book Series

ISSN:2327-5677
EISSN:2327-5685

Editor-in-Chief: Ahmed Driouchi, Al Akhawayn University, Morocco

MISSION

In our changing economic and business environment, it is important to consider the financial changes occurring internationally as well as within individual organizations and business environments. Understanding these changes as well as the factors that influence them is crucial in preparing for our financial future and ensuring economic sustainability and growth.

The **Advances in Finance, Accounting, and Economics (AFAE)** book series aims to publish comprehensive and informative titles in all areas of economics and economic theory, finance, and accounting to assist in advancing the available knowledge and providing for further research development in these dynamic fields.

COVERAGE

- Macroeconomics
- Accounting Standards
- Internet Banking
- International Economics
- Health Economics
- Economics of Innovation and Knowledge
- Managerial Accounting
- Economic Policy
- Taxes
- Applied economics

IGI Global is currently accepting manuscripts for publication within this series. To submit a proposal for a volume in this series, please contact our Acquisition Editors at Acquisitions@igi-global.com or visit: http://www.igi-global.com/publish/.

The Advances in Finance, Accounting, and Economics (AFAE) Book Series (ISSN 2327-5677) is published by IGI Global, 701 E. Chocolate Avenue, Hershey, PA 17033-1240, USA, www.igi-global.com. This series is composed of titles available for purchase individually; each title is edited to be contextually exclusive from any other title within the series. For pricing and ordering information please visit http://www.igi-global.com/book-series/advances-finance-accounting-economics/73685. Postmaster: Send all address changes to above address.

Titles in this Series

For a list of additional titles in this series, please visit:
https://www.igi-global.com/book-series/advances-finance-accounting-economics/73685

Agricultural Finance and Opportunities for Investment and Expansion
Augustine Odinakachukwu Ejiogu (Imo State University, Nigeria)
Business Science Reference • ©2018 • 236pp • H/C (ISBN: 9781522530596) • US $195.00

Regaining Global Stability After the Financial Crisis
Bruno Sergi (Harvard University, USA) Filip Fidanoski (University of New South Wales, Australia) Magdalena Ziolo (University of Szczecin, Poland) and Vladimir Naumovski (University American College Skopje, Macedonia)
Business Science Reference • ©2018 • 383pp • H/C (ISBN: 9781522540267) • US $215.00

Employment Protection Legislation in Emerging Economies
Samir Amine (Universite du Quebec en Outaouais, Canada)
Business Science Reference • ©2018 • 301pp • H/C (ISBN: 9781522541349) • US $195.00

Fractal Approaches for Modeling Financial Assets and Predicting Crises
Inna Nekrasova (Southern Federal University, Russia) Oxana Karnaukhova (Southern Federal University, Russia) and Bryan Christiansen (PryMarke, LLC, USA)
Business Science Reference • ©2018 • 306pp • H/C (ISBN: 9781522537670) • US $215.00

Regulation and Structure in Economic Virtualization Emerging Research and Opportunities
Denis Ushakov (Suan Sunandha Rajabhat University, Thailand)
Business Science Reference • ©2018 • 238pp • H/C (ISBN: 9781522549666) • US $145.00

Accountancy and the Changing Landscape of Integrated Reporting
Ioana Dragu (Babes-Bolyai University, Romania)
Business Science Reference • ©2018 • 303pp • H/C (ISBN: 9781522536222) • US $195.00

Foreign Direct Investments (FDIs) and Opportunities for Developing Economies...
Venkataramanaiah Malepati (University of Gondar, Ethiopia) and C. Mangala Gowri (University of Gondar, Ethiopia)
Business Science Reference • ©2018 • 315pp • H/C (ISBN: 9781522530268) • US $215.00

For an entire list of titles in this series, please visit:
https://www.igi-global.com/book-series/advances-finance-accounting-economics/73685

IGI Global
DISSEMINATOR OF KNOWLEDGE

701 East Chocolate Avenue, Hershey, PA 17033, USA
Tel: 717-533-8845 x100 • Fax: 717-533-8661
E-Mail: cust@igi-global.com • www.igi-global.com

Editorial Advisory Board

Table of Contents

Foreword xv

Preface xvii

Acknowledgment xxviii

Chapter 1
Computer Analysis of Texts in Social Networks, Its Method and Tools: State-of-the-Art Review 1
Pavel P. Makagonov, The Russian Presidential Academy of National Economy and Public Administration, Russia
Alexander Troussov, The Russian Presidential Academy of National Economy and Public Administration, Russia

Chapter 2
Studying the Big Data Paradigm in Dynamics of Its Advance 29
Pavel P. Makagonov, Russian Presidential Academy of National Economy and Public Administration, Russia
Amando Alejandro Ruiz Figueroa, University of the Sierra Sur, Mexico

Chapter 3
Set Classification 44
Ievgen Arnoldovich Nastenko, Igor Sikorsky Kyiv Polytechnic Institute, Ukraine
Oleksandra Olegivna Konoval, Igor Sikorsky Kyiv Polytechnic Institute, Ukraine
Olena Konstantinovna Nosovets, Igor Sikorsky Kyiv Polytechnic Institute, Ukraine
Volodymyr Anatolevich Pavlov, Igor Sikorsky Kyiv Polytechnic Institute, Ukraine

Chapter 4
Multicriteria Synthesis of Neural Network Architecture 84
Albert Voronin, National Aviation University of Ukraine, Ukraine

Chapter 5
Local Forum as a Knowledge Source 100
Pavel P. Makagonov, Russian Presidential Academy of National Economy and Public Administration, Russia
Celia Bertha Reyes Espinoza, Mixtec Technological University, Mexico
Oleg M Dzikun, Russian Presidential Academy of National Economy and Public Administration, Russia

Chapter 6
Using Online Data in Predicting Stock Price Movements: Methodological and Practical Aspects 125
František Dařena, Mendel University in Brno, Czech Republic
Jonáš Petrovský, Mendel University in Brno, Czech Republic
Jan Přichystal, Mendel University in Brno, Czech Republic
Jan Žižka, Mendel University in Brno, Czech Republic

Chapter 7
Vector Distribution of Limited Resources in Complex Systems 160
Albert N. Voronin, National Aviation University, Ukraine

Chapter 8
Mathematical Modeling of Information Warfare in Techno-Social Environments 174
A. P. Mikhailov, Keldysh Institute of Applied Mathematics, Russia
G. B. Pronchev, Lomonosov Moscow State University, Russia
O. G. Proncheva, Keldysh Institute of Applied Mathematics, Russia & Moscow Institute of Physics and Technology, Russia

Chapter 9
A Framework for Analyzing the Impact of Data Analytics and the Internet of Things on Digital Marketing 211
Dimitris K. Kardaras, Athens University of Economics and Business, Greece
Bill Karakostas, VLTN BBVA, Belgium
Stavroula G. Barbounaki, Merchant Marine Academy of Aspropyrgos, Greece
Stavros Kaperonis, Panteion University of Social and Political Sciences, Greece

Chapter 10
Enabling Small-Scale Actors to Operate on Markets of Energy and Ancillary Services 241
Mikhail Simonov, Instituto Superiore Boella (ISMB), Italy & European Commission, Italy
Luisa Tibiletti, Universita di Torino, Italy

Chapter 11
Techno-Social Systems in the Internet as a Tool for Social Adaptation of the Visually Impaired 295
Gennadi B. Pronchev, Lomonosov Moscow State University, Russia
Inna V. Goncharova, Lomonosov Moscow State University, Russia
Nadezhda G. Proncheva, Keldysh Institute of Applied Mathematics, Russia
Danila N. Monakhov, Lomonosov Moscow State University, Russia
Irina V. Vasenina, Lomonosov Moscow State University, Russia
Oksana G. Zubova, Lomonosov Moscow State University, Russia

Compilation of References 320

About the Contributors 341

Index 349

Detailed Table of Contents

Foreword xv

Preface xvii

Acknowledgment xxviii

Chapter 1
Computer Analysis of Texts in Social Networks, Its Method and Tools: State-of-the-Art Review 1
Pavel P. Makagonov, The Russian Presidential Academy of National Economy and Public Administration, Russia
Alexander Troussov, The Russian Presidential Academy of National Economy and Public Administration, Russia

Texts in virtual social networks differ cardinally from those of reviewed and edited publications, as being in fact the materials of non-moderated chat dialog having all the syntactic features, and in many cases, they are hypertexts with, as analysis subjects, quite relative boundaries. Instead of texts the virtual discourse, an object of new type is analyzed. In these conditions, the linguistic analysis is transformed into preliminary linguistic processing the texts and analysis of texts into the analysis of networks participants' interactions. Weak sides of linguistic processing both primary and pervasive are shown concerning the texts in social networks. Many problems appear when analyzing the texts as non-structured big data. A changing of used linguistic tools is linked with the reorientation onto new research customers: companies seeing the business interest in that, state structures, and even onto criminal structures using result of analysis for composing the texts aimed for manipulation of the consciousness.

Chapter 2
Studying the Big Data Paradigm in Dynamics of Its Advance............................29
Pavel P. Makagonov, Russian Presidential Academy of National Economy and Public Administration, Russia
Amando Alejandro Ruiz Figueroa, University of the Sierra Sur, Mexico

The study of the big data subject matter in its advance already has its own history. Assuming as a basis the content analysis of article abstracts on big data, using e-library stocks of Association for Computing Machinery (ACM) and Institute of Electrical and Electronics Engineers (IEEE), one succeeds to monitor the life cycle phases of the big data paradigm and distinguish the stages of developing programs and algorithms from the technology update, including applications and their advanced renewals. In order to carry out the analysis, it is proposed to approximate the curves of cumulative frequencies of words, obtained from the corpus of texts by means of cubic parabolas, their parameters being in good concordance with ones of logistic curves.

Chapter 3
Set Classification..44
Ievgen Arnoldovich Nastenko, Igor Sikorsky Kyiv Polytechnic Institute, Ukraine
Oleksandra Olegivna Konoval, Igor Sikorsky Kyiv Polytechnic Institute, Ukraine
Olena Konstantinovna Nosovets, Igor Sikorsky Kyiv Polytechnic Institute, Ukraine
Volodymyr Anatolevich Pavlov, Igor Sikorsky Kyiv Polytechnic Institute, Ukraine

The classification problem where each object is given by a set of multidimensional measurements that is associated with an unknown dependence is considered. Intersection of sets that define objects from different classes is allowed. In this case, it is natural to found classification algorithms based on the difference between dependencies for the objects belonging to different classes. Two algorithms to convert the set classification problem solution from the initial feature space into (1) the parameters space of the common model structure for all the objects and (2) the parameters spaces of the best structures for each class are proposed, along with a classification algorithm based on the accuracy of object representation by the models based on the structures found for each class. If the objects are described with big data, the approach can be used to transform data into a compact form (model parameters) that preserves the characteristics that are necessary to separate the classes. An approach to solve a problem of clustering sets is proposed. Some examples are given.

Chapter 4
Multicriteria Synthesis of Neural Network Architecture....................................84
Albert Voronin, National Aviation University of Ukraine, Ukraine

Statement of a problem and procedure of vector optimization of the neural-network classifier architecture is considered. As a criterion function, the scalar convolution of criteria under the nonlinear scheme of compromises is offered. Search methods of optimization with discrete arguments are used. The example, neural-network classifier of texts, is given.

Chapter 5
Local Forum as a Knowledge Source 100
Pavel P. Makagonov, Russian Presidential Academy of National Economy and Public Administration, Russia
Celia Bertha Reyes Espinoza, Mixtec Technological University, Mexico
Oleg M Dzikun, Russian Presidential Academy of National Economy and Public Administration, Russia

An internet forum can be used as a crowdsourcing tool for searching for new knowledge and the latest non-standard ideas being a result of forum members' joint creative work. On the basis of these regularities, criteria of the forum maturity in processes of its formation and advance are elaborated. Basing on these results on a 2015 analysis of the forum, formed on the ground of the Universidad Tecnologica de la Mixteca (UTM), the State of Oaxaca, Mexico, a moment when the forum reaches its maturity was revealed. These conceptions are suitable for forming a thesaurus and taxonomy prototype of socio-cultural, environmental, and economic problems in Mixteca region. In its turn, a forum thesaurus gives opportunities for the regional community to understand a degree of its involvement into revealing and discussing the most actual regional problems on the internet.

Chapter 6
Using Online Data in Predicting Stock Price Movements: Methodological and Practical Aspects 125
František Dařena, Mendel University in Brno, Czech Republic
Jonáš Petrovský, Mendel University in Brno, Czech Republic
Jan Přichystal, Mendel University in Brno, Czech Republic
Jan Žižka, Mendel University in Brno, Czech Republic

A lot of research has been focusing on incorporating online data into models of various phenomena. The chapter focuses on one specific problem coming from the domain of capital markets where the information contained in online environments is quite topical. The presented experiments were designed to reveal the association between online texts (from Yahoo! Finance, Facebook, and Twitter) and changes in stock prices of the corresponding companies. As the method for quantifying the association, machine learning-based classification was chosen. The experiments showed that the data preparation procedure had a substantial impact on the results. Thus, different stock price smoothing, the lags between the release of documents and related stock price changes, levels of a minimal stock price change, different weighting schemes for structured document representation, and classifiers were studied. The chapter also shows how to use currently available open source technologies to implement a system for accomplishing the task.

Chapter 7
Vector Distribution of Limited Resources in Complex Systems 160
Albert N. Voronin, National Aviation University, Ukraine

The problem of distribution of the given global resource of the system under the constraints imposed on individual resources is considered. It is shown that the problem lies in constructing an adequate objective function for optimization of the resources distribution under their limitations. For solving the considered problem, the multicriteria optimization approach is undertaken with the nonlinear trade-off scheme. The proposed nonlinear compromise scheme has the property to adapt to the situation of multicriteria decision-making. The adaptation to the situation of a nonlinear scheme is carried out continuously, while the traditional selection of compromise schemes is done discretely that adds to subjective errors the errors, associated with the quantization compromise schemes. Model examples are given.

Chapter 8
Mathematical Modeling of Information Warfare in Techno-Social Environments 174
A. P. Mikhailov, Keldysh Institute of Applied Mathematics, Russia
G. B. Pronchev, Lomonosov Moscow State University, Russia
O. G. Proncheva, Keldysh Institute of Applied Mathematics, Russia & Moscow Institute of Physics and Technology, Russia

The chapter discusses a number of mathematical models of information battle in techno-social environments. Some models take into account such battle factors as the mass information media's incomplete coverage of the society, the individuals' acquisition of the information only after receiving it twice, the individuals' forgetting the information, a priori bias to support a party to the battle, and polarization of the society. For simpler models, the results are described in brief. For more complicated ones, mathematical research has been conducted with the sociological interpretation of the results.

Chapter 9
A Framework for Analyzing the Impact of Data Analytics and the Internet of Things on Digital Marketing..211
Dimitris K. Kardaras, Athens University of Economics and Business, Greece
Bill Karakostas, VLTN BBVA, Belgium
Stavroula G. Barbounaki, Merchant Marine Academy of Aspropyrgos, Greece
Stavros Kaperonis, Panteion University of Social and Political Sciences, Greece

The proliferation of the internet of things will open up new opportunities for implementing the digital transformation of businesses. Available data is expected to rise in unprecedented levels of quantity with the IoT playing an important role towards that end. Data analytics techniques will provide businesses with refined pieces of information in almost all aspects in both B2C and B2B context, thus refining services design and customization with more flexibility and options that focus right at the heart of consumers' needs. Digital marketing depends on these developments. This chapter aims at proposing a framework for analyzing the implications of data analytics and IoT on digital marketing.

Chapter 10
Enabling Small-Scale Actors to Operate on Markets of Energy and Ancillary Services...241
Mikhail Simonov, Instituto Superiore Boella (ISMB), Italy & European Commission, Italy
Luisa Tibiletti, Universita di Torino, Italy

Widespread renewable energy alters infrastructures and business by changing a way to balance between the demand and the offer. In customer-centered model, flexible economic behavior of small-scaled energy actors mitigates variability and uncertainty in flows of power and energy. Flexible cooperative behavior of many intraday market participants has a potential to reduce uncertainty in renewable energy flows. However, owners of small-scale renewable energy plants play limited market role. This chapter presents changed socio-economic and technology contexts and attracts attention to new challenges. New ICT enabler activates role of small-scale renewable energy actors by complementing their physical energy by structured information about the capacity and flexibility. In new market scenario, unpredictability of renewable energy is reduced by adding knowledge and exploiting better flexible behavior. Main conclusion is about using the information about flexibility to activate small-scale actors on real-time markets while improving ecological sustainability.

Chapter 11
Techno-Social Systems in the Internet as a Tool for Social Adaptation of the Visually Impaired.......295
Gennadi B. Pronchev, Lomonosov Moscow State University, Russia
Inna V. Goncharova, Lomonosov Moscow State University, Russia
Nadezhda G. Proncheva, Keldysh Institute of Applied Mathematics, Russia
Danila N. Monakhov, Lomonosov Moscow State University, Russia
Irina V. Vasenina, Lomonosov Moscow State University, Russia
Oksana G. Zubova, Lomonosov Moscow State University, Russia

The chapter deals with issues related to social adaptation of the visually impaired in techno-social systems of the internet. The current legislation providing access for visually impaired people to such techno-social systems is analyzed, as well as the way the legislation is implemented. Traditions and innovations in the field of accessibility of techno-social systems for visually impaired people in Russia are discussed. The opportunities of the electronic banking system of the European Union and Great Britain for the visually impaired are analyzed.

Compilation of References.......320

About the Contributors.......341

Index.......349

Foreword

We live in a world of permanent technological revolution. Digital technologies are a way of boosting productivity, of transforming our societies to sustainable flourishing and of making them more peaceful and just.

It is widely accepted that the growth of the digital economy, the economy that is based on digital computing technologies, has already widespread impact on the whole economy. The digital economy is growing at 10% a year—significantly faster than the global economy as a whole (Boston Consulting Group). Digital transformations affect the whole world, change business models and relationships between business and the state.

Information and communication technologies are main drivers in the creation of information society, have profound effect on all aspects of social organization, including the economy, education, health, warfare, government and democracy.

Techno-social systems, including web-based collaboration tools (such as Facebook, Twitter, blogs, and wiki systems) and proprietary databases having records of actors' activities (like customs declarations for commercial goods), are important drivers of the digital transform. The editors of this book have included content here about the most exciting and current technologies for the use of Techno-social systems in Digital Economy and Society. A good job has been done on the balancing the relevant theoretical aspects of the data mining (including neural networks and mathematical modelling), and use cases across various industries, sectors and geographies.

This book provides timely and up-to-date information about the state-of-the-art and best practices in the area of Techno-social systems for economical and governmental infrastructures, and will help both specialists and non-specialists understand the various technical and scientific advances and challenges, and apply described solutions to their own problems.

Vladimir Mau
The Russian Presidential Academy of National Economy and Public Administration, Russia

Vladimir Mau *was born on December 29, 1959 in Moscow. He graduated from Plekhanov Moscow Institute of the National Economy in 1981. After he carried out scientific researches at the Institute of Economics of the USSR Academy of Sciences, the Institute of Economic Policy of the Academy of National Economy under the USSR Cabinet, the Institute for the Economy in Transition (IET) and taught at Lomonosov Moscow State University, the State University - Higher School of Economics, and the Moscow Center of Stanford University. Since 1991 he participated in the development and implementation of economic reforms in Russia, including working as Advisor to the Chairman of the Russian Government from 1992-1993. In 1997 - 2002 Vladimir Mau was the Head of the Working Center for Economic Reforms of the Russian Government. In 2002, he became the Rector of the Academy of National Economy under the Government of the Russian Federation. In 2010 Vladimir Mau became the Rector of the newly formed Russian Presidential Academy of National Economy and Public Administration (RANEPA). The Academy was established in accordance with the Presidential Decree No. 1140 (September 20, 2010) and the Federal Government Decree No. 1562 (September 23, 2010) on the basis of the existing Academy of National Economy under the Government of the Russian Federation (ANE), the Russian Academy of Public Administration under the President of the Russian Federation (RAPA), and 12 federal educational institutions. Rector Mau is a renowned expert in the field of economic theory, the history of economic thought and national economy. He is the author of 25 monographs, books and textbooks published in Russia and the UK, as well as more than 600 other published works in Russian, English, French, German and Italian. The main results of Professor Mau's research focus on economic history and the history of economic thought in Russia and the USSR; the theory and history of economic policy, including the period of the New Economic Policy; the evolution of the economic system of the USSR; and the experience of reforms in its economic mechanisms. Particular emphasis is placed on analyzing contemporary Russian economic problems and long-term developmental trends. Vladimir Mau was one of the first to investigate the problem of the Russian constitutional economics and develop a new direction in the study of transformational economic processes. This became known as the political economy of reforms. The results of these studies are summarized in the essential monographs "In Search of balanced development: From the History of Development of Soviet Economic Thought in the late 1930s – early 1960s." (1990), "Economy and Power" (1995), "Economic Reform Through the Prism of the Constitution and Politics" (1999), "The Challenge of Revolution: Contemporary Russia in Historical Perspective" (2001), "Great Revolutions. From Cromwell to Putin" (in collaboration with I. Starodubrovskaya, 2001) "Reforms and Dogmas: 1861 - 1929. Government and Economy in the Time of Reforms and Revolutions" (2013). Vladimir Mau is also the editor-in-chief of the scholarly journal "Economic Policy"; chairman of the Editorial Board for the journal "Logos"; a member of the editorial board for academic publications such as "Economic Issues", "Journal of Economic Transition" (USA), "Finance and Business".*

Preface

INTRODUCTION

Nowadays, most of the digital content is generated within public and enterprise techno-social systems like Facebook, Twitter, blogs, wiki systems, and other web-based collaboration and hosting tools, office suites, and project management tools, as well as proprietary data bases. These applications have transformed the collaboration environment from a mere document collection into a highly interconnected social space, where documents are actively exchanged, filtered, organized, discussed and edited collaboratively. In these techno-social systems "everything is deeply intertwingled" using the term coined by the pioneer of information technologies Ted Nelson (Nelson, 1974): people are connected to other people and to "non-human agents" such as documents, datasets, analytic tools and concepts. These networks become increasingly multidimensional, providing rich context for understanding the role of particular nodes that represent both people and abstract concepts.

TECHNO-SOCIAL SYSTEMS, BIG DATA, AND DIGITAL TRANSFORM

In techno-social systems infrastructures are composed of many layers (such as Internet communication protocols, markup languages, metadata models, knowledge representation languages which have spanned over two decades) and interoperate within a social and organizational context that drives their everyday use and development. Abstract concepts become the foci of social interactions. Techno-social systems are primary generators of Big Data about actors, documents, events, and the relations between actors and the thing they create and do. The ability to automatically analyze the structure of techno-social spaces to discover local and global structures and to provide recommendations for decision making, becomes very attractive for organization, businesses and governing bodies.

Techno-social systems should be considered as a core part of Big Data and Digital transform paradigms. Techno-social systems, Big Data and Digital transform paradigms should be evaluated in the context of the data bases evolution. Since 1980s the dominant view of databases was that one type of databases is suitable for all types of data and applications. “The last 25 years of commercial DBMS development can be summed up in a single phrase: “One size fits all”. This phrase refers to the fact that the traditional DBMS architecture (originally designed and optimized for business data processing) has been used to support many data-centric applications with widely varying characteristics and requirements” (Stonebraker & Çetintemel, 2005).

Until the mid-1990s, the only market requiring databases, was business data processing, particularly operational transaction management. Then data warehouses came on the scene when the retail sector started to put historical sales data into a data warehouse. Enterprises started to look at business data processing as a potential input to any type of business decision (e.g., what can we offer a specific segment of our customers), not just decisions that were accounting-related (e.g., how did the business do last month). Just like Big Data today, it reflected a new attitude by business executives towards computer-generated data. All of a sudden, it became imperative to keep data in storage for a longer time (instead of deleting it) and to mine the data for new business insights.

What started in specific industries has spread, within a decade, to all sectors of the economy: “Since 2000, basically the entire world has realized that their data management problem is the same as the business data processing problem” (Press, 2015).

Techno-social systems bear most of the general characteristics of Big Data; for instance, in these systems frequently it is easier to predict agent’s actions than to explain them. Mining of techno-social systems constitutes a new distinctive branch of Business Information Systems.

This book covers theoretical and practical aspects of mining techno-social systems which have potential for creation of scalable methods, systems and applications for business, governance and economics.

THE CHALLENGE OF BUILDING IN-HOUSE SOLUTIONS

In her interview on key principles for designing business intelligence tools, Amy Gershkoff, who was at that time Director of Customer Analytics & Insights at eBay, contended that “off-the-shelf business intelligence tools do not meet the needs of clients who want to derive custom insights from their data” (Gershkoff, 2014). Therefore, medium-to-large organizations frequently go for building custom, in-house solutions. Solving of engineering problems of data integration might be a complicated task, however, in building of such solutions the focus is on Smart analytics. This book is do-it-yourself guide for building in-house solutions.

Of course, there are millions of various use-cases and analytic tasks, but the number of typical combinations of data models and algorithms probably can be measured by thousands, there are hundreds of building blocks consisting of only dozens of data models and popular algorithms.

To bring data to our formal reasoning we need first build data models adequate to the mining tasks. Identification of the most generic models applicable for many data types and mining tasks, will simplify knowledge transfer between various domains and will reduce cost of building and maintenance of the software solutions.

In other words, if you can't use somebody's else solution, and go for building in-house solution, there is an increased need for borrowing and reuse of tried-and-tested data models and to benefit from knowing the solutions built on these models. The bigger the area covered by a particular model, the bigger are the chances for successful reuse of the solutions, tried-and-tested in other fields.

ABOUT MODALITIES OF DATA SETS USED IN ECONOMIC RESEARCH AND PUBLIC ADMINISTRATION

In this book the focus is on two interrelated areas – national economies and public administration. The quest for finding appropriate data models for a particular domain invites considerations on salient features of data in this domain, which in turn requires understanding of data modalities (see Lahat et al., 2014).

Techno-social systems play an ever-increasing role in the functioning of national economies and in Public Administration.

For instance, mining of Internet forums is essential for functioning of Public Administration.

Many data sets and mining tasks on the surface are quite different and seemingly are unrelated to techno-social systems. "Big Data frequently come in tabular form of rows and columns of numbers, special codes and short textual descriptions, in strict structured, disciplined formats generated by a variety of transactional and operational business systems" (Maruev et al., 2014b). For instance, customs declarations for commercial goods have a tabular form where each column describes a particular feature of the declaration, including the traders, the carrier, the type of the goods, etc. (Maruev et al., 2014a).

Collections of customs declarations also have different nature, different modality, and different use than the documents in techno-social systems which are exchanged, filtered, organized, discussed and edited collaboratively. However, deep mining of customs declarations involves the same tasks and application of the same methods as in the mining of techno-social spaces: discovery of patterns of relations between the actors (such as traders, carriers, insurers, customs officers), the artefacts of the international trade (such as the nomenclature of goods, taxation, convoying of transports, etc.), and the terms used in goods description. Many tasks, like checking if textual descriptions of goods match digital codes in the nomenclature of goods, could be addressed by measuring network connectivity of nodes representing words and commodity codes in a network model of customs declaration data.

We identify the two most ubiquitous modalities of data sets used in economic research and public administration:

1. Natural language textual descriptions;
2. Records of actors' activities.

THE IMPORTANCE OF GENERALIZATION IN BUILDING COMPUTATIONAL MODELS

Data sets in these domains describe complex systems, many mining tasks are "directed to understanding the structure and functioning of complex systems at various size scales. … It is more important to understand the organizational principles of such systems on the basis of their connectivity than to understand the role of their individual components" (Estrada, 2018).

Network models lend themselves as an adequate tool to study such complex systems; and network models for techno-social systems proper, understood in the most exact sense of this term, become almost undistinguishable from the network models of such complex systems (Maruev et al., 2015).

In case of techno-social systems proper, like Twitter or Facebook, the interactions between actors happen within these technical system. In case of customs declarations, interactions between actors typically happen outside of the system, the system only has records about these interactions.

The path of the human mind is essentially inductive: that is to say, it goes from the real to the abstract. The understanding of the general should be conquered as a higher degree of something already known and easier, that is to say as a 'generalization'. (Giovannini, 1942)

COMPUTATIONAL MODELS OF TECHNO-SOCIAL SYSTEMS

Building and processing of data models requires certain generalization of a mathematical type. Generalization which provides the shift of attention from individual cases to all the possible ones, as well as the extension and adaptation of the model to any of them. David Hilbert, one of the most influential and universal mathematicians of the 19th and early 20th centuries, said that "The art of doing mathematics is finding that special case that contains all the germs of generality" (Reid, 1970).

In this book the focus is on the mining of the data, not on the engineering problems of functioning techno-social system. When we move to data models, distinctions regarding the media of communications (within or outside the system) might become irrelevant. The fact that both modalities (1) and (2) are present is important. In this book we want to put many use cases, involving processing of natural language data combined with the data about actors' activities, under one heading of Techno-social systems. The use of this umbrella term might simplify knowledge transfer between various domains, and reduce cost of building and maintenance of the software solutions.

ORGANIZATION OF THE BOOK

The book is organized into 11 chapters. A brief description of each of the chapters follows.

Chapter 1 is titled "Computer Analysis of Texts in Social Networks, Its Method and Tools: The State-of-the-Art Review". In this chapter a study is represented of social networks language features, object under studying being not well edited text of the only author, but many short sayings and not large comments, where besides a text other means of expression are used, when the literacy level is not important and deviations from the grammar norm even are used like an expression mean to underline the status of saying author. In that connection requirements are changing to text study instruments along with notions about studied object boundaries, especially taking into account the hypertext nature of discussions in social networks. The chapter is of review kind and suitable for both an acquaintance with problems of linguistic studying the social networks texts in the Internet and software developers with an objective to take into account the language heterogeneity in the boundaries of the only object under studying.

In Chapter 2, titled "Studying the Big Data Paradigm in Dynamics of Its Advance", it is shown that on a basis of the studying the life cycle initial stage for close subject field it is possible to predict with high accuracy the ending time of main development stages for this subject field. It is useful when planning the financial supporting the chosen direction researches and their practical applications. Time distribution of curves for accumulated frequencies of words in articles on themes of this field was taken as basic model. For more broad Big Data knowledge field the dynamic model pointed has far complex cumulative nature. However studying the homogeneous word clusters singled out inside this theme is available to reveal sub-fields, where timelines of passing their life cycles stages can be estimated too.

Chapters 3-4 describe important methods for mining techno-social systems. Chapter 3 offers an approach for a very large problem class of decision making under ambiguity. It is assumed, that an ambiguity can be overcome if the object is described not by a single, but by a set of observations, each of which is recorded in different environmental states. The set, obtained in such circumstances, is unique and represents detailed information for reasoned decision making. The authors present a range of algorithmic instruments for decision making, which operate on structures and parameters of models, obtained through observation sets of classification objects. If objects are described by Big Data, the suggested approach can be used for transformation of data into compact form (model structures and parameters). These data maintain the object properties, which are necessary for decision making. An approach to solve a problem of clustering sets is proposed. The approach method is illustrated by a number of examples. This study appeals to students, researchers and specialists in decision-making spheres of modern economical and governmental infrastructures or any other area, where classification is necessary on the basis of object monitoring results or image processing.

Chapter 4 establishes the need for optimization of multicriteria synthesis of neural network architecture. An artificial neural network can serve as a part of a techno-social system for modern economical and governmental infrastructures. It is inspired by the way biological nervous systems, such as the brain, process information. Artificial neural networks, like people, learn by example. It is configured for a specific application, such as pattern recognition or data classification, through a learning process. Neural network classifiers are an important kind of artificial neural networks. They are applicable in technical and medical diagnostics, classification of various information sources, etc.

The author presents a method for choosing the optimal neural network architecture that ties up such contradictory criteria as 1) the misclassification probability and 2) the time it takes to train the neural network. Generally, realization of considered in-process stages of vector optimization allows determining such architecture of neural network classifier, at which the contradictory criteria of efficiency of its functioning are systemically tied up, and the resulting architecture is compromise-optimal.

The chapter should be useful for specialists in the study of complex systems and students in related disciplines.

Chapters 5 and 6 deal with mining of on-line text sources. Chapter 5 presents an analysis of Internet forums (online discussion sites where people can hold conversations in the form of posted messages) concerned with themes actual for only one geographical region or a close social community. Internet forums of this type do not pursue the generality of the audience, their objective is in resultant looking for efficacious solutions of local problems as at scanty forums the life cycle of a message is longer comparing with large social networks. A local forum message becomes interesting for the "meaty" study only when most of the comments for it will be received. An Internet forum can be used as crowdsourcing tool to search for new knowledge as a result of forum members' joint creative work. So it is important to determine the moment when a discussion on local or close social problem is near to solve it. To analyze the success of forum work it's desirable to be sure, that a degree of maturity for forum is reached. On the basis of regularities derived for bonds among objects of the complex system, criteria of the forum maturity are elaborated. Using these results, a moment was determined, when the forum of the Technological University of the Mixteca in Mexico reaches its maturity. As was shown, a corpus of texts at that forum devoted to local problems has holistic features. To simplify the consideration of diverse authors' messages on one theme a transition from forum frequency dictionary to the word-combinations (bigrams), linked with a forum subject matter, were revealed. These conceptions are suitable to form a thesaurus and the taxonomy prototype for socio-cultural, environmental and economic problems in region of the Mixteca, Mexico. The forum thesaurus opens opportunities to study a degree of involvement of regional community into debate of the actual regional problems in the Internet.

Chapter 6 debates about methodological and practical aspects of using online data in predicting stock price movements.

A lot of research has been focusing on incorporating the vast amount of online available data into models of various social and economic phenomena. The data generated not only by domain experts but also by ordinary people can provide a new perspective and potentially complementary information to conventional quantitative evidence. The data often comes from non-traditional and contemporary information sources and environments, like social networks or microblogging sites. Typically has this data a form of unstructured texts that are published by different types of subjects, without the time and spatial limits. Because a large amount of data is often freely available, finding proper methods for collecting, storing, and analyzing it must be found and systems implementing them need to be developed. The chapter focuses on one specific problem coming from the domain of capital markets where the information contained in online environments is quite topical. The information contained in online environments can help, e.g., in explaining less rational factors as influential for asset pricing and capital market volatility. The chapter presents the result of experiments that were designed with the goal of revealing the association between texts published in online environments (Yahoo! Finance, Facebook, and Twitter) and changes in stock prices of the corresponding companies at a micro level. As the principal method for revealing and quantifying such association, the machine learning-based classification was used. From the experiments, it was obvious that the data preparation procedure had a substantial impact on the results. Thus, different stock price smoothing approaches, the lags between the release of documents and related stock price changes, levels of a minimal stock price change, different weighting schemes for the structured document representation, and various classification algorithms were studied. It has been found that at least part of the movement of stock prices is associated with the textual content when selecting a proper combination of data processing parameters. The chapter not only describes the theoretical background of the domain, methods, and results but also shows how to use currently available open source technologies to implement a system for accomplishing the task.

In Chapter 7, the problem of such resource distribution of the controlled system between the individual elements (objects) is considered, which provides the most effective functioning of the system as a whole. The problem of allocating of limited resources is a main problem of economics. It is believed that the proper distribution and redistribution of resources – this is just the economics. Similar problems arise in other subject areas, in particular, in techno-social systems for modern economical and governmental infrastructures. The art is to allocate properly limited resources, depending on the circumstances. In simple cases, the problem can be solved subjectively, on the basis of the experience and professional qualifications of a decision maker. However, when there is a large number of objects and for important cases, the price of the error of management decisions sharply increases.

The author presents an analysis of the development of the formalized methods of decision making support, for competent resource distribution between objects, taking into account all the given circumstances, which in important cases becomes urgent. In the present Chapter, for solving the considered problem, the approach of multicriteria optimization, using the nonlinear trade-off scheme, is used.

The chapter should be useful for specialists in the study of complex systems and students in related disciplines.

Chapter 8 is devoted to the problem of analysis of information processes in a society. The main attention was paid to information warfare in techno-social environments. The authors proposed a number of mathematical models that describes affect to the result of information warfare. Different parameters were analyzed, such as polarization of a society, propaganda, etc. Some sociological interpretation is given for the results of the mathematical analysis. For example, moderate political polarization favors the side that runs more intensive propaganda. However, the advantage of stronger propaganda is impaired if the polarization is great enough, because neither media nor individuals can reassure their radical opponents. The results are interesting and useful from practical point of view. For example, this can help in carrying out the most effective agitator or advertising campaign. The chapter will be useful for students and researchers in various fields: applied mathematics and mathematical modeling, sociology, politology, modern economical and governmental infrastructures. The paper will also be useful to political technologists and marketers, who organize agitation companies.

Chapter 9 addresses the need to systematically analyze and evaluate the impact of the Internet of things (IoT) and data analytics on digital marketing. It introduces the concept of the IoT, its enablers and its adoption inhibitors and presents its potential in digital marketing. This chapter proposes a framework that draws on the Virtual Value Chain and the Customer Service Life Cycle models and illustrates how data analytics techniques can be used to analyze the masses of data that users generate on the Web. Real time data regarding customers' behavior can be collected from the network of interconnected IoT devices. It suggests that this data can be represented as a graph of interrelated digital marketing Key Performance Indicators (KPIs). Data analytics can be used to analyze the interrelationships of KPIs and develop highly personalized digital advertising content to the right customer, at the right time, utilizing the most appropriate digital media. This chapter utilizes the DEMATEL multicriteria method in order to exemplify the proposed approach. This chapter is useful for both academics and professionals in the areas of digital marketing and data analytics.

Chapter 10 addresses the issue of inclusion of small-scale actors in the renewable energy use scenario. The authors argue that the transition to the 100% renewable energy scenario imposes the adoption of fully decentralized control approach, which has impact in terms of security of supply of intermittent energy flows. Therefore, authors discuss about the technology enablers supporting the transition towards such a scenario and the techniques supporting business operations.

The authors suggest that the flexibility can be adopted at the demand-side in the generation-led energy scenario in order to optimize collectively intermittent energy resources.

This chapter will be useful to experts in energy informatics, in energy markets, to energy engineers, to students, and to general public, especially to people interested in Modern Economical and Governmental Infrastructures, for example e-energy Infrastructures, so called "Smart Grids", to people that use Multi-Agent Systems for collective resource optimization, and to general public interested in better efficient energy use.

Chapter 11, titled "Techno-Social Systems on the Internet as a Tool for Social Adaptation of the Visually Impaired", is devoted to the problem of the barrier-free environment creation. The authors undertook a serious work on study of techno-social systems, created on the basis of multimedia Internet technologies, which can be a very effective means of smoothing social inequality for the visually impaired. The paper reviews the virtual social environments existing in Russia and used for the visually impaired, the regulatory framework for the support of disabled people. A historical sociological digression into the research problem was made. The comparative analysis of the barrier-free environment in Russia, the European Union and Great Britain is of particular interest, that undoubtedly made the article more interesting and relevant. Chapter of the book is of great interest for specialists dealing with the problems of social stratification of modern society, the use of techno-social systems for smoothing this social stratification. The paper will also be useful to economists working on problems of increasing the economic efficiency of socially-oriented business.

Alexander Troussov
The Russian Presidential Academy of National Economy and Public Administration, Russia

Sergey Maruev
The Russian Presidential Academy of National Economy and Public Administration, Russia

REFERENCES

Estrada, E. (2018). *Applications of Networks to Real-World Problems*. Retrieved from http://www.estradalab.org/

Gershkoff, A. (2014). *Interview: Amy Gershkoff, Director of Customer Analytics & Insights, eBay on How to Design Custom In-House BI Tools*. Retrieved from https://www.kdnuggets.com/2014/07/interview-amy-gershkoff-ebay-in-house-BI-tools.html

Giovannini, A. (1942). L'errore nelle matematiche. Periodico di Matematiche, 4(22), 57-65.

Lahat, D., Adali, T., & Jutten, C. (2014). Challenges in Multimodal Data Fusion. *22nd European Signal Processing Conference (EUSIPCO-2014)*, 101-105.

Maruev, S., Stefanovsky, D., Frolov, A., Troussov, A., & Curry, J. (2014a). Deep Mining of Custom Declarations for Commercial Goods. *Procedia Economics and Finance, 12*, 397–402.

Maruev, S., Stefanovsky, D., Frolov, A., Troussov, A., & Curry, J. (2014b). Multidimensional Networks for Heterogeneous Data Modelling. *Proceedings of the International Conference on Intelligent Information and Engineering Systems INFOS 2014*, 67-77.

Maruev, S., Stefanovsky, D., & Troussov, A. (2015). Semantics of Techno-Social Spaces. In J. Zizka & F. Darena (Eds.), *Modern Computational Models of Semantic Discovery in Natural Language*. IGI Global. doi:10.4018/978-1-4666-8690-8.ch008

Nelson, T. (1974). Computer Lib/Dream Machines. Self-Published.

Press, G. (2015, July 20). Turing Award-Winner Stonebraker On The Future Of Taming Big Data Forbes. *Forbes*. Retrieved from https://www.forbes.com/sites/gilpress/2015/07/29/turing-award-winner-stonebraker-on-the-future-of-taming-big-data/2/#64779c7a19a7

Reid, C. (1970). *Hilbert: With an appreciation of Hilbert's mathematical work by Hermann Weyl*. Springer-Verlag Berlin Heidelberg. doi:10.1007/978-3-662-28615-9

Stonebraker, M., & Çetintemel, U. (2005). "One Size Fits All": An Idea Whose Time Has Come and Gone. *21st International Conference on Data Engineering (ICDE'05)*. 10.1109/ICDE.2005.1

Acknowledgment

The editors would like to acknowledge the help of all involved in the collation and review process of the edited book, without whose support the project could not have been satisfactorily completed.

We wish to thank all of the authors for their insight and excellent contributions to this edited book.

Thanks go to all those who provided constructive and comprehensive reviews. Although all reviewers provided invaluable contribution to selection, developing and compiling quality research articles for publication, some of the reviewers must be mentioned as their reviews set the benchmark. Reviewers who provided the most comprehensive, critical and constructive comments include Gennadi B. Pronchev of Lomonosov Moscow State University, Igor Varlamov of National Defense University of Ukraine, Islam Choundhury of Kingston University, London, Marco Mussetta of Politecnico di Milano, Sergey Mostovoy of National Aviation University, Ukraine, Marek Miśkowicz, Polish Academy of Science (AGH), Ilias Petrounias of the University of Manchester, Natalia L. Smakotina of Lomonosov Moscow State University, and Olga G. Proncheva, Keldysh Institute of Applied Mathematics (RAS) and Moscow Institute of Physics and Technology (SU), Russia.

Special thanks also go to the publishing team at IGI Global, whose wise guidance throughout the whole process from inception of the initial idea to final publication has been invaluable. In particular, Marianne Caesar, Mariah Gilbert and Jan Travers at IGI Global for their assistance with development of the proposals and plans and who carefully and gently reminded us that our project milestones were due.

Finally, we would like to thank members of our families, including Tatiana, Olga, Alexander, Tatiana, Maria and Ekaterina who provided encouragement, support, patience, and strength throughout.

Alexander Troussov
The Russian Presidential Academy of National Economy and Public Administration, Russia

Sergey Maruev
The Russian Presidential Academy of National Economy and Public Administration, Russia
January 2018

Chapter 1
Computer Analysis of Texts in Social Networks, Its Method and Tools:
State-of-the-Art Review

Pavel P. Makagonov
The Russian Presidential Academy of National Economy and Public Administration, Russia

Alexander Troussov
The Russian Presidential Academy of National Economy and Public Administration, Russia

ABSTRACT

Texts in virtual social networks differ cardinally from those of reviewed and edited publications, as being in fact the materials of non-moderated chat dialog having all the syntactic features, and in many cases, they are hypertexts with, as analysis subjects, quite relative boundaries. Instead of texts the virtual discourse, an object of new type is analyzed. In these conditions, the linguistic analysis is transformed into preliminary linguistic processing the texts and analysis of texts into the analysis of networks participants' interactions. Weak sides of linguistic processing both primary and pervasive are shown concerning the texts in social networks. Many problems appear when analyzing the texts as non-structured big data. A changing of used linguistic tools is linked with the reorientation onto new research customers: companies seeing the business interest in that, state structures, and even onto criminal structures using result of analysis for composing the texts aimed for manipulation of the consciousness.

DOI: 10.4018/978-1-5225-5586-5.ch001

INTRODUCTION

Texts found in virtual social networks fundamentally differ from those found in publications that have been subjected to editing and reviewing processes. Social network texts are texts that are retrieved from non-moderated chat-dialogue and that have specific syntactic structure. In many cases, they are hypertexts that have notional boundaries when taken as objects of research analysis. When researchers shift from the analysis of professionally created texts to the analysis of texts that are created by Internet users in a variety of virtual social networks, they face challenges associated with both research object and the shift in the pragmatic character of (research customer) expectations related to the research results. Texts created in virtual social networks have their own specific characteristics in terms of authorship, stimuli and agendas for altering vocabulary as well as of the ways they convey meaning, employ specific grammar and select topics for discussion.

The tools of linguistic analysis were developed a long time ago with the primary focus on the lexical analysis of literary fiction, authentication of the texts authorship and, later, creation of computer-assisted translation and automated text referencing and indexing. With the rapid development of mass media, new goals for linguistic analysis emerged: processing large volumes of text, creating and indexing large e-libraries, speech recognition, information searching, computer-assisted document classification and referencing, computer managed linguistic processing, creating online dictionaries, constructing linguistic processors to ensure users' communicating with automated intellectual systems, and extracting fractographic information from informal texts, to name but a few. A significant change in linguistic analysis, its tools and objectives was stimulated by the sharp increase in the volume of information found on the Internet (proliferation of news channels, e-libraries, non-structured texts stores, anti-plagiarism software development, etc.) All this, coupled with the use of computer technologies and networks, led to the change in the linguistic analysis toolkit. Pre-processing services became available and the field of corpus linguistics flourished. When applied to the above-mentioned tasks, the linguistic analysis toolkit relies on a systematically developed theory and is complemented by specific software.

The development of social networks prompted the need to revise the methods of computer linguistic analysis given the new object of research and its new tasks. Before the appearance of the Web, computer linguistic research related to the area of corpus studies could have focused, for example, on the work of a specific writer. A social network on the Internet (or a virtual context) comprises many users, who, united by a common goal or interest, create their content. Specific "thematic" online forums, that have recently experienced rapid development, likewise belong to this category. In his "Socio-Dynamics of Culture," Moles (2008) divided society into readers and writers. Currently, with the emergence of social networks, the volume of material written by the former readers far outstrips the amount of material published in official publications, either literary or scientific. The texts created by such "readers" can be easily lost unless special search algorithms are applied.

GENERAL CONTEMPORARY APPROACH TO SOCIAL NETWORKS ANALYSIS

The development of social networks is viewed by many representatives of the scientific community as a totally new phenomenon manifesting itself in culture, public life, sociology, and linguistics (e. g. "Internet Communication as New Speech Formation"). New research tasks are being solved with the methods relying on the study of graphs and networks, while tools employed in linguistics, in many cases, are used as auxiliary, interim stages in the general analysis of social networks. In the paper "Methods of Analyses of The Computer Social Networks," Batura (2012) defines the major directions in this area of research: structural, resource, normative and dynamic (with the key tools for analyzing the social networks being graph and stochastic models, models of network evolution, methods involving ontologies, structural and relational models, machine learning, graph visualization techniques, etc.). The feasible paths for further research are identified as the creation of a synthetic theory of social networks and a greater adaptation of language text processing to the network content.

In the meantime, by content analysis of the social network content, the author means the analysis of general information with arbitrary data types, text analysis, analysis of multimedia, sensory and data-flow analysis. Batura (2012), in turn, justifies the necessity of textual analysis information in social networks, by explaining that each social network node comprises a large scope of valuable data in different formats (e.g. posts, articles, blogs, etc.). Network content is, thereby, critical to the analysis of social networks especially for the purposes of classification or cauterization. Thus, for instance, searching someone inside a specific social network is somewhat identic to looking for a document in the vast database with many links. This is only one example of how text data can be processed as a part of a network analysis. The author does not speak about the development of linguistic methods used to analyze texts of messages in social networks, but only about adapting the already existing methods of research.

Let us turn to the paper "Analysis of Social networks: Methods and Applications" by Korshunov (2014) published in the Proceedings of the Institute of System Programming (ISP) RAS Automation & Comp Engineering that is a classic example of general research design for analyzing social networks in the paper. The keywords of the paper are a social network, social data, users' data, social analysis, social networks analysis, content analysis, Web services, micro-blogs, computer linguistics, graph theory, machine learning, distributed algorithms, and systems. The paper describes the basic components of ISP RAS technology stack for analyzing users' data from social networks. Special emphasis is placed on tasks, methods, and applications of the data analysis in the network (social connections among users) and textual (users' messages and profiles) data. This includes the identification of the users' demographic attributes, collecting descriptions of events in messages, identification of users of differing networks, identifying communities of users and measuring information impact among them. Moreover, the authors discuss approaches to receiving initial data for analysis, namely, collecting the real data by means of employing Web-interfaces of social services as well as generating random social graphs. They describe each developed tool in terms of its functionality, areas of application, and main steps of the used algorithms as well as the results of experimental research. From the standpoint of a general scheme of processing though, linguistic analysis is only one stage of processing and analysis of the social network texts.

Another view of the problem is offered by Gorchinskaya (2015) who highlights the pragmatic aspect of social networks analysis. Here, social networks are viewed as a "free" source for locating information about social networks members in order to solve a wide range of business tasks including but not limited to fighting counterfeiting and fraud, brand management, advertising of goods and services, and finding new markets. In her article, Gorchinskaya (2015) mentions that Big Data technologies provoked interest in searching for additional information about customers: their interests, social status, professional field, conjugal status, education level, social circle, musical preferences, and language use specifics. Such data extracted from social networks can be received indirectly and employed in various areas. For example, the problem of extending a client is solved in the following way: a company provides basic data about its clients (name, last name, birth date, the city of residence) and wants to find them based on this information. To solve this problem, it is necessary to collect data about each client from social networks, identify him or her, complete data, and create a uniform profile for each client.

Below is the description of the commonly employed scheme for analyzing textual information from social networks, engendering Big Data:

- Some text from a message is selected (perhaps, as a part of site monitoring);
- The lexical content of the text message is then compared to various dictionaries in several subject fields, as well as with different messages taken from Big Data store, news, and companies websites or from a corpus of texts connected to a particular author, publishing house or website.

- Information about the author or a website is extracted or the cluster that the author of the text message belongs to is identified based on this data set. The characteristics of the text are subsequently identified with the help of large databases and/or knowledge bases and are classified in terms of a particular cluster they belong to.
- In the latter case, the characteristics belong to specific subjects, encompassed by the site, genres, aspects of language style, tonalities of materials;
- Social networks graph, to which the author of the message belongs, is built or corrected based on all-encompassing analysis of all the data.

Here, the data or knowledge base is formed in advance in offline regime from a "natural source" as it is, or, as Gorchinskaya (2015) puts it, from a free source (the Internet), from the materials of a big social network or from a variety of specialized networks. This database is formed already using Big Data instruments such as MapReduce and Hadoop or, sometimes, their analogs, privately developed to solve specific problems on an individual computer. Big Data are stores of knowledge created as a result of preliminary work on information accumulation from a practically unlimited source - the Internet - with the help of machine learning and expert support in the fields including linguistics, psycholinguisticsб and sociology.

At this point, the discussion can cover not the linguistic analysis but the linguistic processing of texts coming from social networks. The term "analysis" is mainly referred to the final stages of the corporate activities in a particular area, whose products attract customers' interest. Linguistic processing is characterized by different levels (depth) and various functions. In technical documents and papers compiled by linguistic software producers, it is practically impossible to find detailed descriptions of linguistic processing of social networks texts. Certain advances made in methods and algorithms now generally become commercial products. In these papers, there are only some mentions of linguistic methods employed by commercial companies or descriptions of stages of texts processing that hint at a specific sort of processing that has been applied to particular texts. Thus, the notion of text analysis from social networks as an object of research significantly differs from a traditional idea of both the object of research and its methods. In the new paradigm of social networks research, texts play a notable, though an auxiliary role, compared to the members of such social networks. Here texts, to varying degrees, function as their authors' attributes, that help to study links in a network, but they are not considered as distinct systems that require separate research focus.

Systematic, detailed research of new problems in the field of linguistic analysis only takes its first steps. There is still no consensus regarding the minimum or maximum parameters of a text employed to solve a local problem or study a narrow subject field. In the initial period of studying social networks texts on the Internet, the largest unit for the study was the total content of a website or one of its parts. Currently, depending on research aims, a unit in linguistic analysis can account for the whole corpus of texts. For example, if it is necessary to localize a query in time or inside a community discussing a particular issue, or the speed of discussion topic changes, it is impossible to do this without comparing different texts within one or between several websites or at least within one forum topic. In this regard, the title of the paper "Constructing the Texts' Corpus for Tuning a Tonal Classifier" by Rubtsova (2015) speaks for itself.

Some papers take separate messages (posts) as objects of their research, others focus on the aggregate body of material produced by one particular blogger. However, the established opinion is that in virtual social networks the object of research is a hypertext united by a particular and well-commented theme with links and related citations. As all of the World Wide Web can be viewed as a unified hypertext, restrictions of spatial-temporal boundaries are proposed in order to include messages into the corpus of texts under analysis or into a collection of texts that were topically selected. At times net restrictions according to the "six handshakes" principles are mentioned, but the majority of these discussions are ignored and the task lies in analyzing materials of just one site or excerpts from one site or forum. Often small texts sizes (e.g. in Twitter) simply push researchers to analyze not one text but multiple exchanges of information on a particular topic. As a result of short text analysis, a new understanding of discourse connected to such texts has recently emerged. New problems have arisen in connection with new phenomena in social networks language. The degree of multi- and inter-disciplinarily research is increasing.

VIRTUAL DISCOURSE AND HYPERTEXT AS NEW OBJECTS OF LINGUISTIC ANALYSIS

Many linguists argue that virtual discourse should be considered as a form of communication that takes place in the context of multiple and fragmentary discourses which is constantly expanding and transforming into a hypertext. The text ability to adapt its linear structure to the non-linear one allows ensuring the functioning of the large volume of information in e-space. According to Ryazantseva (2010), a hypertext is interpreted not technologically but is understood as a specific discursive act, "specific type of creating and perception of written communication, forming a new rhetoric of intellective text and new functional stylistics", whereas its result is a semantic network of interrelated texts. She argues that hypertext properties include "specific information environment in which human learning and educational activities take place" as well as "communicative environment, that connects verbal and nonverbal forms of communication (multimedia space)" and lastly, "operative environment, that facilitates copying, altering and deleting text fragments, as well as creating the associative links among them" (ibidem).

Asmus (2005), in turn, mentions a new type of discourse characteristic of the present culture. The distinguishing traits of this discourse are its virtual nature and heterogeneous texts that compose it. According to Asmus (2005), these texts are associated with different discourses (political, scientific, domestic, etc.) and with different data formats (visual, audio, etc.). Her theoretical research results derived from analyzing graphic, lexico-semantic and syntactic means of expression, formalize many manifestations of texts features, connected to the influence of online discourse, characterized by its radical openness (of texts, data banks, link references) that gives participants the opportunity to add, alter and delete the initial text. Within the frameworks of this study, the most important conclusion reached by Asmus (2005) is that a phenomenon of changing the text model in the Internet-discourse still remains the subject of linguistic analysis independent from computerized research methods. Lexicographical studies rely on the "manual" text processing and conclusions are drawn on the basis of probative examples.

Experience of other authors shows that when they conduct manual text processing, they try to avoid situations, where the texts under investigation have heterogeneous content or authors. In this respect, only the materials of personal sites, especially blogs are selected for research and only the language aspects of the main author (blogger) are analyzed. When the study subject is language features of a semantic network, all the generalizations are made in regard to characterizing an average network participant without distinguishing them by language use models. Thus, being applied to social networks instead of texts analysis, virtual discourse becomes the object of the research. Virtual discourse is viewed as fusing text and context, linguistic and socio-cultural components. It is an object, whose tonality (emotional coloring) of messages and non-dialogue characteristics of participants are as important as its text component.

The contemporary Russian linguistics discourse is often approached from the standpoint of the activity theory approach. In this respect, discourse is structurally viewed as a totality of text and context, of linguistic and socio-cultural components. Rusakova (2007) distinguishes several approaches to interpreting discourse, citing numerous discourse analysis papers and inter-disciplinary research in this area: linguistic, semiotical, socio-communicative, post-modern and critical. Among these, two approaches of special interest in the frame of this research: a) approach connected with the linguistic analysis of texts, including socio-linguistics methods, cultural linguistics, cognitive-linguistics, lingo-synergetics and other areas of linguistics; b) approach based on socio-communicative interpretations of discourse.

According to Moroslin (2009), real-time electronic communication on the Internet represents a complex combination of various discourses: interpersonal communication (everyday discourse), official exchange of information and information queries (business discourse), and discussion of academic and scientific problems in newsgroups or at conferences (academic discourse). If a message contains an evaluation of some news event, one detects its "tonality" (emotional coloring analysis) and degree of similarity between positions of message and news piece authors, the result is then saved in the statistical generalization of discussion participants' opinions. Together with this, statistical data on ratings of goods and services are accumulated. In these conditions, linguistic analysis transforms into preliminary linguistic text processing and texts analysis itself transforms into the analysis of networks participants' interactions. Formation of the graph models becomes the main tool and linguistic analysis serves mainly for characterizing the connections among knots of graphs.

In order to corroborate the above-mentioned theoretical approaches, let us consider the results of several search queries into ACM e-library. The first query can be formulated as follows

linguistic +social +networks +analysis.

RESULTS OF CLUSTER ANALYSIS OF WORDS FROM TEXTS STORED IN E-LIBRARY ACM

Let us consider the result of cluster analysis of words from 94 texts extracted from the store of e-library at the Association for Computing Machinery (ACM), namely of ACM Digital Library (http://dl.acm.org/). The query consisted of the following words: +analysis +texts +social +networks +tool. For that collection of texts, the first 176 most commonly found keywords were selected, that were capable of forming word combinations-concepts (n-grams). Text files were grouped by the year of publication. As a result, all the rows of a resulting matrix of "word or word combination — texts of the same year" happened to be temporal rows according to the year of publication of the selected words.

Figures 1, 2 and 3 show temporal changes in word usage that are useful while analyzing them together, in terms of their correlation and frequency occurrence. They are also analyzed together to measure their correlation and even coincidence by the frequency of occurrence. Thus, in Figure 1, the words "social" and "network" have practically the same frequencies of occurrence by year. This proves that it would be correct to shift from analyzing words and their combinations obtained by joining words (well correlated in all the texts) into one concept, to n-grams analysis. However, among words with the highest frequency of occurrence (in 94 texts), there are such as GRAPH and NODE(S). This means that since 2012, social networks analysis has,

Figure 1. Matched growth of social networks, their graph analysis and machine learning methods over period 2011—2016

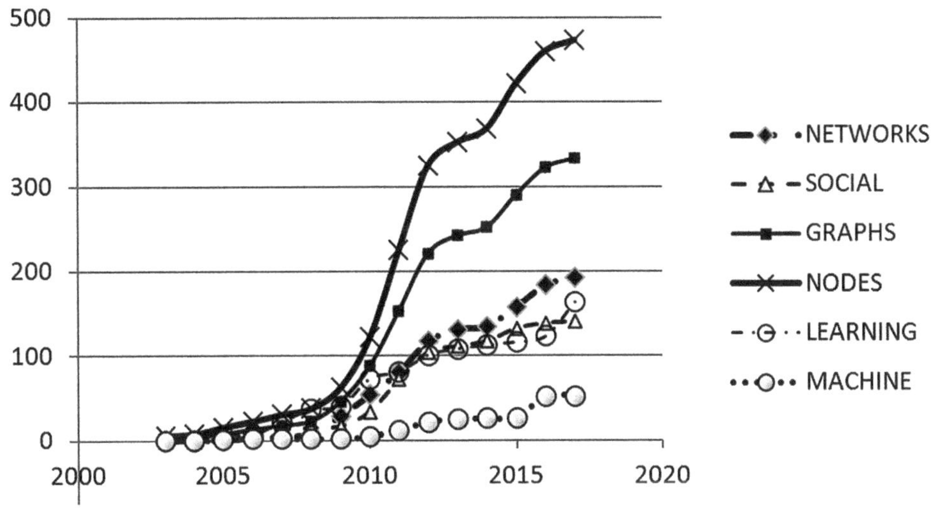

to a large extent, transformed into graph analysis. Good correlation of temporal rows for the above-mentioned words with the words MACHINE and LEARNING attests to transition (since 2012) to research methods which are not viewed as methods of linguistic analysis, but function as a superstructure built on these methods and are connected with the recognition of site users or site(s) attributes.

Figure 2 presents distributions for EVENT(S), FORUM VIRTUAL, DISCUSSION, FILTERING. Their behavior allows putting forward a hypothesis about the close correlation between mass-media discussions of some events and the corresponding increase of forum members' activity. The results of discussions may be moderated (filtered).

Figure 2. To discussion of news and actual events in networks over period 2011—2016

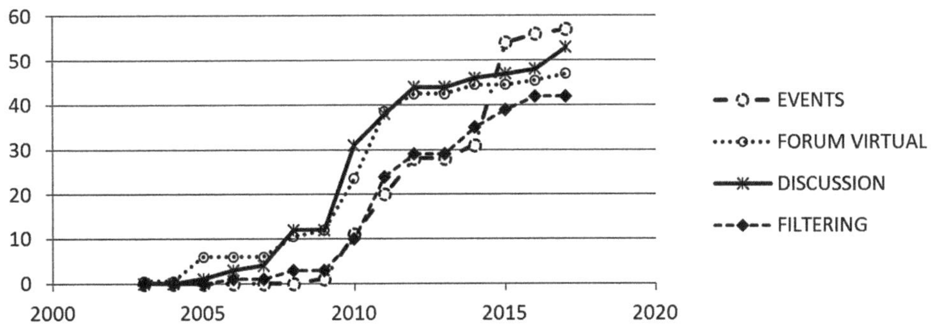

Figure 3 shows distributions for LATENT, KNOWLEDGE, INTERACTIONS, SNA. In this case, an abbreviation SNA stands for *social network analysis*, in addition, the abbreviation may stand for *social networking sites* or *social networking service*. From the same words, it is also feasible to assemble phrase-hypothesis like *«social networks analysis for revealing hidden links inside them»* given that social network analysis (SNA) is a process of studying not the texts, but social structures using graphs and network theory. Here individual actors, Internet users or social network objects function as network nodes, while connections and relationships between the participants' interactions function as arches or frames that link them. The most frequent terms in the first 94 most representative texts confirm the fact that linguistic analysis of social networks is fading in importance in the west, being replaced by social networks analysis which employs graphs. There has been an advent of commercialization and a shift of focus from research into the linguistic analysis of social networks to the development of pragmatic applications.

In the e-library of the Institute of Electrical and Electronics Engineers (IEEE), the area of linguistic analysis has been represented very poorly throughout the past three years. While searching literature using keywords such as "social networks texts linguistic analysis", a number of papers concerning both theoretical and applied research can be found, that have been previously published mostly in ACM. For instance, the above-mentioned query generates only two results:

1. Learning to Recommend Descriptive Tags for Questions in Social Forums. Found in ACM Transactions on Information Systems (TOIS). By Jialie Shen, Liqiang Nie, Tat-Seng Chua, Xiangyu Wang, Yi-Liang Zhao. Issue Date: 2014-01.
2. Maximum likelihood analysis of conflicting observations in social sensing. Found in ACM Transactions on Sensor Networks (TOSN). By Dong Wang, Lance Kaplan, Tarek F. Abdelzaher. Issue Date: 2014-01.

Figure 3. To discussion of hidden interactions in social networks

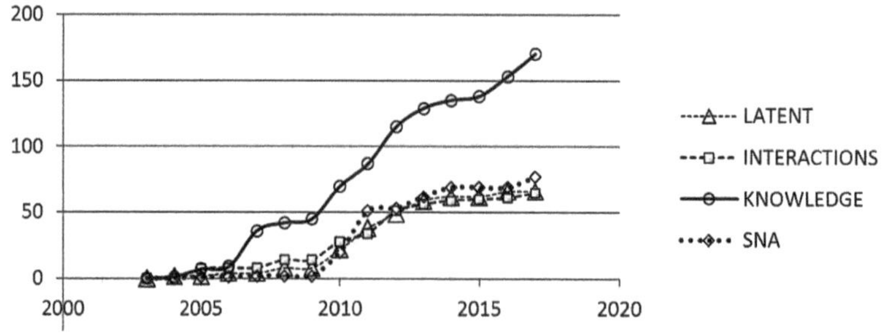

A more detailed search in ACM e-library, depending on the character of a search query, showed from 16 up to 282,116 results. Table 1 shows the summary of reports by queries in ACM.

As soon as the word combination "linguistic + tools"+ "social +networks" was deleted (combinations "linguistic + tools" or "social +networks" were preserved), the number of documents increased dramatically, indicating that themes (areas) were separate.

Next query in ACM e-library was limited by searching the articles published over the period of 2014—2017 using an only one-word combination: *discourse+linguistic+analysis.*

During that search, the authors selected the first 100 articles by their relevance and examined the correlation coefficient between the words discourse, linguistic, social network, parsing (or parser). It turned out that those texts had a negative correlation coefficient between linguistics and discourse: –0.363.05, and –0.22 between linguistic & social network. In the same texts correlation, coefficient between linguistic & content is almost zero but it can be negative as well: –0.013.72. At the same time, the correlation coefficient between the words discourse & parsing (resolving a sentence into its grammatical elements) and also parsing & social network were –0.414 and 0.405 correspondingly. This may attest to the interest in the analytical process of social networks sites content analysis, and in their use for data mining.

However, the interest in parsing is not connected with the subsequent analysis of textual information. The end result of parsing is an e-table or a database being initial material for analysis, including linguistic analysis. The discourse, where social networks are not present and linguistics is not involved is not the focus of the present study. Therefore, the specific focus should be placed on the analysis of Russian sources, where significant emphasis is placed on the toolkit of linguistic

Table 1. A summary of reports by queries into ACM

Search Queries	Results Found
+linguistic +tools +social +networks +analysis	16
linguistic+tool +social +networks +analysis	80
+linguistic +social +networks +text+analysis	1820
+linguistic +WEB +analysis	5430
+linguistic +social +networks +analysis	5500
+linguistic +text +analysis	8031
virtual +networks +text+analysis	6378
+social +network +text+analysis	6378
+tool+social +network +text+analysis	282,116

analysis of social networks texts. Thus, there is a gap in Russian research that lies not in program realization but in the scale of applying the program-algorithmic complexes to solving practical problems.

According to Moroslin (2009), it is possible to determine the following directions in the research field of Russian-speaking Internet:

- Analysis of online language in terms of its accordance to the norms of the standard Russian literary language and the influence of the latter on the former;
- Formation and functioning of special computer discourse in chats, blogs, and forums;
- Analysis of the hypertext systems and methods of their realization in the Russian-speaking Internet;
- Peculiar organization of Web-pages as a specific kind of text;
- Specific aspects of mass-media functioning on the Internet;
- Socio-linguistic and psychological aspects of Internet users;
- Specific aspects of the functioning of online literary fiction, its language, and style;
- Formation of computer terminology in the Russian language and features of professional computer slang.

These themes can be found in titles of algorithms and programs both in Russia and internationally.

REVIEW OF PROGRAMS FOR LINGUISTIC ANALYSIS AND TEXT PROCESSING

It is feasible to roughly divide the text analysis methods into three groups: statistical, linguistic and hybrid, where the last group comprises linguistic and the statistical stages of analysis in a different order. Statistical analysis of formal aspects, independent of text contents is effectively used by many researchers. Statistical analysis of network texts themselves may be preceded by content-analysis of a significant number of social networks, when a basic list of words is compiled, which is then searched for in a message or in a flow of messages. Further, the word search proceeds without linguists' participation. Therefore, at this stage, statistical methods and methods of recognition are used. Altogether, a hybrid technology of analysis emerges. While discussing this specific technology in scientific and engineering journals, the problems mentioned here, relate to the volumes of information stored, and even more to the insufficiency of "expert" database, lack of a systematic refilling capacity and the rate of thematic change. Thus, the output is the estimation of the rate of problem-solving and not the result.

Tests were not performed for the programs of real data social networks analysis listed below, so the authors rely on reviews of these programs contained in the following sources:

- (Ustalov, 2014), founder of NLPub project, report;
- Description of commerce program software for linguistic analysis and text processing, connected with the search portal AskNet (http://asknet.ru/products.htm);
- "Linguistics and Texts Processing" (Seleznev, 2013).

Apart from comparative descriptions of program products in the first two sources, there are links to program load modules from various parts of the world.

NLPub is a well-established set of tools used to analyze texts in social networks when solving the network current problems. The English version of NLPub description can be found here: NLPub:About. ("https://nlpub.ru/index.php?title=NLPub:Описание&oldid=1958"). A synopsis of NLPub toolkit linguistic resources contains brief characteristics of the resources dedicated to the following problems of texts treatment: graph analysis, morphologic analysis, syntactic analysis, spelling check, grammar check, hyphenation, concordance building, keyword extraction, automated referencing, thematic classification, thematic modelling, named essence extraction, relation extraction, tonality/sentiment analysis, information search, machine translation, integrated packages. Among others, there are also links to commercial products such as WordSmith Tools, AntConc Stanford CoreNLP, Pache OpenNLP, Twitter NLP and Part-of-Speech Tagger, NLTK, MBSP and PatternMBSP with the same functions. These resources, at the very least, allow building a linear frame of linguistic text processing in Russian, English and a series of other European languages, as well as to solve various applied tasks. In the NLPub–ATT project (automated text treatment), tools have been developed for text processing using a natural language. These tools consist of linguistic processors that take turns in the processing of the incoming text: when one processor starts operating, the other processor stops. The authors of the define four major components: graphematic, morphological, syntactical and semantic analyzers.

A wide range of problems is solved by means of Asknet (search) program products. It is a metasearch engine and Internet service for processing the meaning of non-structured text information and Internet-services with the same objective. The program products by Search are commercial search systems that search by queries using a natural language. They are created to realize complex intellectual processes of morphological, syntactical, semantic and statistical analysis of text information and users' queries.

The paper by Seleznev and Vladimirov (2013) is an unbiased critical overview, that, to some extent, relates to the problematics of social networks texts; some of the authors' comments regarding software usage technology are important for understanding the situation with social networks texts analysis. Notably, the authors criticize attempts to create universal analysis modules and suppose that "modules optimized for one task are not optimal for other tasks" meaning that the quality of the system performance is largely determined by the quality of the analysis. As mentioned above, the processing of the text occurs in several stages, with the output of one stage being transmitted to the input of the next stage. Here, it is necessary to point to a paradox: one and the same piece of input data can be associated with various possible results and, on the contrary, one and the same set of results can be associated with different pieces of input data. It follows, then that the scope of data increases largely with every new stage.

Seleznev and Vladimirov (2013) likewise argue that the so-called "canonical" text processing tasks can be addressed without specific machine linguistics. Thus, for instance, they refer to the example of spam filtering that involves sorting text documents by two criteria: spam or non-spam. In order to perform this task, a special form of machine learning is required that could analyze document content (words and phrases). Another way to perform the task is to check the source of the text document on its relation to the so-called "blacklist" that contains data about all the sources that deliver spam. The authors suggest changing the traditional scheme of the multi-stage work of text analysis by dividing it into two stages: first, performing a surface scan and identifying key fragments of the text; second, performing a detailed analysis with the use of a fundamentally different scenario, according to which the higher-level modules turn to the downstream modules in order to obtain clarifying information. For example, in the task of extracting information during surface scanning, references of persons are identified, and then the semantic module refers to the downstream syntax module with the query what links there are for each found mentioning.

It is also important to point out the relevance of tasks for VEB monitoring systems to eliminate intentional distortions, including the necessity to solve the problem of deobfuscation of words. These words were disguised by authors to avoid effective linguistic analysis of messages, that contain either an uncensored or destructive quality in terms of their impact on network participants. The authors call into question the possibility of creation and use of universal modules of computer linguistic analysis of texts, explaining, however, that many problems can be solved without accounting for the specific features of natural language. These remarks can be further seen in authors' works - reviewers of existing software.

Researchers of virtual discourse try to limit the scope of their inquiry down to the analysis of texts that do not have any significant differences in their language. Therefore, only the author's messages are subjected to linguistic analysis on personal websites or blogs, and this allows researchers to use the old analytical tools created before the era of social networks. Nevertheless, the contemporary linguistic analysis is carried out by means mainly suitable for the analysis of the "monologue par." (the texts created by a single author, usually a blogger (blog owner) or regular Twitter user). The language of the communicative space as the language of a fully-developed dialogue does not yet have universally recognized closed processing systems.

A considerable number of examples have been accumulated, that prove a limited usefulness of the linguistic analysis current purposes to carry out deep texts processing of social networks. In the (anonymous) paper "Normalization and Lemmatization of the Text Using the Thesaurus" (http://www.solarix.ru/for_developers/docs/text-normalization.shtml], section "Purpose of Deep Normalization Algorithm"), it is argued that "the normalization process realized in a grammatical dictionary, allows one to remove from the source text grammatical information (cases, numbers, verbal forms and tenses, voices of participles, gender, etc.), leaving only the semantic component (Koziev, 2010).

Further on, there is the argument against deep text normalization that is given as follows:

the other two algorithms – stemming and lemmatization - are trying to achieve the same effect, but the depth of text conversion in them is less. The other side of the coin is the more significant costs of computational resources are needed for performing all the stages of the deep normalization algorithm. (Koziev, 2010)

The frequent use of stemming instead of lemmatization only slightly worsens the statistics of the usage frequency, which can often be tolerated for the following reasons:

- As a result of the rejection of lemmatization in favor of stemming, the processing time of texts increases only slightly, if at all, moreover, this only concerns old words inherited from the old grammar, and old words are usually not so significant for interested social network members or social network viewers in specific subject areas;
- If statistics of words in the text from a given list are required, it is generally possible not to do text stemming, but only perform the stemming of words in a given list and count found words (with the help of a program) and whether it coincides in its core part with a stem from the given list.

The question arises as to the purpose of spelling check (if literacy can be a search factor in social networks). Correction of the text will deprive it of belonging to the social network, where even deliberate deviations from the rules of grammar are quite numerous and more than a thousand slangs of various kinds exist. In addition to this, certain problems arise in the analysis of texts that account for a large volume of unstructured data. If one considers a large fragment of the Web as a body of texts, then the problem of result representation arises. In respect to large corpora, the problem that was previously irrelevant grasps much more attention: search can produce hundreds or even thousands of results (of usage contexts) that are impossible to view within a limited period of time. The specific systems are being developed that allow to group search results and automatically break them into subsets (search results clustering) or issue the most stable word collocations together with the statistical evaluation of their significance in order to solve the above-mentioned problem. In the meantime, search for collocations, word combinations, n-grams, and not for the totality of words, still remains a tool for processing text corpora, though it is clear that multigrams are a more powerful search tool.

LINGUISTIC NEEDS FOR SEARCH ENGINES

Search algorithms on the Internet for queries are the result of the search engines' needs analysis. Big social networks have their own tools for the linguistic processing of social networks, but these tools (except for phenomenological manifestations) are a trade secret, and it is hardly possible to see any of meaningful discussion in publications. However, it is clear that in these algorithms there exist the necessary procedures for lemmatization as well as other stages of search flow and site-content processing, including social network sites.

Fuzzy search algorithms (also known as search by similarity or fuzzy string search) are the basis of spell checking systems and fully-fledged search engines like Google or Yandex (Kotov & Tselih, 2004). The resulting output, for example in Yandex, is formed by processing the history of the user's interests, as well as the record of the user's, ignoring of individual sites. In Google, hints are also formed based on the statistics of similar searches, although sometimes this leads to incorrect formulations regarding companies' or individuals' reputations. Often, hints are used to suggest the continuation of a query phrase based on statistics of queries with similar beginnings. Similarly, there are hints in which an attempt is made to replace a rare word (interpreted as erroneous) with the more common one, accompanied by the appeal "Perhaps you are looking ...".

A relatively new step in linguistic processing is stop-words filtering procedures. However, in addition to the obvious set of auxiliary words, the further increase in the words list excluded from search queries is determined by a subjective choice. Nevertheless, the procedure itself can be successfully implemented in the processing of the corpus of texts of narrow subject areas. There, this procedure facilitates the simplification of the text preparation for meaningful analysis. Indeed, almost all irregular verbs are ancient, often included in the Swadesh list, and therefore can be excluded from the content analysis. In this case, deep processing may be necessary. Moreover, in many cases, while retaining only the words belonging to a narrow subject area in the analyzed texts or when analyzing social network texts in small collections, different word forms only uncritically increase the volumes of frequency lists, but their retention improves the understanding of words in word combinations.

When lemmatizing (putting words into their standard dictionary form.), word combinations lose their meaning. When a deep normalization of the text takes place, including, for example, the conversion of verbal forms into nouns, a distortion of the text can occur to a level that does not allow restoring the meaning of the utterance. In the aforementioned anonymous work (for developers), "Lemmatizer" in the grammar dictionary presents a visual comparison of all the available types of lemmatization of a Russian text for the same sentence. There is a difficulty finding an adequate translation for a Russian text because the deep normalization results in losing the meaning of the entire utterance. However, given a very high degree of homonymy in the English language, readers can try to evaluate the results of normalization for phrases like *I play the best part of the play, and have a rest.*

LINGUISTIC PROBLEMS OF SOCIAL NETWORKS TEXTS RESEARCH

The texts of social networks have their own specifics related to online communication:

- They use mostly colloquial style, everyday vocabulary, lack thoroughness of formulation, allow for computer and network jargon; often, for the sake of compressing expressive means, they use ideograms, smileys, and special punctuation in the hope of matching their vocabulary and style with that of the recipient of the message;
- They are not subject to strict censorship and have special circumvention methods (obfuscation) of automated moderation and filtering;
- When it is not the case of "communication for the sake of communication," these texts contain condensed knowledge (cognitive component), suitable for the formation of a public opinion or a solution to a problem when crowdsourcing.

The linguistic study of the language may include:

- Research from the author's point of view (structural-semantic approach),
- Research from the point of view of the message recipient (communicative and psycholinguistic approaches), and
- Research from the position of the cognizer (discursive, cognitive and linguistic-cultural approaches).

It is necessary to use an integrated approach that takes into account all aspects of the linguistic problems of analyzing virtual discourse materials. From the standpoint of the authors and recipients of messages, an important role is played by publications related to the issues of text creolization, communicative mimicry, and the resulting problems of manipulating consciousness. From the standpoint of the linguists conducting research, literature related to the genres existing in social networks, cultural studies perspective and folksonomy are important.

Creolization of Texts and Communicative Mimicry in Social Networks

In "The Theory of Language," Asmus (2005) argues that "the rate of speech is close to its oral variety" and that those participating in chats are somewhat disadvantaged because they cannot use the real paralinguistic means such as speech timbre, accent, emotional connotation, voice timbre, gestures, and mimics, to name but a few. This disadvantage is partially compensated by standardized emotional codes called "smileys." Nevertheless, attempts to assign and fix the designation of certain emotional states for certain emoticons, were unsuccessful (Danilova, 2016).) Practice shows that smileys are only informing about the author's emotional attitude of the author, simply conveying the direction and strength of his or her emotions (notably, the look of the smiley does not matter). In addition to the "smileys" used for the timbre of voice compensation, the upper register (CapsLock) is used to accentuate parts of messages in virtual communication. A phrase or parts of it written in capital letters is interpreted as an increase in 'voice-volume'. The impossibility to transmit color, sound, movement via online communication is compensated by verbal and sign analogs - a large number of exclamation marks, the use of obscenities (most often transmitted using Latin letters), and other means from other speech genres.

In the works of Russian linguists, this phenomenon is called creolization, or, in some cases, text carnivalization (Asmus, 2005) and is examined in details. Since text creolization is a concept developed by Russian researchers, their definition of creolized texts is one of the most neutral and comprehensive. Thus, Nezhura (2012) defines creolized texts as the texts the textures of which comprises "two or more -

homogeneous parts (verbal language (verbal) and non-verbal (belonging to other sign systems, rather than natural language))." This definition emphasizes the multi-code character of such texts, a combination of symbols and various semiotic systems: a phenomenon which is flamboyant in terms of language design and carnivalesque in its nature (specific punctuation, mathematical symbols, the presence of emoticons and smileys.) The graphical heterogeneity of the text is used to explain the motivation for using graphic inserts in the text. The lexical-semantic means of expressing the carnivalesque are directed toward identification of "one's own" in the virtual world. The use of certain words and expressions becomes an ethical form and marks a user's belonging to a certain social group. In the context of online communication the identification of "one's own" is determined by speech behavior, such as the use of abbreviations denoting various concepts in certain fields of activity, computer jargon, or "user's jargon" that constitutes an actively transforming vocabulary layer that can be comprehensible to a specialist possessing the relevant knowledge and a computer user possessing the relevant level of proficiency.

The vocabulary of computer jargon is heterogeneous in functional and stylistic terms and in the degree of its expressiveness. However, about one-third of all the jargon units are a semantic innovation. The main mechanism for the formation of transferable jargon meanings is the metaphor. In the conditions of online communication, the development of new word meanings in the language occurs due to the emergence of specific meanings in general literary or slang lexemes. Affixation, truncation, word-building, and abbreviation are the most common ways of word formation. In the wording of jargon, the manifestation of a playful, expressive function can be better distinguished than in other areas of language. The borrowing of jargon is carried out from the source language (English) into the recipient language (Russian), followed by the adoption of the phonetic, graphics, lexical-semantic and grammatical aspects of the source language. A distinctive feature of computer jargon word-building is its high vividness, with the casual and somewhat rough coloring of the user's attitude to reality. This leads to the dominance of expressive function over the nominative. It is necessary to note that these results have been obtained manually, without designing and applying the new computer tools. The linguists do not compare the language features of participants who belong to different subcultures in the real world. However, the difference in interlocutors' subcultures can be seen on answers@mail.ru, where people with more knowledge in a particular issue ("expert" or "guru") help those who ask for help ("pupil"). They provide their expertise not in the formal academic style, but by offering useful content information that contains sublanguage of a particular Internet subculture. Mimicry begins where the participant in a dialogue values his status in the network at the entry stage. In Responses@mail.ru, for example, participants who have reached the level of "guru" no longer worry about the impression they make on other participants.

Homogeneous texts can provide the raw material for the study of communicative mimicry, which is used by companies that promote their products or services through social networks. This is an example of a new type of "consumer-company" communication, in which companies simulate a casual two-way "communication for the sake of communication" characteristic of social networks. However, communication on Twitter accounts remains focused on the target audience to attract potential customers' attention to the company's product with a profit-making goal. Customers in a social network enter into a dialogue more easily than in other circumstances. Twitter pagers make the very situation of everyday communication with users of the network (with their potential or real customers) more casual in character. An analysis of what is now termed CD - corporate discourse, was made by Romashova (2014). According to the results of research on Twitter texts, the use of social networks as new channels of promotion by corporations essentially changes the genre structure and style of traditional advertising, as well as the style of the company's PR releases and journalistic texts (Goroshko & Polyakova, 2015). This factor should be considered by the copywriter who makes up the texts for Twitter accounts.

Thus, it can be argued that companies have mastered a simple but effective way of influencing a wide range of potential customers by switching to their manner of communication on the network, and linguistic analysts are ready to provide consulting services to copywriters that compose Twitter accounts texts. Companies that are particularly advanced and successful in the synthesis of texts aim to influence the target audience so that they compose texts employing mind manipulation techniques.

Technology for Behavior Management in Social Networks

There are many publications on the use of social networks for mind manipulation (manipulative psychological impact) (Chusavitina et al.,2015; Smirnova, & Dvorjanchikov, 2015; Andreeva, 2015). Investigating the technologies of manipulation shows the importance of compiling texts aimed at influencing the target audience. For linguists, it is particularly important to identify these texts at a stage when they are hardly distinguishable from "normal" discourse texts. Linguistic analysis with the use of time series analysis and analysis of local areas of social networks, a kind of "small worlds" showed that the creators of mind manipulation texts have a well-developed technology of gradual, step-by-step change in the vocabulary, leading a member of the target audience to the desirable mental state. The implementation of this manipulative technology requires the application of psychological and linguistic techniques, such as tone management, as well as the know-how in the field of Internet technologies.

Technologies for managing behavior in social groups are known and used for benign purposes, (e.g. in the education system) and commercial or even criminal purposes (Makagonov, Dorado, & Espinoza, 2014). In academic discourse, they are described by mathematical models of the imitative behavior of the individual, who is guided both by his personal attitude to the issue under discussion and by the attitude of the subjects surrounding him to this issue. To predict the risk of occurrence of undesirable consequences as a result of analysis of retrospective information, an analysis of the texts using specialized dictionaries is needed. The name of the article by Savva and Davydova (2015) “Linguistic Analysis of Slang in Automated Search for Distribution of Drug Addiction Dissemination in Virtual Social Networks”, speaks for itself. The compilation of these dictionaries can be done manually.

Linguo-Culturological Features of Word Coinage in Social Networks

In addition to the organized integration of companies and other user-organizations into social networks and related developments containing a linguistic component, unorganized users show considerable activity in self-organization. These phenomena attract linguists’ attention due to their novelty and language development potential. Thus, linguists take interest in the social networks’ trend to use precedent statements as special tools that enhance the expressiveness of messages when discussing a particular topic (referring to fragments of the language experience of the message recipient actualizes both conceptually significant and emotion-evaluation attributes). In cases of high popularity, tags become phraseological units.

Prior to the study of social networks, the precedent statement was not considered as a textually independent representative unit of individual vocabulary. Its mechanisms of functioning in individual linguistic capacity were not studied. As shown by Pavlikova (2005), the signs, actualized by this or that precedent statement, do not normally coincide in English and Russian linguistic consciousness. The results of the study of precedent statements in social networks are diverse, but they all demonstrate an increased interest in this language tool from a significant mass of participants in social networks, as well as a difference in the practice of application in different languages. Russian linguists regard intertexts as constituent elements of the semantic memory of native speakers of the Russian language (or, culture) and point to their impact on social networks participants. Moiseev (2011) looked at the specifics of the process of the transition of precedent phenomena to the composition of phraseological units of the English language, formed from precedent names, precedent situations, precedent statements and precedent texts. A more disputable point that linguists argue upon is the discourse about the creative activity of social networking participants in enriching Internet-genres. In the same work, Asmus (2005), divided online communication (based on the communicative goal, the sphere of communication and author-reader image) into several genres: e-mail, chat, forums or virtual conferences, electronic boards, homepages, games and entertainment projects. Other approaches to the evaluation of Internet genres can be found in Andreeva (2013), for example.

Folksonomy and Other Examples of Social Networks Participants' Activity

Let us show that the creativity of the network participants is capable of generating important means for the search processes and structures that cannot emerge outside the activity and self-organization of participants in the social network. The most advanced form of self-organization is the types of resources in the WEB 2.0 format, which is defined as the methodology of system design attracting users to filling and multiple reconciliations of information material. As a result, projects, and services are actively developed and improved by the users themselves: blogs, wiki-projects, and social networks.

According to Guy and Tonkin (2006) and Suvorov (2013), consumers of information can play an active role in web communication. The end information user can take part in the classification of information resources, assigning classification tags to documents or canceling already assigned tags, which, in his or her opinion, do not correspond to the actual content of the information resource. Thus, the information consumer acquires the features of the manufacturer or the quality controller. In order to index the document, the consumer uses the folksonomy method, which is a kind of joint categorization of information. Despite all the advantages of folksonomy, there is a problem of insufficient accuracy of tags. On modern resources that allow using the "national classification", you can see different forms of words, nouns in singular and plural, abbreviations, words with misspellings in the role of tags. Moreover, an extra difficulty is that as tags can be in different languages, there is no control over synonyms and homonyms. Information consumers are in different contexts, each has its own level of interpretation, so there is no standard level of indexing. Most tags define the contents of the document, but some can determine the formal sides of the document. For example, they can determine the type of document or with the help of what or by whom it was created. According to Peters (2006), it is not desirable to work with the only folksonomy within the professional environment; instead, its methods need to be combined with other indexing methods. Currently, there are two trends in the development of the World Wide Web: the semantic web and the social web. The semantic web provides better connectivity and relevance of information on the World Wide Web through the introduction of new metadata formats. The social web relies on streamlining the information on the Web, carried out by the users of the Web. Within the second direction, developments that are part of the semantic web are actively used as tools (RSS and other formats of web feeds, OPML, microformats such as XHTML). There is also a popular concept of Web 2.0, which summarizes several directions of the World Wide Web development.

CONCLUSION

Social networks turned out to be so innovative in the sphere of information processes that classical methods of linguistic analysis were not ready to adjust social networks to solve economic, cultural, and social problems. The need of analyzing the social network to address these problems has morphed into the need to use social networks for resolving them. Moreover, some of the social, economic and governance-related problems arose precisely as a result of the emergence and rapid development of social networks. A significant part of these problems was solved by adopting the classical methods of linguistic analysis. Therefore, differences in the texts (or rather, discourses) of social networks from the former objects of linguistic analysis were not taken into account at the initial stages. An important point was the commercialization of the analysis of social network texts as part of the services rendered to economic agents and public services. This led to the scarcity of information related to the methodologies of linguistic analysis and to the growth of semi-advertisement publications on technologies for analyzing the characteristics of social networks in general while keeping the issues related to social network research secret.

Therefore, many of these issues are described in academic and technical publications on a declarative level neglecting the details of the software implementation. In this regard, the above-presented discourse has already been covered in scientific publications though in the form of some generalizations. These generalizations needed to be compared in terms of their consistency. This review also includes materials that have received high ratings from the scientific community (the number of copies and citations). Linguistic analysis of the texts turned into the analysis of virtual discourse, which was the object of a new type. Virtual discourse is determined not only by the words used but also by the relationships between the objects that generate them. This phenomenon is caused by the generation of texts of social networks, the connections between the elements of which are known and are amenable to analysis and significantly affect the generated texts. Contrast to the classical tasks of linguistic analysis of texts associated with large volumes (collections, text corpora, libraries), the tasks of linguistic analysis of social network texts are related to analyzing the characteristics of the networks as such to solve practical problems. They represent input data for the next stages, and therefore the results of the linguistic analysis, in this case, are not conclusions of an article or a thesis presented in the form of unstructured text in natural language, but summary tables or more complex databases featuring a predetermined structure.

While processing Internet texts and especially while searching for social networking texts, some problems emerged despite the fact that they did not seem critical in the classical methods of text analysis. There was no problem of stop words; the problems of removing and/or analyzing official words did not seem significant. In articles describing software packages, it is shown that there is no ideal standard text processing system. Several counterexamples to the statement "In our days there are a large number of systems and modules for initial preparation of texts" are given in this chapter. With regard to the analysis of comparatively short texts extracted from social networks and having a good technical condition, it can be concluded that the need for separate text processing steps can be reasonably challenged. It turned out that in the analysis of texts of social networks, statistical methods can be relevant even with very weak linguistic preparation of texts for analysis.

In the modern products designed for social networks analysis, the linguistic part is associated with the processing of two objects that contain different texts in character and volume. It mainly contains well-structured and formalized information, and represents a data storage that includes text components. This part accumulates data during the entire lifetime of the repository, and therefore in the algorithms and programs of this part, special attention is paid to the program for processing and storing large data. The second smaller part serves to replenish the first after processing. Its main characteristics are that these are small-volume texts that are stored on the Internet or in the process of monitoring the flow of messages from within social virtual networks. To process the texts of this second part, the materials of the first part are actively involved in classifying and recognition learning of the texts from the second part. At the same time, the variety of character and vocabulary of the texts of the second part requires flexible adjustment of the processing frame or the specialization of the processing centers according to the nature of the input material and the produced results.

The accessibility of linguistic data with the emergence of electronic resources radically changed the requirements for the evidence base linguistic research: in the given time it is not enough to give a few exotic examples in support of the proposed concept; instead, it is necessary to provide a complete sample of the language data. However, working with megabytes of "raw" texts is no less difficult than searching for examples manually. The use of text corpora makes it possible to observe the behavior of linguistic units in a natural linguistic environment, unlike artificially constructed contexts. In addition, case studies using statistical methods make it possible to formulate, confirm or disprove a certain hypothesis about a particular linguistic phenomenon using a large volume of material. The shortcomings of technical solutions and the word processing algorithms stimulate social network analysts (dealing with narrow subject areas) to look for simplified solutions that is using statistical methods while minimizing the use of linguistic methods. For example, a single dictionary stemming of the dictionary, rather than the text being analyzed, allows the compilation of a frequency list of n-grams without significant processing of the analyzed text.

REFERENCES

Andreeva, A. O. (2015). Manipulation in the Internet network. In Информационная безопасность и вопросы профилактики киберэкстремизма среди молодежи [Info safety and problems of preventing the cyber-extremism among youth] (pp. 21-28). Academic Press.

Andreeva, V. A. (2013). Genres and types of a text in scientific and media discourses. In P. A. G. Orel (Ed.), Inter-U anthology of scientific works [Межвузовский сборник научных трудов] (pp. 283–287). Academic Press.

Asmus, N. G. (2005). *Linguistic features of virtual communicative space*. PhD thesis abstract. Retrieved from http://www.lib.csu.ru/texts/diss/002160.pdf (in Russian)

Batura, T. V. (2012). Methods of social networks analysis. *Info Technologies*, *10*(4), 13–28. (in Russian)

Chernyavskaya, V. E. (2013). Linguistics of text. Linguistic of discourse. PH Flinta. (in Russian)

Chusavitina, G. N. (2015). Info safety and problems of preventing the cyber-extremism among youth. In Информационная безопасность и вопросы профилактики киберэкстремизма среди молодёжи [Materials of Intra-U conf.]. St. Tech. Univ.

Danilova, V. A. (2016). *Influence of Social Networks Language upon Verbal and Witten Speaking of the pupils*. Retrieved from http://rodniki.asu.ru/wp-content/uploads/2016/02/Данилова.pdf (in Russian)

Goroshko & Polyakova. (2015). To assembly of genres typology in Social Media. *Speech Genres, 2*(12), 119-128. Retrieved from http://docplayer.ru/29050008-Internet-zhanry-udk-81-38-bbk-81-e-i-goroshko-t-l-polyakova-harkov-ukraina.html (in Russian)

Guy, M., & Tonkin, E. (2006). Folksonomies Tidying up Tags? *D-Lib Magazine, 12*(1). Retrieved from https://cyberleninka.ru/article/ n/internet-memy-problema-tipologii

Ilvovsky, D., & Chernyak, E. (2014). Systems for automated text processing. Открытые системы. СУБД, 1. Retrieved from https://www. osp.ru/os/2014/01/13039687/

Kolokoltseva, T. N. (2012). Internet communication as new speech formation. In Интернет-коммуникация как новая речевая формация. PH Flinta.

Korshunov, A., Bekoborodov, I., Buzun, N., Avanesov, V., Pastukhov, R., Chikhraze, C., . . . Kuznetsov, S. (2014). Social networks analysis: methods and applications [Анализ социальных сетей: методы и приложения]. In *Transactions of the ISP RAS. Automatics & comp engineering* [Труды ИСП РАН. «Автоматика. Вычислительная техника»] (pp. 439-455). Academic Press. Retrieved from https://cyberleninka.ru/article/n/analiz-sotsialnyh-setey-metody-i-prilozheniya

Kotov, E. M., & Tselykh, A. N. (2004). Formation of info systems and search by similarity [Построение информационных систем и поиск по сходству. Автоматика]. *Вычислительная техника*. Retrieved from https://cyberleninka.ru/article/n/postroenie-informatsionno-poiskovyh-sistem-i-poisk-po-shodstvu

Koziev, E. (2010). *Normalization and lemmatization of the text using the thesaurus*. Retrieved from http://www.solarix.ru/for_developers/docs/text-normalization.shtml

Lemmatizer in grammar dictionary. (2017). Retrieved from http://www.solarix.ru/for_developers/api/lemmatization.shtml

Makagonov, P. P., Dorado, R. M. V., & Espinoza, C. B. R. (2014). Measure of Mutual Influence among Members of a Social Network. In Modeling and Data Analysis [Моделирование и анализ данных] (2014, N°1, pp. 64-73). Academic Press.

Mitina, O. V., & Evdokimenko, A. S. (2010). *Methods of text analysis. Methodological cases and program realization* [Методы анализа текста и программная реализация]. Retrieved from https://psibook.com/articles/ metody-analiza-teksta-metodologicheskie-osnovaniya-i-programmnaya-realizatsiya.html

Moiseev, M. V. (2011). Phraseologisation of precedent-related phenomena of the English Language [Фразеологизация прецедентных феноменов в английском языке]. In Gerald of the Omsk St. U, (2011. N° 3, pp. 262-268). Academic Press.

Moles, A. A. (2008). *Sociodynamics of culture*. PH BCG. (in Russian)

Moroslin, P. V. (2009). Internet language as object of linguistic researches [Язык Интернета как объект лингвистических исследований]. In Gerald of the Peoples' Friendship U of Russia (РУДН). Series Linguistics, (2009, No 3, pp. 10-17). Academic Press.

Nezhura, E. A. (2012). New types of creolized texts in communicative space of the Internet [Новые типы креолизованных текстов в коммуникативном пространстве интернета]. Language Theory and Intercultural Communication [Теория языка и межкультурная коммуникация], 2, 47-52.

Pavlikova, S. K. (2005). *Russian and English precedent sayings: Comparative analysis* [Русские и английские прецедентные высказывания: Сравнительный анализ] (thesis). Москва.

Pervushin. (2013). *Design and working up the program system for graphematic analysis of texts in Russian* [Проектирование и разработка программной системы графематического анализа текстов на русском языке] (Magister thesis).

Peters, I. (2006). Against folksonomies: Indexing blogs and podcasts for corporate knowledge management. *Preparing for Information 2.0. Online Information 2006. Proceedings*, 93-97.

Potapova, R. K. (2005). New info technologies and linguistics [Новые информационные технологии и лингвистика] (4th ed.). PH KomKniga.

Romashova, V. (2014). Pragma-stylistic features of Russian corps. Twitter-communication [Прагмастилистические особенности особенности Твиттер-коммуникации Российских корпораций]. In Communicative Studies [Коммуникативные исследования] (2014, N° 2. pp. 134-140). Academic Press.

Rubtsova, Y. V. (2015). Formation of texts corpus for tuning a tone classifier [Построение корпуса текстов для настройки тонового классификатора]. Software & Systems, 1(109).

Rusakova, O. F. (2007). Main variations of contemporary political discourse theories: background of classifications [Основные разновидности современных теорий политического дискурса: опыт классификаций]. Sci YB, the Institute of philosophy and law. Ural dept of RAS. —2007.

Ryazantseva, T. I. (2010). Hypertext and e-communication [Гипертекст и электронная коммуникация]. PH BCG (ЛКИ).

Savva, Yu. B., & Davydova, Yu. V. (2015). About slang linguistic analysis problem in the task of automated searching for threats of dope habit dissemination in virtual social networks [О проблеме лингвистического анализа сленга в задаче автоматизированного поиска угроз распространения наркомании в виртуальных социальных сетях]. In Int. sci-tech. conf «Info systems and technologies».

Sedunov, A. A. (2007). A model of graphematic analysis in the system of natural language processing [Модель графематического анализа в системе обработки естественного языка]. In Gerald of VSU, Series System Analysis & Info Technologies. (2007, № 2, pp. 69-77). Academic Press.

Seleznev, K., & Vladimirov, A. (2013). Linguistics and text processing [Лингвистика и обработка текстов]. In *Open Systems* [Открытые системы] (2013, № 04). Retrieved from http://linter.ru/ru/press-center/detail/27/1660/

Smetanin, N. (2011). Fuzzy search in text and in a dictionary [Нечёткий поиск в тексте и словаре]. Retrieved from https://habrahabr.ru/users/ntz/topics/

Smirnova, N. S., & Dvoryanchikov, N. V. (2015). Studying manipulative impacts strategies realized by totalitarian sects via Internet network (e-resource) [Исследование манипулятивных стратегий воздействия, реализуемых тоталитарными сектами посредством сети Интернет]. In Psychology & Law [Психология и право] (2015. № 2.). Academic Press.

Suvorov, K. B. (2013). *Folksonomy as a method of social classifying Web resources* [Фолксономия как метод социальной классификации веб-ресурсов]. Retrieved from http://www.rusnauka.com/6_PNI_2013/Informatica/3_129815.doc.htm

Ustalov, D. (2014). NLPub: A Catalogue and a Community for Russian Linguistic Resources. In *Selected Papers of XVI All-Russian Scientific Conference «Digital libraries: Advanced Methods and Technologies, Digital Collections»* (pp. 56-60). CEUR-WS.org. Retrieved from http://ceur-ws.org/Vol-1297/056-60_paper-10.pdf

KEY TERMS AND DEFINITIONS

Folksonomy: Folksonomy is the result of personal free tagging of information and objects done in a social environment by the person consuming the information for one's own retrieval.

Linking or Syntactic Word: We consider the words to be linking or syntactic if they are non-derivative, or if they are derivative, they contain parts of significative words that have almost lost their meaning within the context.

Stemming: A stemming algorithm is a computational procedure which reduces each word of its derivational and inflectional suffixes.

Chapter 2
Studying the Big Data Paradigm in Dynamics of Its Advance

Pavel P. Makagonov
Russian Presidential Academy of National Economy and Public Administration, Russia

Amando Alejandro Ruiz Figueroa
University of the Sierra Sur, Mexico

ABSTRACT

The study of the big data subject matter in its advance already has its own history. Assuming as a basis the content analysis of article abstracts on big data, using e-library stocks of Association for Computing Machinery (ACM) and Institute of Electrical and Electronics Engineers (IEEE), one succeeds to monitor the life cycle phases of the big data paradigm and distinguish the stages of developing programs and algorithms from the technology update, including applications and their advanced renewals. In order to carry out the analysis, it is proposed to approximate the curves of cumulative frequencies of words, obtained from the corpus of texts by means of cubic parabolas, their parameters being in good concordance with ones of logistic curves.

INTRODUCTION

When analyzing an advance of studies, it is important to monitor the life cycle of a subject matter in the close field. In our case for these aims it was required to clarify the phase of life cycle, where the Big Data paradigm is situated.

DOI: 10.4018/978-1-5225-5586-5.ch002

As well known, a quiverish scientific idea on the science front line becomes a paradigm in that moment or period of time, when resources of science and technology are at the level high enough to advance the idea as long as the self-organization of scientific community generates necessarily some critical host of persons adhering this idea. Right after the moment mentioned articles of *normal science* appear, they pick up and advance the idea. If the critical host of adherents is not reached or if the idea is scarified by opponents and rejected at the popularity growth stage, in these conditions no new paradigm arises.

Life Cycle Model for a Topic in Close Scientific Field

Seemingly, any paradigm should have its own empiric model too. When considering the life cycle of a project or an enterprise, their cycle stages are determined and all the cycle is described using some parameter A, its model being, in its turn, the S-like curve of one from two kinds: a curve of intensity, increasing from zero and then diminishing as far as zero or a curve of cumulative frequency for A parameter. For an enterprise start and finish dates of its life cycle may be fixed, so instead of logistic curve the model is more suitable in the form of increasing part of cubic parabola between left minimum and right maximum (see Figure 1).

Figure 1. Cubic parabola P and logistic curve L as models of cumulative frequencies curve, when an inflection point of P is congruent with the same one of L and for both curves slopes of a tangent are the same too

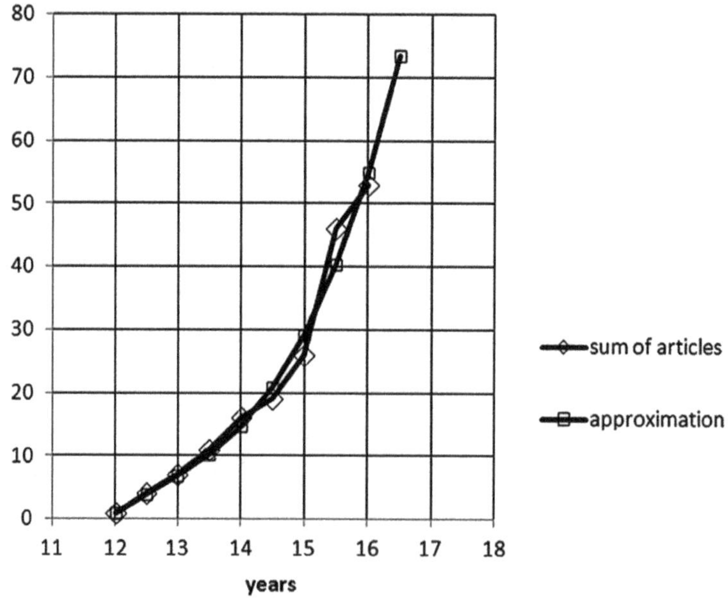

To get a paradigm advance successfulness parameter, the scientific texts, to this paradigm related, are the best source. These texts from the close subject matter field are more content-analyzable by virtue of: a) their better self-organization; b) greater language discipline, the authors of scientific articles showing; c) more strict procedure of selecting articles before publishing them.

The dynamics of new paradigm advance can be represented as the cumulative frequency of publications in scientific magazines or of reports on scientific conferences — on themes reflecting an intension of the paradigm. Representative excerpt of displays for the paradigm given in its time outlook as a rule has the appearance near to logistic curve or, in case of *young* paradigm, not reached its mature age, excerpt is well approximated by J-like curve with the outlook to become advanced into S-like one. Most commonly this J-like curve has an initial point related to time moment of the first scientific message appearing, from where a counting of the new paradigm life cycle is possible. If excerpt is formed from data not having, for some reasons, an initial phase of paradigm advance, the curve may have the appearance as an upper branch of logistic function with not enough clear expressed way-out onto horizontal asymptote.

Let's consider the simplest admissible math overviews of above mentioned heuristic models, both J-like and S-like.

Simplistically each complete model (of J- or S-like kind) can be represented as a segment of cubic parabola between left minimum and right maximum on a graph for following function:

$$F(t) = -a_3 \cdot t^3 + a_2 \cdot t^2 - a_1 \cdot t + a_0, \tag{1}$$

where $a_3 > 0$, $a_2 > 0$.

Taking into account signs (-) and (+) before coefficients a_3 and a_2 in (1), this segment of the curve has on itself the inflection point between left minimum and right maximum:

$$T_{ip} = \frac{1}{3} \cdot \frac{a_2}{a_3}. \tag{2}$$

For the curve of cumulated frequencies there is a logistic dependence (3) generally recognized as proper math model:

$$f(t) = L_{\min} + \frac{1}{1 + \exp\left[-k\left(t - T_{ip}\right)\right]}, \tag{3}$$

where

T_{ip} = inflection point abscissa;
k = inflectional tangent to a curve.

In common case an empirical curve is situated between horizontal asymptotes L_{min}, L_{max}:

$$f(t) = L_{min} + \frac{L_{min}}{1 + \exp\left[-k\left(t - T_{ip}\right)\right]}. \tag{4}$$

And so a slope ratio (otherwise slope tangent) of the logistic curve is determined by (5):

$$\mathrm{tg}\varphi = 0.25 \cdot k \cdot L_{max} \quad \text{or} \quad k = \frac{4\mathrm{tg}\varphi}{L_{max}}. \tag{5}$$

Cubic parabola (1) and logistic curve (3) or (4) have a center of symmetry in the inflection point.

Having inflection points of both curves superposed and coefficients a_2, a_3 from (1) and k parameter from (5) come in an agreement up to coincidence of the curves tangents, we get central parts of the curves as, in essence, close models for the paradigm life cycle. For initial left part of the graph more realistic model is (1), whereas for right one — asymptotic branch of logistic curve.

J-like curve for the new paradigm in the earliest phase of its advance can be approximated by cubic parabola as well, but with coefficients a_3, > 0 $a_2 < 0$. Then the point of minimum corresponds to beginning of curve branch going away into infinity. That is, the curve corresponds to early initial phase of life cycle distant from the inflection point to an extent, when this point is not felt in a model given.

Numerical experiments showed: incomplete models (for excerpts with no data related to early times of life cycle) can be described well by ascending branch of quadratic parabola:

$$F(t) = b_2 \cdot t^2 + b_1 \cdot t + b_0 \tag{6}$$

with maximum in the point:

$$T_{max} = -\frac{1}{2} \cdot \frac{b_1}{b_2}. \quad (7)$$

Represented hypothetical dependences are monitorable not for any subject field. Our experience of constructing an ontology of close subject fields, for instance in case of International Civil Aviation Organization (ICAO) normative documents, has shown: texts of administrative-technical contents can have unpredictable returns to the themes, considered formerly, in connection with circumstances, anew arose, or emergency situations, when it is required to alter instructions and other normative documents/ In these cases curves of cumulative frequencies have several inflection points, the intensity of publishing having accelerations and decelerations as well.

Ever before, other researchers collided with similar situations, see, for instance (Vesnina, 2005), (Maruev, 2006). As they showed, the interest of a society in the scope of training the specialists is better monitored not by life cycle economic indices, but by number of guide-books published, in time sequences of publications:

$$y = a \cdot t \exp\left(-bt\right), \quad (8)$$

where

y = estimate criterion for prospectivity of technology studied;
a, b = caliber coefficients;
t = registration moments (model time).

A substitution of the efficient t in model function (8) onto t^2 only replaces lightly the inflection point to the right, a value of cumulative frequencies still being much less than a half of maximum, i. e. comparing with right asymptote level in the inflection point.

Let's assume, in the initial point $x_{min} = a$ even one article of normal science didn't appear yet and for new articles the cumulative frequency of their arrival $y_{min} = y(x_{min}) = 0$, but in this moment an article at the science front line has been issued or remarked thereby initiating the new paradigm.

As the life cycle advancing, the curve for cumulative frequency goes through inflection point (x_{ip}, y_{ip}) and reaches the maximum point (x_{max}, y_{max}). Such S-like curve of life cycle can be represented as cubic parabola of the following form (see Figure 1):

$$y\left(x\right) = -d\left(x - a\right)^2 \left(x - 3b\right). \quad (9)$$

Taking here d =0.2, a = 3, b = 5, we get ratios:

$$y = -0.2x^3 + 4.8x^2 - 23.4x + 32.4$$

$$y_{\min} = y\left(a\right) = 0; y_{\max} = y\left(2b + \frac{1}{3}\right) = 100;$$

$$x_{ip} = b + \frac{2}{3}a; y_{ip} = y\left(x_{ip}\right) = 50.$$

Let's accept horizontal asymptotes for logistic curve as equal to ordinates of minimum and maximum for cubic parabola: $Y\left(-\infty\right) = 0; Y\left(+\infty\right) = y_{\max}$.

Logistic curve of the form (4) together with cubic parabola have mutual inflection point and the same slope tangent in this point if following equalities are fair:

$$L_{\min} = 0; L_{\max} = y_{\max}; k = \frac{4}{3} \cdot \frac{\left(3b - a\right)}{y_{\max}}; h = x_{ip}.$$

For cubic parabola of the form (1) its coefficients are linked with presentation (9) using following ratios:

$$a_3 = d; a_2 = \left(2a + 3b\right)d; a_1 = 6abd; a_0 = 3a^2bd.$$

As monitoring the paradigm advance, a success in many respects is determined by choosing the most informative themes and terms corresponding to studies being long-lived for the paradigm given, but not in general use in a broader field of study. If some themes are essentially shorter in a life and ends their life-cycle in the limits of current time, when the chosen paradigm is advanced, these themes should disrupt a simple J- or S-like form of the curve. If one succeeds to reveal clearly the theme resulting in this effect with no reasons to exclude that theme from consideration of it as paradigm, there is lower validity degree of hypothesis, that an object, chosen to study, is a paradigm carrier in the close scientific field. If distortions of the curve for cumulative frequencies don't allow to approximate it successfully using proper cubic or quadratic parabola, for instance, with a determinacy coefficient exceeding 0.96, the hypothesis (that subject matter given represents an united paradigm) should, if not be rejected, then at least, get the lowered degree of confirmability.

Consider that the paradigm itself perhaps occupies not so close subject field, if according to this paradigm theoretical studies are transformed smoothly into solving technological and/or applied problems on the basis of theoretical groundworks.

Let's carry out a stronger formalization for representing the paradigm life cycle using the curve of cumulative frequencies. In this statistical model a wrongly chosen initial point is assumed for *normal science* advancing on the basis of the *new science* breakthrough article or the article being on science front line in some subject field. This initial point corresponds less to an appearance moment of the first article, forming the paradigm, than a period of accepting an article idea by scientific community, ready to advance the new science on its base. Hence, most commonly one chooses as initial point (x or t) the moment of the first article appearance with a reference onto the science front line article, containing a new idea stating. If at once several articles of the *normal science* appear, for better approximating the model it's to choose the initial point (x -1), i. e. by 1 earlier, just that point, when a refilling of a source (collection of articles) under study took place, if this refilling did not contain the article on desired close subject matter.

The curve of cumulative frequencies for a life cycle of organization, enterprise or project commonly has the terminating point corresponding to time, when their functionality ceases officially. For the paradigm its lifetime normally cannot be fixed exactly. So right branch of the logistic curve is a better paradigm behavior model, comparing with cubic parabola of the form (1). The cubic parabola maximum falls on time, when the logistic curve verges towards 96% of its asymptote. Thereby it is useful to have both models for the curve of cumulative frequencies: cubic parabola and logistic curve, when inflection point coordinates and slope tangents in this point are congruent, maximum and minimum of a polynomial having the same ordinates as logistic curve asymptotes.

VLSI FAULT TOLERANCE AS AN EXAMPLE OF THE MODEL FOR CLOSE SUBJECT MATTER

Formerly we considered the closed subject matter field «Very Large Scale Integration (VLSI) & Fault Tolerance» in the frames of a topic *Parallel, Concurrent, Distributed & Simultaneous (PCDS) Computing* (Figueroa & Makagonov, 2007). By data about publishing the articles in 1997—2003 period curves like cubic polynomial and logistical curves for life cycle of the theme *PCDS, VLSI Fault Tolerance* have been constructed, including the curve of cumulative frequencies for articles in IEEE magazines and the following has been shown: a) in the middle of 2019 *PCDS* theme life cycle will be over according to cubic polynomial approximation or will reach 95% saturation when logistic approximating; b) in 2016 the publication of articles on the theme *VLSI Fault Tolerance* will end or their accumulation will reach the 95% level.

Having carried out in 2016 a partite analysis for the number of publications on *VLSI* and *Fault Tolerance* themes, we have got following results, taking into account data for 12 years after analyzing the articles, collected up to the middle of 2004.

Partite analysis gave ending forecasts by years: 2016 for *VLSI* and 2021 for *Fault Tolerance.* Consider: a number of articles on *VLSI* exceeds a number of articles on *Fault Tolerance* only slightly. As joint counting the articles on *VLSI* and *Fault Tolerance*, a deadline of life cycle ending, when cubic approximation was in use, should be in 2019. In the event, a deadline of life cycle by data for period 1994—2004 was vastly close to that for period 1997—2016. It gave us grounds to consider practical behavior models for cumulative frequencies of *normal science* yielding power as acceptable when forecasting the paradigm advance in close subject field. On these grounds we have carried out an analysis of publishing dynamics on interesting for us theme *big data*.

COMPARING THE COLLECTIONS OF SCIENTIFIC TEXTS ON BIG DATA

In E-Libraries of ACM and IEEE

One from our intermediate aims is in comparing the vocabularies on Big Data subject matter in two representative e-libraries of ACM and IEEE. Each of them forms collections of texts by somewhat different way: a distinction being possible in scientific orientation of Big Data paradigm adherents in their zones of interest, as well in expressing an interest to exactly the same subject matter, but in various periods.

Complete excerpts of articles containing, in the certain form, a word combination *big + data* on the moment of middle 2016, was 1141 units for IEEE and 1844 ones for ACM. As seen, volumes of both totalities are practically comparable. For IEEE articles, by half a year periods quantized, models have been got for distributions of articles, word combinations *big + data* and amounts of significant words with high values of the determinacy coefficient. Parameters of models, by cubic parabolas (1) approximated, are given in Table 1.

For three various characteristics a match-up of model parameters is practically close to be ideal, the determinacy coefficient pointing at very well conformity of distributions with their cubic polynomials them approximating. The results allows us to conclude: a community of scientists, whose publications are being selected into e-library of IEEE, up to end of 2017 will accomplish not less than by 96% (taking

Table 1. Cumulative frequencies distribution models for articles on Big Data in e-library IEEE, by their main characteristics

Distribution by Half-Year Periods	Point of Minimum	Inflection Point	Point of Maximum	Determinacy Coefficient R^2
Number of articles	2012.1	2014.8	2017.5	0.9926
Number of significant words	2012.0	2014.9	2017.8	0.9938
Number of word combinations *big + data*	21012.0	2014.7	2017.4	0.9938

into account polynomial and logistic approximations for the curve of cumulative frequencies) their scientific activity in the Big Data field.

When analyzing abstracts of articles from e-library ACM we observe a diverse picture (see: http://dl.acm.org/). Normalized curves of cumulative frequencies for two main concepts are represented on Figure 2. As the 1st concept (a word combination *big + data*), existing in each text), is accepted, 2nd one being compounded using special terms (names), such as Large, R, HADOOP, Scalable, DATASETs, Platform, Variety, Ghemawat, Refine, Categories, SoCC etc, these designations eing formed by words with high, more 0.9, correlation in all the texts of main, the most multiple cluster of articles. Let us mark here: SoCC means Big Data system created, as a

Figure 2. Normalized curves of cumulative frequencies for Big Data (lower curve) and for the second, by occurrence, concept (upper curve, practically all along)

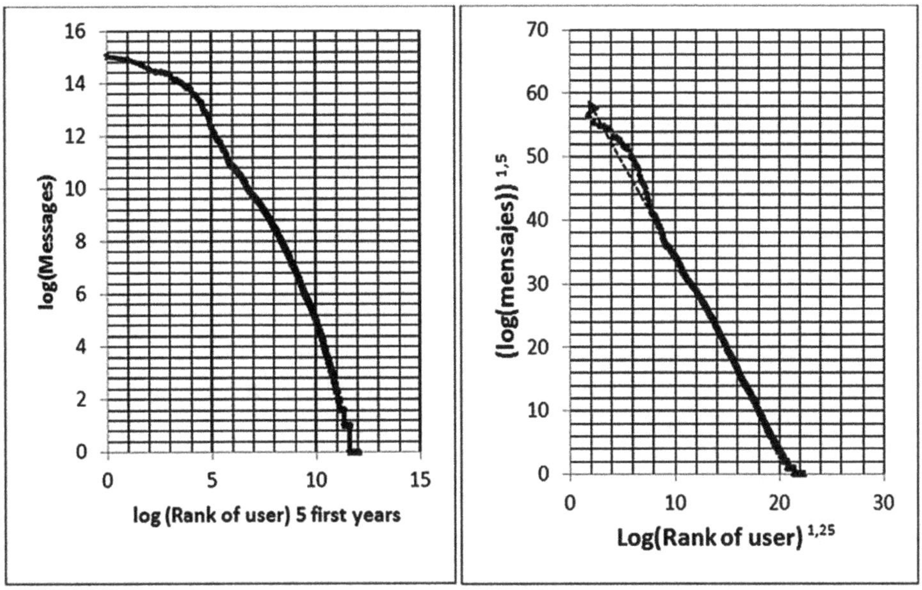

result of co-sponsoring, by ACM's Special Interest Groups on Management of Data (SIGMOD) and personally by Sanjay Ghemawat, one from the most popular authors on Big Data in ACM, see for instance a resource http://dl.acm.org/pubs.cfm. As well let us mark: 2nd concept contains words, hardly reducible into a comprehend combination. However, their joint substitution into the retrieval request results gives in delivering the sensible article titles like *The Family of MapReduce and Large Scale Data Processing Systems* (by Sakr *et al.*, 2014), *Towards Automatic Optimization of MapReduce Programs* (by Babu, 2010.), or *Handling big data: research challenges and future directions* (Anagnostopoulos *et al.*, 2016).

As Figure 2 displays, on framed segments A and C normalized curves of cumulative frequencies for *big data* concept (lower curve) and for the second, by occurrence, concept (upper curve practically all along) slope descents are seen and even outlets onto horizontal asymptote (in case of A) of S-like parts pertaining to both curves, whereas for 2nd concept the same curve slope descents are seen on segments B and D.

To build a fast prototype of *big data* ontology, matrices were compounded for word occurrence frequencies in analyzed texts, by months and years of publication, using the results of analyzing the abstracts of texts from e-library ACM, the first (the highest) level of commonality or abstractiveness for ontology concepts of Big Data paradigm being possible to single out.

This level contains four branches by concept sets differed, the branches spanning various study directions from elaborations of initial algorithms up to applied practical realizations of program-algorithmic and technological elaborations. These directions are divided provisionally by four branches represented in Table 2, Table 3, Table 4, and Table 5.

As may be supposed, in Table 5 names, closed one to another, on themes and directions for advancing the Big Data applications are determined by graduality of elaborating the joint concordant position of authors in relation to both priorities among claimed applications and their structuredness.

As well, a chronological sequence of concept appearances in ACM texts by years is interesting, see Table 6.

Further, in Table 7 concept models with the life cycles, well approximated by cubic polynomial (1), are represented. In the Table there are formulae, where time x changes within the range of 9.0…16.5. This corresponds to period 2009—2016, fractional part showing the year allotments in decimal notation. R^2 means the determinacy coefficient for approximating polynomial, related to the factual distribution of cumulative frequencies.

Big Data and NoSQL concepts, not included in Table 7, are given by J-like curves going away into infinity, these curves having no inflection points at the right of initial minimum. In Table 8 they are represented as cubic polynomials.

Table 2. Main directions for elaborating big data concepts of 1st and 2nd kinds. Information and algorithmic problems of big data in science and technology.

Big Data **Approach**	*Big Data* **Science**
Big Content for Sensitive *Data*	*Big* amounts of recorded *data*
big linked *data*	*big* meta *data*
Big heterogeneous data	Big data enabled tools
Big data domains	*Big data* flow
Big data set	*big* complex *data*sets
Big connected *data*	*Big* dynamic distribution *data*
big fast *data*	*Big* mobility *data*
Very large *data* base (VLDB)	multi-source *big* infrastructure *data*
Big data Software Engineering (BIGDSE)	hadoop distributed file system
Big open linked *data* (BOLD)	*big* trajectory *data*
Big textual data	*Big* uncertain *data*
big streaming *data*	

Table 3. Technical and technological types of solving the special problems of IT

Big **Video** *Data*	*Big Visual Data*
Big graphs	*BIG* XML *data*
Big (Internet) *Data*	*big* RDF *data* Resource Description Framework (*Big* RDF *Data* using NoSQL and MapReduce)
Big sparse *data*	Large-scale *data*
Big sensor *data*	*Big* multimedia *data*

Table 4. Technological Solutions taking into account features of usage in applications

Big **Personal** *Data*	*Big* **Public** *Data*
Big bad *data*	*Big data* friendly
Big aerial image *data*	*Big data* Digerati
Big GPS traces *data*	*Big* Massive Open Online Course (MOOC) *data*
Big network *data*	

Not high level of determinacy index for main concept, i. e. for root vertex of Big Data ontology, points onto the circumstance, that the paradigm, being formed, haven't reach the mature condition. This conclusion is not in agreement with result of analyzing the Big Data life cycle characteristics through IEEE texts. To consider

Table 5. Practical applications of Big Data algorithms and technologies

Big **Medical** *Data*	*Big* **Social** *Data*
Big nutritional *data*	*Big* social media *data*
Big genomic *data* *Big* health *data*	*Big* Location-Based Social Networks (LBSN) *data(*
Big* Geo-Social *Data	**Big Data in Social Science**
Big spatiotemporal *data* *Big* spatio-temporal *data* analytics	*Big data* for Musicology, *Big data* history of music
Big transportation *data*	*Big* city *data*
Big* Financial *Data	***Big* Scholarly *Data***
large-scale e-commerce *data*set	***Big* Geodata**

Table 6. The chronology of concept appearances in ACM texts

Years	Concept Names
2009	{TEXT; SCALABLE; SCALABILITY; BOTTLENECK; FAILURES}; {DATA; BIG; LARGER; QUERY; DISTRIBUTED; PARALLEL; NODES}; {MAP_REDUCE; CLOUD; SIGCOMM; ISARD; FRAMEWORK}; { RDBMS}; {HADOOP; SIGMOD; VLDB; SQL; WORKFLOWs; OLAP; UBIQUITOUS; DBMS; BI}
2010	RDF; HDFS; LEARNING; KNOWLEDGE;
2011	{NOSQL; API}; {VERTEX(s); HBASE}; MARKET; {STREAM (s); TWITTER}; PIG; NEURAL; {SIGKDD; URBAN; GPS; GEOGRAPHIC}; MEDICAL; PIPELINE; GPU; {HEALTH CARE};
2012	ONTOLOGY; KDD; {XML; BIOINFORMATICS}; GIS.

Table 7. Concepts with the life cycles, well approximated by cubic polynomial (1)

Concept	Approximating Cubic Polynomial	R^2
LARGE R, HADOOP, SCALABLE, DATASETS, PLATFORM, VARIETY GHEMAWAT REFINE CATEGORIES SOCC	$F(x) = -0.022\,x^3 + 1.9571\,x^2 - 34.936\,x + 175.08$	0.9932
MAP_REDUCE	$F(x) = -5428\,x^3 + 361.21\,x^2 - 5865.8\,x + 28034$	0.9942
QUERY	$F(x) = -4.5026\,x^3 + 278.33\,x^2 - 4467.5\,x + 21332$	0.9896
PARALLEL	$F(x) = -2.1484\,x^3 + 144.37\,x^2 - 2367.4\,x + 11371$	0.9933
VLDB	$F(x) = -0.8357\,x^3 + 56.292\,x^2 - 925.26\,x + 4456.6$	0.9919
OLAP	$F(x) = -0.2044\,x^3 + 24.528\,x^2 - 466.04\,x + 2412.8$	0.9746
XML	$F(x) = -2.2046\,x^3 + 93.583\,x^2 - 1259.\,x + 5438.7$	0.9374
STREAM(s)	$F(x) = -3.7412\,x^3 + 189.13\,x^2 - 2793.4x + 12747$	0.9888
Relational database management system (RDBMS)	$F(x) = -0.9595\,x^3 + 41.928\,x^2 - 570.59x + 2470.3$	0.982
Database management system (DBMS	$F(x) = -0.9064\,x^3 + 40.861\,x^2 - 563.7x + 2454.4$	0.9923
ACM's Special Interest Group on Management of Data (SIGMOD)	$F(x) = -0.0505\,x^3 + 52.735\,x^2 - 1127.6\,x^2 - + 6046.9$	0.9921

Table 8. Cubic polynomials for J-like curves with coefficients $a_3 > 0$, $a_2 < 0$, R^2 being a determinacy index

Concept	Approximating Cubic Polynomial	R^2
Big&Data	$y = 0.071\,x^3 - 1.9112\,x^2 + 15.657\,x - 36{,}038$	0.9671
NoSQL	$y = 0.5973\,x^3 - 10.382\,x^2 + 16.996\,x + 266.43$	0.9882

a contradiction arisen, let's view the last results of analyzing the ACM abstracts, namely life cycle time parameters of main concepts for texts from ACM. These results are represented in Table 9.

As following from Tables 6,7,9, XML and RDBMS concepts, being born long before Big Data appearance, but already emaciated with reference to this paradigm, are proved to be the most short-living. On the other hand, concepts of *Big* medical (health) *data* kind and ones of spatio-geographic character, arisen later, are being mentioned in texts jointly with main concepts of the most multiple cluster. Thereby applied subject matter extends an active usage of main concepts, hence enlarges their life time.

Thus, the Big Data paradigm is being changed bit by bit with switching onto applied tasks. At the same time it should be noted: studied texts from e-library

Table 9. Life cycle milestones for concepts; in brackets: word usage number, both already fixed and supposed for future

2nd Type Concepts (Besides *BIG DATA*)	S	M (Inflexion Point)	E
LARGE R, HADOOP, SCALABLE, DATASETS, PLATFORM, VARIETY GHEMAWAT REFINE CATEGORIES SOCC	2011 (0)	2030 (294)	2048 (574)
SIGMOD Special Interest Groups on Management of Data	2010 (9)	2050 (1734)	2091 (3483)
MAP REDUCE	2010.5 (0)	2022.5 (15700)	2033 (28629)
RDBMS (Relational database management system)	2011 (0)	2014.5 (95)	2018 (190)
VLDB	2011,5 (0)	2023(2687)	2034 (5225)
PARALLEL	2011.5(0)	2023 (6900)	2034 (13330)
STREAM(s) (In stream *big data* processing)	2012 (0)	2017 (1537)	2023 (3029)
OLAP	2012 (0)	2040.5 (10190)	2069 (19887)
XML	2012 (0)	2014.5 (120)	2017 (249)
QUERY	2012 (0)	2021 (8559)	2030 (16234)
Big medical (health) *data*	2013 (3)	2023 (227)	2033 (448)

Denotations: 2nd type concepts — words and word combinations for concepts, being extra to one of 1st type (*BIG DATA*), in texts of articles;

S, M, E — year of start, middle, end correspondingly for concept life cycle

IEEE don't reflect sufficiently applied matters in a frequency list of significant words. That explains essentially shorter Big Data paradigm life cycle, estimated by publications in e-library IEEE.

The 1st word cluster from ACM abstracts contains the lexicon in general use of the Big Data paradigm adherents. From 125 words of this cluster 85 ones matches up to words from the first type in IEEE sources. Naturally, it is possible to carry out more subtle comparative analysis of word clusters from abstract text corpora for each e-library used. But, it's obvious: the text corpus from ACM e-library will contain more multiple clusters of words-concepts linked to applied problems.

CONCLUSION

A science hasn't elaborated the normatives for that, how many confirmed facts are required to conclude confidently: the hypothesis is becoming an empirical law. However a successful verification, executed here on the basis of analyzing the texts repeatedly by topics *VLSI* and *Fault Tolerance* after the 1st analysis 12 years ago, i. e. on the basis of the latest new data, seems to be a strong argument in favor of accepting the cubic parabola model, alongside the logistic one, as the main models for the life cycle of close scientific subject matter.

In spite of numbers comparability for Big Data articles extracted from e-resources ACM and IEEE, a quantitative analysis of both text corpora reveals an essential difference in their subject matters. IEEE publications on *big data* subject matter in their overwhelming majority deal with *big data* technologies and algorithms, but from the middle of 2011 a new subject matter arose, it being linked with *big data* applications of medical, urban and similar social-oriented profiles. At outgoing wave rear front line of *pure big data* topics the readiness of program-algorithmic component in *normal science* became near to completion. At that in ACM texts a gradual change of Big Data paradigm takes place with switching onto applied tasks.

During linguistic analysis of texts difficulties, linked with the frequency analysis of vocabulary, when abbreviations, matching up to the same ones, but in other knowledge fields, appeared or software, procedure names, having ciphers inside the word, encountered. Not for a while yet many text analysis systems do not perceive the terms like Neo4j, B2B as one orthographic or lexical words. When constructing the fast prototype of Big Data paradigm ontology, sometimes it is hard to expiscate a sensible name for the specific concept, composed of a few words. Usually this concept is composed with words, being well correlated all over the corpus of texts under analysis. However, when writing these concepts into search system, one may get article names, where the most part of concept words is represented, so the article name itself may be used as one from concept names.

REFERENCES

Anagnostopoulos, I. S., Zeadally, E., & Exposito, E. (2016, April). Handling big data: Research challenges and future directions. *The Journal of Supercomputing*, *72*(4), 1494–1516. doi:10.100711227-016-1677-z

Maruev, S. A. (2006). *A formal theory of labor technological competences and its applications*. PH of the Research Center on quality problems of human resource development. (in Russian)

Mohammed, E. A., Far, B. H., & Naugler, C. (2016, April). Applications of the MapReduce programming framework to clinical big data analysis: Current landscape and future trends. *The Journal of Supercomputing*, *72*(4), 1–23.

Ruiz Figueroa, A., & Makagonov, P. P. (2007). Models of hard- and software advance based on the parallel computation study. *Interciencia, 32*(3), 160-166. (in Spanish)

Sakr, S., Liu, A., & Fayoumi Ayman, G. (2014). The Family of MapReduce and Large Scale Data Processing Systems. *Journal ACM Computing Surveys, 46*(1). Retrieved July 22, 2014, from https://arxiv.org/pdf/1302.2966.pdf

Shivnath Babu, S. (2010). Towards Automatic Optimization of MapReduce Programs Conference. *Proceedings of the 1st ACM Symposium on Cloud Computing*.

SIGMOD. (2014). *Proceedings of the 2014 ACM SIGMOD International Conference on Management of Data*. ACM.

Vesnina, I. F., & Maruev, S. A. (2004). Analysing the life cycle of education program on a base of life cycle data for technologies under study. In State Regulating the Economics at Regional Level. Moscow: PH of the All-Russian State Tax Academy (ARSTA). (in Russian)

Chapter 3
Set Classification

Ievgen Arnoldovich Nastenko
Igor Sikorsky Kyiv Polytechnic Institute, Ukraine

Oleksandra Olegivna Konoval
Igor Sikorsky Kyiv Polytechnic Institute, Ukraine

Olena Konstantinovna Nosovets
Igor Sikorsky Kyiv Polytechnic Institute, Ukraine

Volodymyr Anatolevich Pavlov
Igor Sikorsky Kyiv Polytechnic Institute, Ukraine

ABSTRACT

The classification problem where each object is given by a set of multidimensional measurements that is associated with an unknown dependence is considered. Intersection of sets that define objects from different classes is allowed. In this case, it is natural to found classification algorithms based on the difference between dependencies for the objects belonging to different classes. Two algorithms to convert the set classification problem solution from the initial feature space into (1) the parameters space of the common model structure for all the objects and (2) the parameters spaces of the best structures for each class are proposed, along with a classification algorithm based on the accuracy of object representation by the models based on the structures found for each class. If the objects are described with big data, the approach can be used to transform data into a compact form (model parameters) that preserves the characteristics that are necessary to separate the classes. An approach to solve a problem of clustering sets is proposed. Some examples are given.

DOI: 10.4018/978-1-5225-5586-5.ch003

INTRODUCTION AND HISTORY OF SOLUTIONS

An important role in the functionality of techno-social systems in Modern Economical and Governmental Infrastructures plays by decision support making systems. The mathematics of such decision-making is most often classification methods. The system operation conditions in these areas are characterized by a high degree of task subjects' behavior ambiguity and the presence of hidden variables, knowledge of which is essential for making management decisions. It is for such decision-making tasks the approach proposed by the authors is intended.

Historically, pattern recognition problem considers a classification object as a single multidimensional point (observation) in a feature space, this condition will hereinafter be denoted for reference in this text as (*). At the same time, if the "portraits" of objects are insufficiently informative, the well-known issue of ambiguity solution of classification problem arises. Difficulties in recognizing become even more obvious if the object feature values can vary depending on the magnitude of some uncontrolled parameter or, in general, on the environment state. The problem stems from the possibility of feature value areas partial intersections in the original space of measured variables for objects of different classes in the various environment states, that leads to the obvious ambiguity of the classification result.

A possible way out is to describe the object not by one, but a certain number of measurements taken for the different environmental states. Such a set of measurements makes it possible to presence the classification object more accurately as a certain set of its states in the original multidimensional space. As a consequence, we turn to a new class of classification problems where objects are defined by sets of multidimensional measurements, we denote the specified condition for a reference in this text as (**).

However, the solution of problems class (**) meets certain difficulties because of an overwhelming majority developed approaches to solve the recognition problem assume a single measurement of the object features, in addition, the areas partial intersections of the original feature space for classification objects from different classes are allowed. These conditions do not allow one to direct use the individual observations for object classification, but require the development of special approaches where it is possible to operate with measurement sets or with characteristics derived from these sets or with parameters of various expedient expansions of obtained characteristics in model range. Thus, approaches to solve the problem under condition (**) are divided in two groups: direct solution of problem (**) and approaches that consider reducing the problem in wording (**) to the problem in formulation (*).

A classical approach to solve the problem class (**) was developed for two types of objects: objects specified by one-dimensional feature $z(t)$ (Figure 1) and objects specified by the values of multidimensional feature **z** on image plane (Figure 2).

To write the classification problem in the form of statement (*) for the first type of objects, the curves are determined by the values of features z_1 as the values of $z(t_1)$, the values of z_2 as $z(t_2)$, ..., the values of z_n as $z(t_n)$. To write this problem in the form of statement (*) for the second type of objects, the variables z_{ij} are defined as the different image features (*i=1,..,m*) at the object point with the coordinates of the given pixel (*j=1,..,n*). The features are interpreted as random quantities, the problem of the classifier searching is reduced to obtain the distributions

Figure 1. To problem of curves recognizing

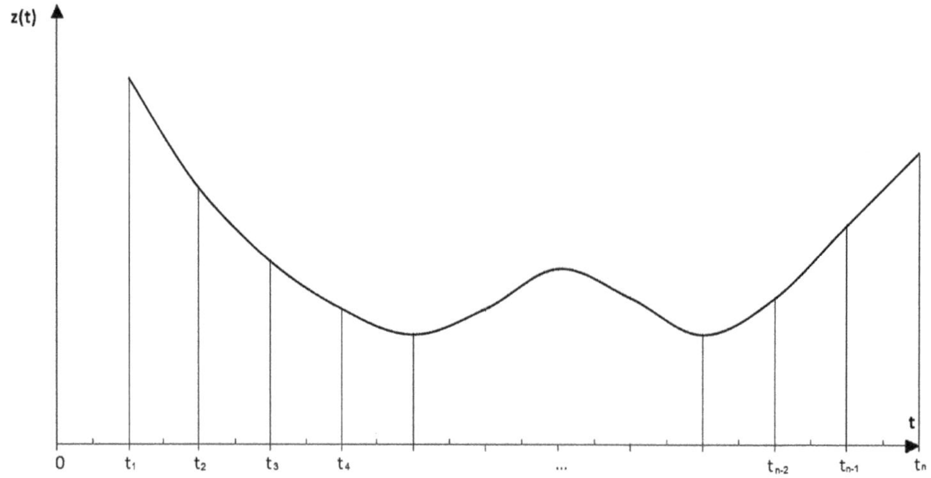

Figure 2. To problem of planar forms recognizing

of features values in classes and to calculate the discriminant function allowing to separate these objects (Fukunaga, 1990). A positive experience of such problem solving by comparing the distribution functions for various images in the low-dimensional case is shown in Shakhnarovich, Fisher and Darrell (2002) and Aranjelovic, Shakhnarovich, Fisher, Cippola and Darrel (2005). However, the need of taking into account more of the dependent features, requires the creation of a multi-multi-dimensional density with dimension $m*n$ where m is the dimension of feature vector and n is representation discreteness of the object. The complexities of such approach are well known, additionally, the necessary amount of training information required to create the above-mentioned multidimensional densities as a rule is not available. Such circumstances reduce the efficiency of density function instruments in the original feature space for objects classification.

Let's consider in more details the occurrence circumstances of problem (**).

Set, which characterizes an object, can be a result of feature measurements registered in various observation condition or of multidimensional monitoring. Diagnosis of human cardiovascular system state by analyzing the monitoring or multiple of pressure-pulse measures, obtained in various conditions, is an illustration of problem under the specified conditions. Another example of problems for the present object type is the classification (diagnosis analysis) of objects images in medical applications. These objects are defined by a pertaining point set (pixels). Each point has multiple characteristics contained in DICOM data format. In general, this means that objects, which have to be classified, are defined by feature matrix in which object is specified not by one string, as usual, but by some number of them. Wherein the quantity of such strings can be different for each object (each string is one multidimensional measurement). The same matrix is formed when the disease clinical parameters are recorded under different conditions or are the monitoring data. Measure conditions can be unknown that means a possible presence of hidden variables, which influence the object. An example of two such objects designated by sets "1" and "2" in feature space x_1, x_2 is shown in Figure 3.

The singularity of this problems class is the fact that the measurement sets representing the objects can intersect (like in Figure 3) up to the identity of some string subsets of the feature matrix belonged to objects of different classes. Here are some articles where considers this problems class: authors of Voitikova and Khursa (2013), Nastenko, Pavlov and Nosovets (2014) considers diagnostics and prognosis of disease by repeated observations or monitoring of features, authors of Biuk and Loncaric (2001), Shakhnarovich et al. (2002) considers observation and authentication applications, authors of Samsudin and Bradley (2010), Wang et al. (2011) considers problem of image-based pathology.

Figure 3. An example of an observations location of different classes of objects in the source features space

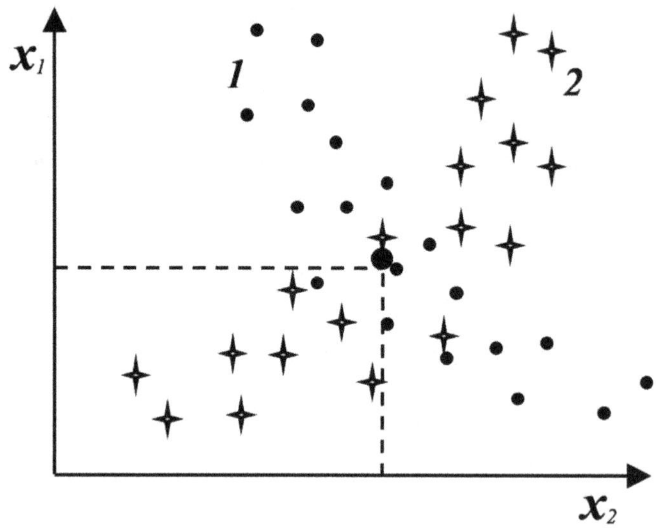

This class of problems naturally called as Set Classification Problems (SCP). According to Jung and Qiao (2014): "Set Classification Problems arise when classification tasks are based on sets of observations as opposed to individual observations" (p.1). "The classification rule in need is learned from sets of observations and also should be able to predict a single class label for a new set of observations" (p.3). At the same, time this term (SCP) was previously applied to a slightly different formulation of the Set Classification Problem (Ning & Karypis, 2009). Learning is performed here by the sets of multi-labeled observations and all the individual observations from the sets that should be classified by definition belong to the same (unknown) class.

However, it is obvious that such formulation is a particular case of a more general problem that is considered in the work of Jung and Qiao (2014) and this paper, when there is no need for the belonging of set individual observations to one class, but belonging the whole set to the class is necessary.

Moreover, learning is also carried out by sets of observations as a whole. Therefore, the authors consider it reasonable to apply the term Set Classification Problem in both cases. If it is necessary to emphasize the peculiarities of learning procedure, we will use Set Classification with Learning by Sets (SCLS) in a first case and Set Classification with Learning by Sets of Multy-Labeled Observations (SCMLO) in the second.

Please note that both of these statements can get closer if for the individual observation of the learning sample in SCLS problem, a measure of the membership of a particular class is introduced, equal to the frequency of observation presence in the sets of a particular class. The identity of observations in various patterns (e.g. in normal and tumor tissue) can be established by the presence of them in some sub-domain of measurements. An example of such observations identity could be the presence of some normal cell nuclei in a sample of the tumor tissue.

Among the works directly solving SCP can be specify (Biuk & Loncaric, 2001; Shakhnarovich et al., 2002; Aranjelovic et al., 2005) that united by the observation and authentication applications. This subclass of problems is distinguished by the fact that a separate class is presented by a specific person or otherwise a set of images that refers to the same person. Having a number of other sets of images, it is necessary to establish the identification of the person being represented or to determine whether the object belongs to the existing classes. The methods are based on one or another transformation of image sets to some more compact form that is compared with another form representing the class.

In the work of Biuk and Loncaric (2001), where the images are a fixed sequence of the representation of the person with a turn from left to right, each image is transformed into eigenimages (eigenfaces) and a vector trajectory is formed in the eigenspace. The comparison of trajectories provides the basis for assigning an object to class, or to refuse classification. In works of Shakhnarovich et al. (2002) and Aranjelovic et al. (2005) the probability density of features is another compact form of representing the images. Approaches in these cases have shown that are operable because of conditions for the formation of images (Biuk & Loncaric, 2001) and methods for transforming the feature space (Shakhnarovich et al., 2002; Aranjelovic et al., 2005). The above circumstances made it possible reducing the problem to the low-dimensional case.

An effective approach to convolution of the compared information is developing by authors Wang, Wang, Shan and Chen (2017), Tan and Gao (2017) and Wang, Guo, Davis and Dai (2012). The problem of closeness measure of covariance matrices of images that lie on a specific Symmetric Positive Definite (SPD) Riemannian manifold solves here. This allows obtaining good results in problems where it is possible to form features with a distinct linear dependence as a basis for the distinctive ability of classes.

Summarizing the review above, an obvious conclusion can be made that in the case of an arbitrary non-linear dependence of features representing objects in the sets of observations, it is necessary to propose a generalization approach that allows to base the classification system on the forms and parameters of these dependencies.

Other works that are close to the proposed approach are discussed in next section.

THE FORMAL PROBLEM STATEMENT

The fact of the existence of some set of classes $D = \left\{\bar{D}^1, \bar{D}^2, \ldots, \bar{D}^K\right\}$ is given. These classes are finite or infinite sets of objects: $\bar{D}^1 = \left\{\bar{d}^1\right\}$, $\bar{D}^2 = \left\{\bar{d}^2\right\}, \ldots,$ $\bar{D}^K = \left\{\bar{d}^K\right\}$.

It is known that sets $\bar{D}^i \cap \bar{D}^j = \varnothing$ when $i \neq j$. Classes $\bar{D}^1, \bar{D}^2, \ldots, \bar{D}^K$ are given as their approximations $D^1 \subset \bar{D}^1$, $D^2 \subset \bar{D}^2$, ..., $D^K \subset \bar{D}^K$ through the truncated sets of objects that belong to these classes: $D^1 = \left\{d^1\right\} \subset \left\{\bar{d}^1\right\}$, $D^2 = \left\{d^2\right\} \subset \left\{\bar{d}^2\right\}$, .., $D^K = \left\{d^K\right\} \subset \left\{\bar{d}^K\right\}$, where the mentioned sets are: $\left\{d^1\right\} = \left\{d^1_1, \ldots, d^1_{n_1}\right\}$, $\left\{d^2\right\} = \left\{d^2_1, \ldots, d^2_{n_2}\right\}$, ..., $\left\{d^K\right\} = \left\{d^K_1, \ldots, d^K_{n_K}\right\}$.

It is obvious that since $\bar{D}^i \cap \bar{D}^j = \varnothing$ is true, $D^i \cap D^j = \varnothing$ is also true when $i \neq j$.

It is suppose that classified objects d are given by the sets of measurement vectors $\left\{\boldsymbol{z}\right\}_d$ in finite dimensional space $Z \subset R^M$ of variables $\left(z_1, \ldots, z_M\right)$, where vectors $\boldsymbol{z}$ form sets (domains) $\bar{Z}^1, \bar{Z}^2, \ldots, \bar{Z}^K$ appropriate to the classes $\bar{D}^1, \bar{D}^2, \ldots, \bar{D}^K$. As was pointed out above, a partial intersection of the $\left\{\boldsymbol{z}\right\}_d$ sets belonging to different classes is possible in the Z space (according to Figure 3) resulting a possible partial intersection the sets (domains) $\bar{Z}^i$.

It is necessary to develop the best classification rule for dividing the objects of initial sets $\left\{\bar{D}^1, \bar{D}^2, \ldots, \bar{D}^K\right\}$ based on the learning subsets of objects d from different classes $Z^1 \subset \bar{Z}^1$, $Z^2 \subset \bar{Z}^2$, ..., $Z^K \subset \bar{Z}^K$.

WAY TO SOLVE THE PROBLEM

Let's consider other possible ways of solving the problem. First, formalize data at the input of our problem. Let in space $Z \subset R^M$ is given the learning subsets $Z^1 \subset \bar{Z}^1, Z^2 \subset \bar{Z}^2$, ..., $Z^K \subset \bar{Z}^K$ of objects $\left\{d^i_j\right\}$, where *i* is a class index, *j* is a class object index. Each object d^i_j is defined in space Z by subsets $Z_{d^i_j}$ of multidimensional observations (vector-rows) $\boldsymbol{z}_t$ of an feature matrix *M*, $Z_{d^i_j} = \left\{\boldsymbol{z}_t\right\}_{d^i_j}$. Let the data matrix is ordered by classes, denote n_k the number of objects in class k, $n = \sum_{k=1}^{K} n_k$ is the number of matrix objects. Let's write further the number of observations in each class. If this number in each object of class k is the same and equal to N_{W^k}, then $N_k = n_k \cdot N_{W^k}$. If number of observations in objects d_i^k is different and equal $N_{W_i^k}$, then $N_k = \sum_{i=1}^{n_k} N_{W_i^k}$ .Here indices W^k and W_i^k denote the learning subsets of observations in corresponding classes and individual objects of class k, respectively. The total number of observations (rows) in the data matrix is

$$N = \sum_{k=1}^{K} N_K = \sum_{k=1}^{K} \sum_{i=1}^{n_k} N_{W_i^k} .$$

The essential further is that for each object d_i^k is known not one, but some subset of observations $Z_{d_i^k} = \{z_j\}_{d_i^k}$, here

$$j = \sum_{p=1}^{k-1} N_p + \sum_{q=1}^{i-1} N_{W_q^k} + 1, \ldots, \sum_{p=1}^{k-1} N_p + \sum_{q=1}^{i} N_q^k ,$$

where i is the number of the object in class k. It's also essential that, in the general case, the objects existence domains d_i and d_j, $Z^{d_i}, Z^{d_j} \subset Z$ represented in learning subsets by vectors $Z_{d_i} = \{z_t\}_{t \in d_i}$, $Z_{d_j} = \{z_t\}_{t \in d_j}$ can intersect partially, and these objects can belong to the different classes. Then it is possible to consider the following two ways to convert the statement (**) to the classification problem in conditions (*). One of them is to find for objects d_j^k a convolution $z_{d_j^k}^{\theta} = \sum_{z \in W(k,j)} \theta \cdot z$ of observations subset $Z_{d_j^k} = \{z\}_{d_j^k}$ in such a way that it identically determines the object d_j in its class k within original feature space $z_1, \ldots, z_M$. Such convolution determination (parameters θ) should be followed by the best object classification condition in present convolution class. The simplest convolution variant is objects presentation by their centroids. Two sets (points and stars), which represent two objects of different classes, are shown in Figure 3. The example shows the low efficiency of object presentation by centroids: the centers ones coincide on features, and the objects in such representation are indiscernible. As for the possibility of constructing classifiers or separating such objects by complex boundaries based on the initial features: we take into account that coinciding subset measurements of objects of different classes in any new space of transformed original features will be also coincide. Hence, there are no classifiers or boundaries of any complexity level which can differentiate such objects in original features space.

The second approach takes into account that dependence of initial features and the presence of a measurement set for each object provides an opportunity of modeling the characteristic relationships that underlie the phenomena under study. The structure features and the parameter values of these models can be used as the basis for classification system. Thus, the sense of the approach is the solution the SC problem in the parameters space of classification objects models.

The idea to solve the problems in the space of objects model parameters is not new. This approach was used to the problems of identifying regression models' parameters which are such that in the best way to solve the approximation or prediction problems. The tasks of information compression are similar to this idea. The same applies to the classical approaches of solving the classification problem in formulation (*). Let's demonstrate the possibility of applying the same principle in SC problem.

Let the object d is defined by a set of points $Z_d = \{\boldsymbol{z}\}_d$ of unknown object's characteristics $f_d(z_1,\ldots,z_M) = 0$ in the initial feature space $z_1,\ldots,z_M$. It is supposed to be as many object's characteristics as the number of given objects:

$$f_d(z_1, z_2, \ldots, z_M) = 0, d = 1, \ldots, n. \tag{1}$$

Now consider the case, when among the initial variables $z_1,\ldots,z_M$ it is possible to distinguish the output variable y. Let's X denotes the new feature space of generalized variables $x_1, x_2, \ldots, x_m$ derived from the initial space $Z \subset R^M$. It is assumed the possibility representing of characteristics (1) that based on the $Z_d = \{\boldsymbol{z}\}_d$ sets as linear convolutions by generalized variables $x_1, x_2, \ldots, x_m$. Then, characteristics (1) can be found in the following form:

$$y = a_0 + \sum_{i=1}^{m} a_i \varphi_i(z) = a_0 + \sum_{i=1}^{m} a_i x_i, \tag{2}$$

where m denotes the space dimension of the generalized variables x_i, $i = 1, \ldots, m$ in which representing now the d objects.

Then the solution of the classification problem can be transferred to the parameter space $A \subset R^m$ and the values of the vector parameters $\boldsymbol{a} = (a_0, a_1, \ldots, a_m)$ of the $y = a_0 + \sum_{i=1}^{m} a_i x_i$ characteristics will define the objects in this new space. Single vectors $\boldsymbol{a}_d$ unambiguously define the objects d due to an absence of completely coincided $Z_{d_j} = \{z\}_{d_j}$ subsets. And now there is an opportunity to classify the d objects already as $\boldsymbol{a}_d$ points in the parameters space A.

An objection about the use of this approach can be associated with a possible violation of the compactness hypothesis and the attendant problems associated with the choice of proximity measure in the resulting space A in solving the classification problem. However, as will be shown, this circumstance can be taken into account by selecting the appropriate an external criterion for modeling (2). The example presented in Figure 3, Figure 4, Figure 5 shows the possible effectiveness of this approach.

Figure 4. Object Models in the space of initial features

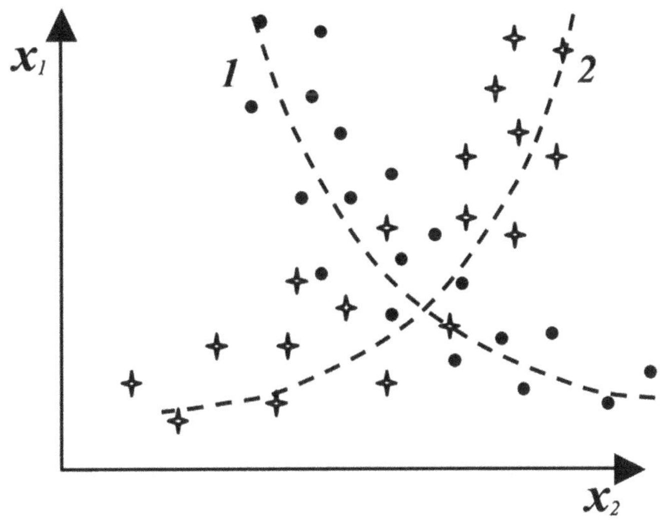

Figure 5. Objects representation in the models parameter space

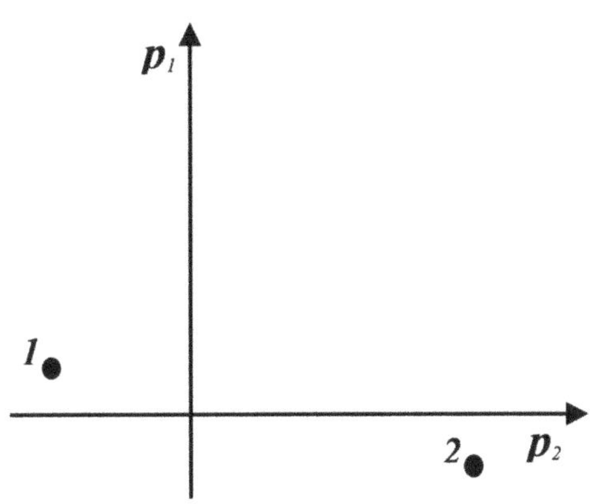

As can be seen two objects that are defined by their sets of measurements are inseparable in the space of initial features. When models had been created on the basis of every set (Figure 4) in the models parameter space (hyperbola parameters $x_1 = 1 / (p_1 x_1 + p_2) + k$) the indicated objects are already divided efficiently (Figure 5). The separation efficiency is higher than more differs the structure and / or parameter values of constructed models. Hence, the classification problem solution is advisable to move from original features space to the space of object models parameters.

Then indicate the articles that most closely approached the realization of this idea. A solving the problem of diagnosing cardiac muscle disruptions on the basis of signs that were received as parameters of the electrocardiogram signal expansion into the orthogonal discrete Kravchuk series is shown in work of Zabara, Filimonova and Zelensky (2009). The degree of approach conformity to solve the SC problems allowed to make the transition in the parametric space using fairly simple mathematical tools in a work of Voitikova and Khursa (2013). Here, the problem of forecasting the acute hypotensive episode was considered when observing cardiac patient. The context of problem is described in detail by Moody and Lehman (2009). The observation was carried out for patients in the intensive care unit for a main disease. Some patients had at least one acute hypotensive episode during the observation period. Other patients the problems with pressure were not experienced. These groups of patients formed a 2-class learning sets with a high and low risk of developing menacing hypertension. The used discreteness of pressure measurements of time series data was every 15 minutes. The received measurement sets were used to construct linear regressions of systolic, diastolic and pulse pressure. Then, in the 4-dimensional parameter space of obtained models a classification system was constructed by the support vector method. A fairly high indicator of correct classification 93% was obtained. It should be note that the problem was solved for a fairly rough division into classes (two classes) which made it possible to obtain a high-quality classification based on the linear regression parameters values. However, a more detailed approach to assessing the functional state of the cardiovascular system (5 or more classes) requires the construction of nonlinear models of the dependence of the pulse, systolic and diastolic pressure parameters (Nastenko, Pavlov & Nosovets, 2014). Therefore, it is desirable to offer a more general approach allowing to search the nonlinear structures and to orient the objects modeling on the quality of set classification problem solution. Such requirements can be satisfied within the theory of Group Method of Data Handling algorithms (Ivakhnenko & Stepashko, 1985, Madala & Ivakhnenko, 1994). Next, approach implementation variants are highlights:

- The models of all objects (of all classes) are creating on the same structure, while the model parameters can reflect the characteristic features of classes.

Then the modeling problem decision concerning of structural synthesis is directed for searching of exactly such structure for all objects. Each object can now be represented by a point in parameter space of obtained models. Classification problem will be solving in this space;

- The classes differences structural do not allow to display their particular qualities within a single structure object models. In this case, the object models are created in each class on the basis of optimal structure for each class. Herewith, optimality is formulated in terms of a) cumulative accuracy of class object models and b) class objects separability from all other classes. Classification problem is solved according to the used external criteria: classification can be performed in accordance with the accuracy of representation of object by the model for each found class structure or can be solved by classifiers in the parameter space of class structures by the principle "one against all" or by classifiers in the space of parameters of the "united" structure.

ALGORITHMIC DECISIONS

Algorithmic decisions of structural parametric synthesis are indicated for the above-mentioned cases.

Algorithms Search of the Best Common Structure

Algorithms search of the best common structure are offered in two implementation variations:

- Combinatorial algorithm of Group Method of Data Handling (COMBI GMDH), focused on obtaining the smallest cumulative error of all models. The algorithm guarantees a global optimum when searching for structure of models, but the necessity of full enumeration of all candidate structures restricts the rational use of algorithm with the number of arguments no more than 6-9. In higher dimensions, you should use multi-layer or multistage algorithms (Ivakhnenko & Stepashko, 1985).
- Recurrence additive multiplicative multistage algorithm GMDH (RAMMA GMDH), which implements shortened enumeration of structures.

Combinatorial Algorithm of Group Method of Data Handling

The algorithm task is to find a structure (non-linear basis $\phi_i(z) = x_i, i = 1,...,m$) that best represents in some meaning the dependencies

$$y_d = a_{d_0} + \sum_{i=1}^{m} a_{d_i}\phi_i(z) = a_{d_0} + \sum_{i=1}^{m} a_{d_i}x_i,\ d = 1,...,n. \tag{3}$$

from the experimental data $Z_d = \{z\}_d$. Formalization of a concept of "best meanings" and their correct use in the structural-parametric synthesis of models is substantiated in Group Method of Data Handling theory. Optimality is understand here as an achievement of the best value of the "external criterion" in the process of structures enumeration when synthesizing the model (Ivakhnenko & Stepashko, 1985).

According to Knyshov, Nastenko, Kondrashova, Nosovets and Pavlov (2014) to adapt the COMBI algorithm for solving our problem it is necessary to:

- Determine the external criterion of the algorithm for finding the best general structure for objects models of all classes $d = 1,\ldots,n$;
- Choose a rational approach calculating the parameters of particular models in order to minimize the calculating time of the optimal structure;
- Determine the search order of particular models.

Selection of External Criterion

The model parameters are calculate on training data sample and the best structure is choose based on minimum of external criterion in accordance with principles of GMDH (Ivakhnenko & Stepashko, 1985; Madala & Ivakhnenko, 1994). This means that such a common structure $\phi_i(z) = x_i, i = 1,...,m$ is search for all $d = 1,\ldots,n$ models which parameters $a_{d_0},..,a_{d_m}$, $d = 1,...,n$ found from the training sample will most accurately represent all object models (3) in the sense of the external criterion.

For each object $d = d(k,i)$, where *k* is a class number, *i* is an object number in the class, a set of its learning observations is indicated $W(k,i) = A(k,i) + B(k,i)$, where $A(k,i), B(k,i)$ are training and testing observation samples. Accordingly, $W(k) = A(k) + B(k)$, $A(k)$, $B(k)$ - are sets of learning, training and testing object observations of class *k* and $W = A + B$, A, B are observation sets from learning, training and testing samples of objects of all classes, respectively.

We will use further one of the simplest forms of the external criterion because of a weak point of COMBY algorithms is a total amount of calculations. This form is a corrected accuracy criterion:

$$Cr = \alpha \cdot \Delta_A^\gamma + (1-\alpha) \cdot \Delta_B^\gamma , \tag{4}$$

where α is the weight of training sample errors, (1- α) is the weight of testing sample errors, the error criterion calculated for all models at training observations:

$$\Delta_A^\gamma = \left(\frac{\sum_k^K \gamma_k \sum_j^{n_k} \sum_{i \in A(k,j)} \left(Y_{kji} - \sum_q^M x_{iq} a_{kiq}^A \right)^2}{\sum_{i \in A} (Y_i)^2} \right)^{-1/2} , \tag{5}$$

Δ_A^γ is weighted in classes with coefficients γ_k, the error criterion for models found on training samples and counted on test observations:

$$\Delta_B^\gamma = \left(\frac{\sum_k^K \gamma_k \sum_j^{n_k} \sum_{i \in B(k,j)} \left(Y_{kji} - \sum_q^M x_{iq} a_{kiq}^A \right)^2}{\sum_{i \in B} (Y_i)^2} \right)^{-1/2} . \tag{6}$$

Δ_B^γ is weighted in classes with the coefficients γ_k, *k* is the index of the class, *j* is the index of object in class, *i* runs through all observations of the object *j* of class *k* on samples *A* for (5) or samples *B* for (6), respectively. Since the centered values of variables are use in calculations there is no need centering the output values Y_i in the formulas (5,6). In notation of the parameter vector $\boldsymbol{a}_{kj}^A$ and the individual parameter a_{kjq}^A, index *A* indicates the parameters are found on training sample of object.

Parameters Calculation and Search Order Selection of the Particular Models

COMBI algorithm finds the best structure as a part of complete polynomial:

$$y = a_0' + \sum_{i=1}^{M} a_i' z_i + \sum_{i=1}^{M}\sum_{j=1}^{M} a_{ij}' z_i z_j + \sum_{i=1}^{M}\sum_{j=1}^{M}\sum_{k=1}^{M} a_{ijk}' z_i z_j z_k + \ldots, \tag{7}$$

where the number of the composite sums is p, the number of the terms of polynomial (7) $m = C_{M+p}^{M} - 1$, the number of the sub-polynomials of polynomial (7) $q = 2^m - 1$.The structural elements of the complete polynomial we call as the generalized variables (GV) and denoted them as $x_i, i = 1, \ldots, m$. In a new notation, expression (7) will have a linear form:

$$y = a_0' + \sum_{i=1}^{m} a_i' x_i \, . \tag{8}$$

To find the parameters of a certain sub-polynomial (9) with the corresponding collection GV x

$$y_k = a_0 + a_1 x_{i_1} + \ldots + a_{\tilde{m}} x_{i_{\tilde{m}}} \tag{9}$$

and with the length $\tilde{m}$ it is necessary forming an information matrix $(X^T X)_{\tilde{m} \times \tilde{m}}$, and solving the normal system of equations, having obtained a solution

$$\boldsymbol{a} = (X^T X)^{-1} X^T Y \, . \tag{10}$$

It is possible to organize the enumeration of sub-polynomials of polynomial (7) without optimizing this process: first will search all linear models, second all quadratic ones, etc. to polynomials of degree p. The number of operations (and the computation time) for calculating (10) for (9) will be proportional $\tilde{m}^3$ with this approach. However, it is possible to reduce the computational complexity by an order of magnitude up to $\tilde{m}^2$ (Ivakhnenko & Stepashko, 1985) by organizing the sequences of embedded structures and using the recurrence formulas of Bordering

Method for Least-Squares Method (LSMB) to calculate the parameters. The rationale for applying the scheme for models enumeration with parameters calculating by LSMB for combinatorial algorithm of GMDH was proposed by Stepashko (1981).

To use of LSMB requires the enumeration organization in such a way that particular models are selected for calculating the parameters in the order that forms a complex of successively embedded structures $(x_{i_1}),(x_{i_1},x_{i_2}),..., (x_{i_1},x_{i_2},....,x_{i_k})$. The mechanism of embedded complexes formation of the additive structures of form

$$Y_k = a_{d1}x_{i_1} ... + a_{d(k-1)}x_{i_{k-1}} + a_{dk}x_{i_k}, d = 1,...,n$$

is evident from the tree graphical representation of the complete enumeration of additive models (Figure 6).

Here, also a binary counter is given, when adding to the last bit of which 1, a sequential, right-to-left path along the enumeration tree is generated. The counter establishes a correspondence between its decimal value, as the model number when circumventing the tree and units in it, as indicators (by location of bit) of entering in the model of the corresponding GV.

The tree branches from root x_p to the end sheet x_1 form embedded structures. Consider the current state of the counter on that part of the tree that "grows" from

Figure 6. The tree of complete enumeration of additive models

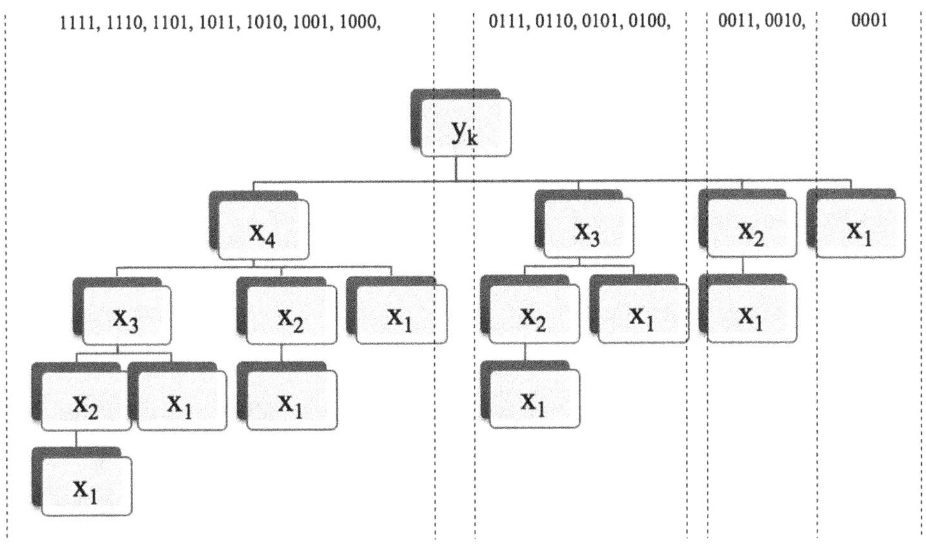

root p at level k. Let the sum "modulo 2" of the current and subsequent states of the counter be a value with only one unit in any of bits. Then, two indicated states of the counter reflect the embedded structures, and the vertices on the tree satisfy the condition of contiguity and are on the same branch at levels k and $k+1$ of the tree. If the amount differs from the specified value, then the second counter state moves the location to another branch of the tree. The sum "modulo 2" that representing the state of the counter with two units in any digits indicates the transition to the next branch on the left at the same level k, with the common of tree branching for the previous state at level k-1. The sum "modulo 2" representing the state of the counter with three units indicates the transition of the current state on the tree to the next branch on the left at level k-1 with the common ancestor of the previous state on this branch at level k-2. And so on. These properties make it easy to define the branches of embedded structures of the enumeration tree and to forget information in the nodes for recurrent calculation at the moment when all the descendants of each ancestor are counted.

It is possible now to use the recursive formulas of the LSMB for calculating model parameters for additive embedded structures corresponding to branches of the enumeration tree. In each tree vertex it is calculated:

1. The information matrix and its inverse for each object d.
2. A vector of model parameters $\boldsymbol{a}_d$ on a given structure on training samples for each object d.
3. The value of the selection criterion Cr_i characterizing the structure.
4. The number s, equal to the number of already calculated descendants for each ancestor.

In this way, each vertex $i = 1,...,q = 2^m - 1$ of the tree is calculated. The tree circumventing is completed when the current state of the counter reaches the maximum value. In the end, the structure for which the selection criterion has adopted the minimum value is selected. Let's show the implementation of LSMB in the algorithm for some branch of enumeration tree.

Suppose that on level k-1 of the tree we have some additive structure $x_{i_1},...,x_{i_{k-1}}$, the corresponding information matrices $G_{k-1} = (X^T X)_{(k-1)\times(k-1)}$ and its inverse $G_{k-1}^{-1} = (X^T X)_{(k-1)\times(k-1)}^{-1}$ have been calculated. For structure $x_{i_1},...,x_{i_{k-1}}, x_{i_k}$ of the next level k of the enumeration tree, we know the information matrix of the next step G_k. The parameters $\boldsymbol{a} = G_k^{-1} X^T Y$ recurrent calculation of the model $Y_k = a_1 x_1 ... + a_{k-1} x_{k-1} + a_k x_{i_k}$ the GMDH COMBI algorithm requires an appropriate mechanism LSMB for calculating the matrix $G_k^{-1} = (X^T X)_{k\times k}$ (Stepashko, 1981). Briefly, this mechanism:

At step k the information matrix of the previous calculation step is known

$$G_{k-1} = \begin{vmatrix} g_{1,1} & \cdots & g_{1,k-1} \\ \cdots & \cdots & \cdots \\ g_{k-1,1} & \cdots & g_{k-1,k-1} \end{vmatrix}.$$

If the matrix of the next step G_k is written in block form $G_k = \begin{vmatrix} G_{k-1} & u_k \\ v_k & g_{kk} \end{vmatrix}$,

where $v_k = (g_{k,1},\dots,g_{k,k-1})$, $u_n = (g_{k,1},\dots,g_{k,k-1})^T$, then the inverse matrix of step k - matrix G_k^{-1} can be written as

$$G_k^{-1} = \begin{bmatrix} G_{k-1}^{-1} + \dfrac{G_{k-1}^{-1} u_k v_k G_{k-1}^{-1}}{g_k} & -\dfrac{G_{k-1}^{-1} u_k}{g_k} \\ \dfrac{v_k G_{k-1}^{-1}}{g_k} & \dfrac{1}{g_k} \end{bmatrix},$$

where $g_k = g_{kk} - v_k G_{k-1}^{-1} u_k$

It should be noted that it is possible to reduce the dimension of the information matrix due to calculations in centered variables $Y = y - \overline{y}_A$, $X_{i_k} = x_{i_k} - \overline{x}_{A,i_k}$, where index A denotes the training sub-sample, (further, A index is omitted). The free term will be equal to zero in the resulting models, the criteria value for these models will change to a constant, which will allow one to find the best structures of the model in a centered form. It is possible to classify objects directly in the parametric space of a centered version of data after determining the best structure for centered models $Y_k = a_1^k x_{i_1} + \dots + a_k^k x_{i_k}$. However, if necessary, we can find the free member of models replacing the centered values of variables through initial values and their averages, then we get

$$(y - \overline{y}) = a_1^k (x_{i_1} - \overline{x}_{i_1}) + \dots + a_k^k (x_{i_k} - \overline{x}_{i_k}).$$

Hence, taking into account equation $y = a_0^k + a_1^k x_{i_1} + \dots + a_k^k x_{i_k}$ we find $a_0^k = \overline{y} - a_1^k \overline{x}_{i_1} - \dots - a_k^k \overline{x}_{i_k}$. As a result, the algorithm for determining the structure of the parametric feature space for classification problem is reduced to the following stages:

1. Data preprocessing:
   a. the generalized variables matrix formation;
   b. the transition to a matrix of centered variables.
2. Formation the maximum size of an information matrix.
3. Organization the enumeration of structures with the formation of embedded structures on the enumeration tree. For each generated structure, the following actions are performed:
   a. the formation of information matrix of given structure for each object d, using the result of clause 2;
   b. the model parameters calculation on this structure for each object using LSMB;
   c. the calculation of the value external criterion of the structure.
4. The best structure selection by minimizing of the external criterion value.

Using the Results

Based on the results above, we obtain the optimal structure $(x_{i_1}, x_{i_2}, ..., x_{i_k})$ and perform the recalculation of the parameters $\boldsymbol{a}_d$ for n models

$$Y_k = a_{d_1} x_{i_1} ... + a_{d_{(k-1)}} x_{i_{k-1}} + a_{d_k} x_{i_k}, d = 1, ..., n$$

on the whole learning sample W of the matrix of centered data. The obtained vectors $\boldsymbol{a}_d$ form the feature matrix of classes $k = 1, ..., K$ of objects $d = 1, ..., n$ in the parameter space A. Then, it is necessary to analyze the properties of the classes in A in order an appropriate classification algorithm choosing.

Recurrence Additive Multiplicative Multistage Algorithm GMDH

The main difference from the previous algorithm is that it implements shortened enumeration of structures. Models are searched in formulas class

$$y_1 = a_0 + a_1 x_{i_1}, ..., y_k = a_0 + a_1 x_{i_1} + ... + a_k x_{i_k}, ...,$$

where generalized arguments x_{i_j} are chosen from complete polynomial term set (7) of specified degree *p*. Here z_j, $j = 1, ..., m$ are extended set of original variables.

It consists of transformations $z_j', (z_j')^{-1}, (z_j')^{1/3}, (z_j')^{-1/3}$, $j = 1, ..., M$ of original variables z_j' for the possibility of presence in the models the arguments both positive and negative rational degrees. The best generalized variable is added into the structure as an individual polynomial term of (7) on each stage according to the value of the external criterion. So RAMMA GMDH includes the following stages:

1. **The Matrix Formation of Expanded Set Of Initial Features:** It is suggested extending initial features set z by additional variables $1/z, z^{1/3}, z^{-1/3}$ to provide the better of solution accuracy.
2. **Generalized Variables Matrix Calculation:** Each GV is one of the terms of the polynomial (7) or one of the possible products of the extended set variables raised to a power that is limited by the maximal polynomial power p. If there are m variables in the initial extended matrix, then the best way to generate GVs is to form a sequence of numbers in ($p+1$) notation without those which sum of digits is more than p. The amount of the numbers is calculated as $S = C_{m+p}^{m} - 1$ and is the quantity of terms in the polynomial. Obtained S numbers in ($p+1$) notation are the GVs where the bit number corresponds to the variables from the extended matrix and the bit value demonstrates the power of each extended variable in the current GV. A similar approach was used in work of Stepashko (1981).
3. **Information Matrix Calculation:** To avoid repeated calculations $X^T X$ for each object structure parameters at each stage of algorithm the maximum size information matrix is calculated.
4. **Structures Generation and Parameters Evaluation:** Model generation at the stage k is performed using the $y_k = a_0 + a_1 x_{i_1} + \ldots + a_k x_{i_k}$ formula where $x_{i_1}, \ldots x_{i_{k-1}}$ were obtained at the previous stages and the x_{i_k} is determined at the current stage.

To generate the GV for the current stage model, the enumeration tree is used (Figure 7). For this, movement along the tree nodes from left to right and from top to bottom is realized. For the tree depicted in Figure 7, the corresponding image of the polynomial terms will be the set displayed in Table 1. In order to move along a given tree from left to right and from top to bottom it is necessary to ascend the table from the bottom up, first by rows, the sum of the values of which is 1, then, where it is 2 and further (up to $p+1$). There are two parameters in the algorithm that control the number of structures surviving a stage: F_1, F_2. The F_1 is used at

Figure 7. Enumeration tree of the multiplicative terms

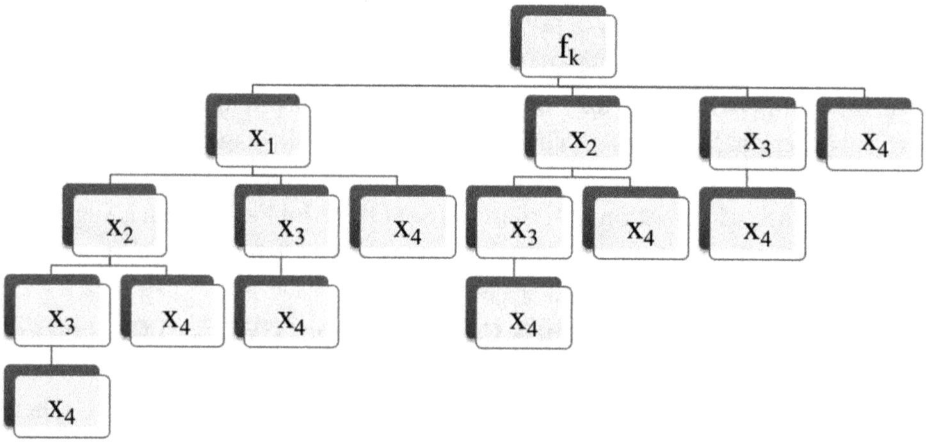

Table 1. The polynomial terms scheme

Z_3	Z_2	Z_1
0	0	1
0	0	2
0	0	3
0	1	0
0	1	1
0	1	2
0	2	0
0	2	1
0	3	0
1	0	0
1	0	1
1	0	2
1	1	0
1	1	1
1	2	0
2	0	0
2	0	1
2	1	0
3	0	0

the first stage and the F_2 – at the others. Additionally, the F number of best structures are retained and is given as the result when the algorithm stops.

Since models $y_k = a_0 + a_1 x_{i_1} + \ldots + a_k x_{i_k}$ are formed by the sequential addition of new generalized variables, they form complexes of embedded structures. Therefore, LSMB is used to calculate model parameters similarly to the version of COMBI in Section 1.1.2.

5. **The External Criterion Used:** It is possible to offer more complex, but more effective external criteria in connection with the possibility in RAMMA to organize a reduced search of model structures:
5. a. **Combined Accuracy Criterion:**

$$Cr_{sel} = (1-\beta)\cdot\left(\alpha\cdot\Delta_A^{\gamma} + (1-\alpha)\cdot\Delta_B^{\gamma}\right) + \beta\cdot\left|\frac{\Delta_B^{\gamma} - \Delta_A^{\gamma}}{\Delta_B^{\gamma} + \Delta_A^{\gamma}}\right|, \tag{11}$$

where meanings α, γ, Δ_A^{γ}, Δ_B^{γ} were specified (5), (6) in section 1.1.1., the new additive component of criterion (11) with respect to the corrected accuracy criterion is the balance criterion, β is the weight of the balance criterion in the combined criteria.

b. **Separability Criterion:** Since, the final goal is classification, it is logical to assess the quality of the desired structure in terms of its separating ability. Therefore, it is proposed to calculate the external criterion, which is based on the relation of the sum of the variances of objects within classes to the value of the variance between the centers of classes in the space of the parameters the object models of the constructed structure.

$$Cr_{sep} = \frac{\frac{1}{K}\sum_{j=1}^{K}\frac{1}{n_j}\sum_{r_i\in R_j}^{n_j}\left\|\boldsymbol{a}_i - \bar{\boldsymbol{a}}_j\right\|^2}{\frac{1}{C_K^2}\sum_{i=1}^{K}\sum_{j=i+1}^{K}\left\|\bar{\boldsymbol{a}}_i - \bar{\boldsymbol{a}}_j\right\|^2}, \tag{12}$$

where C_K^2 is the number of combinations from K to 2.

Taking into account the variance for each of m coordinates ($p = 1,\ldots,m$, where m is the dimension of the space A= R^m) and understanding the norm as the Euclidean distance (13), expression (12) takes form (14). Here, for convenience, the re-designation was introduced: the current number of class q was transferred as the superscript

$$\left\|\boldsymbol{a}_i - \bar{\boldsymbol{a}}_j\right\|^2 = \sum_{p=1}^{m} (\boldsymbol{a}_{ip} - \bar{\boldsymbol{a}}_p^q)^2; \tag{13}$$

$$Cr_{sep} = \frac{\frac{1}{K}\sum_{q=1}^{K}\frac{1}{n_q}\sum_{i=1}^{n_q}\sum_{p=1}^{m}\left(a_{ip} - \bar{a}_p^q\right)^2}{\frac{1}{C_K^2}\sum_{i=1}^{K}\sum_{j=i+1}^{K}\sum_{p=1}^{m}\left(\bar{a}_{ip} - \bar{a}_p^q\right)^2}. \tag{14}$$

Search Algorithm of the Each Class Best Structures

Generally, the need to take into account the specificity of classes requires a description of objects belonging to different classes by the different structures. This demands suggesting new algorithms for obtaining the optimal structures for every class as well as the ways of their application to classification. Therefore, algorithm (next version RAMMAs) that search for the structures most appropriate for the separation of each class in the parameter space is proposed. The quality of each structure at each class evaluated here.

As you can see, both algorithms have much in common. The main modification concerns changes in external criteria. It takes into account NRMS $E\left(k\right)$ and dispersion $D\left(k\right)$ components in models parameter space and should be calculated separately for each class k as:

$$Cr\left(k\right) = \beta E\left(k\right) + \left(1 - \beta\right) D(k), \tag{15}$$

where β defines the weighs ratio of the criterion components.

$E\left(k\right)$ accounts for current class k and other classes k':

$$E\left(k\right) = \left(\frac{Err\left(k\right) + Err\left(k'\right)}{\sum_{i\in A}\left(Y_i\right)^2}\right)^{1/2} \tag{16}$$

The notations of $Err\left(k\right)$ and $Err\left(k'\right)$ imply that:

$$Err(k) = \gamma_k \sum_{j}^{n_k} \sum_{i \in A(k,j)} \left(Y_{kji} - \sum_{p}^{M} x_{ip} a_{kjp}^{A} \right)^2 . \quad (17)$$

$$Err(k') = \gamma_k' (\sum_{q=1}^{k-1} \sum_{j}^{n_q} \sum_{i \in A(q,j)} \left(Y_{qji} - \sum_{p}^{M} x_{ip} a_{qjp}^{A} \right)^2 + \sum_{q=k-1}^{K} \sum_{j}^{n_q} \sum_{i \in A(q,j)} \left(Y_{qji} - \sum_{p}^{M} x_{ip} a_{qjp}^{A} \right)^2 . \quad (18)$$

The class coefficients y_k and y_k' are equal to 1 and 0 in general, but could be given manually if it is necessary.

The determination of the optimal structures S_i°, $i = 1, \ldots, K$ when $\beta = 1$ implies using the accuracy measure of object representation via obtained classes structures.

The dispersion part of criterion (15) characterizes the divisibility capability of the structure. It is based on the dispersion minimization in the classes and the classes centers distance maximization:

$$D(k) = \frac{\alpha \cdot D^{in}(k) + (1-\alpha) \cdot D^{in}(k')}{Dist(k)}, \quad (19)$$

where α allows accounting the object dispersion relative to the classes centers with a different power when the structure is determined. The dispersions inside class k and other classes k' are:

$$D^{in}(k) = \frac{1}{n_k} \sum_{i=1}^{n_k} \sum_{p=1}^{m} \left(a_{ip}^{k} - \bar{a}_{p}^{k} \right)^2 , \quad (20)$$

$$D^{in}(k') = \sum_{j=1}^{k-1} \frac{1}{n_q} \sum_{i=1}^{n_q} \sum_{p=1}^{m} \left(a_{ip}^{q} - \bar{a}_{p}^{q} \right)^2 + \sum_{j=k+1}^{K} \frac{1}{n_q} \sum_{i=1}^{n_q} \sum_{p=1}^{m} \left(a_{ip}^{q} - \bar{a}_{p}^{q} \right)^2 . \quad (21)$$

The distance between the class center k and the center of class k' (a union of all the points except those which belong to class k) is:

$$Dist\left(k\right) = \sum_{p=1}^{m}\left(\overline{a}_p^k \quad \overline{a}_p^{k'}\right)^2, \tag{22}$$

where $\overline{a}_p^{k'}$ is the centre of class k'.

As a result, the approach allows obtaining as many structures as the classified classes, and each of the structures is the most relevant for the corresponding class.

The determination of the optimal structures S_i°, $i = 1,\ldots,K$ when $\beta = 0$ implies development of classifying system that utilizes the "one-vs-all" principle in the space of obtained structures.

EXAMPLE: THE HUMAN CARDIOVASCULAR SYSTEM FUNCTIONAL STATE CLASSIFICATION PROBLEM

Problem Description

The challenge was inspired by a real-world classification problem of determining the cardiovascular system functional states based on the measurements of pulse and pressure in different circumstances. Group of 96 patients is given, each of them belongs to one of five functional classes of cardiovascular system states:

1. Arterial hypertension.
2. Isolated systolic hypertension.
3. Normal regulation.
4. Heart failure of low levels.
5. Heart failure of high levels.

Sets of 3-dimensional measures of diastolic pressure, systolic pressure, heart rate (DIA, SYS, HR) are given for every patient in quantity of 4 to 151, received in various conditions. The objects number in classes and the values boundaries of observations number in each class are given in the Table 2.

The goal is to construct the functional states classifiers of the cardiovascular system: arterial hypertension, normal regulation, isolated systolic hypertension and heart failure of various degrees.

It is not possible to solve our problem by constructing classifiers in the space of initial features due of the intersection of measurement domains belonging to objects of different classes. The intermixing degree of the objects measurement of different classes is shown in Figure 8 in the projection on the plane HR-SYS. Here,

Table 2. The objects number in classes and the boundary values of the observations number in objects

Class N°	1	2	3	4	5
Class name	Arterial hypertension	Isolated systolic hypertension	Normal regulation	Heart failure of low degrees	Heart failure of high degrees
Number of objects	10	11	25	22	28
Min number of measurements	4	4	4	4	4
Max number of measurements	151	114	42	45	41

Figure 8. The location of the objects observations of different classes in initial feature space

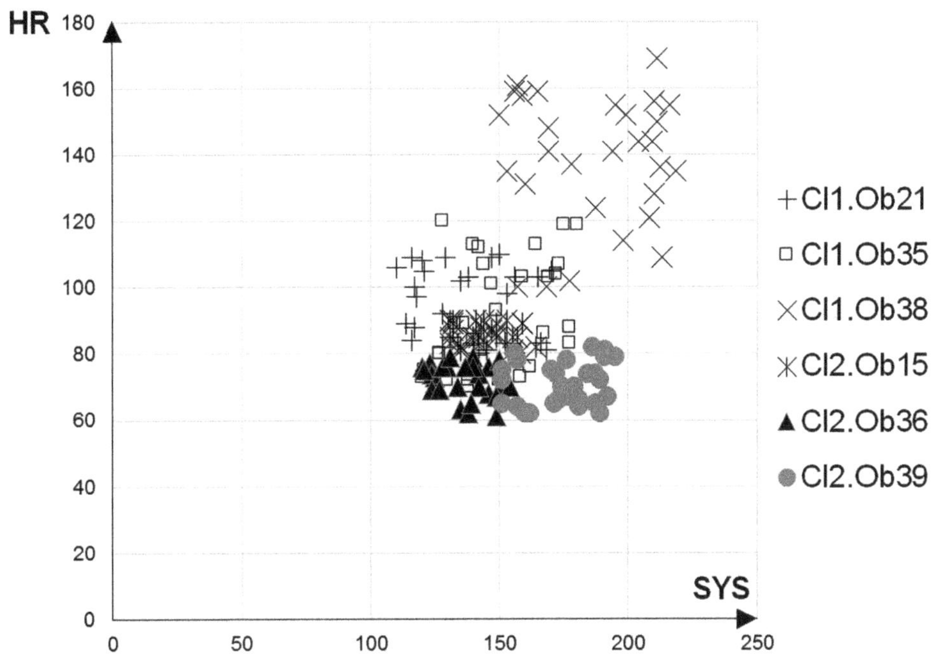

you can see the measurement sets for objects of the classes "Arterial hypertension" and "Isolated systolic hypertension" for 3 objects from each class.

Below in Figure 9, the same 6 objects are presented in the parameter space of the general structure obtained using the external separability criterion.

As can be seen, now these objects are spaced quite conveniently, even for linear separation.

Figure 9. The location of the objects observations of different classes in the parameters space of common structure

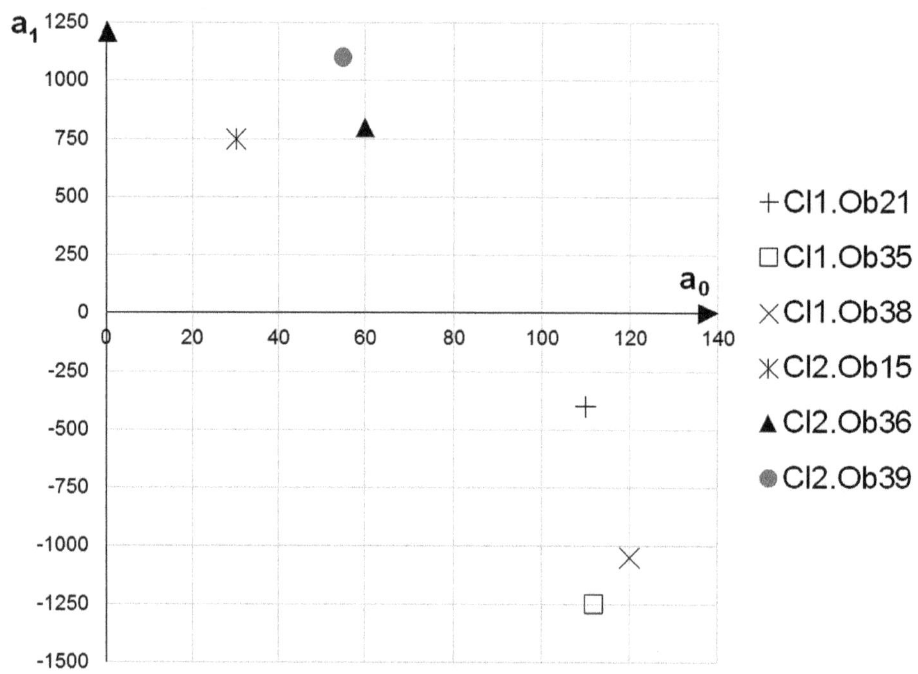

Objects Modeling and Solving the Classification Problem

An obvious fact that the fixed us parameters of the cardiovascular system functional state are dependent on each other was used to solve the problem. It is further proposed to transfer the solution from the initial features space in the parameter space of the objects models to be classified. Among the possible variants of modeling objects in explicit form by the functions of the type $y = f(x)$, we choose dependence the form $DIA = f(SYS, HR)$.

Two examples are considered below: the classifiers modeling for the above five classes on the basis of a common unified structure of object models, then the possibility of significantly improving the classification results by using a special structure for some separate class is shown.

Solving the Problem Using a Common Structure

Let's consider here the classifiers modeling that should be constructed on the basis of transition to a parameter space of a single common structure most suitable for a model's description of all objects of the learning sample. If such a structure exists at a sufficiently good value level of the external criterion then it is possible to expect a high quality of the classification problem solution.

Using RAMMA GMDH software provides the possibility of next variants of the single best structure for all object models are calculated: optimal in the combined total accuracy of object models and optimal in classes separation in the parameter space. And it is possible to take into account each of above criteria in different weight ratios in a unified form of the external criterion.

The calculation was carried out with the following values of the algorithm parameters: the maximum of polynomial degree was equal 4; all possible variants of the input features set extension were used; the number of selected models in the buffer of the best models was equal 5; the number of results from the first level of the generalized variable formation which passed to subsequent network levels was equal 4, the number of results from the subsequent levels of formation of the generalized variable passed to subsequent network levels was equal 3; when using the combined criterion of the accuracy of the weight of the training error and the inconsistency of the training and testing errors were equal 0,2; the coefficients of the classes were considered the equal.

Then the results for two calculated variants follow: the optimal structure calculating in accordance the external criterion for the combined accuracy of models (23) and the optimal structure calculating in accordance of external criterion for classes separability in model parameters space (24):

$$DIA = a_0 + a_1 \cdot HR^{-1} \cdot SYS^{3/2}, \tag{23}$$

$$DIA = a_0 + a_1 \cdot HR^{-1} \cdot SYS^{2}. \tag{24}$$

Then the parameter vectors $\boldsymbol{a}_i = (a_1,\dots,a_p)_i$ are calculated for each structure $i = 1,\dots,\sum_{k=1}^{K} n_k$, where K - the number of classes, n_k - the number of objects-sets in each class. The vectors found $\boldsymbol{a}^*$ form the rows of a new feature matrix $M(N \times p)$, $N = \sum_{k=1}^{K} n_k$, that is used to calculate the classifiers of cardiovascular system functional states. The classifiers modeling was performed in the parameter space of objects using the software algorithms GMDH Shell DS 3.8.3 (2017). Here, classifiers are constructed for each class separating it from all other classes and, if necessary, the classifiers found can be integrated into the system. The classifiers system $K_j(\boldsymbol{a})$ $j = 1,\dots,K$ relates an object d^* with a vector of values of parameters $\boldsymbol{a}^* = \{a_{0i}^*, a_{1i}^*\}$ to the class r starting from the maximum value $K_j(\boldsymbol{a})$ at the point of its parameters $\boldsymbol{a}^*$:

$$r = \max_{\arg j} K_j(a^*), j = 1,...,K. \quad (25)$$

The following are the arguments which have guided authors in selecting a tool for classifier constructing.

GMDH algorithms belong to the group of structural-parametric synthesis methods with an implicit penalty for the complexity of model. Algorithms provide a gradual complication of the model structure as long as an improvement in the value of the algorithm external criterion is observed. Achieving an external criterion minimum (maximum) is indicates the model optimal complexity. The variety of GMDH algorithms is determined by the algorithm purposes (approximation, prediction, classification), the class of functions on which the models constructing (polynomials, functions with delays, etc.), the way of forming the particular descriptions (models), the mechanism for calculating parameters, the selecting external criteria. Among other methods, GMDH algorithms are distinguished by a number of advantages - speed, nonlinear models construction, solving the overfit model problem. Details of this algorithms class can be found in works Ivakhnenko and Stepashko (1985) and Madala and Ivakhnenko (1994).

The following are the classifier formulas separating each class from all other classes and the percentage of correctly classified objects. Since the examples are illustrative for the application of the method provides only the total indicator of the correctly classified objects number by each classifier is given.

The Calculation Results of Classifiers in the Parameters Space of the Common Structure That Was Obtained in Accordance With the Accuracy External Criterion

1. The classifier formula that differentiates the state "Arterial hypertension":

$$y_1 = 1.24124 - 57.781 \cdot a_0^{-1} \; Y = 1{,}24124 - \frac{57{,}9781}{x_{a_0}},$$

the percentage of correctly classified objects P= 91.7%, the sensitivity S=1.

2. The classifier+ formula that differentiates the state "Isolated systolic hypertension":

$y_2 = 1.25964 - 50.8624 \cdot a_0^{-1}$, P= 67.7%, S=1.

3. The classifier formula that differentiates the state "Normal regulation":

$$y_3 = 1.27877 - 48,3245 \cdot a_0^{-1} + 8.61784 \cdot 10^{-06} \cdot a_1 \cdot a_0^{-1} Y = 1,24124 - \frac{57,9781}{x_{a_0}},$$

P= 69.8%, S=0.80.

4. The classifier formula that differentiates the state "Heart failure of low degrees":

$y_4 = 0.763324 - 15.992 \cdot a_0^{-1}$, P= 57.3%, S=0.5.

5. The classifier formula that differentiates the state "Heart failure of high degrees":

$y_5 = -0.817229 + 72,105 \cdot a_0^{-1}$, P= 100%, S=1.

The Calculation Results of Classifiers in the Parameters Space of the Common Structure That Was Obtained in Accordance With the Separability External Criterion

1. The classifier formula that differentiates the state "Arterial hypertension":

$y_1 = 8.63029 - 2.671315 \cdot a_0 - 1.15282 \cdot a_1$ $Y = 1,24124 - \frac{57,9781}{x_{a_0}}$, P=98.9%, S=1 .

2. The classifier formula that differentiates the state "Isolated systolic hypertension":

$y_2 = -0.604812 + 0,0154266 \cdot a_0 + 60.6143 \cdot a_1$, P=73.96%, S=0.9 .

3. The classifier formula that differentiates the state "Normal regulation":

$$y_3 = 50.3725 - 25.88254 \cdot a_0 - 0.272351 \cdot a_0^2 - 921..465 \cdot a_1^2$$

$Y = 1,24124 - \frac{57,9781}{x_{a_0}}$, P=72.92%, S=0.92 .

4. The classifier formula that differentiates the state "Heart failure of low degrees":

$y_4 = 52.1111 - 6.54505 \cdot a_0 - 101.021 \cdot a_0^{-1} - 4.81616 \cdot a_0^{-1} \cdot a_1$, P=69.79%, S= 0.95 .

5. The classifier formula that differentiates the state "Heart failure of high degrees":

$y_5 = -112.732 + 92.697 \cdot a_0 - 24.1956 \cdot a_0^2$, P=98.96%, S=1 .

Improving the Classification Results by Using a Special Structure for Separate Class

It should be noted that the sense of obtaining the common structure for object models lies in the convenience of converting individual classifiers into a single system for K classes. Since all classifiers are constructed in the same space and at the same value level for the "own" class it is natural to resolve classifier conflicts, when constructing the classification system, directly comparing their values. However, at a low quality of the individual classifiers obtained on common structure it becomes necessary to sacrifice this convenience and to construct individual classifiers using their specialized structures. As it is obvious, the quality of classifiers based on individual structures increases, this is shown in example below. The system solution must be implemented in the "united" parameters space of all class structures in this case.

Further on the example of the class "Isolated systolic hypertension" it is shown the possibility to obtain higher classification results for individual classes. Using algorithm RAMMAs

GMDH software we calculate the best model structure for only objects of this class according to the external separation criterion. The resulting structure has form

$$DIA = a_0 + a_1 \cdot HR^{-1/3} \cdot SYS^{-2}. \tag{26}$$

Then get the values of the parameter vectors $\boldsymbol{a}_i = (a_1,...,a_p)_i$ for the all objects models of the learning sample and form the feature matrix in the parameter space of the found structure.

Using the algorithms of the software GMDH Shell, we construct a classifier that differentiates a given class from all other classes. The resulting classifier has the form

$y_2 = 0.168683 + 1.334134E - 09 \cdot a_0 \cdot a_1 - 3.42306E - 07 \cdot a_1$, P=81.3%. S=0.91

As can be seen, the obtained result improved the version of the general structure for the total criterion of accuracy by 13.6% and for the separability criterion by 7.4% with more balanced indicators in classes. The solution methodology shown above is given by example with not too large samples of data. Nevertheless, this approach is perspective for converting the "big data" sets defining objects into a parameter vector of their models, which preserves the target information: the differences of classes.

Next, is given a possible version of the transition formalization to the parameter space for one of the classifying images problems

TRANSITION FORMALIZATION TO THE PARAMETER SPACE FOR THE IMAGE-BASED PATHOLOGY CLASSIFICATION PROBLEM

Install the following correspondence between mathematical and physical entities:

Objects or patterns for which the relation to the class is known is some set $X_i = \left\{x_{i1}, \ldots, x_{in_i}\right\}$ of segmented images of the cell nucleus x_{ij}, belonging to the same example of tissue; the total number of patterns is *N*; this object (pattern) X_i can also be called a "set of observations"; observation is a separate image of the cell nucleus x_{ij}; multidimensional measurement is a computed vector of characteristics $\boldsymbol{z}_{ij} = \left\{z_1, z_2, \ldots, z_p\right\}_{ij}$ that determines the state of each nucleus.

Denote values of the vector components $\boldsymbol{z}$ for observation x_{ij} as z_{ijq}, $q = 1, \ldots, p$, for an individual object-sets X_i as z_{ijq}, $q = 1, \ldots, p$, $j = 1, \ldots, n_i$, for all objects X_i, $i = 1, \ldots, N$ (all tissue examples) as z_{ijq}, $q = 1, \ldots, p$, $j = 1, \ldots, n_i$, $i = 1, \ldots, N$. Then, it is possible to set the dependency for each object X_i, $i = 1, \ldots, N$ in the form $\boldsymbol{F}_i(\boldsymbol{z}) = 0$, or in the scalar case $F_i(\boldsymbol{z}) = 0$ or more habitual in a form resolved with respect to a some variable z_s:

$$z_{is} = F_i(\boldsymbol{z}), \tag{27}$$

where *s* is the index of the variable from the vector of initial features with respect to which the model of the object is constructed.

If the dependence (27) will be sought in the form $z_{is} = \sum_{j=1}^{p} a_{ij}\phi_j(\boldsymbol{z})$ each object (a set of images or a set of subareas of one image) can be determined not by a set $\left\{x_{i1}, \ldots, x_{in_i}\right\}$, but only some multi-dimensional point or vector $\boldsymbol{a}_i = \left\{a_{ij}\right\}_{j=1,\ldots,p}$.

As a result, we are able to solve the Set Classification Problem by each suitable conventional method of multidimensional observations classification with a known correspondence to the class. Herewith, an important role for the quality of the classifiers obtained is plays a good selection of structure $\phi_j(z), j = 1, \ldots, p$, which in turn is determined by the applied variant of the external criterion.

Note the effectiveness of the approach considered in each individual problem will depend on the severity of correspondence between the dependencies characteristics of the initial features and the classes of the problem under consideration. In the particular case, the variables vector z may consist of the distribution parameters of the image features. Obviously, in the case of independent features, there is a natural application of the frequency approach, construction of probability densities, etc.

RECOMMENDATIONS AND METHOD PERSPECTIVES

This section is the discussion result, contains recommendations on additional refinements of algorithmic implementations of the work current version and general considerations on research expansion in this area. Some obvious aspects of the proposed approach implementation are not included in the work and under certain conditions will require to independently work the researcher on their development and its application.

A significant number of classification objects with a high-dimensional space of input features will require a significant computational resources, therefore need to develop the algorithmic solutions the modeling problem from the point of view of organizing distributed computing. This conclusion seems obvious because of the calculating "simultaneously" of all the object models (or the object models of a particular class) within the framework of one optimization computational procedure. However, the parallelizing of computations is not a problem, since the calculation of the parameters for each object on the selected structure can be performed independently.

The approach application in image-based pathology classification problem requires the proposals for the rational mechanisms of determining the initial feature space for the analyzed images. Such considerations are not trivial, since many procedures for reducing the original space provide for the orthogonalization of the output variables, which makes it impossible to apply the approach proposed by the authors. The direct application of factor analysis procedures (FA with orthogonal rotation), principal component analysis (PCA), and canonical discriminant analysis

(CDA) are useless for determine the initial space due to form an independent set of components. However, the same mechanisms can be useful if the variables they form can be associated with some informative variable that was not subjected to the specified transformations. The structures and parameters of such relationships for different objects can be used as the basis for the classifying systems.

Denote the prospects for the work development.

1. As we mentioned the approach is interesting to the task of image processing. In addition, this approach will show the new opportunities when using different external criteria, which allows to produce structures with the greatest efficiency in serving the purpose of classification or decision-making problems.
2. The applying condition for the proposed technology is the existence assumption for the classification objects the statistical dependences in an explicit form that are restoring in the work. In the future, to consider a more general approach, taking into account the relationships between the variables in an implicit form and propose appropriate algorithmic solutions, is supposed.
3. It is possible to designate the prospects of the proposed approach as a tool for "Big Data" tasks, not limited to SC problem. The proposed algorithms searching for optimal structures and models carry the meaning of a purposeful convolution of initial sets into a condensed form with the target information preservation (determined by an external criterion) in the structure and parameters of the object models. It could be pointed out that this tool is of independent interest, when it is possible to consider not the original sets, but their models, for storage, transmission and target application. Obviously, the inverse problem of reconstructing initial sets is incorrect, but it is possible to obtain some realization of their projections related to the applied external criterion. To do this, you must have the values of independent variables, the model of the object for each of the dependent variables, and the variability of the modeling error. Note that in order to be able to correctly reproduce the initial information by simulation methods, it is necessary to have a model that gives an output unbiassed estimator that generally is not performed in implementing the principles of GMDH. However, in order to fulfill this condition, it is sufficient to recalculate the model parameter estimates on the found structures for each object for the entire learning sample, and that is proposed in the work under consideration.

SET CLUSTERING

Formally, Set Classification Problems (SCP) contain both SCP with supervisor (Supervised Learning), and SCP without it (Unsupervised Learning). Let's briefly outline our vision of the latter problems. We will call them, as Set Clustering Problems (*SClP*). Below is one of the possible options for transition to a parametric space for solving cluster analysis problems.

As before, we assume that each clustering object is given by some set of observations, recorded for different states of the medium. The areas partial intersection that represent the objects of clustering in the feature space, is allowed. The basic assumptions for applying one version of the approach developed are three:

1. The existence of a statistical relationship between the features that characterize objects.
2. The uniform structure existence (call it the kernel of clustering), on the basis of which the obtaining sufficiently precise descriptions for the objects of clustering is possible.
3. The differences in the parametric representation of objects give the expected effect of object clustering.

Conditions 2 and 3, as obviously, are not something strict, formal, as it is not defined what to consider as "sufficiently precise descriptions" and "expected effect". However, the clustering problem formulation in essence does not give a unique solution, and any clustering is subject to a rather complex stage of interpreting the results, which is the decisive argument in assessing the utility or weak applicability of the approach. When apply of cluster analysis tools, one always has to rely on the significant role and intuition of the analysis operator, heuristics have been and will be an essential component of the corresponding algorithms.

In these assumptions, the object clustering can be performed using the following two-step mechanism:

1. The problem of finding common structure to adequately describe all the objects of the clustering problem solves. To do this, apply the above version of the modeling algorithm with the use of the external accuracy criterion. Based on the solving results, we obtain the model parameters of each object. The parameter values will be the feature values in the new feature space of clustering problem.

2. At the discretion of the operator-researcher, object clustering is performed by any of the analysis appropriate methods, an interpretation is given to the clusters obtained, and the result of clustering is estimated.

Now, introduce the concept of the cluster kernel (CK), as a mechanism (structure, model) that is behind the union of individual multivariate observations into the objects set. In some cases, such as postulated in p.1 of assumptions, the kernel of clusters will coincide with kernel of clustering.

An obvious, the generalization of the problem statement in par.1 is to find the number and type of kernels of the clustering problem, bearing in mind the simultaneous determination of the number and composition of clusters and the kernel for each of them. In some cases, it will be convenient to call them the cluster kernel of a first kind (CK1K).

If the data for clustering are obtained as a result of an active experiment on the objects, the number of experimental conditions for each object observations is set to be the same and equal to m, and each of the observations is recorded under the corresponding identical conditions, then the new space is formed from the initial variables, but by repeated them multiple to m in the appropriate experimental conditions. Thus, the new dimension of the resulting object clustering space is $m*n$, where n is the dimension of the initial space. The object information in this space (multidimensional observations related to this object) is concentrated in one multidimensional point in the expanded space of dimension $m*n$. Therefore, clustering can be implemented by usual methods of cluster analysis.

In the case of cluster intersections, the clustering problem turns into its most complex variant - the mixture separation problem. In a general way, this problem requires the development of solving methods.

When the clustering problem objects are representable by a multidimensional point, the cluster kernel can be considered as some mechanism (structure, model, or multidimensional point) that can be used as a basis for objects simulation in this cluster. If the shape of clusters is close to the spherical models, then the cluster centroid can serve as the cluster kernel. If the clusters are of a certain functional nature, then the kernels will be the corresponding hyper surfaces. Objects of this type can be considered as the cluster kernel of the second kind (CK2K). In parallel with the clustering problem solution, it is possible to consider the problem of finding the cluster kernels of the second kind. Obviously, these objects (cluster kernel, kernel of clustering) play a special role in classification algorithms with the teacher, when the results of clustering are used to formulate Supervised Learning tasks.

To be continued.

CONCLUSION

A new approach to solve the problem of object classification that are defined by observation sets is proposed. Approach is based on transferring the problem solution from the initial features space to the model structures parameter space of classification objects. To search such model structures, GMDH algorithms were developed. Algorithms use two types of external criteria: combined total accuracy criterion and separability external criterion in parameter space of the found structures. Both can be taken into account in different weight ratios in a unified form of external criterion.

Two algorithms transferring the solution of set classification problem from the initial feature space into the parameters space of model structures is proposed to account for varying degrees of differences between the class structures. The individual classifiers and the classification system are constructed in parameter space of the optimal common structure of classification objects models in the first case. The second option requires the use when the significant structural differences in the object models of different classes lead to a poor classification in the parameter space of overall structure. It is suggested here to take into account their specifics by defining the best structure of objects for each class separately.

In this case, the classification system can be implemented also in two approaches: the object class is determined by the model accuracy maximum at the class structures when every structure is found by the accuracy external criterion, the second approach is based on transferring the problem solution from the initial features space into the spaces of object model parameters of class structures, wherein the structures should be obtained here in accordance with the separability criterion. Two variants of system solutions are also possible here: the classifiers are constructed in the parameter space of found structures on "one-vs-all" principle, the system refuses classification in a case of classifier conflict; the individual classifiers and the classifier system should be constructed in the "united" parameters space of model structures of objects of all classes. The last two variants are close in the sense that both are realized on structures found in accordance with the separability criterion and the accuracy estimate of the first of them is the accuracy lower bound of the second.

The approach can be used to solve a wide range of SCP problems because of the offered transition from the original features space to the object model parameters allows one to implement a complete set of developed methods for objects, specified by one multidimensional measurement. Besides, it has good perspectives for converting Big Data that can be used to specify the objects (a sets of measurements) into a compact form (model parameters) while preserving the characteristics necessary for class separation. The approach to clustering objects, which are given by sets of observations, is proposed.

REFERENCES

Aranjelovic, O., Shakhnarovich, G., Fisher, J., Cippola, R., & Darrell, T. (2005). Face recognition with image sets using manifold density divergence. In *Proceedings of the Computer Vision and Pattern Recognition Conference* (pp. 581--588). Piscataway, NJ: IEEE.

Biuk, Z., & Loncaric, S. (2001). Face recognition from multi-pose image sequence. In *Proceedings of 2nd Int'l Symposium on Image and Signal Processing and Analysis* (pp. 319-324). Pula, Croatia: IEEE.

Fukunaga, K. (1990). *Introduction to statistical pattern recognition*. Boston: Academic Press.

Ivakhnenko, A., & Stepashko, V. (1985). *Noise-immunity modeling*. Kiev: Naukova dumka. (in Russian)

Jung, S., & Qiao, X. (2014). A statistical approach to set classification by feature selection with applications to classification of histopathology images. *Biometrics*, *70*(3), 536–545. doi:10.1111/biom.12164 PMID:24588775

Knyshov, G., Nastenko, I., Kondrashova, N., Nosovets, O., & Pavlov, V. (2014). Combinatorial algorithm for constructing a parametric feature space for the classification of multidimensional models. *Cybernetics and Systems Analysis*, *50*(4), 627–633. doi:10.100710559-014-9651-3

Madala, H., & Ivakhnenko, A. (1994). *Inductive learning algorithms for complex systems modeling*. Boca Raton, FL: CRC Press.

Moody, G., & Lehman, L. (2009). Predicting acute hypotensive episodes: the10th annual PhysioNet/Computers in Cardiology Challenge. *Computers in Cardiology*, *36*, 541–544. PMID:20842209

Nastenko, Ie., Pavlov, V., & Nosovets, O. (2014). Modeling of differential diagnosis classifiers of pathological states of the cardiovascular system [in Russian]. *Eastern-European Journal of Enterprise Technologies*, *6*(3), 30–35. doi:10.15587/1729-4061.2014.31079

Nastenko, Ie., Pavlov, V., & Nosovets, O. (2014). Synthesis classifiers differential diagnosis of the circulatory systems pathological conditions in a multidimensional space [in Russian]. *Inductive Modeling of Complex Systems*, *6*, 105–122.

Ning, X., & Karypis, G. (2009). The set classification problem and solution methods. In *Proceedings of SIAM International Conference on Data Mining* (pp. 847-858). Springer. 10.1137/1.9781611972795.73

Samsudin, N., & Bradley, A. (2010). Nearest neighbour group-based classification. *Pattern Recognition*, *43*(10), 3458–3467. doi:10.1016/j.patcog.2010.05.010

Shakhnarovich, G., Fisher, J., & Darrell, T. (2002). Face recognition from long-term observations. In *Proceedings of 7th European Conference on Computer Vision* (pp. 851-868). Copenhagen, Denmark: Springer.

Stepashko, V. (1981). A combinatorial algorithm of the group method of data handling with optimal model scanning scheme. *Soviet Automatic Control*, *14*(3), 24–28.

Tan, H., & Gao, Y. (2017). Patch-based principal covariance discriminative learning for image set classification. *IEEE Access: Practical Innovations, Open Solutions*, *5*, 15001–15012. doi:10.1109/ACCESS.2017.2733718

Voitikova, M., & Khursa, R. (2013). Linear regression modeling of blood pressure data to determine the risk of acute hypotensive episodes [in Russian]. *News of the Academy of Sciences of Belarus*, *1*, 117–122.

Wang, R., Guo, H., Davis, L., & Dai, Q. (2012). Covariance discriminative learning: A natural and efficient approach to image set classification. In *Proceedings of Computer Vision and Pattern Recognition* (pp. 2496–2503). Washington, DC: IEEE.

Wang, W., Ozolek, J., Slepčev, D., Lee, A., Cheng, Ch., & Rohde, G. (2011). An optimal transportation approach for nuclear structure-based pathology. *IEEE Transactions on Medical Imaging*, *30*(3), 621–631. doi:10.1109/TMI.2010.2089693 PMID:20977984

Wang, W., Wang, R., Shan, S., & Chen, X. (2017). Discriminative covariance oriented representation learning for face recognition with image sets. In *Proceedings of IEEE Conference on Computer Vision and Pattern Recognition* (pp. 5599-5608). Honolulu, HI: IEEE. 10.1109/CVPR.2017.609

Zabara, S., Filimonova, N., & Zelensky, K. (2009). The method of selection signals invariant features [in Russian]. *Reports of the Ukraine's National Academy of Sciences*, *3*, 55–60.

KEY TERMS AND DEFINITIONS

COMBI: Combinatorial algorithm of GMDH.
External Criterion: A suitably chosen criterion for model structure evaluating.
Generalized Variable: Member of a complete polynomial of a given degree.

GMDH: Group Method of Data Handling – the structural-parametric synthesis method with an implicit fine for the model complexity.

Learning Sample W: The whole sample of objects for which is known the class accordance.

LSMB: Bordering method for least-squares method.

Model of the Optimal Structure: Is understood in a sense of achieving an extremum of the algorithm external criterion.

Partial Description: Intermediate models considered as applicants for object description.

RAMMA: Recurrent additively multiplicative multistage algorithm of GMDH.

SCLS: Set classification with learning by sets.

SCMLO: Set classification with multi-labeled observations.

SCP: Set classification problem.

Testing Sample B: A sample of objects that using in GMDH algorithms mainly for selection of model structure.

Training Sample A: A sample of objects that using in GMDH algorithms mainly to calculate the model parameters.

Chapter 4
Multicriteria Synthesis of Neural Network Architecture

Albert Voronin
National Aviation University of Ukraine, Ukraine

ABSTRACT

Statement of a problem and procedure of vector optimization of the neural-network classifier architecture is considered. As a criterion function, the scalar convolution of criteria under the nonlinear scheme of compromises is offered. Search methods of optimization with discrete arguments are used. The example, neural-network classifier of texts, is given.

INTRODUCTION

An artificial neural network is an information processing paradigm that can serve as a part of a techno-social system for modern economical and governmental infrastructures. The key to artificial neural networks is that their design enables them to process information in a similar way to our own biological brains, by drawing inspiration from how our own nervous system functions. This makes them useful tools for solving problems like language processing, data mining, etc, which our biological brains can do easily.

An artificial neural network is inspired by the way biological nervous systems, such as the brain, process information. The key element of this paradigm is the novel structure of the information processing system.

It is composed of a large number of highly interconnected processing elements (neurons) working in unison to solve specific problems. Artificial neural networks, like people, learn by example. An artificial neural network is configured for a

DOI: 10.4018/978-1-5225-5586-5.ch004

specific application, such as pattern recognition or data classification, through a learning process. Learning in biological systems involves adjustments to the synaptic connections that exist between the neurons. This is true of artificial neural networks as well.

Neural network classifiers are an important kind of artificial neural networks. They are applicable in technical and medical diagnostics, classification of various information sources, etc. Figure 1 shows the structure of a generalized q- layer neural network classifier with direct connections.

In the figure, $x_1, x_2, ..., x_n$ are the attributes of the classification object that constitute the input vector $x = \{x_i\}_{i=1}^{n}; p_0 = n$ is the number of neural elements in the receptor layer; $p_1, p_2, ..., p_q$ is the number of neurons in each of the hidden (processing) layers q; $p_{q+1} = m$ is the number of neurons in the output layer (the number of classes); $y = \{y_k\}_{k=1}^{m}$ is the output vector of the neural network that assigns the classification object to one of the m classes; $w_1, w_2, ..., w_q, w_{q+1}$ are the vectors of the synaptic weights of the neural network.

Let us present the necessary information from neural networks theory (Bodyansky, E.V. & Rudenko, O.G. 2004), (Borisov, V.S. 2007), (Golovko, V.A. 2001). An artificial neural network is a set of neural elements and connections among them.

Each neuron (Figure 2) has a group of synapses, i.e., unidirectional connections of inputs with outputs of other neurons. Each synapse is characterized by the value of synaptic connection or its weight w_i (it can be found during the neural network training). A neuron has the current state, specified as the weighted sum of its inputs: $s = \sum_{i=1}^{n} w_i x_i$. The output of a neuron is a function of its state, which is called the

Figure 1. The neural network classifier

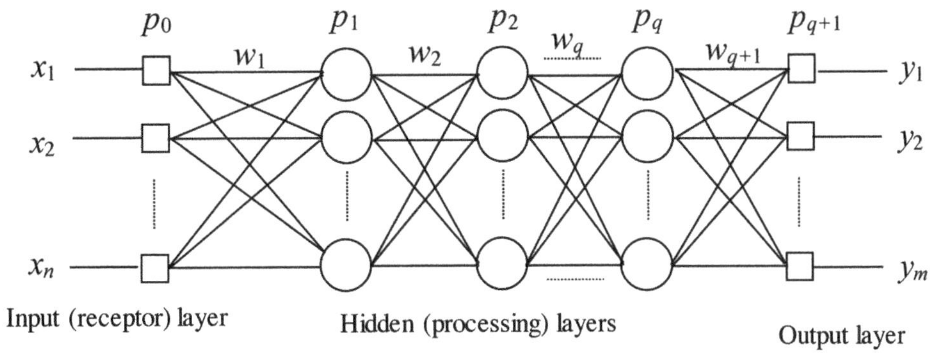

Figure 2. A neuron structure

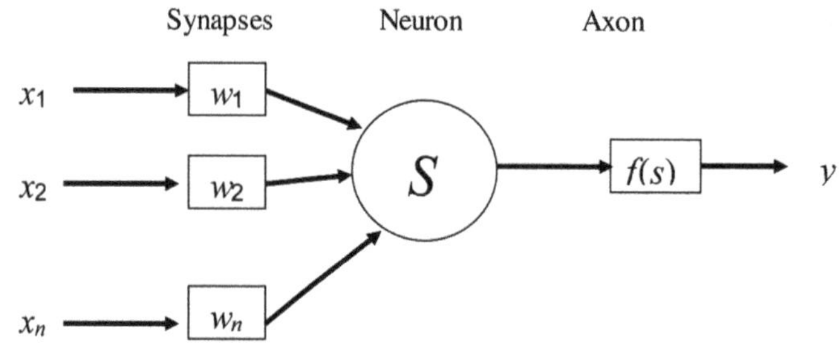

activation function: $y = f(s)$. By means of the axon (output connection of the neuron), an excitation or inhibition signal arrives at synapses of succeeding neurons. Activation functions are threshold or continuous (bipolar sigmoid, Gaussian, etc.). The set of all neurons of an artificial neural network is divided into subsets called layers. A layer is a set of neurons, to which parallel signals from others neurons of the network are applied in parallel at each time step (Golovko, 2001). a vector of activation functions $y = \{y_k\}_{k=1}^{m}$ is produced at the output of the classifier. The number j for which the activity of the output y_j is maximum, i.e., $\max\limits_{k\in[1,m]} y_k = y_j$, corresponds to the number of the class of the classification object.

The number of neurons in the input layer $p_0 = n$ depends on the dimension of the input vector of attributes and is not subject to variations. Similarly, the number of neurons in the output layer $p_{q+1} = m$ is constant and depends on the number of domains (classes), into which the attribute space is divided. The number of processing (hidden) layers q and number of neurons in each of them $p_1, p_2, \ldots, p_q$ constitute the concept of the architecture (Bodyansky & Rudenko, 2004) of a neural network and can be arguments (independent variables) in its optimization.

In this Chapter, the study is restricted to the case where the number q is fixed and prescribed. Then the arguments of optimization of the architecture of a neural classifier are the number of neurons in each of the processing layers which constitute the vector of independent variables $p = \{p_j\}_{j=1}^{q}$. The performance of a neural classifier depends on the choice of the architecture p.

The problem is to choose an architecture such that the neural classifier is characterized by its best properties under prescribed performance conditions.

STATEMENT OF THE PROBLEM

Generally, choosing the architecture can be formally represented as the problem

$$p^* = \arg \underset{p \in P}{extr}\, Y(p) \tag{1}$$

where $Y(p)$ is the objective function; $\underset{p \in P}{extr}$ is the operator of extremization of the objective function with respect to arguments p; and P is the feasible domain of independent variables.

For the constructive solution of the problem, let us formulate additional partial assumptions. Let us associate each property of the neural classifier with a quantitative characteristic $f(p)$ as the performance criterion. One of such criteria characterizes the misclassification probability. In what follows, we determine this criterion experimentally. Let us represent it approximately as the number of classification errors $e(p)$ divided by the total (sufficiently large) number of tests N:

$$f_1(p) = \frac{e(p)}{N} \tag{2}$$

As the number of neurons in processing layers grows within some reasonable limits, the classification accuracy is assumed to increase and the value of this criterion to decrease. The maximum admissible network error should be known from physical considerations and be specified as the constraint $f_1(p) \le A_1$.

The second criterion characterizes the time it takes to train the neural network for the given architecture p. This time closely correlate with the total number of neurons in the hidden layers of the classifier. Therefore, we will represent this criterion as

$$f_2(p) = \sum_{k=1}^{q} p_k \tag{3}$$

Note that this criterion characterizes also the time it takes for a signal to pass through the neural network from the input to the output. As the number of neurons grows, the value of the criterion increases. The maximum admissible value of the second criterion is determined by the admissible time of neural network training and is specified as the constraint $f_2(p) \le A_2$.

There are also other criteria to characterize various properties of a neural classifier. In this Chapter, we will restrict ourselves to the two above-mentioned basic criteria, meaning that other properties of the classifier can also be considered.

The feasible domain of the optimization arguments is represented by a parallelepiped

$$P = \left\{ p \middle| 0 \le p_k \le P_u, k \in [1, P_u], u \in [1, q] \right\},$$

where P_u is the maximum number of the neurons in the u -th layer.

Since both included in consideration criteria are subject to minimization (when the criterion is less the better is the corresponding property of the classifier), the operator of extremization of the objective function becomes $\underset{p \in P}{extr} = \underset{p \in P}{\min}$.

Thus, both criteria are contradictory, non-negative, to be minimized and limited. There are all prerequisites for the scalar convolution of criteria by nonlinear compromise scheme to be used as the objective function (Voronin, A.N. at al 1999), (Voronin, Albert, 2017).

NONLINEAR SCHEME OF COMPROMISES

This Chapter deals with a nonlinear compromises scheme in the problem of multicriteria optimization of neural network classifiers. Finding a multicriteria solution is inherently a compromise and is based on using subjective information. The essence of the concept "compromise" is the answer to the question: how many units of winning on one of the criteria we are ready (according to the decision-maker) to pay for the inevitable loss of one unit on other criteria (other) in a given situation? Given this information and a compromise scheme selected, it is possible to pass from the general vector expression to the scalar convolution of partial criteria, which provides a basis for a constructive apparatus to solve multicriteria problems.

Solving the problem is based on the hypothesis that there exists a utility function (Fishburne, 1978) appearing in the decision-maker's brains during the solution of a specific multicriteria problem. A compromise scheme in the form of a scalar convolution of criteria is considered as a mathematical model of the utility function. We may state that virtually all the approaches to determining the scalar convolution of criteria are reduced to constructing one mathematical model or another of the decision maker's utility function. The problem is to approximate correctly the utility function and to construct a substantional mathematical model as a scalar convolution, adequate to the given situation, to solve different multicriteria problems.

In our case, the subject of the research is such a fine substance, like an imaginary utility function that appears in the brains of decision-makers during the solution of a specific multicriteria problem. Moreover, each a decision-maker has a utility function of his own. However, you can get the background to identify the content type of the model of the utility function, if detect and analyze some general patterns observed in the process of multicriteria decision-making by various decision-makers in different situations.

In the problem of vector optimization the scalar convolution Y has the meaning of a target (objective) function. As a result of its extremization with respect to arguments x it turns out a compromise-optimal vector of arguments x^*. Here we consider the problem of vector optimization, assuming for definiteness that all the criteria $y(x)$ are to be minimized. Then mathematically, the vector optimization problem can be represented as

$$x^* = \arg\min_{x \in X} Y\left[y\left(x\right)\right].$$

In what follows, convenient is to operate with relative values of the criteria. If the criterion vector $y(x)$ is normalized by restrictions vector A,

$$y_0\left(x\right) = \left\{y_k\left(x\right) / A_k\right\}_{k=1}^{s} = \left\{y_{0k}\left(x\right)\right\}_{k=1}^{s},$$

then a scalar convolution $Y[y_0(x)]$ is applied.

Now we need to determine the choice of the principle of optimality. Finding the extremum of a weighted sum of the partial criteria in decision theory is called the implementation of the Laplace principle. Determination of the multiplicative convolution extremum is carried out in accordance with Pascal's principle. Charnes-Cooper concept (Charnes & Cooper, 1961) requires minimizing the distance from the ideal (utopian) point to the Pareto boundary (the principle of "closer to the ideal point"). These and other optimality principles have their advantages, but do not include estimates of the ratio of the partial criteria and their maximum allowable values (limitations).

The monograph (Voronin, 2017) says:

As a river has its banks, so the criteria have their limitations. Navigation on the rivers and seas is not possible if there is a danger of approaching the shore (reefs, shoals, etc.). Implementing the known principles of optimality does not exclude the possibility of a dangerous approach of certain criteria to their limitations, which is very undesirable. To avoid this danger, we will be guided by the principle of "away from restrictions".

Let us introduce the concept of the intensity of a situation as a measure of how normalized relative partial criteria are close to the limit value (unity):

$$\rho_k = 1 - y_{0k}, \rho_k \in [0;1], k \in [1,s], \rho = \{\rho_k\}_{k=1}^{s}.$$

Let us analyze the logic of the utility function, by which the decision- makers are guided to make decisions at different values of the intensity of the situation ρ.

If we say that the multicriteria decision is made in an intense situation, then in the conditions specified, one or several partial criteria, as a result of the decision, may appear dangerously close to the limit values ($\rho_k \approx 0$). And if one of the criteria achieves the limit (or is outside it), this event will not be compensated by a possible small level of other criteria (violating any of the constraints is usually prohibited).

In such a situation, it is necessary to interfere (in all possible way) the dangerous increase in the most adverse (i.e., the closest to the limit) partial criterion irrespective of the behavior of other criteria. Therefore in rather stressful situations (for small ρ_k) a decision-maker, if he allows the deterioration of the maximum (the most important in the current context) partial criterion by unit, it is only to compensate by a very-very large number of units, which improve other criteria.

And in the first polar case (ρ_k=0), the decision-maker leaves only this unique, most unfavorable partial criterion for consideration and neglects the other. Hence, the minimax Chebyshev model (egalitarian principle) adequately expresses the compromise scheme in an intense situation:

$$x^* = \arg\min_{x \in X} Y[y_0(x)]^{(1)} = \arg\min_{x \in X} \max_{k \in [1,s]} y_{0k}(x)$$

In the less stressful situations and other criteria must be simultaneously satisfied, taking into account the contradictory interests and goals of the system. In this case the decision-maker varies his assessment on the winning one and losing other criteria depending on the situation. In intermediate cases, the schemes of compromise are selected, giving different degrees of partial alignment of partial criteria. With decreasing tension of the situation the preferences on individual criteria are aligned.

And finally, in the second polar case, (ρ_k≈1) the situation is quiet, partial criteria are small and there is no threat of constraints violations. Here, the decision- maker considers that a unit deterioration of any partial criterion is compensated quite well by an equivalent unit improvement of any other criterion. This case corresponds to an economical compromise scheme that provides a minimum, for the given set of conditions, total loss of the partial normalized criteria. Such a scheme can be expressed by the model of integral optimality (utilitarian principle)

$$x^* = \arg\min_{x \in X} Y[y_0(x)]^{(2)} = \arg\min_{x \in X} \sum_{k=1}^{s} y_{0k}\left(x\right).$$

Thus, we have found two reference points (polar parameter values of situation intensityρ), in which the different decision-makers use the same utility functions.

The analysis reveals a pattern, according to which the decision-makers are ranging their choice from integral optimality models in quiet situations to minimax models in stressful situations. In intermediate cases, the decision- maker chooses the schemes of compromise, giving various degrees of satisfaction to certain criteria in accordance with his individual preferences, and in accordance with a given situation. If we take the conclusions from this analysis as a logical basis for formalizing the choice of a scheme of compromise, we can present various constructive concepts, one of which is the concept of a nonlinear compromise scheme (Voronin, 2017).

The presented analysis makes it possible to replace the problem of choosing a compromise scheme with the equivalent problem of synthesis of a unified scalar convolution of partial criteria, which in various situations would express different optimality principles. This is the key moment of research. Let us formulate requirements for the synthesized function $Y(y_0)$:

- It should be smooth and differentiable;
- In stressful situations should express the principle of minimax;
- In calm conditions should express the principle of the integral optimality;
- In intermediate cases, should lead to a Pareto optimal solution, giving a variety of satisfaction measures to partial criteria.

This universal convolution should express a compromise scheme adaptable to a situation. We may say that adaptation and adaptability are the main substantial essence of studying multicriteria systems. The scalar convolution should include the explicit characteristics of the situation intensity ρ.

One can consider several functions that satisfy the above requirements. Among the possible functions meeting the above requirements, we choose the simplest:

$$Y\left(\alpha, y_0\right) = \sum_{k=1}^{s} \alpha_k \left[1 - y_{0k}\left(x\right)\right]^{-1}; \alpha_k \geq 0, \sum_{k=1}^{s} \alpha_k = 1, \tag{4}$$

where α_k=const are formal parameters defined on a simplex and having double physical meaning. On the one hand, these are weight coefficients that express the preferences of decision-makers in partial criteria. On the other hand, these are coefficients of a substantional regression model based on the concept of a nonlinear compromise scheme.

Thus, a nonlinear compromise scheme corresponds to the model of vector optimization, which explicitly depends on the characteristics of the situation intensity ρ:

$$x^* = \arg\min_{x \in X} \sum_{k=1}^{s} \alpha_k \left[1 - y_{0k}\left(x\right)\right]^{-1}. \tag{5}$$

In contrast to the linear model, defined in a small neighborhood of a working point, the nonlinear model of decision-maker's utility function is defined on the whole feasible region of solutions X and does not require coefficients α_k to be recalculated if the situation varies.

From the expression (5) we can see that if any relative partial criterion, for example $y_{0i}(x)$, approaches the limit (unity), i.e., the situation becomes intense, the corresponding term $Y_i = \alpha_i / [1 - y_{0i}(x)]$ in the sum being minimized increases so that the minimization of the whole sum reduces to the minimization of only this worst term, i.e., of the criterion $y_{0i}(x)$. This is equivalent to the action of minimax model. (To eliminate the possibility of division by zero in stressful situations in the optimization algorithm according to the formula (5) we can apply the following rule: if $y_{0i}(x) \geq 0,95$, we take $y_{0i}(x) = 0,95$).

If the relative partial criteria are far from the unity, i.e., the situation is quiet, the model (5) operates equivalent to the model of integral optimality. In intermediate situations, different degrees of partial criteria alignment are obtained.

The proposed nonlinear compromise scheme has the property to adapt to the situation of multicriteria decision-making. Wherein adaptation is carried out continuously, while traditional compromise scheme choice occurs discretely, whereby errors are added to subjective error associated with quantization of compromise schemes.

The design of nonlinear compromise scheme is convenient by the fact that it does not require obligatory normalization of criteria. An equivalent form of the scalar convolution on nonlinear compromise scheme for the minimized criteria is

$$Y[y(x)] = \sum_{k=1}^{s} \alpha_k A_k \left[A_k - y_k\left(x\right)\right]^{-1}.$$

Moreover, the non-linear scheme does not require and binding to a single extremization method, for example, to minimize criteria. For maximized criteria the scalar convolution form on nonlinear compromise scheme is

$$Y[y(x)] = \sum_{k=1}^{s} \alpha_k A_k [y_k(x) - A_k]^{-1}.$$

At the same time, regardless of the scalar convolution type the model of vector optimization for nonlinear compromise scheme remains unchanged: $x^* = \arg\min_{x \in X} Y\left[y\left(x\right)\right]$.

Returning to the problem of optimizing the architecture of the neural network classifier, we write down a scalar convolution by the nonlinear scheme of compromises in unified version as

$$Y(p) = Y[f(p)] = \frac{A_1}{A_1 - f_1(p)} + \frac{A_2}{A_2 - f_2(p)} \tag{6}$$

where $f(p) = \{f_r(p)\}_{r=1}^{r=2}$ – a two-dimensional vector of the partial criteria. Taking into account (2), (3) and (4), the expression (1) for the problem of optimizing the architecture of neural classifier is transformed into

$$p^* = \arg\min_{p \in P} \left[\frac{A_1}{A_1 - e(p) / N} + \frac{A_2}{A_2 - \sum_{k=1}^{q} p_k} \right] \tag{7}$$

It is easy to see that in (7) the dependence $e(p)$ is a priori unknown. To determine it a special experimental procedure should be organized in the given conditions. Therefore, the method of vector optimization of neural classifier architecture that is set out in this Chapter is called the theoretical-experimental method.

METHOD OF SOLUTION

Among the multicriteria optimization problems are such that by physical nature their arguments can only take discrete values. By special normalization the discrete values usually can always be reduced to integer ones. Such problems are much more complicated then continuous multicriteria problems and for their solutions different approaches should be applied.

The set of valid discrete values can be infinite, finite or even consist of only two values, such as 0 and 1. In the first case the problem degenerates into a continuous optimization problem. To solve this problem in (Voronin et al., 1999) effective and formalized algorithms and software are suggested. In the latter case an integer programming takes place with Boolean variables and specific methods (logic synthesis of finite automata, Rvachev functions and so on.).

From our point of view, the most interesting and informative is a case when the set of admissible discrete values is not so great that the task degenerated into a continuous one, but not so small that it could be solved by simple sorting options. Such is the problem (7) – the problem of nonlinear discrete (integer) programming.

Discrete programming methods do not possess such a unity, as the methods of the calculus of variations, and largely they are a set of special techniques that are suitable for solving particular problems. But their relevance require for their development and improvement since the most important applied problems are reduced, as a rule, to the tasks partially or completely of discrete programming. The complexity of the solution of the discrete (integer) programming increases when the problem is multiobjective.

When the components of possible solutions of multiobjective problems can only take discrete values $p_k^{(P_u)}, k \in [1, P_u], u \in [1, q]$, scalar convolution by nonlinear compromise scheme $Y(p)$ is a lattice function defined on a discrete set P. Optimization of the lattice objective function, built on nonlinear compromise scheme, is reduced to a nonlinear programming problem with discrete (integer) arguments, the solution of which, as noted above, is quite difficult.

To solve this problem, we assume that at a discrete set P there exists an auxiliary area of continuous arguments $p_c \in P_c$, which contains all the discrete points $p_k^{(P_u)}$ and all continuous space between them. In the area P_c the continuous function $Y(p_A)$ is defined, which coincides in points $p_k^{(P_u)}$ with the lattice function $Y(p)$.

This assumption allows us to obtain an analytical solution if in the expression (7) is given the relationship $e(p)$, for example in the form of a regression model. Then you can use a necessary condition for a minimum of functions: $\dfrac{\partial Y(p_A)}{\partial p_c} = 0$. The solution to this system of equations gives a compromise- optimal continual point p_A*. The last step of the algorithm – search on P for the nearest to the p_A* a possible discrete point that will be the desired discrete solution $p*$. In our case, unfortunately, the issuance of analytical relationships is very difficult or impossible.

We consider as the basic a case where the functions $e(p)$ and, therefore $Y(p)$, are not known, but it is possible to determine the values of the function $Y(p)$ at the points $p_k^{(P_u)}$ by experiment (measurement or calculation). Then it is possible to organize a full-scale or numerical simulation, as a result of which the search movement to the desired discrete compromise -optimal point p^* is carried out.

There are various approaches to the search procedure, which should give consistently improving solutions. One of them – a discrete analogue of the simplex-planning Nelder-Mead method (flexible polyhedron method). This is a kind of gradient methods, very often and successfully applied in practice. Second – the nonlocal (dual) approach (Voronin et al., 1999), which is often more effective than gradient methods.

Since in the search procedures are used the local or non-local models of a continuous function $Y(p_A)$, the common for these options is the need to search on P a possible discrete point p_d closest to the continuous solution p_c on the current or the final iteration.

If the number of hidden layers q is small, the solution to this problem is straightforward (simple rounding to the nearest whole number). When multilayer classifiers, we recommend using the following algorithmic method. In the point p_c the center of hypersphere is placed whose diameter increases from zero to until the surface of the sphere touches the nearest discrete points, which thus is identified as p_d. Different software implementations of the algorithm are possible.

VECTOR OPTIMIZATION OF A NEURAL NETWORK TEXTS CLASSIFIER

Neural network classifiers of different types and purposes are known. For example, let's consider in general terms the task of multicriteria optimization of architecture of a neural network texts classifier. The text classification system (Borisov, 2007) consists of two main parts: a frequency analyzer with system dictionary and the actual neural network classifier (Figure 3).

Figure 3. The network texts classifier

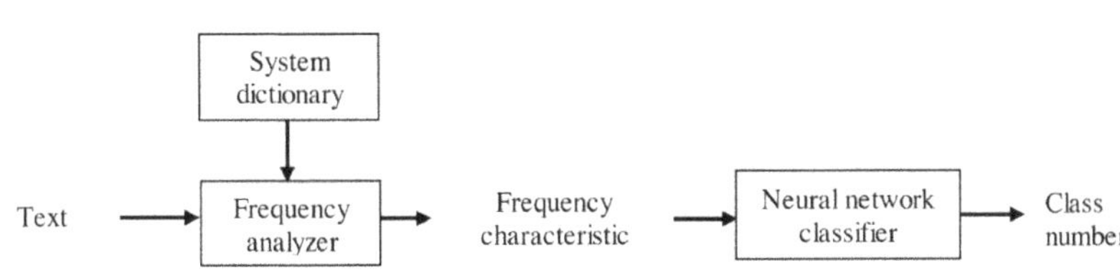

In the system input a text arrives, the output is a number of topic to which the text belongs (business, politics, medicine, sports, just spam, etc.).

Before optimizing the architecture of neural network texts classifier, the following steps must be performed:

1. m classes are defined, with which the system will operate.
2. Appropriate educational texts $t_k, k \in [1, m]$ and validation (test) texts $t_l, l \in [1, L], L \geq m$ are selected.
3. From the many educational texts are specially allocated words $v_i, i \in [1, n]$ and the system dictionary V is formed.
4. Frequency Analyzer determines for each word v_i from the system dictionary V its occurrence frequency x_i in a given text. Frequency characteristic – it is a feature vector $x = \{x_i\}_{i=1}^{n}$ of text attributes t_k, dimension of which is equal to the number of words $v_i \in V$ in the system dictionary.

After receiving the results of frequency analysis of educational texts, you can start learning neural classifier at a certain architecture $p = \{p_j\}_{j=1}^{q}$. The learning process of the neural network is to establish such weighting coefficients $w_1, w_2, \ldots, w_q, w_{q+1}$ of its links in which the maximum error of the network on educational texts for this architecture does not exceed the maximum permissible value. Specific learning algorithms are not considered here.

After performing these steps, you can proceed directly to the theoretical-experimental vector optimization procedure. To optimize the architecture of the neural network classifier we use one of the search methods, e.g, by simplex-planning. Suppose that for a certainty number of processing layers $q = 2$. Then the idea of the method in a continuous manner can be illustrated using Figure 4.

On the plane of the arguments $p_1 - p_2$ in a starting area we build the initial regular simplex, which in two-dimensional case is an isosceles triangle with vertices $p^{(1)}, p^{(2)}, p^{(3)}$. For each of the three architectures of the simplex we provide a process of learning classifier and serve to input a series of test texts t_l. At each vertex of the simplex we experimentally determine the number of classification errors $e^{(1)}, e^{(2)}, e^{(3)}$ in the total number of tests $N = L$. According to the formula (6) we obtain criteria $f_1^{(1)}, f_1^{(2)}, f_1^{(3)}$. According to the formula (7) criteria $f_2^{(1)}, f_2^{(2)}, f_2^{(3)}$ are determined. Formula (6), acting in this case as not an objective, but the evaluation function, for our example has the form

Figure 4. The simplex-planning procedure

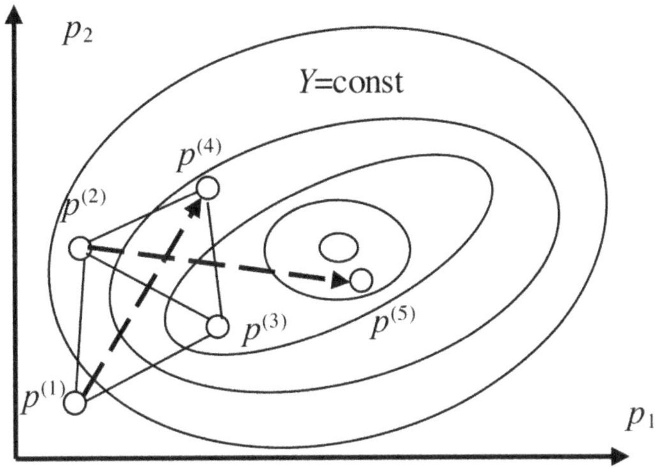

$$Y(p_1, p_2) = \frac{A_1}{A_1 - e(p_1, p_2) / L} + \frac{A_2}{A_2 - p_1 - p_2} \tag{8}$$

For the starting simplex architectures, it gives the values of scalar convolutions $Y^{(1)}, Y^{(2)}, Y^{(3)}$. Comparing these values with each other, we find that one of them, for example $Y^{(1)}$, proved more (i.e. worse) than others. With high probability it can be argued that the architecture $p^{(4)}$ obtained as a mirror image of the worst in the original simplex point $p^{(1)}$ relative to the center of the opposite face, it will be better. By carrying out all the calculations for architecture $p^{(4)}$, we form a new simplex with vertices $p^{(2)}$, $p^{(3)}$ and $p^{(4)}$. Comparing the values $Y^{(2)}, Y^{(3)}, Y^{(4)}$, we find that one of the points, for example $p^{(2)}$, turned out to be worse than others in terms of the second simplex. Displaying this point relative to the center of the opposite face of the second simplex we obtain architecture $p^{(5)}$, etc. up until we obtain an architecture p^* corresponding to the minimum of objective function.

This is only an illustration of the simplex-planning method idea. In fact, this method in the modification of Nelder-Mead provides adaptation of simplexes to the topography of the objective function due to deformation of polyhedron, it has a well developed algorithms and software. In addition, we must not forget that we have the case of optimization with integer arguments, which dictates the need for each received continuous solution p_c search for a nearest discrete solution p_d.

Second, non-local search method, is somewhat more complicated to implement, but it is generally more efficient (Voroninet al., 1999). The method is based on the iterative construction of "floating" with the system of changing basic points, specifying by the experimental results, the non-local model $Y(p)$, wherein a set of reference points compresses and shrinks to the desired point of extremum ("shagreen leather"). At each iteration, both simultaneously and interdependent, is performed a refinement of our understandings of the objective function in the field of extremum, and the definition of such an assessment of extremum arguments that is adequate to the level of these understandings in this iteration. Therefore, non-local optimization method belongs to the class of dual and can be called the dual programming method.

Both search methods provide for a series of experiments. Obtained experimental data can be used to construct analytical regression models of the partial criterion $f_1(p) = e(p) / L$. With these models, you can carry out not a search but analytical vector optimization of architecture of other neural network classifiers of the same kind. If this proves difficult, the search procedure is carried out, but not with the use of full-scale but computational experiment, that is much easier.

Solving the problem of regression models building, we need to set the kind of approximating dependence known up to unknown regression coefficients. Analysis of the problem leads to the assumption that with sufficient accuracy for practical purposes, you can use the linear regression:

$$f_1(p_1, p_2) \approx (a_1 p_1 + a_2 p_2) / L \tag{9}$$

where a_1, a_2 – the regression coefficients determined from experimental data by least squares method. Linear regression model is tested for adequacy by methods of mathematical statistics. If necessary, the model can be complicated.

The above methods involve starting the search procedure on the architecture, which, according to developers, is sufficiently close to the optimum point. If in the search procedure an increase in the number of neurons in the processing layers takes place, the neural network theory characterizes this as a *constructive* approach. When starting with excess number of neurons, this is called *destructive* approach (principle of Rodin: to carve a sculpture, you need to take the whole block of marble and remove from it the unnecessary).

CONCLUSION

Realization of considered in-process stages of vector optimization allows determining such architecture of neural network classifier, at which the contradictory criteria of efficiency of its functioning are systemically tied up, and the resulting architecture is compromise-optimal.

REFERENCES

Bodyansky, E. V., & Rudenko, O. G. (2004). *Artificial neural networks: architecture, training and application*. Kharkov: TELETEH.

Borisov, V. S. (2007). Self-learning texts classifier in natural language. *Cybernetics and Systems Analysis*, (3): 169–176.

Charnes, A., & Cooper, W. (1961). *Management models and industrial applications of linear programming*. New York: Wiley.

Fishburne, P. S. (1978). *Utility theory for decision making*. Moscow: Nauka.

Golovko, V. A. (2001). *Neural networks: education, organization and application*. Moscow: IPRZHR.

Voronin, A. (2017). *Multi-Criteria Decision Making for the Management of Complex Systems*. IGI Global. doi:10.4018/978-1-5225-2509-7

Voronin, A.N. (1999). *Vector optimization of dynamic systems*. Kiev: Tehnika.

Chapter 5
Local Forum as a Knowledge Source

Pavel P. Makagonov
Russian Presidential Academy of National Economy and Public Administration, Russia

Celia Bertha Reyes Espinoza
Mixtec Technological University, Mexico

Oleg M Dzikun
Russian Presidential Academy of National Economy and Public Administration, Russia

ABSTRACT

An internet forum can be used as a crowdsourcing tool for searching for new knowledge and the latest non-standard ideas being a result of forum members' joint creative work. On the basis of these regularities, criteria of the forum maturity in processes of its formation and advance are elaborated. Basing on these results on a 2015 analysis of the forum, formed on the ground of the Universidad Tecnologica de la Mixteca (UTM), the State of Oaxaca, Mexico, a moment when the forum reaches its maturity was revealed. These conceptions are suitable for forming a thesaurus and taxonomy prototype of socio-cultural, environmental, and economic problems in Mixteca region. In its turn, a forum thesaurus gives opportunities for the regional community to understand a degree of its involvement into revealing and discussing the most actual regional problems on the internet.

DOI: 10.4018/978-1-5225-5586-5.ch005

INTRODUCTION

Web Forum as a Crowdsourcing Technology

Recent years has shown that by virtue of the ubiquitous Internet development, it is possible to organize separate discussion and search for a solution for a local territorial and/or social problem, using the creative potential of the territorial or social community. In order to carry out a discussion and search (if possible), one often employs the survey method, but a local web forum specialized on the problem, is the best choice among low-cost tools.

The discussion of a problem at the forum gives the following advantages:

- Openness of questions allows each asked person to freely express his/her own opinion, suggest original ideas, actively consider and estimate the consciousness and propositions of others;
- Absolute voluntariness of participation; self-evident filtration of forummembers.

A web forum can be used as a crowdsourcing tool for searching for new knowledge, the latest non-standard ideas being a result of forum members' joint creative work. Sometimes the mentioned knowledge is new only for the forum community, but in the majority of cases,only forum members or forum managers are interested in gaining the innovations owing to joint search for replies onto questions stirring them.

Forum discussion can bring to light a situation, where an interference of local community or partnership with the state are required to solve the problem, new or out of conscious formerly; for instance see: (Samorodova, 2015;Warner, 2011;Vasilkova, 2015).

A web forum is an open, dynamically upcoming, hence complex, system. In many works, where forums are under analysis, researchers are interested in all stages of their development, when information exchange processes can be represented as "mutual synergetic cycle" inside which people create a continuous flow of the information, placed into the interrelated data repository; for instance see: (Stern, 2013; Paulus, 2007; Zhang, 2007;Wei, 2013;Makagonov, 2014).

However, researchers are more often interested only in analyzing the results of discussions with respect to all the communities, where forums exist. In order to analyze the forum groundwork, it's desirable to be sure, that the main part of the work has already been done, the results of discussions are final and will not undergo any serious changes. This stage is usually highlighted with lowering of the forum members' activity within the limits of a close subject matter when the

Figure 1. Accumulated sum of articles on crowdsourcing at forums in e-library ACM (ordinate) vs last publication year

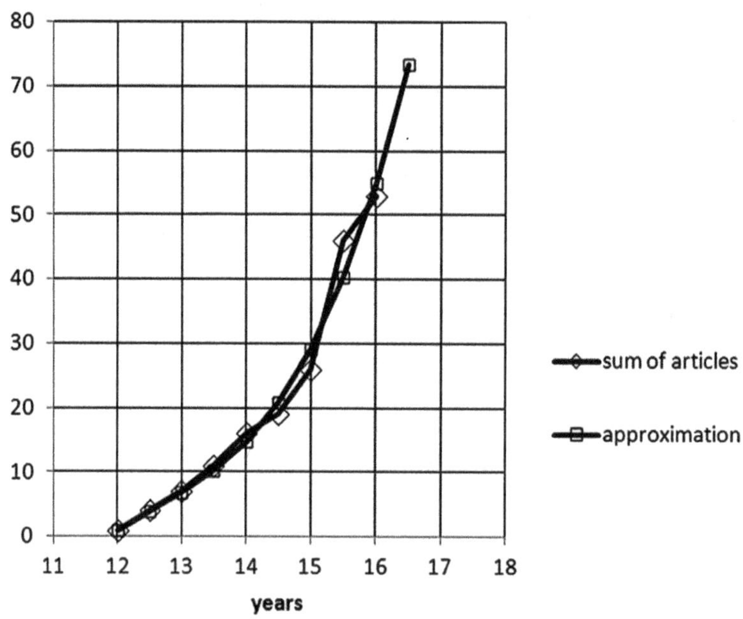

forum fulfilled its mission in that part of work. One can come to this conclusion if there is an opportunity to verify a degree of maturity (or self-orderliness) for forum community given. Otherwise, the cognitive analysis of the discussion contents may become shallow, not exhaustive and incomplete. If forum members exhaust a specific theme, it means the absence of interest in it and accordingly, in the life cycle of the forum. One needs to ascertain that hitherto in scientific literature there was not any information on the forum lifecycle problem, especially on the forum maturity stage as a phase of its development. At least in the e-library ACM, there is no note on this subject matter.

At the same time, an elaboration of the scientific problems in the context of crowd-sourcing is quite prospective. As it is shown in Figure 1, the life cycle curve of the articles on crowdsourcing technology (with using forums in e-library ACM) has the J-like appearance, that reflects the early development stage, being far from an inflection point observable onto S-like curve for accumulated frequencies.

Below in (1), the curve approximating accumulated number s of articles vs the year t of the last publication is represented with determination factor $R^2 = 0.9809$.

$$s = 0.7744\, t^3 - 29.201\, t^2 + 372.64\, t - 1603.9. \tag{1}$$

FORUM MATURITY CRITERIA

1st Type Estimation: By Information Exchange Intensity Among Forum Members – G-H Distribution

Self-orderliness is an important factor that stimulates free creating work in a community. The degree of self-orderliness or maturity of the forum community can be estimated according to the empirical law of interacting the forces, bonds, messages exchange intensity among forum members. Several works (Makagonov, 2014, 2015a, 2015b) prove the following point: for the complex social system, for example, the forum as a social network of a specific form, just the consistency degree of members' interaction parameters with empirical distribution law (2) may act as a criterion of self-organization and maturity:

$$Y^G = A - KX^H, \tag{2}$$

where $Y = \log(F)$; $A = \log(F_0)$; $X = \log(i)$.

F = F (i) is an intensity characteristic for bonds of i-object in the system with the other objects. Inside the forum as a social system authors of judgments are its objects. In this case, the judgments of each forum member themselves play the role of system bonds. Presentation (2) as

$$Y = \sqrt[G]{A - KX^H} \tag{3}$$

corresponds to a certain curve: convex or (in separate rare cases) concave. Transition to (2) allows finding optimal values for G and H when a graph for (2) becomes a practically straight line:

$$u = A - K\,v;\ u = Y^G;\ v = X^H. \tag{4}$$

In its turn, this permits even laymen to visually estimate the approximation quality of dependence (3) under consideration.

For any complex social system, it is possible to reveal the characteristic interpretable as a degree (or force) of a bond among system objects under analysis. Multifarious numerical factors may serve as characteristics of interactions, bonds among forum members. However, it is preferable to use such factors, that differentiate forum members in the process of contacting more clearly, for instance, their activity, number of messages (posts) and their length, etc.

In case this information is inaccessible for some reason or a greater number of resources is required to obtain it, it might be easier to consider subforums or separate themes (topics), when they as objects of the system, are numerous enough: tens and HDs.

For acknowledged maturity of the forum or its independent part, it seems advisable to analyze the combined contents of members' judgments on a given theme (topic). As the forum or a separate theme develops successfully, new judgments strive to add the contents on hand, making it functionally united. These texts are named *holistic* ones. When a holistic text undergoes linguistic analysis, an important aspect lies in using its vocabulary wholly, not fragmentarily.

Obtained texts can be analyzed to reveal a degree of their harmony or perfection by compliance between frequency list of significant words and Zipf—Mandelbrot distribution (Montemurro, 2001) and also by compliance between syntactic words distribution and approximation of *G—H* kind. Commonly used words are named as syntactic ones, if they are lexically dependent (having no nominative function in the language) and express diverse semantic-syntactical relations among words, clauses and parts of the latter. Syntactic words are opposed to significant (self-dependent) ones.

This kind of analysis gives good indices only in holistic texts (Makagonov, 2014). Statistics accumulated on distributions of *G—H* kind up to present time allows to formulate the perfection criteria for a complex system in terms of fuzzy sets: a holistic text, forum members' community and, as long as it exists protractedly, a totality of forum themes or subdivisions. One of those criteria is a determination factor R^2 for the approximation of distribution by (2) with parameters G, H, A, K, found using the least-squares procedure.

Let us accept the following scale for an extent of system perfection (harmonicity, self-sufficiency) or finally with a special reference to the forum — its maturity degree, according to the distribution of *G—H* kind:

- The forum is mature, if $R^2 > 0.98…0.975$;
- The forum is close to becoming mature, if $R^2 > 0.96…0.95$;
- The forum is certainly far from becoming mature if $R^2 < 0.93$.

These limits are based on analyzing the forums having the right to claim for a high level of maturity. The following forums matching this criterion were selected:

- Forums of little and middle towns in Russia: Podolsk, Kashira, Pushkin (see: http://www.inform-podolsk.ru, http://kashira.tv/forum/, https://www.mypushkin.ru/);
- Forum of the municipal settlement Kommunarka (see: http://new.msk.ru/);

- Student community forum of the Southern Illinois University (SIU) in the City of Carbondale, Ill., USA (see: http://www.salukination.net/forumlist.php).

Considered criteria of forum maturity were used further for analyzing development dynamics for a separate forum established on the basis of authors' participation (see: http://foros.utm.mx).

Examples of Mature Forums and Their Parameters in a Presentation of G—H Kind

The distribution of the members' posts (messages) at Podolsk city forum for the first 5 years is presented in Figure 2.

The best approximation of this distribution has the following form:

$$y^{1.5} = 64.083 - 2.9745x^{1.25}; R^2 = 0.9897. \tag{5}$$

Figure 2. Left: The distribution of 4125 members' posts (messages) at Podolsk city forum for the first 5 years; right: Podolsk city forum with approximation formula $y^G = A - KX^H$.

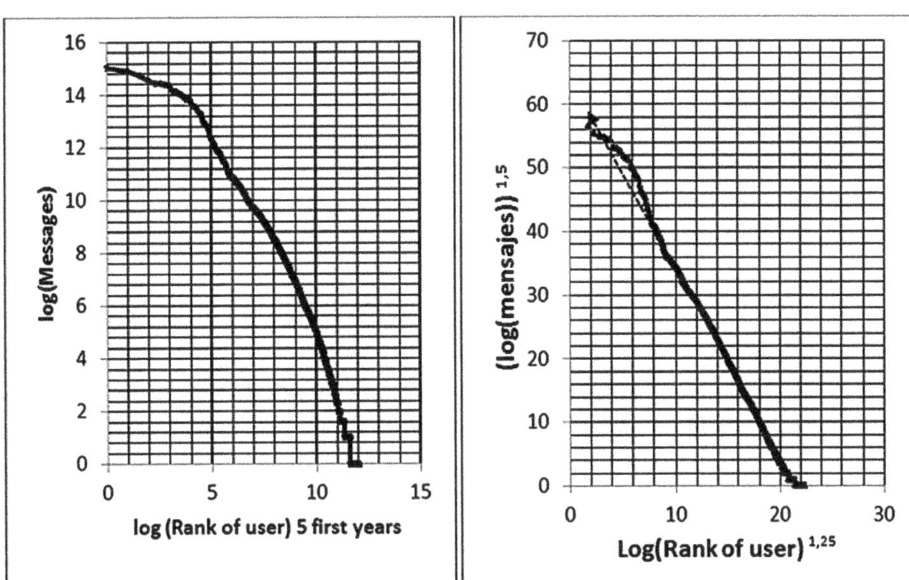

Also let us consider the distribution of posts (messages) for the first 291 members at the forum of the local community in the municipal settlement Kommunarka, Moscow Region. The best approximation of this distribution is presented in the following way:

$$y^2 = -6.4205x^{1.5} + 154.61;\ R^2 = 0.9857. \tag{6}$$

Sometimes it is difficult to collect the information about each forum member. For instance, at the long-lived SIU football forum, there is information about numbers of subforums (including one private for all the comers), posts, views, and replies. It was difficult to collect personal forum data about each member of the forum, but the estimation of the maturity degree of all 9 subforums was enough to estimate the bond intensity by number of themes (from 986 to 9) and posts (from 72,497 to 22) for each of 9 subforums mentioned, excluding an"off-topic" one, containing everything that did not fit any other existing discussion. The following dependencies were established:

$$y^{2.5} = -89.623x + 326.75; R^2 = 0.9792, \tag{7}$$

where

$$y = \log\left(TOPICS\right); x = \left(\ \right)\log\left(SUBFORUMINDEX\right);$$

$$y^{2.5} = -299.76\ x + 1073;\quad R^2 = 0.9833, \tag{8}$$

where

$$y = \log\left(POSTS\right); x = \log\left(SUBFORUMINDEX\right).$$

An approximation of *G—H* kind for thematic distribution by subforums at Kashira forum is of the form:

$$y^{2.25} = -6.2094x^{1.25} + 65.38; R^2 = 0.9951; \tag{9}$$

where

$$y = \log(TOPICS); x = \log(SUBFORUMINDEX)$$

And for message distribution we have got accordingly:

$$y^2 = -11,224x^{1,25} + 128,11;\ R^2 = 0,9821; \qquad (10)$$

where

$$y = \log(POSTS); x = ((\ ))\log((SUB)FORUMINDEX).$$

The best approximation of distribution by topics, at each subforum considered for Pushkin community forum is of the form:

$$y^2 = -14.504x + 71.42, R^2 = 0.9755, \qquad (11)$$

where

$$y = \log(TOPICS); x = \log(SUBFORUMINDEX).$$

For replies (posts) of members on the same topics at the same subforums the approximation is of the form:

$$y^{2.5} = -11.999x^2 + 326.75, \qquad (12)$$

where $y = \log(POSTS); x = (\ )\log(SUBFORUMINDEX)$, the determination factor value being low: $R^2 = 0.9189$.

One can interpret this as weak self-organization of the main and less active mass of forum members. The most active part of the community, i.e. those who suggested topics for discussion, possess high enough self-organization degree. Thus, this example shows the asynchrony in maturing of role forum members and diverse in their activity.

Studying the Dynamics of Forum Progress in Universidad Tecnologica de la Mixteca (UTM), the City of Huajuapan de Leon, Mixteca Region, Mexico

Having known, in what limits lie criteria values for perfect systems of a common kind and mature forums on a close subject-matter, let us consider our forum, established with authors' participation in the frames of the UTM to analyze social-cultural problems in the City of Huajuapan de Leon.

Below in bi-logarithmic scale, the distribution graphs «Rank vs Messages (posts) number» for the Huajuapan community forum are represented during a period of the first two weeks (curve A) and 10 weeks (curve C) from the launching point of the forum life cycle (Figure 3).

The curves A and C together with the curve of intermediate distribution for 6 weeks period (not shown in Figure 3) are in compliance with approximating curves of *G—H* kind and determination factors, represented in the form of formulae in Table 1.

Let us accept the estimation of forum maturity at 10th week as satisfactory, taking into account that the aliasing on the right part of distribution for small samples with an integer step of parameter in hand changing, when a number of messages, posts is equal 1, 2, 3…, gives an approximation error not as a result of distribution

Figure 3. Distribution graphs «Rank vs Messages (posts) number» for the Huajuapan community forum during a period of the first two weeks (curve A) and 10 weeks (curve C) from the launching point of the forum life cycle

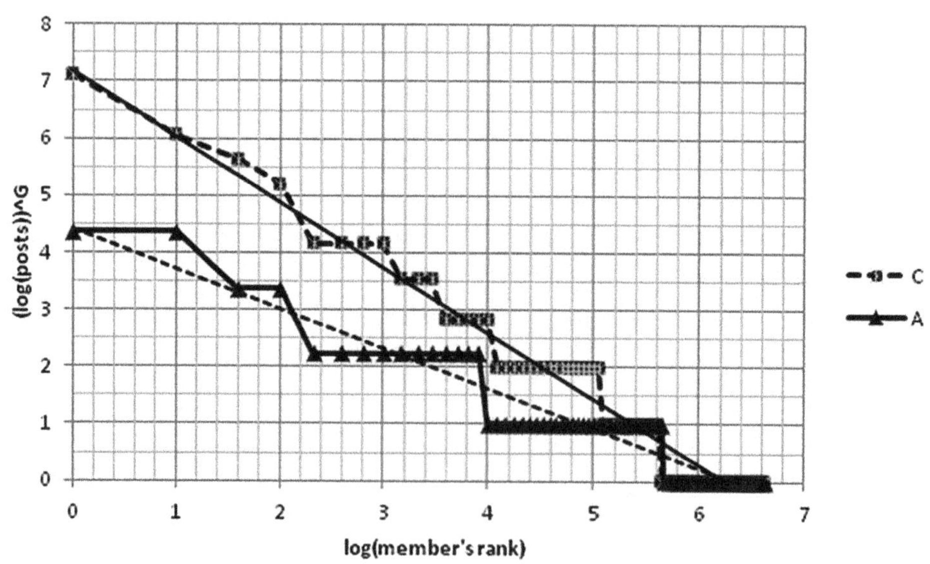

Table 1. Formulae and numerical representation of data for the Huajuapan community forum

Time From the Forum Launching Point, Weeks	Approximations of *G—H* Kind, $y = \log\left(POSTS\right); x = \log\left(MEMBERS'RANK\right)$.	Determination Factor R^2
2	$y^{1.75}\left(2weeks\right) = -0.6994x + 4.419$	0.9137
6 (variant 1)	$y^{1.5}\left(6weeks\right) = -0.8774x + 6.4237$	0.9461
6 (variant2)	$y^{1.5}\left(6weeks\right) = -0.4674x^{1,25} + 5.628$	0.9511
10	$y^{1.5}\left(10weeks\right) = -1.1523x + 7.1953$	0.9621

character distortion, but owing to a fault of approximating the discrete distributions by continuous ones.

For instance, if we take the linear distribution $y = b - ax$ and replace all the fractional values of ordinate by the nearest integer, we will get something like what is shown in Figure 4.

Figure 4. Linear approximation of step-like distribution (see clarification in the text)

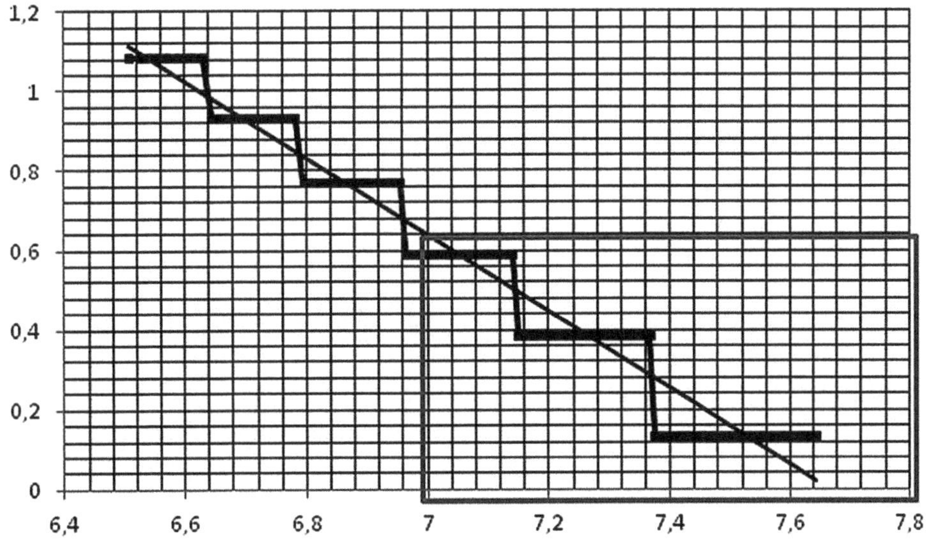

If now we approximate all step-like figures as a straight linc, wc will get the representation in the form:

$$y = -0.9639\,x + 7.388 \qquad (13)$$

with determination factor $R^2 = 0.9622$.

And if we approximate only a part of step-like figures shown in fig. 4 in the right low rectangle, we will get the approximation in the form:

$$y = -0.8856\,x + 6.8088 \qquad (14)$$

with far worse value of determination factor $R^2 = 0.8629$.

Taking into account all the set forth, it should be accepted, that the forum in the City of Huajuapan has reached the maturity levelup to 10th week of its existence, allowing to carry out the content analysis of its texts as the quite formed end-product.

2nd Type Estimation: By Info Contribution of Each Forum Member

Forum members get access not only to statistical data but to posts too: the content of the latter is a characteristic of the bond degree of one post-author with others. Having determined a volume V of each specific member judgments in the form of usage number, one can also estimate the balance of information bonds at the forum.

Let us consider the distribution of the judgments volume among forum-members in the City of Huajuapan.

For each author of a message on each topic a number of significant words as a function of message author's index (rank) is approximated using the following expression of G—H kind:

$$y^{3.5} = -41.636\,x^{1.5} + 841.38, \qquad (15)$$

where $y = \log(V)$.

As the level of the determining factor is quite high ($R^2 = 0.9847$), the value of the exponent G does not exceed 4, but it is high enough to acknowledge the forum as quite mature, although relatively high value of the hybrid criterion R^2 allows supposing that the forum is rather near to low permissible limit of maturity.

ANALYZING THE TEXTS FORMED FROM POLEMISTS' JUDGMENTS DONE DURING DISCUSSIONS ON A CLOSE SUBJECT-MATTER

Text Estimation by Distributions of Significant and Syntactic Words

All the above-represented forum maturity estimations, possessing required quality, allow to pass on to the cognitive analysis of the information accumulated at the forum.

In the work of Soo (2002) is given the following popular academy judgment: "In the Web, making judgments of information quality....is a difficult task for most users because overall, there is no quality control mechanism".

However, as shown in Makagonov (2014), there is an opportunity to estimate not information quality, but the perfection of holistic text structure by determination factor of significant words distribution according to Zipf law in the text and by the same factor – of syntactic words distribution in the text in accordance with "*G—H* law". It is commonly acceptable to estimate the text perfection by consistency degree between the frequency list or all the words and Zipf—Mandelbrot distribution: $F = F_1/(i + B)*K$ or $Y = A - K*\log(i + B)$, where $Y = \log(F)$, $X = \log(i)$ — and i is a frequency rank of the word; F_1, B, K, A being some constants for texts with the volume over 1800 words and with Zipf distribution ($B = 0$) for texts of less volume.

For this distribution it is not important, who is the author of a certain message (post), only a total list of significant words from forum members' messages is taken into account. Here the distribution characterizes perfection degree for the totality of all the texts as united knowledge system by forum members' creative work generated.

For occurrence frequency distribution of all the words from forum messages, including linking words, there is an approximation

$$y = -0.9191\, x + 10.075, \text{ when } R^2 = 0.955. \tag{16}$$

That means that the known criterion works to some extent.

As mentioned above, in a holistic text the perfection degree of content together with its semantic value is linked with perfection factors of frequency list of syntactic words in the text.

Also as an analog of Zipf law for syntactic words, one suggests using the distribution of *G—H* kind, where the exponent *G* must be changed within the limits 1...4 and the exponent *H* must not exceed *G*, quite often accepting a value 1.

Formerly this assertion was verified and precisely rendered on the basis of tales and poetry (Makagonov, 2014) and further, with the use of a series of accomplished scientific works by the great Russian scholars, known as the most significant ones in the culture of such countries, where native languages are English, Russian, German or Spanish. The overall number of the syntactic words in all the posts at the Huajuapan forum is merely 4010. For the distribution "word rank vs frequency" the following approximation is equitable:

$$y^{1.5} = -0.9648\, x^{1.5} + 21.925, \qquad (17)$$

when $R^2 = 0.9917$.

According to this criterion, the combined text of all the forum messages is perfect.

Text Estimation Based on the Golden Section

Let us estimate a perfection of a holistic text at the Huajuapan forum by Golden Section criterion. *The Golden Section*, also known as the *Divine Proportion*, *Golden Mean*, or Golden Ratio, is one of numbers $\varphi = \frac{\sqrt{5}-1}{2}$ or $\Phi = \frac{\sqrt{5}+1}{2}$, so that $\Phi - \varphi = 1$. The *Golden Section* appears while dividing any quantity into two parts: *a* and *b* so that the whole quantity divided by a larger part is equal toΦ and a larger part divided by a smaller part is the same. A lot of people recognize the *Golden Section* as the constant of harmony.

Let us accept:

$$\varphi_1 = \frac{a}{b}; \varphi_2 = \frac{b}{a+b}; \varphi = \frac{\varphi_1 + \varphi_2}{2}, \qquad (18)$$

where *a* and *b* — numbers of word usages of significant and syntactic words correspondingly.

The holistic text ratio φ_1 for more harmonious texts is near to the Golden Section ($\varphi = 0.618$).

In (Makagonov, 2015a, 2015b) the following conclusion was made for texts with not less than 1800 word usages: when the exponent $G \leq 2 \ldots 2.5$ and the deviation of φ_1, φ_2 from the Golden Section lie within the limits 0.73…0.535, the text answers the perfection criterion. For texts that by common agreement are not acknowledged as the most perfect in the given sphere of knowledge or in a given genre even at the national level, obtained values of factors deviated considerably from the limits pointed.

The total number of word usages *a* + *b* at the whole forum is 9417 and 5407 from them are significant, 4010 ones being syntactic. From this follows:

$$\varphi_1 = 0.741631219; \varphi_2 = 0.574174366 \text{ and } \varphi = (\varphi_1 + \varphi_2)/2 = -0.6579027 \qquad (19)$$

As in (17), $G = 1.5$ and the number of words in texts of the whole forum is enough to employ the Golden Section criterion, one can conclude: *a/b* ratio exceeds the acceptable deviation 0.73 by only 0.012.

If we stay within the limits of the fuzzy logic, this deviation may be ignored and one can consider text content of the forum as close to harmonious, explaining the deviation in the following way: the forum contains about ten themes on social, cultural and ecological problems, being relatively close, but still diverse; it is not a success to employ the criterion to the analysis of only one theme, as the number of words in each of them turns out to be less or equal to the critical value of 1800, so it is not a success to divide the whole text by themes for analysis.

A Hybrid Criterion: Rank of Forum Member vs. the Number of Significant Words

Thus far we have analyzed the links between forum members according to the number of messages sent to the fellow members by each forum member, or according to the number of messages mentioned at each sub-forum.

Now let us consider the number of significant words in the messages posted by each forum member as the intensity of links between the forum members in pairs. This will combine two different parts of the forum as a system: on the one hand, there are characteristics of forum members as producers of new knowledge for some narrow domain and/or for a local area; on the other hand, there is the content of the product forum members have generated.

Let us consider the following dependence: the number of significantwords belonging to each message writer on every topic is an index (range) function of a message writer.

The distribution of the convex curve type has been obtained. It is transformed by the formula (2) and approximated by the expression:

$$\left(\log\left(the\ \ number\ \ of\ \ words\right)\right)^{3.5}$$
$$= -41.636 \times \left(\log\left(author's\ \ index\right)\right) * 1.5 + +841.38\ ;$$

$$R^2 = 0.9847\ .$$

Content Analysis of Texts on the Forum and Formation of Thesaurus Prototype

We do not imply a comparison of sites and forums between each other as a necessary content analysis of forums, but only an opportunity to analyze contents of the forum to increase its efficiency. Old local forums (for instance, in Russia), deeply structured by topics, contain many themes (hundreds) and much more messages (hundreds of thousands). But at these forums as well, the valuable messages can often be lost if the forum structure allows alteration of places for materials allocation. New forums with a little number of members have quite a close subject matter (for instance, the town football club) or in no way can clarify it.

Firstly it is useful for tenuously structured forums to introduce the hypertext technology inside the forum to increase the efficiency of searching for a close topic for forum members. So there are many arguments in favor of including content analysis statistical tools into an envelope of the local forum to support its folksonomy, reflect the forum structure in hypertext and accelerate searching within the forum. Here it turns out to be a good idea to single out sections (subforums), where themes, each active participant is interested in, are being discussed. It is desirable for the forum structure to be transparent, as this simplifies the work with data.

Let us consider such analysis procedure as an example of the UTM forum for the Mixtec region. Environmental, social, and cultural problems of the Mixtec region are mentioned here as the most interesting for discussion in the local community. Self-motivated forum members have introduced two following groups of discussion topics.

Topics of the first and most popular group are below.

1. Abastecimiento de Agua (Water supply).
2. Centros De Acopio (Landfills).
3. Diffucion Preservacion Cultural (Dissemination and conservation of culture).
4. Globalizacion Ayuda Perjudica Cultura (Does Globalization assist the culture or damage it?).
5. Rescate Gastronomia (Gastronomy saving).
6. Usos y Costumbres(Customs and Traditions)
7. Migracion (Migration).

Topics from this group occurred in the clusters partially reduced while sometimes partially united.

In the second group there are topics not included into the most popular clusters: Social Otros (Social Climbers and Others); Cultura Otro Tema (Theme: Different

Culture); Artesanias Conservacion (Folk Crafts Conservation); Ecologico Otra Situacion (Other Environmental Situation); Recursos Forestales (Forest Resources); Mas Alla De Las Palabras (Behind the Words); Pensemos Verde (Green Thoughts). These topics are somewhat different from the matters of mainstream ones.

The smaller-in-size matrices of the "text–word" type were obtained for every cluster of forum topics. These matrices can be used to carry out the drilldown of clusters of forum members according to narrower subjects and the drilldown of domain vocabularies for each of the word clusters singled out before. This can be used as a basis for creating rapid prototypes of top layers of each cluster's ontology.

Let us return to first seven themes opened for discussion at this forum. For these themes, one can single out subthemes touched in forum discussions. It would be better if the opportunity to do it would be given to the experts on Mixtec region problems. Our task is to reveal stable word combinations with a lower generalization level than phraseological units of common vocabulary, but sufficient for conformity with forum thesaurus concepts or even suitable to form hierarchical network like the taxonomical or ontological one on the basis of statistical analyzing of a corpus of messages appeared at the forum.

In order to solve this task, all the functional words were deleted from word frequency lists in all the texts. Further, an occurrence matrix for each significant word in each text and a matrix of occurrence frequency for these words were formed. After clustering the given matrices it became clear that the resulting clusters are of weak saturation and inside them there are, in fact, only vector-rows, corresponding to the appearance of one word in many texts, or only vector-columns, corresponding to the appearance of a group of words in one text. This is shown in Figure 5.

Figure 5. Graphic presentation of the fragment of "texts – words" matrix. The contoured rows correspond to words, the chosen columns correspond to texts.

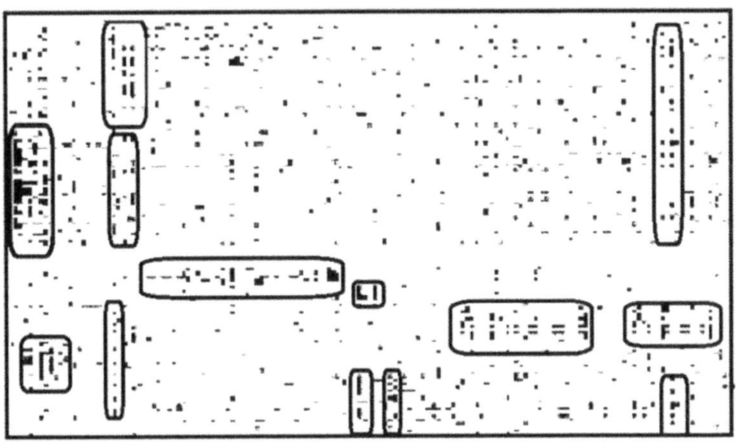

In this situation, instead of singling out informationally rich blocks, another approach was used. The filtration of initial "texts—words" matrix was carried out, where only words with major values of ratio A/B were saved, "A" being the standard deviation of each word frequency in all the texts and "B" being an arithmetical mean for this A/B distribution frequency.

Rare usage of a term by the small number of authors in relation to the general number of participants discussing a close theme became the reason to exclude these words from bigram search at this stage of studies. On the contrary, high-frequency part of the dictionary substantially corresponds to a common vocabulary and is out of interest when forum subject thesaurus is being formed. For common vocabulary the arithmetical mean is high, so the normed standard deviation of these words has means close to 1, not falling into the selected range 4…8.

In the forum dictionary stable word combinations (bigrams), with forum subjects linked, were semi-automatically revealed. Results were represented as lists, their titles corresponding to text files names of separate messages: the first part of the name corresponded to a theme within the limits the author had allocated his message at the forum, and second one corresponded to the author's avatar (nickname). A list body contained all the bigrams revealed during statistical content analysis and a number of their mentions in the text. These bigrams had no functional words, but for native speakers, it was not difficult to restore them to make a word combination more habitual for perception. As an example, Table 2 shows the list of bigrams from the alphabetically first file.

Algorithms for searching bigrams are simple, so we do not describe them and only mention in application program packages. In this case, the construction of bigrams for small (up to 500 units) collection of short texts may be carried out

Table 2. The list of bigrams

Text File Name	AbastecimientoAguaAraceli_Cruz_.txt	
Bigrams found in file texts	Basura Ríos	Garbage Rivers
	Concientización Tarea	Consciousness Task
	Contaminación Agua загрязненностьводы	Water Contamination
	Gobierno Ciudad администрация города)	City Administration
	Lugar Dejar	Garbage Leave
	Ríos Evitar	Rivers Elude
	Tarea Campaña	Campaign Task
	Tarea Gobierno	Management Task
	Tirar Basura	Garbage Disposal

semi-automatically, if functional words are deleted and the stemming volume is minimal. Obvious and main steps of the algorithm are as follows:

- To form dictionaries of 1st and 2nd words admissible in bigram on the basis of the list with words frequencies of text-corpus studied;
- To divide the text by word sequences having no punctuation symbols between them and enumerate these fragments;
- For all the fragments in the cycle, it is necessary to find the fragment by its first word, containing this word and in case of success, in the cycle manner to search for the second word by following words of the fragment.

From 313 words, selected within $4 < x_n < 8$ criterion with the use of the presented algorithm, more than 145 bigrams were obtained, some of them appeared not only in different texts but in different themes. These bigrams obviously belong to close subject fields — the most attractive themes under discussion at the forum. The bigrams given below are distributed in seven main themes of the forum and reflect discussion content by directions the authors of messages have identified themselves. Let us enumerate them being preliminary grouped in seven discussion directions according to authors' allocations.

Theme 1 - Water Supply: City Administration; Campaign Task, Create Awareness, Env Year, Consciousness Task, Water Contamination, Garbage Collecting, Garbage Eject, Garbage Leave, Rivers Elude, Behavior Culture, Respect Situation.

Theme 2 - Garbage Problem: Garbage Centers, Utilizing Industry, Main Problem, Awareness Importance, Garbage Quality, Waste Recycling, Separate Garbage, Garbage Sorting, Let Assort, Separate Allocation, Final allocation, Hardless Work, Handling Project, Family Training, School Task.

Theme 3 - Culture Distribution: Culture Saving, Mixtecs Culture, Health Value, Knowledge Deficiency, Natural Drugs, Env Situation, Treat Skill, Save Drugs, Cultivate Drugs, Use Plants, Ancestry Knowledge, Medical Grasses, Family Cultivate, Culture Important, Traditional Physic, Stomach Pain, Stomach Camomile, Brew Tea, Family Drug, Important Elude.

Theme 4 - Globalization & Culture – Assistance or Damage: World Development, Drugs Case, Culture Advance, Important Culture, Natural Drugs, Medical Plants, Treat Maladies, Medical Traditions, Cultural Diversity, Cultural Identity, Diversity Sense, Oahaca Mixtecs, Know Culture, Criterion Lack, Identity Criterion, Importance Identity, Culture Loss, Culture Proliferation, Milieu Phenomenon, Embodiment Globalizing, Evil Globalizing, Defense Force,

Basic Roots, Economic Development, Cultural Rcsplcndcncc, Know Level, World Level, Opinion Globalization, Country Tourism.

Theme 5 - Gastronomy Save: Cookery Save, Course Required, Main Consumption, Gastronomical Resplendence, Proliferation Level, Oaxaca Identity, Gastronomical Identity, World Level, Resplendence Diversity, Courses Resplendence, Courses Diversity, Recipes Loss, Traditional Courses, Traditional Drugs, Realize Force, Course Salvage, Knowledge Lack, Identity Style, Regional Gastronomy, Gastronomy Save, Time Lack, Social Significance, Bring Alternatives, Preparing Way, Important Traditions, Administration Assistance, Regional Food.

Theme 6 - Customs & Habits: Social Advantage, Custom Save, Social Party, State Community, Realize Customs, Realizing Way, Region Selecting, Integrated Value, Consumption Expanding, Sale Places, Allow Produce, Improve Product, Save Culture, Community Habitants, Rescue Culture.

Theme 7 - Migration (Emigration): Several Consequences, Entails Effects, Reason Lack, Administration Task, Family Lack, Life Quality, True Quality, Provide Quality, Foreigner Lifestyle, Private Life, Family Life, Seems Commune, Senior Pupils, Globalization Proposes, World Proposes, Adjacent Country, Gives Advantage, Realize Training, Unbiased Estimate, Provide Advance, Economic Development, Alter Country, Community Most.

As it was found while clustering, some texts, basing on their content, had fallen into clusters where the majority of self-identifications did not coincide with the basic themes of the corresponding cluster.

It is quite expected, as themes 1, 2 and 3, also 4, 5 and 6 have many points of contiguity in their content. For instance, 1st cluster contains 8 texts on theme 1, two texts on theme 6 and 1 text per themes 2 and 3. 2nd cluster practically fully consists of texts on theme 6, while 4th cluster contains 5 texts on theme 3, 4 texts on theme 4 and one text on theme 6.

Taking into account this connection, while hierarchically structuring all subject matters, we suggest dividing them into 4 main themes:

- Environmental conditions in the region (themes 1, 2);
- Culture proliferation and saving in globalizing conditions (themes 3, 4 and partially 6);
- Mixtec emigration problems in families and the region on the whole.

Each bigram can be considered as a concept of the prototype or as entering that prototype but at the lower community level.

Basing on some bigrams it is not difficult to form multigrams where content is opened wider, but this step demands a review of their availability in some text at the forum.

The list of bigrams obtained while analyzing the texts (see Table 2) and structure of the matrix "texts—words" show: these materials of the forum can be used to form a hypertext e-book. Besides, one-word concepts should be linked with corresponding text, its name being in a title of the column containing the word given and bigram being included into hypertext owing to its link with list name. Represented ways of analysis allow forming a structure with the depth of no more than 3 levels, namely:

Zero Level: Forum;

1st Level: Theme, that was announced by the administrator-moderator of the forum or one of four main themes proposed above;

2nd Level: Concepts that were proposed by forum participants and supported in their messages;

3rd Level: Texts with a hyperlink from 2nd level concepts and/or conceptions, used when detailing the theme at conception level or in the description of specific cases (situations) typical for the theme under discussion within the limits of one text.

Among bigrams constructions, it is crucially important to have links to some forum members and messages. These links can be actually considered as tags prototypes inside the forum and while creating a forum thesaurus links can be used to form inter-forum hypertext bounds. At this point,it should be taken into account that a link can be connected with a relation of both kinds, positive or negative, to a mentioned message, mainly the message being under discussion in the theme.

Formerly, as it can be seen in the article (Makagonov, 2008), the authors have noticed that the majority of Internet users stop searching after browsing first 300 messages and almost never reach 500 messages. When the number of messages at the forum increases significantly, the search within its limits becomes baffling. So we consider advisable to introduce a forum hypertext organization on the basis of prototype thesaurus formed hierarchically as an object that increases search efficiency inside the forum. This thesaurus, according to the above-considered construction way, can be allocated among forum documents and recommended to forum participants for studying and review of its structure and content.

For the convenience of this analysis, it is advisable to use not only materials at the forum but also the materials that are formed according to the already mentioned results as prototypes (of thesaurus, taxonomy or ontology) with the hierarchical structure of conceptions in respect to terms and word combinations. So, even without experts on problems under discussion, an ontology prototype may be formed using results of carried out statistical analysis of forum texts.

For an external expert it can be difficult to conduct a cognitive analysis of discussions at the forum, if forum participants are sharing the opinions they already understand: many facts or agreements in a given subject field are well-known in their circle of intercourse and taken into account, while an outside specialist is out of subject and weakly grasps the specificity of the problem under discussion at the local level.

The inquiries using revealed word combinations (bigrams) have shown that all the themes are opened broadly, but in some other aspect to which we have not encountered any appropriate mentioning. It is true for all the cases except an inquiry about Mixtec culture, although this word (Mixteca) was added artificially into all the inquiries.

This testifies to the existence of problems that are not discussed yet, on other regional sites, though they are quite actual at the global level, but without connection to Mixteca region.

In respect to messages, instead of general arguments and discourses, main assertions in favor of a specific text are supported with examples that argue the thesis under discussion. However, lack of descriptions (as new cases are different from the already represented due to the expiry of messages flow) testifies to the point that the considered case is the most indicative of the most typical at the given forum.

From all the imaginable multitude of problems, connected with each theme, those that are most typical for the region are discussed at the forum and now forum materials are suitable for analyzing by local authorities and public organizations.

As an example, we can mention the following discussion at the forum of the City of Huajuapan de Leon: school leavers and U-graduates, their emigration from Mixteca region to the USA. While talking about youth conformism, discussion members implicate the following fact as being well-known: in the last decades, the region lost more than 40% of populationin consequence of labor migration to the USA. As a result, young people have numerous examples of available opportunities for getting work. Although it might be connected with hard labor, this brings hope to help their relatives, who stayed at home. On the other hand, forum members talk about the negative side of migration, without expressing the negativity clearly, as all of them already know that the program of creating the U-network in boroughs of the State of Oaxaca is aimed only at raising the socio-cultural level of the state population, including Mixteca region. At the same time, forum members also suggest measures for lowering migration flow, namely, creating workplaces in boroughs of the State of Oaxaca.

CONCLUSION

A great number of scientific and other texts appear on the Internet, the majority of then demand the estimation of the quality of presented sources and materials, but in fact, they are not passing through any examinations, though they are easily accessible for students' milieu. The last point, in its turn, can have various negative consequences.

Forum maturity criteria proposed hereto, allow estimating the quality of text materials for their holism and self-sufficiency for studying a close subject field. For linguistic analyzing of a holistic text of this kind, it is very important to use the whole text vocabulary dictionary, not only fragments or separate examples.

Forum maturity criteria recommended hereto, are useful for express-analysis of social networks and materials that circulate in them.

Abidance to the proposed criteria does not guarantee full fading of forum activity but it is a necessary condition for a situation when both interaction system of forum members on the one hand and text material they have generated on the other one, are meaningful for holistic texts.

In this case forum data can claim to be considered as a material, enough for forum analysis, as a tool for solving problems, conducting analysis of links among forum members on the one hand and full(not fragmentary) cognitive analysis of the forum text corpus and also for forming its ontology and solving all the range of partial problems on the other hand. Indirect signs of theme exhaustiveness are as follows: essential lowering of the messages flow on a specific theme, lowering of information exchange dynamics and absence of dynamics in conditions having generated a discussion.

From the technical point of view, the use of statistical methods for content-analysis of the forum and arrangement of its results as a hierarchic hypertext scheme among forum documents is not onerous but will be quite useful for increasing the efficiency of forum members' familiarization with the most interesting information.

These conceptions are suitable for forming a thesaurus and taxonomy prototype of socio-cultural problems in the Mixteca region. In its turn, a forum thesaurus gives opportunities for the regional community to understand a degree of its involvement into revealing and discussing the most interesting regional problems on the Internet.

REFERENCES

Dunlap, R. (1997). The Golden Ratio and Fibonacci Numbers. World Scientific Publishing. doi:10.1142/3595

Forum of Kommunarka settlement. (n.d.). Retrieved from http://new.msk.ru/

Forum of Pushkin Town. (n.d.). Retrieved from https://www.mypushkin.ru/

Forum of the City of Kashira. (n.d.). Retrieved from http://kashira.tv/forum/1

Forum of the City of Podolsk. (n.d.). Retrieved from http://www.informюpodolsk.ru

Forum of the Huajuapan de Leon town. (n.d.). Retrieved from http://foros.utm.mx/

Jun, Z., Ackerman, M., & Adamic, L. (2007). Expertise networks in online communities: structure and algorithms. In *Proceedings of the 16th Inter. Conference on World Wide Web (WWW '07)*. ACM.

Makagonov, P. (2015). Model of the Empirical Distribution Law for Syntactic and Link Words in Perfect Texts. . In Modern Computational Models of Semantic Discovery in Natural Language. IGI Global. doi:10.4018/978-1-4666-8690-8.ch002

Makagonov, P. (2015a). The evaluation of quality of a complex system based on the distribution of links between its objects. In The Modeling and Data Analysis (2015, N°1, pp. 27-40). Academic Press.

Makagonov, P. (2015b). Quality evaluation of texts on geosciences based on linguistic criteria. In X. I. I. Inter (Ed.), Conf. New ideas in Earth Sciences, S-XV, Numerical methods and mathematical modeling (pp. 280–281). Academic Press. Retrieved from https://cloud.mail.ru/public/ Vh7tiAF22PFz/eng.pdf

Makagonov, P., Espinosa, S. Z., & Sboychakov, K. (2008). Application of document «search image» from digital library on museum site to simplify disclosing in Internet the document itself. In *XV Jubilee Intern. Conf. «Crimea 2008». — Libraries and Info resources in a contemporary world of science, culture, education and business*. Sudak.

Montemurro, M. (2001). Beyond the Zipf—Mandelbrot law in quantitative linguistics. Physica A 300, Statistical Mechanics and its Applications, 300(3), 567-578.

Paulus, T. M. (2007). Online but off-topic: establishing common ground in small learning groups. In *Proceedings of the 8th Inter. Conference on Computer supported Collaborative Learning (CSCL'07).* Inter. Society of the Learning Sciences. 10.3115/1599600.1599710

Rieh, S. Y. (2002). Judgment of information quality and cognitive authority in the Web. *Journal of the American Society for Information Science and Technology, 53*(2), 145–161. doi:10.1002/asi.10017

Saluki Forum of South Illinois. (n.d.). Retrieved from http://www.salukination.net/forumlist.php

Samorodova-Bogatskaya, L. (2015). Tradition and Innovation: Cyber-Landsgemeinde and Crowdsoursing as Modern Realization of Democratic Technologies. Int. J. of Applied and Fundamental Research, 2.

Stern & Pallickara. (2013). On the role of topology in autonomously coping with failures in content dissemination systems. In *Proceedings of the 2013 ACM Cloud and Autonomic Computing Conference (CAC '13)*. ACM.

Vasilkova, V., & Koltsov, A. (2015). Crowd sourcing as a new socio-communicative technology. In *Discussion.* Ekaterinburg: PH Institute of Modern Government Technologies.

Warner, J. (2011). Next steps in e-government crowdsourcing. In *Proceedings of the 12th Annual International Digital Government Research Conference: Digital Government Innovation in Challenging Times*. ACM.

Weimer, M., & Gurevych, I. (2007). Predicting the Perceived Quality of Web Forum Posts. *Proceedings of the Conference on Recent Advances in Natural Language Processing (RANLP)*, 643-648.

KEY TERMS AND DEFINITIONS

Bigrams: A bigram or digram is a sequence of two adjacent elements from a string of tokens, in our case these being words.

Determination: Coefficient: (of the approximation reliability), R2, also designated as R^2, indicates how well data points fit a line or a curve.

DOD: The list of words of the domain-oriented dictionary. DOD is formed from word frequency list of the whole by elimination linking or syntactic words. DOD represents domain knowledge, contains new words, concept-words, and a lot of them (nearly half of the list) are *hapax legomena* (a word occurring only once in a text collection).

Golden Section: Also known as the divine proportion, golden mean, or golden ratio, is one of numbers $\varphi = \frac{\sqrt{5}-1}{2}$ or $\Phi = \frac{\sqrt{5}+1}{2}$, so that $\Phi - \varphi = 1$. The golden section appears when we divide any quantity into two parts a & b so that the whole quantity divided by a larger part is equal to Φ and a larger part divided by a smaller part is the same. A lot of people recognize the Golden Section as the constant for harmony.

Linking or Syntactic Word: We consider the words to be linking or syntactic if they are non-derivative, or if derivative, contain parts of significative words having practically lost their meaning within the context of the text document under our investigation.

System Harmony: Should be defined by two criteria: minimum deviation of the main attribute of the objects from the Zipf law, and minimum deviation of links between the objects and the distribution law of links between the system elements in pairs.

Zipf Law: Is known as a phenomenological model of the "object rank–frequency of occurrence" or "rank-dimension" type with a very low probability of deviation for perfect systems. That is why the deviation of the practical distribution from the Zipf one can be taken as the criterion of the system ideality.

Chapter 6
Using Online Data in Predicting Stock Price Movements:
Methodological and Practical Aspects

František Dařena
Mendel University in Brno, Czech Republic

Jonáš Petrovský
Mendel University in Brno, Czech Republic

Jan Přichystal
Mendel University in Brno, Czech Republic

Jan Žižka
Mendel University in Brno, Czech Republic

ABSTRACT

A lot of research has been focusing on incorporating online data into models of various phenomena. The chapter focuses on one specific problem coming from the domain of capital markets where the information contained in online environments is quite topical. The presented experiments were designed to reveal the association between online texts (from Yahoo! Finance, Facebook, and Twitter) and changes in stock prices of the corresponding companies. As the method for quantifying the association, machine learning-based classification was chosen. The experiments showed that the data preparation procedure had a substantial impact on the results. Thus, different stock price smoothing, the lags between the release of documents and related stock price changes, levels of a minimal stock price change, different weighting schemes for structured document representation, and classifiers were studied. The chapter also shows how to use currently available open source technologies to implement a system for accomplishing the task.

DOI: 10.4018/978-1-5225-5586-5.ch006

INTRODUCTION

A lot of research has been focusing on incorporating the vast amount of data available online into models of various social and economic phenomena in miscellaneous fields of science. The data, which is generated not only by domain experts but also by regular people, can provide new perspectives and potentially complementary information to conventional quantitative and objective evidence (Kearney & Liu, 2014). The data often comes from non-traditional and contemporary information sources and environments, like social networks or microblogging sites. The data typically has a form of unstructured texts that are published by different types of subjects, without the time and spatial limits.

On one hand, there are many logical reasons for this trend: there is a lot of data freely available, many different sources can be combined together, the data is often accessible immediately, in real time, and the variety of data items, opinions, and perspectives can be great. On the other hand, collecting, storing, and processing such data relate to several problems: tools for collecting the data need to be available, it is necessary to handle multiple systems and data formats, it is necessary to consider differences in data quality, reliability, objectivity etc.

One of the domains, where using online data is very topical and plays an important role in analyzing the studied systems, is the field of capital markets. Here, the data provided by digital media can help, e.g., in explaining less rational factors such as investors' sentiment or public mood as influential for asset pricing and capital market volatility (Bukovina, 2016).

One of the greatest advantages of using online resources for decision making support in the domain of capital markets is the timeliness of the information, which is particularly important for investment decisions. The quality of the messages posted in online environments (such as microblogs or discussions in social networks) is, however, generally low. That is why Internet postings have been the least frequently studied source of textual sentiment (Kearney & Liu, 2014). Despite all difficulties, content generated by web users has become a widely accepted resource for determining sentiment or opinions related to different aspects of the public mood (Tumasjan et al., 2011). It has been also shown that a large number of people participating in a content generation process enables the creation of artifacts that are of equal or superior quality than those made by experts in the respective field (Gottschlich & Hinz, 2014). Messages from millions of people are also unlikely to be biased (Mostafa, 2013).

There exist numerous studies focusing on the usefulness of textual data for predictions related to stock prices. Majority of them focused on an aggregate level (e.g., the level of a stock market index), worked with a single source of texts (e.g., newspaper articles or financial reports), or required additional expert knowledge (e.g., a list of words or expressions that are usually related to positive and negative stock price movements).

In our work, we focus on analysis at the micro level, namely at the level of individual companies. The goal is to determine whether there are some associations between the content of online texts related to a company and the movements of the stock prices of that company. We also wanted to avoid the necessity of using various lexicons provided by domain experts, which might perform poorly in previously unknown situations (Eisenstein, 2017). In our research, we also combine documents from three different sources, Yahoo! Finance, Facebook, and Twitter collected over a period of about 8 months. A machine learning-based approach is applied in order to find out whether the content plays an important role in revealing the document-stock price movement association.

Section Background gives a brief overview of the current state of research in the field of capital markets where text data is used as one of the possible sources of data. The Experimental Procedure Background section describes the considerations related to individual aspects of the problem that include the data and its processing. Section Experiments contains a detailed characterization of the conducted experiments together with their variable parameters. In section Results, specific values obtained from all conducted experiments and some statistical measures derived from them are presented and discussed. The last section, Implementation of the Procedure, focuses on the technological background of the research and describes the technologies and tools used in the research.

BACKGROUND

Most of the past research in the domain of capital markets utilized structured data, which is often objective, to analyze the impact of volatile data on business (Groth & Muntermann, 2011). Including other information sources and types into various models can provide another insight and potentially complementary information to quantitative data. This supplementary information source is typically unstructured texts as the textual form is the most typical form used by people to convey messages. The texts are published by different types of subjects, in many forms, with different frequency, quality, quantitative characteristics etc.

Decisions of investors in capital markets are based on information that is available to them. The investors can behave both rationally and irrationally, depending on the availability of information and the mental state of every person. It might be expected that rational decisions are based on objective and often quantitative facts coming from reliable sources. Irrational actions can be a result of sudden decisions, affect caused by opinions of other people, or when working with imprecise, incomplete, or irrelevant information. Thus, both objective and subjective resources are interesting and should be taken into consideration.

Objective facts, good writing style, argumentation, or reliability are mostly typical for newspaper articles, books, scientific papers, annual reports, theses, or other professional texts. On the other hand, texts like blog posts, personal e-mails, customer reviews, or questions to open-ended questions in a marketing survey are written informally by normal people, without the time and spatial limits, are shared with their friends or interest groups, and often contain a certain portion of subjective information.

It can be assumed that subjective information, such as the sentiment and mood of the public can influence financial decisions to a similar extent as news. Bollen, Mao and Zheng (2011) found that the collective mood in Twitter messages correlates to the value of the Dow Jones Industrial Average.

Wuthrich et al. (1998) investigated whether the content of newspaper articles can predict changes in selected composite indices of major stock markets in Asia, Europe and America. Their approach is based on training data from 100 days and a set of more than four hundred phrases (like "bond strong", "dollar falter", or "property weak") provided by a human expert. Knowledge of the phrases that are related to an index movement can thus also explain the movement. The achieved prediction accuracy of the proposed approach was between 40 and 47%. However, a great portion of additional outcomes was only slightly wrong, which enabled achieving a trading strategy comparable to or better than human managers.

Schumaker and Chen (2007) studied 484 companies from the S&P 500 for five weeks in 2005. They analyzed the impact of slightly more than 9,000 financial news articles on stock price movements. In their experiments, a Support Vector Machine derivative was used to predict a stock price after the publication of a newspaper article. Three different representations of textual data (Bag of Words, Noun Phrases, and Named Entities) were used separately or combined with stock price information. The achieved directional accuracy lied in the interval 56 to 58%.

Rao & Srivastava (2014) studied several characteristics of Twitter messages in a period of 14 months and their relation to stock price movements for 13 major stock market indices. They found a strong correlation (up to 0.88) between returns and twitter sentiments. The sentiment was determined using Twittersentiment API provided by the Stanford NLP research group (Go, Bahyani & Huang, 2009). To validate the causative effect of tweet feeds on stock movements they used the econometric technique of Granger's Causality Analysis (Granger, 1969).

Most of the studies analyzed sentiment primarily at an aggregate level, based on the existence of specific words or expressions identified by rules or lexicons. Despite numerous attempts and application areas summarized by Hagenau, Liebmann and Neumann (2013), prediction accuracies for the direction of stock prices following the release of corporate financial news rarely exceeded 58%. The same authors achieved the accuracy of about 76% for one data set by employing a particular combination of advanced feature generation and selection methods together with exogenous market feedback.

Compared to other research, we analyze data from multiple sources using a common methodology employing both the dictionary-based and content-based approaches. Besides popular newspaper articles, we employ also data from Twitter and Facebook. On Facebook, we distinguish two types of documents – posts created by company representatives, and comments created by other Facebook users. Unlike other studies, that focus on an aggregate value representing stock price movements we focus on the level of individual companies.

THE EXPERIMENTAL PROCEDURE BACKGROUND

To be able to make a conclusion whether there exists or there does not exist an association between stock prices and texts published online different approaches might be applied. The most straightforward one would require a human expert who will thoroughly read all of the documents, look at the corresponding stock prices and their movements, and assess how the objective and subjective facts from the documents are related to stock prices. To be able to prove such an association, enough quantitative evidence must be ideally given. Obviously, it is usually not feasible to choose this approach from many reasons (unavailability of human experts, time constraints, mental limits etc.). Instead, an automated procedure based on algorithmic steps where the findings can clearly be substantiated by undeniable facts is favorable. In order to make the results more reliable, it is good to support them with a sufficient amount of data.

Data Used in the Experiments

In the experiments, we used data related to so-called blue chip (large and famous) companies because there is a higher probability of availability of a sufficient amount of related data. The analyzed companies were selected from Standard & Poor's 500 and FTSEurofirst 300 indices as they contain a sufficient number of listed, both US-based and European, companies.

In order to analyze the relationship between stock price movements and facts and opinions expressed by Internet users, two types of data were needed – stock prices at desired moments in time, and texts containing information related to the selected companies.

The information about stock prices can be obtained at stock exchanges or in specialized Internet data sources. For the research, only historical data is needed (no live feeds). Table 1 contains several sources that of such data. The differences are in prices of the data, covered stock exchanges, the length of the history, and others. It is generally quite a complicated task to obtain reliable and high-quality data so banks and hedge funds spend thousands of dollars a month to get it (Lukebuehler, 2013). Although sometimes contains some mistakes, Yahoo! Finance is relatively credible and reliable source that enables obtaining the stock price data free of charge (Caltech, 2017). It contains daily data for many stock exchanges around the world, with a long history. For every working day and company, opening, highest, lowest, closing, and adjusted closing stock prices are available together with traded volumes.

Texts related to the investigated companies may be found in many different sources. Usually, the objective ones are typically found on news servers. Examples of them can be found in Table 2. It is obvious that not all servers are focused on news related to European companies. Also, their popularity expressed in terms of Alexa rank (http://alexa.com) is different. It can be assumed that more visited ones can influence a higher number of investors. From the available financial news servers Yahoo! Finance was selected. It contains news aggregated from several sources (unlike, e.g., Reuters.com), is one of the most visited servers (measured by the Alexa rank), contains also recommendations of financial analysts, and is accessible free of charge.

Texts containing also subjective opinion are usually located in places where the content is created by individuals without many constraints imposed on the content. These places include social networks, microblogging sites, instant messaging

Table 1. Selected sources containing information about stock prices

Name	Price	Frequency	History	Area
Yahoo! Finance	free	Daily	max	World
Quant Quote Free	free	Daily	1998	S&P 500
CSI data	paid	Daily	10/30 years	World
Quant Quote	paid	minutes, seconds, tick	1998	USA
Tick Data	?	minutes, tick	?	World
NYSETAQ	paid	Tick	1993	USA
Compustat	paid	Daily	1960	?
CRSP	?	Daily	100 years	USA
Xignite	?	Daily	1993 USA, 2000 other	World
Nanex	paid	Tick	2004	USA

(Caltech, 2017; lukebuehler, 2013)

Table 2. Selected news servers together with their characteristics in March, 2016 (Alexa – global Alexa rank of a server; Europe – indicates whether a server provides information about stocks in Europe; RA – shows whether a server contains recommendations of analysts).

Source Name	URL	Alexa	Europe	RA
Bloomberg Business	http://www.bloomberg.com	338	no	no
CNBC International	http://www.cnbc.com	704	no	no
CNNMoney	http://money.cnn.com	85	no	yes
FINVIZ.com	http://finviz.com	4,857	no	yes
Google Finance	https://www.google.com/finance	1	yes	no
MarketWatch	http://www.marketwatch.com	784	no	yes
Motley Fool	http://www.fool.com	1224	no	yes
Morningstar	http://www.morningstar.com	2,660	no	yes
MSN Money	http://www.msn.com/en-us/money/markets	15	no	no
Reuters.com	http://www.reuters.com/finance/markets	398	yes	yes
Seeking Alpha	http://seekingalpha.com	1,402	no	no
Wall Street Journal	http://www.wsj.com/news/markets	384	no	yes
Yahoo! Finance	http://finance.yahoo.com	5	yes	yes

platforms, sites for multimedia sharing, or discussion forums. A list of most popular can be found in Table 3.

Some of the listed sites focus on users from China. The content is not expected to be related to western companies so the sites can be eliminated. Instant messaging services are not able to provide data and are thus useless as well as services enabling photo and video sharing. From the remaining ones, Facebook, Tumblr, Twitter, LinkedIn, and a Google+, Facebook and Twitter seem to be a reasonable choice for obtaining a sufficient amount of relevant text data from enough users. The data is freely also available through an API with sufficient search capabilities.

On Facebook, companies have their profile pages. From the investigated companies, only 55% had such a page. There is a sequence of documents, called posts, arranged according to the time of their publishing in a timeline. The company representatives create these short postings. Other Facebook users may comment the posts on at any moment. The comments, however, do not have necessarily relate to a particular post (e.g., users are just complaining about company products/services). Twitter is a microblogging site enabling users to publish short messages (up to 140 characters), called tweets. Other users may follow their favorite users (i.e., receive

Table 3. Selected social networks and similar sites containing opinions of people

No.	Name	Users	Area	Type
1	Facebook	1,550	World	social network
2	WhatsApp	900	World	instant messaging (IM)
3	QQ	860	Asia	instant messaging
4	Facebook Messenger	800	World	instant messaging
5	Qzone	653	China	social network
6	WeChat	650	China	instant messaging
7	Tumblr	555	World	microblogging site
8	Instagram	400	World	photo and video sharing
9	Twitter	320	World	microblogging site
10	Baidu Tieba	300	China	communication platform
11	Skype	300	World	video, VoIP, instant messaging
12	Viber	249	World	VoIP, instant messaging
13	Sina Weibo	222	China	microblogging site
14	LINE	212	World	video, VoIP, instant messaging
15	Snapchat	200	World	photo and video sharing, inst. messaging
16	YY	122	China	social network
17	VKontakte	100	Russia	social network
18	Pinterest	100	World	photo sharing
19	BlackBerry Messenger	100	World	video, IM
20	LinkedIn	100	World	professionals' social network

(Statista, 2016)

their tweets), answer them, or send them new messages. Twitter provides a searching capability with quite a lot of possibilities. In this work, tweets containing the user name of a company (a query contains, e.g., "@google"), mentioning a company (e.g., "Google"), replies to the tweets of a company (e.g., "to: google"), and tweets from the company timeline were used. Because the amount of data on Twitter is extremely massive, only 21 representative companies from different industries were investigated.

The data was collected in the eight-month period in years 2015 and 2016. Together with them, the 100 most liked comments from Facebook pages were retrieved, too. Twitter data was collected every six hours because the amount of generated data is quite large and Twitter does not allow retrieving more than 100 tweets at a time. Table 4 contains the total and average numbers of data items analyzed in the experiments.

Table 4. Amounts of data from different sources (from 2015-08-01 to 2016-04-04).

Document Type	Total Number	Daily Average/Company	Monthly Average/Company
Yahoo! Finance articles	81,519	0.40	12.55
Facebook posts	134,941	0.71	21.97
Facebook comments	2,222,362	17.59	545.43
Tweets	3,887,527	774.29	24,003.00

Quantifying the Association Between Stock Prices and Texts

The presented problem belongs to a group of tasks that are described by series variables whose values are recorded over a period of time. A simple time series can be described as a discrete function Y taking its values y_t at certain time points t, $Y = \{y_t: t \in T\}$, where T stands for an index set of a given stretch of time. Except for the scalar values, the general function Y may also return vectors y_t, which is here a case of text comments that accompany the stock-price time series.

The content and meaning of the documents written in a natural language is given by the words and their combinations included in them. It is expected that the documents' content is somehow related to the values of the stock prices and a method for quantification of such mutual dependency needs to be found.

The stock price values can be expressed as a time series $S = \{s_t: t \in T\}$, and similarly the content of the documents as $D = \{w_t: t \in T\}$, where w_t stands for a vector from term-document matrix (Eldén, 2007). Words are included in the vocabulary, which is shared by the all investigated documents. Both time series, i.e., S and D share the same time dimension.

However, it is not clear when the values of one series react to the values of the other. It can be assumed that the time series are shifted in time relative to each other, which is known as a lagged relationship. In this chapter, we study how financial markets react to news, which is a long-lasting question in finance (Wong, Liu & Chiang, 2014).

For quantification of the possible interdependency between values returned by two functions Y_1 and Y_2, the statistical theory offers computations of so-called correlation values provided by a correlation function $C(Y_1, Y_2)$. Statistical methods include several possibilities for the calculation of correlation between series of values, for example, perhaps the most popular Pearson's correlation coefficient (Benesty et al., 2009) based on the rate between the covariance of two variables and the product of their standard deviation.

However, the problem is complicated by the fact that w_l is not a scalar value and it is not clear how to transform it into just one number. This chapter suggests a viable procedure, which is heavily applied in the machine learning domain. We might hypothesize that there exists a function that is mapping values of one variable to the values of another variable. In our case, *S* and *D* represent the variables. However, the function is not known and has to be found in a process generally known as the training. A critical aspect is to quantify how well (i.e., with what correctness or error) the found function performs because a correct mapping for all instances is usually not found for many reasons. If the performance of the function approaches to some ideal (errorless) performance, there can be supposed that there exists a clear association between the two variables. This association is then expressed by the found function. On the other hand, when the found function is not able to correctly assign an appropriate value, the association probably does not exist or cannot be expressed by the selected function at all or under given circumstances.

The problem can belong to the class of classification or regression problems (Matloff, 2017) depending on the properties of the target variable, i.e., the stock prices. When considering continuous values, the problem is referred to as the regression. In case of categorical/discrete values, we talk about classification.

The absolute values of stock prices are not of the highest importance for our task because stocks can be traded at different price levels. Rather, the price changes between certain moments in time are more interesting. Because the absolute changes can be again proportional to the price levels, relative changes can be considered. In order to simplify the problem even more, the stock price changes can be divided into several classes depending on their movement direction, i.e., increase, decrease, or invariable behavior. Having, for example, these three types of stock price movements it is quite easy to interpret the task of quantifying the association between documents' content and stock price movements as a classification problem. For the quantification of the association, the performance of the function, which is known as a classifier, can be used. Such a performance might be measured, e.g., by classification accuracy which is a number between 0.0 (totally wrong) and 1.0 (totally right).

To find the classifier, so-called training data (Witten, Frank & Hall, 2011) is needed. The training set must contain instances of documents where a previously known stock price movement type is available. The movement type of a stock price will be later used as a label for the document. During training, i.e., the process of building a classifier, rules that enable mapping documents with a similar content to the same labels are expected to be found.

To create the training set of documents and train a classifier, the data needs to be converted to a form suitable for a given algorithm. The following sections, focusing on texts and stock prices (that are the basis for determining labels) describe this process.

Handling Stock Price Data

Stock price values are numbers expressing the prices (for example, in US dollars) at which stocks are sold and purchased at stock exchanges in certain time moments. Because the prices are usually volatile, which means that they are changing very quickly during trading periods (opening hours of a stock exchange), only some of the values are important, especially for historical data. Typically, the prices at the beginning and end of a trading day (opening and closing prices), minimal (low), and maximal (high) prices in a day are considered (Ang, 2015). Sometimes, a market price doesn't give a true picture about a firm's equity value because some corporate actions, such as stock splits, that occurred at any time before opening the next day affect a stock price. The price then needs to be adjusted, especially when working with historical data (http://www.investopedia.com/terms/s/splitadjusted.asp).

In an investigated period, the stock prices can increase or decrease or, which is very rare, remain on the same level. Naturally, the prices change very quickly, although often at small rates, reflecting many different events, habits, or sentiment (Blau & Griffith, 2016). These movements can have a reason but there is also evidence that price movements might be completely random (Borch, 1963). Than it is not necessary to include them in reasoning about the data.

Not all changes are, however, important. Instead, trends, cycles, or their combinations are more interesting (Patel et al., 2015). These movements can be revealed by smoothing, i.e., replacing the original values by other values not showing that high volatility. After application of a smoothing, the "noise" is eliminated and the data better represents real and significant changes.

Good candidates for smoothing are moving averages that substitute the original data by sequences of averages calculated from subsets of the data sets. Moving averages of different types have been widely used in technical analyses studying stocks markets (Chen, Su & Lin, 2016; Huang & Ni, 2017).

A moving average calculation can work with sequences of subsequent values of different lengths. Short moving averages are more sensitive to changes than long ones (Wang et al., 20014). Generally, there are two distinct groups of smoothing methods – averaging methods, and exponential smoothing methods. Both method calculate a new value based on n last original values. In our problem, n stands for a number of days since only one stock price value of a given type per day is available.

Simple Moving Average – SMA, an averaging method, relies on calculating the simple arithmetic mean of n successive values of past data. The Exponentially Weighted Moving Average – EWMA, an exponential smoothing method, assigns exponentially decreasing weights to older values. The values can be calculated according to the following formulas (NIST, 2016):

$SMA_t = (price_t + price_{t-1} + \dots price_{t-n+1}) / n$

$EWMA_t = \lambda \bullet price_t + (1 - \lambda) \bullet EWMA_{t-1}, \lambda = 2 / (n+1)$

In our experiments, besides working with the original stock prices, both types of moving averages based on two different periods, 5 and 20 days, were considered for calculations in order to include averages with different sensitivities.

Changes in these average values are then better indicators of the important changes in prices, see Figure 1. On the left side of the graph, the price is decreasing with a small increase followed by an even bigger decrease. Both moving averages, here SMA working with 5 and 20 days, express the same though the latter is smoother. On the right side of the graph, the price is oscillating quite significantly while a slightly decreasing trend is noticeable at the beginning and an increasing trend is apparent at the end. The shorter moving average, SMA(5), was able to capture both trends whereas the longer moving average captured only the increasing trend of the entire part of the time series.

At any time, a change that has occurred since the previous moment can be detected. Obviously, very small changes, e.g., in the order of tenths or hundredths of a percent, are usually not important. The question is how big a change needs to be to be considered significant? Wuthrich et al. (1998) found that appreciation and depreciation take place when the market moves up or down by at least 0.5%. However,

Figure 1. A graph showing stock price development and its smoothing (using Simple Moving Average, SMA, working with 5 and 20 days). The smoothing can better reveal trends in the data. Here, the trend derived from SMA(5) is expressed by the arrows. Three trend types (increase, stagnation, and decrease) based on a minimal price change are shown.

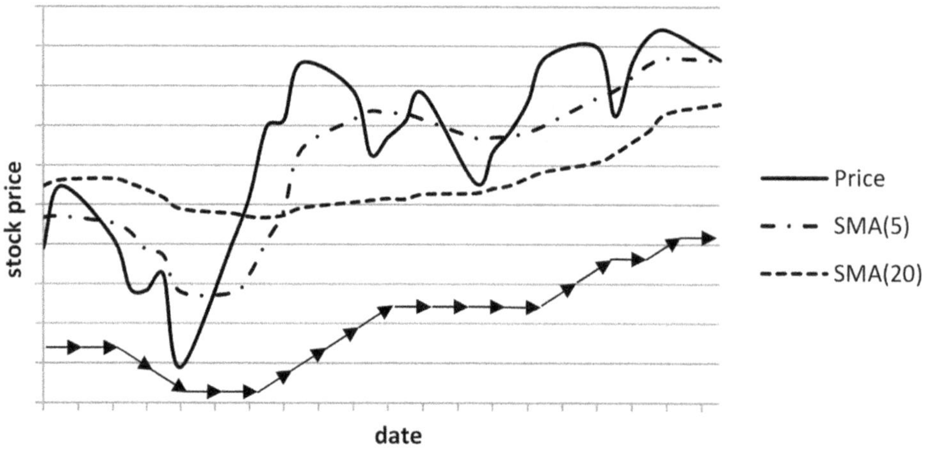

the same authors observed that the average change in market indices is often much more, about 1.5%. A certain threshold can be then determined to distinguish between important and unimportant movements. Positive and negative changes above this threshold, in other words, price increases and price drops (decreases), respectively, can then represent the classes (categories) for the stock prices data set.

Preparing the Text Documents

Text documents generally contain some information that has a relationship to reality. The reality is described, evaluated, judged, or compared. Understanding the messages conveyed in the documents helps with understanding or predicting the world without explicitly observing and studying it. This then has a strong impact on decisions made by people.

For example, reading customer reviews of a product might influence purchase behavior (Weisstein et al., 2017) or looking at customer reviews of a hotel accommodation at a travelers' website might predict the business performance of a hotel (Ye, Law & Gu, 2009).

Information that can contain objective facts, but also personal attitudes, feelings, assumptions, current mood, etc. is generally expressed by the words contained in the text and their combinations. In order to have an impact on decisions, the message needs to be understood by a person. In case of computers, the situation is quite different. A perfect understanding of the meaning of a text and its relation to reality is, though, a complicated task. Such a task is often not faultlessly accomplished even by human experts.

However, for many problems, a perfect and complete comprehension of the text is not needed. It is, for example, possible to determine the main topic of a scientific paper on the basis of the presence of some keywords in the text (Conway, 2009). Similarly, according to a few properties (contained words, number of words, text visibility, the presence of hyperlinks, etc.) an e-mail can be classified as spam or non-spam (Aski & Sourati, 2016).

In the last years, a lot of research has been devoted to extracting useful knowledge (e.g., sentiment or included topics) from texts written in natural languages. This discipline, known as text mining (Feldman & Sanger, 2007), is a branch of computer science that uses techniques from data mining, information retrieval, machine learning, statistics, natural language processing, and knowledge management (Berry & Kogan, 2010). The discipline focuses not only on the specification of some general classes of problems, but also on methods for representation of text data, application or adaptation of existing algorithms, development of new algorithms, and finding new applications in many scientific fields.

Many text mining methods today rely on the availability of a sufficient amount of suitable data from which a model representing a real-world problem can be learned. These data-driven methods often use an algorithmic approach that tries to find a new function that models the data. This approach, referred to as called *machine learning*, can be successfully used on large complex data sets and as a more accurate and informative alternative to data modelling on smaller data sets (Breiman, 2001). At the end of the last century, machine learning gained its popularity and became a dominant approach to text mining.

Textual documents contain mostly unstructured information, which is not suitable, in terms of effectivity and efficiency, for most of the knowledge discovery procedures. Texts are therefore usually converted to a more appropriate structured representation.

The quality of text mining outputs heavily relies on the application of various text preprocessing techniques. Their goal is to infer or extract structured representations from unstructured plain text data (Feldman & Sanger, 2007). Preprocessing methods include, e.g., online text cleaning, white space removal, case folding, spelling errors corrections, abbreviations expanding, stemming, stop words removal, negation handling, and feature selection (Carvalho & Matos, 2007; Clark, 2011; Haddi & Liu, 2013). Some of the natural language processing techniques, such as tokenization (including stemming) or part-of-speech tagging, are a subset of these methods requiring knowledge of the language to be processed (Feldman & Sanger, 2007). The application of these techniques influences what will be the features characterizing the documents and what will be their quality.

A widely used structured format is the vector space model proposed by Salton & McGill (1983). Every document is represented by a vector where individual dimensions correspond to the features (terms) and the values are the weights (importance) of the features. All vectors then form so-called term-document matrix where the rows represent the documents and the columns correspond to the terms in the documents. The values in the matrix correspond to the importance of words contained in the documents. Such a simple approach, known as the bag-of-words approach, is popular because of its simplicity and straightforward process of creation while providing satisfactory results (Joachims, 2002). The terms might be, however, also multi-word expressions or be derived from the original words.

The weight w_{ij} of every term i in document j is given by three components (Salton & McGill, 1983):

- A local weight lw_{ij} representing the frequency of terms in every single document,
- Global weight gw_i reflecting the discriminative ability of the term, based on the distribution of the term in the entire document collection,
- A normalization factor n_j correcting the impact of different document lengths.

Popular weights include *term frequency* (the number of occurrences of a term in a document) and *term presence* (1 if a term is included in the document, 0 otherwise; this is, in fact, a binary weight) for the local weight (Singhal, 1997), *inverse document frequency* for the global weight (Robertson, 2004), and the *cosine normalization* (Chisholm & Kolda, 1999) as the normalization factor.

The texts of collected documents were modified in the way that all HTML tags, @ and # characters (denoting user names and hashtags), and other non-alphanumeric characters were removed, selected emoticons were replaced by artificial terms representing positive and negative sentiment, all URLs were replaced by a single artificial term, and the text was converted to lower case. The minimal length of processed words was 2, and the minimal document frequency of terms (the number of documents where a term occurred) was 10 for Yahoo! Finance articles and 5 for the other collections.

The texts were converted to vectors using the bag-of-word approach to become acceptable for machine learning algorithms. As for weighting schemes, three possibilities were investigated – simple term presence, term frequency with the inverse document frequency weight (tf-idf), and tf-idf with cosine normalization. In order not to bias a classifier against one bigger class the numbers of documents from both classes (increase and decrease) were balanced in terms of instance numbers.

EXPERIMENTS

For the training phase of the experiments, a sufficiently large amount of training instances (text documents) had to be prepared and appropriately labeled (using the information about stock price movements). For each text document, the date of its publication and a related company was known. It was then possible to determine the stock price movement trend (increase, decrease, or stagnation) for that company for a corresponding date and use it as a label for the document. Generally, the publication date and the date related to a stock price movement do not have to be the same, which enables to consider also a time lag.

Then, a classifier mapping the document features to the labels derived from stock price movements is learned. To measure the quality of the induced classifiers, i.e., their ability to assign correct labels for unknown documents, they are examined on test samples that are distinct from the training ones and for which correct answers are known. The strength of the relationship between the input (the content of documents) and output (the label representing stock price movements) might be then expressed by some classification performance measures because they contain information on how well a classifier is able to assign a correct label to a document based on the values of its attributes. High values of these measures demonstrate that there exist attributes or their combinations that are accurately able to distinguish between instances of different classes.

The values representing correctly and incorrectly classified examples are used to compute measures of classifier effectiveness. In the two-class classification, the classes are often labeled as positive and negative. The positive and negative examples that are classified correctly are referred to as true positive (TP) and true negative (TN), respectively. False positive (FP) and false negative (FN) represent misclassified positive and negative examples.

Commonly accepted classifier performance evaluation measures include accuracy, precision, recall, and F-measure combining the values of TP, TN, FP, and FN into a single measure (Sokolova, Japkowicz & Szpakowicz, 2006).

Experimental Parameters

Four different data sources (Yahoo! Finance newspaper articles, Facebook posts and comments, and tweets) were processed separately. Because of the computational complexity, a manageable amount of documents was selected – a maximum 200 most retweeted tweets and 40 most liked Facebook comments for every company in every day. A number of Facebook posts and Yahoo! Finance articles was not that high and no preselection was thus performed.

The stock price data needed to be transformed using moving averages and a suitable class label for training a classifier was assigned to every text. In order to transform the stock price data and to determine a class label of a document D_i related to company C_i, released at time T_r, representing a change in stock price of company C_i at time T_c the following aspects and parameters needed to be determined:

- Concrete values of stock prices to be considered – here, adjusted closing values, simple moving average (SMA) and exponential moving average (EWMA), both based on 5 and 20 days were analyzed (the methods are later referred to as SMA(5), EWMA(5), SMA(20), and EWMA(20)); for days when no value was available (weekends, holidays), the price was calculated as the arithmetic average of the last closing value and the first following opening value.
- The lag between publication of texts at date T_r and a stock price movement at T_c – lags of 1, 2, and 3 days were investigated.
- The minimal relative difference in stock prices at T_c and T_{c-1} to be considered significant – changes of 1, 2, 3, 4, and 5 percent were investigated. If a price change is within the percentage limit it is considered constant and all documents related to the specific date are labeled by the stagnation class label. If the price change is above the limit in the positive direction, i.e., increased

more than, e.g., 3%, documents are labeled as increase. In the remaining case, the price decreased significantly and the corresponding documents are labeled by the decrease label.

The data was massively unbalanced in terms of class labels distributions. The reason is that a large majority of documents belonged to days when no significant change in stock prices occurred. Unbalanced data biased or useless results in terms of accuracy would be achieved without further data set adjustment (Kubat, Holte & Matwin, 1998). Because significant increases or decreases in prices are more interesting than remaining approximately on the same level, documents labeled as stagnation were excluded from further processing and the interdependence between texts and stock price movements was analyzed only in periods with significant price changes. In order not to bias a classifier against one bigger class, the numbers of documents from the remaining classes (increase and decrease) were balanced.

The data was split into training and test sets in the proportion 65:35 percent. This means that 65% of the documents were randomly selected and used for inducing a classifier. The remaining 35% documents were then supplied to the classifier and the assigned label was compared to the real label.

Many different classifiers can be trained on the data. We focused on six of them that are often used in sentiment analysis and text classification (Pang, Lee & Vaithyanathan, 2002; Žižka & Dařena, 2015a) and are implemented in Python's scikit-learn package (Lorica,2015): Multinomial Naïve Bayes (with $\alpha=1$, i.e., Laplace smoothing), Bernoulli Naïve Bayes, Maximum entropy (Logistic regression), CART decision tree, Random forest, and Linear SVC (Support vector machine with a linear kernel).

RESULTS AND THEIR DISCUSSION

Using combinations of all possible parameters of the class label assignment procedure, i.e., five options for stock price value transformation (adjusted close, simple and exponential moving averages working with 5 and 20 days), three options for the lag between publication of a document and related stock price movement (1, 2, or 3 days), and five options for class determination (change 1-5 percent), 75 data sets were prepared. These data sets containing documents labeled differently were then encoded using the three weighing schemes (term presence, tf-idf, and tf-idf with cosine normalization) into three different representations which were subsequently supplied to six classifiers. The correctness of class label assignment was recorded and selected classification performance metrics were calculated. To achieve sufficiently general results, collections of less than 500 documents were excluded from detailed analyses of the experiments.

Selected measures of the most important classification performance metrics and data set properties for all experiments can be found in Table 5. The values are based on experiments using all possible combinations of parameters and classifiers. Because the collections were almost perfectly balanced in terms of class distribution in the data sets, the values of accuracy, precision, recall, and F-measure reached almost the same values. Thus, in the following text, only the values of accuracy are presented.

It is obvious that the classification accuracy varies quite considerably from its minimal to maximal values, e.g., from 0.543 to 0.814 in case of Yahoo! Finance articles. Because the same data was processed in all experiments, the difference must be caused by different values of parameters of the proposed procedure. A detailed exploration of the used algorithms and all parameters was therefore conducted in order to reveal how individual parameters influence the classification process. For every variable parameter, average accuracies for all experiments where the value of the parameter was fixed were calculated. For example, the average accuracy for all experiments where the smoothing method was *AdjClose* was calculated. Then, the average accuracy for all experiments where the smoothing method was *SMA(5 days)* was calculated etc. If the average accuracy for *SMA(5)* was higher than for *AdjClose*, we can assume that *SMA(5)* is a better method for handling stock price values.

It was found that only the smoothing method and classification algorithm had a significant impact on accuracy values. Higher accuracies were achieved for *SMA(20)* and *EWMA(20)* and for *Linear SVC*, *Maximum Entropy*, and *multinomial Naïve Bayes* classifiers across all data sources. The average accuracies from all experiments using the combinations containing only these values for respective parameters increased from 0.64 to 0.72 for Yahoo! Finance articles, from 0.85 to 0.61 for Facebook posts, from 0.60 to 0.67 for Facebook comments, and from 0.67 to 0.70 for tweets.

Table 5. Classification performance and data set characteristics for all experiments with data from all sources.

	Average Accuracy	**Min. Accuracy**	**Max. Accuracy**	**Accuracy Variance**	**Average Number of Documents**	**Average Number of Attributes**
Yahoo! Finance articles	0.637	0.543	0.814	0.003	10,911	13,597
Facebook posts	0.582	0.502	0.694	0.001	14,191	6,743
Facebook comments	0.604	0.523	0.786	0.003	43,037	10,456
Tweets	0.666	0.553	0.839	0.002	35,768	8,459

The remaining parameters did not have a significant impact on the classification accuracy. For example, for all possible values of the minimal price change (1-5%), the average accuracy achieved for Yahoo! Finance articles ranged from 0.631 to 0.644.

For further detailed analysis, aiming at better evaluation of the impact of the remaining parameters, only the experiments where *SMA(20)* and *EWMA(20)* were used for smoothing and *Linear SVC*, *Maximum Entropy*, and *multinomial Naïve Bayes* were used for classification were considered. The values of the achieved average accuracies can be found in Table 6a-6e.

The stock price data is generally highly volatile and the movements are sudden, unanticipated, and sometimes random. Thus, trends that are more meaningful can be discovered with an application of a smoothing. This has proven to be a reasonable step

Table 6a. Classification performance and data set characteristics for all experiments with data from all sources: Lag in Days

	1	2	3
Yahoo! Finance	0.741	0.718	0.713
Facebook comments	0.671	0.675	0.655
Facebook posts	0.645	0.598	0.596
Tweets	0.676	0.699	0.705

Table 6b. Classification performance and data set characteristics for all experiments with data from all sources: Minimal Price Change

	1	2	3	4	5
Yahoo! Finance	0.696	0.733	0.714	0.728	0.747
Facebook comments	0.629	0.663	0.668	0.686	0.719
Facebook posts	0.601	0.607	0.600	0.603	0.636
Tweets	0.714	0.713	0.704	0.654	0.660

Table 6c. Classification performance and data set characteristics for all experiments with data from all sources: Classifier

	LinearSVC	MaxEnt	NB-multi
Yahoo! Finance	0.725	0.721	0.710
Facebook comments	0.659	0.667	0.670
Facebook posts	0.599	0.606	0.615
Tweets	0.702	0.695	0.693

Table 6d. Classification performance and data set characteristics for all experiments with data from all sources: Vector Type

	tf-idf-cos	tf-idf-no	tp-no-no
Yahoo! Finance	0.711	0.728	0.717
Facebook comments	0.668	0.665	0.664
Facebook posts	0.582	0.585	0.585
Tweets	0.691	0.700	0.699

Table 6e. Classification performance and data set characteristics for all experiments with data from all sources: Smoothing Method

	sma(20)	ewma(20)
Yahoo! Finance	0.720	0.718
Facebook comments	0.665	0.666
Facebook posts	0.607	0.607
Tweets	0.702	0.691

in improving the classification accuracy for most of the data sources significantly. Moving averages based on 20 days had more positive impact than moving averages based on 5 days, which means that a greater smoothing had a more positive impact than a smaller one. The type of the moving average used in calculations (simple or exponential) was not considerably important.

When looking at the distance between the moments of publication of documents and related stock price changes, the strongest correlation was found for shorter time spans for the Yahoo! Finance articles and Facebook posts and comments (1 day, or 1-2 days, respectively) and longer (2-3 days) for tweets. The source of the documents is thus another interesting factor. A possible explanation of the finding might be in the nature of the documents and their sources. As it takes some time to publish a newspaper article, the time distance between an article and a related price movement is rather short. Texts that are published very quickly, such as tweets, might anticipate a price movement earlier. Facebook posts that are often prepared by company representatives are usually not published timely so their nature is in this respect more similar to newspaper articles. In addition, the comments written by other people can sometimes be immediate but sometimes are delayed.

For all data sources, except Twitter, a higher considered minimal stock price changes lead to better results in terms of classification accuracy. We can assume that substantial changes are accompanied by an exceptional content of documents making them more distinguishable from the documents published when no or small price changes happened. From all of the experimental parameters, the minimal percentage of stock price change was the one that influenced the size of data set the most. When a higher minimal relative change was considered a smaller number of documents labeled as increase or decrease were available, which is quite natural (there are fewer periods with large changes than periods with small changes). Thus, a meaningful threshold should be used in practical applications in order to balance the accuracy of predictions and a number of cases to be considered relevant.

The impact of different weighting methods was very low; the average accuracies lied in an interval of about 1%. Thus, the weighting scheme can be considered an unimportant factor of data preprocessing.

IMPLEMENTATION OF THE PROCEDURE

The chapter should not only describe the theoretical background of the domain and methods and simply present some results, but also show how to use currently available open source technologies to implement a system for accomplishing the task. The activities, technological considerations, and tools related to data collection and analysis are thus presented in this section.

The complete source code implementing the tasks can be found on Github (see https://github.com/jontesek/mendelu-finance-analyzer). It is divided into three basic modules:

- **DataGetter:** Retrieving data from Yahoo! Finance, Facebook, and Twitter, and storing it to a database.
- **DataProcessor:** Reading data from the database and generating text files for further processing.
- **AnalyzingPipeline:** Converting texts to their structured representation (vectors) and performing classification.

Data Collection

Firstly, the chosen data sources and possibilities they provide are described.

Yahoo Finance

There is a homepage for each company listed on the stock exchange (e.g. for 3M Company it is https://finance.yahoo.com/quote/MMM) on Yahoo! Finance. The page contains a lot of information, such as price charts, financial ratios and statements, analysists recommendations, and other. News articles are located directly on the homepage and consist of a headline and a short description. They both link to a full version of the article, which is either placed directly on Yahoo! Finance or on another service (in total more than 42 different services present their articles on Yahoo! Finance). In the first case, the structure of a generated HTML web page is always the same, so it is possible to acquire the text using web scraping. In the second case, the situation is more complicated, because each service has a unique HTML structure and therefore cannot be parsed in a common way. Therefore, we chose to examine only the articles fully available on Yahoo! Finance. We also downloaded the number of shares on Facebook by querying a public API (http://graph.facebook.com/<article url>).

Yahoo! Finance also provides historical stock prices (https://finance.yahoo.com/quote/MMM/history), which can be downloaded as a CSV file by sending a HTTP GET command in format:

```
http://realchart.finance.yahoo.com/table.csv?s=ABT&d=3&e=9&f=20
16&g=d&a=3&b=6&c=1983&ignore=.csv
```

where s determines the stock symbol (ticker) of a company, a, b, c an initial month, day, and year, and d, e, f a final month, day, and year for the period of data collection. The data contain only values for working days. We saved all available values: Open, High, Low, Close, Adjusted Close (close price adjusted by dividends and splits) price, and Volume – the number of company stocks traded on the exchange during the day.

Facebook

Because Facebook offers no search capability, we decided to focus on fan pages of the examined companies. We wanted to download company posts and user comments. Data from Facebook may be downloaded using the Graph API, which enables applications to read and write into "social graph" of Facebook. The API is based on REST (Richardson & Ruby, 2007) and returns data in the JSON format (Bray et al., 2014). We are interested in the node *Page,* which offers many fields including the posts. You can get at maximum 100 posts per one request. For requesting data from the API, it is necessary to use an access token. It can be obtained on the basis of an APP_ID and APP_SECRET after creating an Application in Facebook Developers section.

We downloaded posts by sending the following HTTP GET request:

```
https://graph.facebook.com/2.3/intel/posts/?limit=90&date_
format=u&since=<timestamp>&fields=id,created_
```

```
time,message,shares,likes.limit(0).summary(true),comments.
limit(100).summary(true)
```

It means to get 90 (limit) newest posts from page "*intel*" which were created since <*timestamp*> (a UNIX timestamp – a number of seconds passed since 00:00 UTC 1. 1. 1970). We wanted to get the following fields for each post: ID, publication time, text, number of shares and likes. We also wanted to retrieve the most 100 popular comments (ordered by the number of likes).

Twitter

Statuses from Twitter may be obtained by using two types of API. The first is a classical REST API, which is limited by a number of requests an application can send to Twitter servers. For search, it is 450 requests per 15 minutes. The second option is to use a Streaming API, which is focused on processing tweets in real-time. It is based on a long-term HTTP connection and can be used to bypass the limits of REST API. We decided to download Twitter data only for a small amount number of companies (21). The reason is that we wanted to focus also on other sources of data and that downloading tweets for all companies would require a huge amount of storage space. Therefore, we decided to use REST API, because its limits did not hold us back.

The Twitter API provides many different endpoints from which the desired data can be accessed via an URL in the format https://api.twitter.com/<version>/<endpoint>. For authentication, OAuth protocol is used – we used an application token. The Search API enables the access to tweets at maximum one week old and a response may contain at maximum 100 tweets. We used the following HTTP GET request (an example for searching tweets about the Google company):

```
https://api.twitter.com/1.1/search/tweets.
json?q=Google&lang=en&result_type=mixed&count=100&since_id=123
```

The example means that we wanted to get 100 (*count*) tweets corresponding to the given query (*q*) that are written in English (*lang*). Popular as well as recent tweets (*result_type*), whose ID is larger than 123 (*since_id*), are included. For downloading tweets from company profiles, another endpoint, by which it is possible to get last 3200 tweets while one response may contain at most 200 tweets, is used. The limit is 300 requests per 15 minutes. We used the following HTTP GET request:

```
https://api.twitter.com/1.1/statuses/user_timeline.
json?count=200&since_id=123&screen_name=google
```

That means that 200 (*count*) newest tweets from the profile of Google (*screen_name*) which have their ID higher than 123 are retrieved. Requests to the Twitter API return data in the JSON format and contain many different fields (see https://dev.twitter.com/overview/api/tweets). We saved the following: ID, text, publication time, number of likes and shares (so-called "retweets"), if it is a response to another tweet, location, and information about the author: ID, location, number of followers, number of users he follows, and number of published tweets.

Data Downloading

Downloading of the data may be performed by various programming languages and tools. We chose Python mainly because of the presence of many available packages for working with data from the Web. We used the object-oriented approach so the resulting program module consists of classes defining methods for data manipulation. The scripts using these classes for downloading the data were periodically (once a day) run by the CRON (Unix-like task scheduler) on a Linux server.

Text-Preprocessing Using Python

We used three parameters influencing the values of training data vectors – a minimal percentage of a price change, a delay in days, and a smoothing method. Based on the combination of their values, a class (*decrease* or *increase*) was assigned to a document according to a stock price movement of the related company.

We thus had 75 versions of training sets where texts. The textual part of the data was a subset of all available texts based on the presence of a significant price movements related to the texts; individual sets also differed in the values of class labels associated to the texts.

Each data source was processed separately. To assign a correct label, the following steps needed to be performed for every company:

- Getting values of stock prices: for every day in the observed period, a given price type (Adjusted Close, SMA(5), SMA(20), EWMA(5), or EWMA(20)) was assigned to every date.
- Calculating the percent difference of stock prices in subsequent days and assigning a label according to the intensity of the movement.
- Retrieving all documents from the database.
- Looking at a date in a desired distance from the publication of every document and assigning a label according to the respective stock price movement.

- Preprocessing the documents (removing non-alphanumeric characters, replacing emoticons, URLs, transforming to lower case etc.).
- Writing the data to a text file with the name matching the following template:

```
<source>_<all|company>_<smoothing>_<lag>_<minimal price
change>.text
```

Converting Texts to Vectors Using VecText

For converting text data to vector numerical data, VecText (https://sourceforge.net/projects/vectext/) was used. The application has many options that influence the conversion process and results. The minimal word length was set to 2 and the minimal document frequency 10 for Yahoo! Finance articles, and 5 for the remaining documents. The program was called for each text file. The following example shows generating a vector file from a set containing Yahoo! Finance articles. The parameters were generated by the script (AnalPipeline/src/docs_to_vectors_bulk.py):

```
params = '--logarithm_type="natural" --min_document_
frequency="10"
--input_file="article_all_ewma_1_1.text" --output_
format="SVMlight"
--min_word_length="2" --encoding="utf8" --normalization="none"
--case="lower case"
--subset_size="100000" --output_decimal_places="6" --create_
dictionary="no"
--output_file="article_all_ewma_1_1_tp-no-no" --class_
position="1"
--local_weights="Binary (Term Presence)" --global_
weights="none" --n_grams="1"
--output_dir="\outputs\vec_text\article" --sort_
attributes="none" --print_statistics'
command = 'perl vectext-cmdline.pl ' + params
return_code = subprocess.call(command, shell=True)
```

Output files had a SVMlight (sparse matrix) format. The values of all specific parameters were included in the file name (e.g., *article_all_ewma_1_1_tp-no-no*).

Classification Using Scikit-Learn

The resulting files in the SVMlight format were then automatically processed by the following machine learning algorithms available in the scikit-learn Python library: Multinomial Naïve Bayes, Bernoulli Naïve Bayes, Logistic Regression, Decision tree (CART), Random Forest Classifier, and Linear SVC.

Each file was loaded and the data was divided into training (65%) and testing (35%) sets:

```
data_matrix = load_svmlight_file(' article_all_ewma_1_1_tp-no-
no')
X_train, X_test, y_train, y_test = cross_validation.
train_test_split(data_matrix[0], data_matrix[1],
test_size=0.35, random_state=38)
```

The split (training and test set) is random, but a parameter *random_state* was specified, so the result will be identical on the same data and platform.

Each classifier was then trained and tested:

```
def classify_data(clf_obj, X_train, X_test, y_train, y_test,
save_model_filepath=False):
    # Train model.
    start_time = time.time()
    clf_obj.fit(X_train, y_train)
    train_runtime = round(time.time() - start_time, 6)
    # If desired, save model to disk.
    if save_model_filepath:
        joblib.dump(clf_obj, save_model_filepath)
    # Test model.
    start_time = time.time()
    y_predicted = clf_obj.predict(X_test)
    test_runtime = round(time.time() - start_time, 6)
    # Evaluate model.
    accuracy = metrics.accuracy_score(y_test, y_predicted)
    precision = metrics.precision_score(y_test, y_predicted,
average='weighted', pos_label=None)
    recall = metrics.recall_score(y_test, y_predicted,
average='weighted', pos_label=None)
    f1_score = metrics.f1_score(y_test, y_predicted,
```

```
average='weighted', pos_label=None)
    # Get the number of tested samples for class 1 and 2.
    conf_matrix = metrics.confusion_matrix(y_test, y_predicted,
labels=[1, 2])
    cl_1_count = conf_matrix[0][0] + conf_matrix[0][1]
    cl_2_count = conf_matrix[1][0] + conf_matrix[1][1]
    # Return data.
    tested_counts = [cl_1_count, cl_2_count]
    results = [accuracy, precision, recall, f1_score, train_
runtime, test_runtime]
    eval_data = [y_test, y_predicted]
    return results, eval_data, tested_counts
```

The results of classification of the test data were evaluated using the metrics *Accuracy*, *Precision*, *Recall* and *F1 score*. Except the first one, the values were weighted by the support (the number of instances for a given class). The output is a CSV file where every row represents an experiment (the application of a classification algorithm) on a data file and every column represents the characteristics of the experiment:

```
timestamp, input file name, document type, company, smoothing
method, lag in days, minimal price change, vector, type, total,
samples, number of features, number of class 1 test samples,
number of class 2 test samples, algorithm name, accuracy,
precision, recall, F1 score, training time, testing time
```

Analyzing Experimental Parameters Using MS Excel

The CSV with the experimental results was imported to Microsoft Excel 2017 spreadsheet calculator and further analyzed to evaluate the impact of individual parameters. We used the *Pivot Table* tool that allows users extract the significant characteristics from a large, detailed data set and to cross-analyze data from different perspectives. The pivot table allows the user place selected attributes to columns and rows and analyze the observed values on their intersection in the data field. In Figure 1, different smoothing methods, lag in days, and minimal price change in rows are combined with different classifiers in columns and the values of accuracy in the data field of the pivot table. The bold values are the averages of the subordinate values. The overview of the whole dataset gives the pivot chart on the right side.

The highest values of accuracy for EWMA(20), 1 or 2 days lag, and 2 or 4 percent of a price change for the Multinomial Naïve Bayes classifier can be identified.

This tool helped us to identify the best combinations of classifiers and smoothing methods. For further analysis, we used only the filtered dataset (with the selected values of experimental parameters). The selected statistical characteristics of the results for the classification of Yahoo! Finance articles can be found in Figure 3.

Figure 2. The application of Pivot Tables in MS Excel for analyzing the experimental results.

Accuracy avg / Row Labels	LinearSVC	MaxEnt	NB-multi	Grand Total
ewma20	**0.720298805**	**0.720374252**	**0.712143952**	**0.71760567**
1	**0.733320436**	**0.736002862**	**0.755273494**	**0.741532264**
1	0.725738397	0.718002813	0.708509142	0.717416784
2	0.740902475	0.754002911	0.802037846	0.765647744
2	**0.72488128**	**0.727524688**	**0.720022685**	**0.724142884**
1	0.690011223	0.694500561	0.667190423	0.683900736
2	0.72674219	0.72674219	0.713697219	0.722393867
3	0.726851852	0.718364198	0.701388889	0.715534979
4	0.755919854	0.770491803	0.797814208	0.774741955
3	**0.711424172**	**0.708402458**	**0.68858915**	**0.70280526**
1	0.667009328	0.674547877	0.637007424	0.659521543
2	0.715483017	0.713718571	0.70327893	0.710826839
3	0.7141339	0.712716968	0.698193411	0.708348093
4	0.704310868	0.683667274	0.662416515	0.683464886
5	0.756183746	0.757361602	0.74204947	0.751864939
sma20	**0.730797748**	**0.721766867**	**0.708246187**	**0.720270267**
1	**0.750712251**	**0.740740741**	**0.731718898**	**0.741057297**
1	0.750712251	0.740740741	0.731718898	0.741057297
2	**0.723521903**	**0.711916343**	**0.69490324**	**0.710113829**
1	0.707432264	0.703703704	0.673378076	0.694838015
2	0.762612613	0.743243243	0.710810811	0.738888889
3	0.700520833	0.688802083	0.700520833	0.696614583
3	**0.731180353**	**0.723882407**	**0.711557412**	**0.722206724**
1	0.685108792	0.691337054	0.658214026	0.678219957
2	0.742871436	0.732532933	0.705352676	0.726919015
3	0.755082742	0.741843972	0.711583924	0.736170213
4	0.730496454	0.720364742	0.729483283	0.726781493
5	0.742342342	0.733333333	0.753153153	0.742942943
Grand Total	**0.725023329**	**0.721000929**	**0.710389958**	**0.718804738**

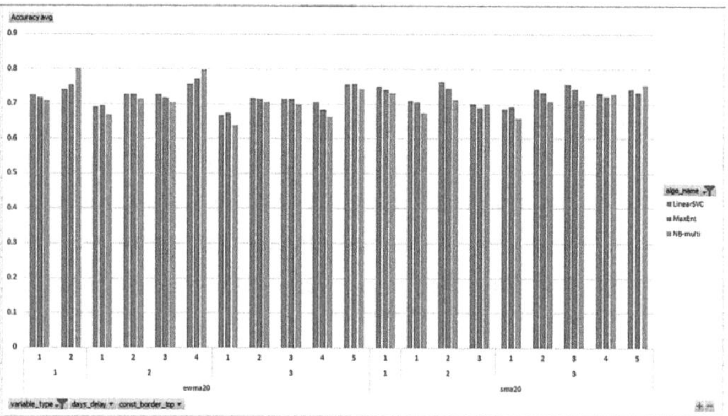

Figure 3. Obtaining important statistical characteristics of the experimental results using MS Excel.

Row Labels	Accuracy max	Accuracy avg	Accuracy min	Accuracy varp
LinearSVC	0.792349727	0.725023329	0.660536836	0.000917653
MaxEnt	0.779202279	0.721000929	0.62295082	0.001321222
NB-multi	0.81420765	0.710389958	0.626156482	0.001863961
Grand Total	**0.81420765**	**0.718804738**	**0.62295082**	**0.001405713**
Row Labels	**Accuracy max**	**Accuracy avg**	**Accuracy min**	**Accuracy varp**
tf-idf-cos	0.794759825	0.710647055	0.62295082	0.001598535
tf-idf-no	0.81420765	0.728420895	0.626156482	0.00121756
tp-no-no	0.812227074	0.717346265	0.640890919	0.001239898
Grand Total	**0.81420765**	**0.718804738**	**0.62295082**	**0.001405713**
Row Labels	**Accuracy max**	**Accuracy avg**	**Accuracy min**	**Accuracy varp**
ewma20	0.81420765	0.71760567	0.62295082	0.001649284
sma20	0.77972973	0.720270267	0.640625	0.001104109
Grand Total	**0.81420765**	**0.718804738**	**0.62295082**	**0.001405713**

CONCLUSION

The paper presented the result of experiments that were designed with the goal of revealing the association between texts published online and changes in stock prices of the corresponding companies at a micro level. To make the association quantifiable, the two time-series (texts and stock prices) needed to be transformed so quantitative analysis was possible. We considered four different methods of stock prices smoothing, three different lags between the release of documents and related stock price changes, five levels of a minimal stock price change to consider the change as significant, and three different weighting schemes for structured document representation used in the machine learning procedure. From these parameters, the smoothing method played the most important role. It was found that smoothing the stock price data with moving averages based on the 20 preceding days led to better results than in the case of using only 5 days. Such smoothing removed excessive price oscillations which are quite typical for this type of data. On the other hand, some of the important changes, especially when followed by another change in the opposite direction might be lost.

We demonstrated that it was possible to reveal an association between texts published in newspapers and on social networks and microblogging sites with the application of the machine learning-based classification. The content of the documents contributed to distinguishing between positive and negative stock price movements. All classifiers used were able to confirm the positive association between texts and stock price movements with all data sets prepared for the conducted experiments. Some of them, namely Linear SVC, Maximum Entropy, and multinomial Naïve Bayes classifiers outperformed the others in terms of the achieved accuracy. The difference between the maximal and minimal achieved accuracies for the same data was between about 20 and 30%. It was therefore obvious that the data preparation procedure had a substantial impact on the results. By further analysis of variable parameters, the values for which better results were accomplished were to be identified.

The chapter does not contain only the theoretical background, design and results of the experiments, but also a description of the technical solution of the entire process. A reader can thus understand what technological considerations needed to be done and what tools are available and can be successfully used.

Of course, there are many aspects that influence stock price movements and that are not included in online texts. It is, therefore, clear that the documents' content cannot explain or predict all movements. However, at least part of these movements is associated to the texts and can be used as part of a more complex model of economic phenomena.

Future research might include a tighter interconnection with other aspects of the financial markets domain, including, e.g., other external market and economy information and industry specifics. From the machine learning perspective, processing the data in a stream using, e.g., a moving window approach (Žižka & Dařena, 2015b), processing unbalanced data, or including additional features such as the dynamics of Facebook posts and comments likings, Yahoo! Finance articles sharing or tweets popularity are possible ways.

ACKNOWLEDGMENT

This research was supported by the Czech Science Foundation [grant No. 16-26353S "Sentiment and its Impact on Stock Markets."

REFERENCES

Ang, C. (2015). *Analyzing Financial Data and Implementing Financial Models Using R*. Springer. doi:10.1007/978-3-319-14075-9

Aski, A. S., & Sourati, N. K. (2016). Proposed efficient algorithm to filter spam using machine learning techniques. *Pacific Science Review A. Natural Science and Engineering*, *18*(2), 145–149.

Benesty, J., Chen, J., Huang, Y., & Cohen, I. (2009). *Pearson Correlation Coefficient*. Springer. doi:10.1007/978-3-642-00296-0_5

Berry, M. W., & Kogan, J. (2010). *Text Mining: Applications and Theory*. Chichester, UK: Wiley. doi:10.1002/9780470689646

Blau, B. M., & Griffith, T. G. (2016). Price clustering and the stability of stock prices. *Journal of Business Research*, *69*(10), 3933–3942. doi:10.1016/j.jbusres.2016.06.008

Bollen, J., Mao, H., & Zeng, X. (2011). Twitter mood predicts the stock market. *Journal of Computational Science*, *2*(1), 1–8. doi:10.1016/j.jocs.2010.12.007

Borch, K. (1963). *Price movements in the stock market. Econometric research program, research paper no. 7*. Princeton University. doi:10.21236/AD0407934

Bray, T. (2014). *The JavaScript Object Notation (JSON) Data Interchange Format. Request for Comments: 7159, Internet Engineering Task Force*. IETF.

Breiman, L. (2001). Statistical modeling: The two cultures (with comments and a rejoinder by the author). *Statistical Science*, *16*(3), 199–231. doi:10.1214s/1009213726

Bukovina, J. (2016). Social media big data and capital markets – An overview. *Journal of Behavioral and Experimental Finance*, *11*, 18–26. doi:10.1016/j.jbef.2016.06.002

Caltech. (2017). *Historical Stock Data — Caltech Quantitative Finance Group*. Retrieved October 1, 2017, from http://quant.caltech.edu/historical-stock-data.html

Carvalho, G., de Matos, D. M., & Rocio, V. (2007). Document retrieval for question answering: a quantitative evaluation of text preprocessing. In *Proceedings of the ACM first Ph. D. workshop in CIKM* (pp. 125-130). ACM. 10.1145/1316874.1316894

Chen, C., Su, X., & Lin, J. (2016). The role of information uncertainty in moving-average technical analysis: A study of individual stock-option issuance in Taiwan. *Finance Research Letters*, *18*, 263–272. doi:10.1016/j.frl.2016.04.026

Chisholm, E., & Kolda, T. G. (1999). *New term weighting formulas for the vector space method in information retrieval*. Computer Science and Mathematics Division, Oak Ridge National Laboratory. doi:10.2172/5698

Clark, E., & Araki, K. (2011). Text normalization in social media: Progress, problems and applications for a pre-processing system of casual English. *Procedia: Social and Behavioral Sciences*, *27*, 2–11. doi:10.1016/j.sbspro.2011.10.577

Conway, M. (2010, April 01). Mining a corpus of biographical texts using keywords. *Literary and Linguistic Computing*, *25*(1), 23–35. doi:10.1093/llc/fqp035

Eisenstein, J. (2017). Unsupervised Learning for Lexicon-Based Classification. In *Proceedings of the Thirty-First AAAI Conference on Artificial Intelligence* (pp. 3188-3194). Association for the Advancement of Artificial Intelligence.

Eldén, L. (2007). *Matrix Methods in Data Mining and Pattern Recognition*. Philadelphia: Society for Industrial and Applied Mathematics. doi:10.1137/1.9780898718867

Feldman, R., & Sanger, J. (2007). *The text mining handbook: advanced approaches in analyzing unstructured data*. Cambridge, UK: Cambridge University Press.

Go, A., Bhayani, R., & Huang, L. (2009). *Twitter Sentiment Classification using Distant Supervision*. Retrieved September 14, 2017, from http://s3.eddieoz.com/docs/sentiment_analysis/Twitter_Sentiment_Classification_using_Distant_Supervision.pdf

Gottschlich, J., & Hinz, O. (2014, March). A decision support system for stock investment recommendations using collective wisdom. *Decision Support Systems*, *59*, 52–62. doi:10.1016/j.dss.2013.10.005

Granger, C. W. J. (1969). Investigating Causal Relations by Econometric Models and Cross-spectral Methods. *Econometrica*, *37*(3), 424–438. doi:10.2307/1912791

Groth, S. S., & Muntermann, J. (2011). An intraday market risk management approach based on textual analysis. *Decision Support Systems*, *50*(4), 680–691. doi:10.1016/j.dss.2010.08.019

Haddi, E., Liu, X., & Shi, Y. (2013). The role of text pre-processing in sentiment analysis. *Procedia Computer Science*, *17*, 26–32. doi:10.1016/j.procs.2013.05.005

Hagenau, M., Liebmann, M., & Neumann, D. (2013). Automated news reading: Stock price prediction based on financial news using context-capturing features. *Decision Support Systems*, *55*(3), 685–697. doi:10.1016/j.dss.2013.02.006

Huang, P., & Ni, Y. (2017). Board structure and stock price informativeness in terms of moving average rules. *The Quarterly Review of Economics and Finance*, *63*, 161–169. doi:10.1016/j.qref.2016.04.012

Joachims, T. (2002). *Learning to classify text using support vector machines: Methods, theory and algorithms*. Kluwer Academic Publishers. doi:10.1007/978-1-4615-0907-3

Kearney, C., & Liu, S. (2014). Textual sentiment in finance: A survey of methods and models. *International Review of Financial Analysis*, *33*, 171–185. doi:10.1016/j.irfa.2014.02.006

Kubat, M., Holte, R. C., & Matwin, S. (1998). Machine learning for the detection of oil spills in satellite radar images. *Machine Learning*, *30*(2-3), 195–215. doi:10.1023/A:1007452223027

Lorica, B. (2015). *Six reasons why I recommend scikit-learn*. Retrieved February 14, 2017, from https://www.oreilly.com/ideas/six-reasons-why-i-recommend-scikit-learn

Lukebuehler. (2013). *Source of historical stock data – Stack Overflow*. Retrieved September 16, 2017, from http://stackoverflow.com/a/17263126

Matloff, N. (2017). *Statistical Regression and Classification: From Linear Models to Machine Learning*. Boca Raton, FL: CRC Press.

Mostafa, M. M. (2013). More than words: Social networks' text mining for consumer brand sentiments. *Expert Systems with Applications*, *40*(10), 4241–4251. doi:10.1016/j.eswa.2013.01.019

NIST/SEMATECH. (2016). *e-Handbook of Statistical Methods*. Retrieved December 14, 2016, from http://www.itl.nist.gov/div898/handbook/

Pang, B., Lee, L., & Vaithyanathan, S. (2002). Thumbs up?: sentiment classification using machine learning techniques. In *Proceedings of the ACL-02 conference on Empirical methods in natural language processing* (*vol. 10*, pp. 79-86). Academic Press. 10.3115/1118693.1118704

Patel, J., Shah, S., Thakkar, P., & Kotecha, K. (2015). Predicting stock and stock price index movement using trend deterministic data preparation and machine learning techniques. *Expert Systems with Applications*, *42*(1), 259–268. doi:10.1016/j.eswa.2014.07.040

Rao, T., & Srivastava, S. (2014). *Twitter sentiment analysis: How to hedge your bets in the stock markets. In State of the Art Applications of Social Network Analysis* (pp. 227–247). Springer.

Richardson, L., & Ruby, S. (2007). *RESTful Web Services*. Sebastopol, CA: O'Reilly.

Robertson, S. (2004). Understanding inverse document frequency: On theoretical arguments for IDF. *The Journal of Documentation*, *60*(5), 503–520. doi:10.1108/00220410410560582

Salton, G., & McGill, M. J. (1983). *Introduction to Modern Information Retrieval*. McGraw Hill.

Schumaker, R. P., & Chen, H. (2009). Textual analysis of stock market prediction using breaking financial news: The AZFin text system. *ACM Transactions on Information Systems*, 27.

Shevlyakov, G. L., & Oja, H. (2016). *Robust Correlation: Theory and Applications*. John Wiley & Sons. doi:10.1002/9781119264507

Singhal, A. K. (1997). *Term Weighting Revisite* (Doctoral dissertation). Faculty of the Graduate School of Cornell University.

Sokolova, M., Japkowicz, N., & Szpakowicz, S. (2006). Beyond accuracy, F-score and ROC: a family of discriminant measures for performance evaluation. In *Australasian Joint Conference on Artificial Intelligence* (pp. 1015-1021). Academic Press. 10.1007/11941439_114

STATISTA. (2016). *Leading global social networks 2016*. Retrieved March 11, 2016, from http://www.statista.com/statistics/272014/global-socialnetworks-ranked-by-number-of-users/

Tumasjan, A., Sprenger, T. O., Sandner, P. G., & Welpe, I. M. (2011). Election forecasts with Twitter: How 140 characters reflect the political landscape. *Social Science Computer Review*, *29*(4), 402–418. doi:10.1177/0894439310386557

Wang, L., An, H., Xia, X., Liu, X., Sun, X., & Huang, X. (2014). Generating moving average trading rules on the oil futures market with genetic algorithms. *Mathematical Problems in Engineering*.

Weisstein, F. L., Song, L., Andersen, P., & Zhu, Y. (2017). Examining impacts of negative reviews and purchase goals on consumer purchase decision. *Journal of Retailing and Consumer Services*, *39*, 201–207. doi:10.1016/j.jretconser.2017.08.015

Witten, I. H., Frank, E., & Hall, M. A. (2011). *Data Mining: Practical Machine Learning Tools and Techniques*. Amsterdam: Elsevier.

Wong, F. M. F., Liu, Z., & Chiang, M. (2014). Stock market prediction from WSJ: text mining via sparse matrix factorization. In *2014 IEEE International Conference on Data Mining* (pp. 430-439). IEEE.

Wuthrich, B., Cho, V., Leung, S., Permunetilleke, D., Sankaran, K., & Zhang, J. (1998). Daily stock market forecast from textual web data. In *1998 IEEE International Conference on Systems, Man, and Cybernetics* (vol. 3, pp. 2720-2725). IEEE. 10.1109/ICSMC.1998.725072

Ye, Q., Law, R., & Gu, B. (2009). The impact of online user reviews on hotel room sales. *International Journal of Hospitality Management*, *28*(1), 180–182. doi:10.1016/j.ijhm.2008.06.011

Žižka, J., & Dařena, F. (2015a). Automated Mining of Relevant N-grams in Relation to Predominant Topics of Text Documents. In *International Conference on Text, Speech, and Dialogue* (pp. 461-469). Springer.

Žižka, J., & Dařena, F. (2015b). Revealing potential changes of significant terms in streams of textual data written in natural languages using windowing and text mining. In *Artificial Intelligence and Natural Language and Information Extraction, Social Media and Web Search FRUCT Conference* (pp. 131-138). Academic Press. 10.1109/AINL-ISMW-FRUCT.2015.7382982

KEY TERMS AND DEFINITIONS

Classification Accuracy: The rate between the sum of the number of true positives + true negatives (the objects that were correctly assigned to a class) and the sum of true positives + false positives + true negatives + false negatives (all objects that were classified), when answering questions (that is, classifying).

Correlation: A dependence or association (causal or not) between two random variables measuring the degree to which two variables move in relation to each other.

Machine Learning: Machine learning is a branch of artificial intelligence (subfield of computer science) that focuses on studying and developing algorithms that can learn from data. Machine learning enables making decisions that are not based on explicitly programmed instructions and thus improving performance of machines based on past experience. It covers a wide variety of tasks that can be distinguished according to the information that is available to the machine during learning.

Natural Language Processing: A field of computer science and linguistics concerned with the interaction between computers and human (natural) languages.

Stock Market: The collection of markets and exchanges where the issuing and trading of stocks of publicly held companies, bonds, and other sorts of securities take place.

Supervised Learning: A learning method (algorithm), which uses a feedback between a trainer and trainee. The trainer knows the right answers (data labels) while the trainee learns the correct answers using the feedback for corrections to eliminate its mistakes.

Text Mining: Text mining (sometimes also text data mining) is a discipline that focuses on extraction of useful knowledge from text data. It relies on the methods similar to those from data mining but includes also specialized methods that need to be applied to texts before employment of the data mining algorithms. Typical text mining tasks include document classification, information retrieval, document clustering, or information extraction. Text mining uses methods and techniques from artificial intelligence, machine learning, natural language processing, linguistics, statistics, and many others.

Chapter 7
Vector Distribution of Limited Resources in Complex Systems

Albert N. Voronin
National Aviation University, Ukraine

ABSTRACT

The problem of distribution of the given global resource of the system under the constraints imposed on individual resources is considered. It is shown that the problem lies in constructing an adequate objective function for optimization of the resources distribution under their limitations. For solving the considered problem, the multicriteria optimization approach is undertaken with the nonlinear trade-off scheme. The proposed nonlinear compromise scheme has the property to adapt to the situation of multicriteria decision-making. The adaptation to the situation of a nonlinear scheme is carried out continuously, while the traditional selection of compromise schemes is done discretely that adds to subjective errors the errors, associated with the quantization compromise schemes. Model examples are given.

INTRODUCTION

In various areas of management and economics the problem of such resource distribution of the controlled system between the individual elements (objects), which provides the most effective functioning of the system under the given conditions, is urgent (Voronin, 2017). The problem of allocating of limited resources is a main problem of economics. It is believed that the proper distribution and redistribution of resources – this is just the economics. Similar problems arise in other subject areas, in particular, in techno-social systems for modern economical and governmental

DOI: 10.4018/978-1-5225-5586-5.ch007

infrastructures. The art is to allocate properly limited resources, depending on the circumstances.

Often the problem is solved subjectively, on the basis of the experience and professional qualifications of a decision maker (DM). In simple cases, such approach may be justified. However, when there is a large number of objects and for important cases, the price of the error of management decisions sharply increases. The development of the formalized methods of decision making support, for competent resource distribution between objects, taking into account all the given circumstances, becomes urgent.

One of such circumstances is usually resources limitation. The most prevalent is the case of upper limitation of a total (global) system resource to be distributed among the individual objects. The problem of redistribution of resources, while decreasing the previously planned level of projects funding, is considered, in particular, inVoronin (2004).

In practical cases, constraints are imposed not only on the global resource, but also on the individual resources, given to individual objects. The constraints may be imposed both from below and from above. Such constraints either are known in advance, or are determined by technical and economic calculations or by peer review methods. One should distinguish the conditional limitations (when the violation of limits is not desirable) and limitations unconditional (when their violation is physically impossible).

Example 1

To run several flights to different cities the airport has a certain fuel resource to be distributed between the aircrafts. For every flight there is a lower limit below which the fuel providing is pointless, because the plane just will not fly to its destination. This is the essence of the lower limit for every individual resource. If the given flight obtains the fuel above the certain lower limit, it has, on the one hand, an opportunity to maneuver freely by echelons, bypass a thunderstorm, going away to an alternate airfield, etc. On the other hand, the partial resource cannot be increased unlimitedly too, since there is an upper bound of the resource. This is understandable, since every aircraft has a certain capacity of tanks and physically it cannot take on board more fuel.

But usually the upper limit is introduced as conditional and assigned by the flight plan. Taking into account this set of constraints, it is required to allocate the global resource of fuel between flights to ensure the most effective operation of the airport as a whole.

Example 2

In the planning and designing organization the order for the development of several projects is received. To fulfill the order, the specific funding is provided, which is to be distributed among the individual projects. For every project the minimum level of funding, below which fulfillment of the project is impossible, is known. Usually there are protected items of the estimate – the salary of employees, rent, utility payments, cost of an absolutely necessary equipment, etc. It is clear that, with minimal funding the quality of the project would be appropriate. The funding increase makes the development of the project more effective. But it is possible to increase the funding amount to the certain limit, constraint by the total estimated cost of the project. Exceeding this limit is called the non-purposeful spending funds and threatens sanctions. Taking into account the mentioned limitations from above and below, it is necessary to distribute the global amount of funding between projects so, that the work of the planning and designing organization as a whole would be the most effective.

It easy to see, that for all the individual resources the sum of the constraints from below is a lower bound for the global resource, and the sum of the constraints from above restricts the global resource from above.

The problem lies in constructing an adequate objective function to optimize resource distribution under the condition of their limitation. A simple uniform distribution in this case is not suitable, since it can put some objects on the verge of the impossibility of their functioning, while other objects obtain an unreasonably great resource.

In the present work for solving the considered problem, the approach of multicriteria optimization, using the nonlinear trade-off scheme (Voronin, 2017), is used.

PROBLEM FORMULATION

Since the considered problem is urgent for different domains, we shall present the problem formulation in a general form (Figure 1).

The global resource R is given, which is to be allocated, and $n \geq 2$ elements (objects) O_1, O_2 ... O_n of the system, every of which is provided with the individual resource r_i, their set forming the vector $r = \{r_i\}_{i=1}^{n}$.

The formula for determining the domain of this vector has the form

$$r \in X_r^{\circ} = \left\{ r \middle| 0 \leq r_i \leq R, i \in [1, n] \right\}. \tag{1}$$

Figure 1. Resource distribution

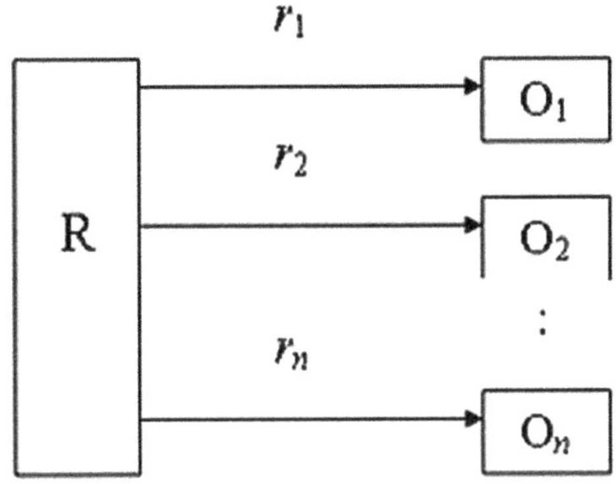

At the same time, the condition

$$\sum_{i=1}^{n} r_i = R. \tag{2}$$

holds true.

For every object it is known (or determined by the peer review method), the maximum permissible value of the resource $B_{i\min}$, below which the given object can not function. Thus, the given system is constraint from below

$$r_i \geq B_{i\min}, \sum_{i=1}^{n} B_{i\min} \leq R, i \in [1, n]. \tag{3}$$

At the same time, for every object the quantity $B_{i\max}$ is known, which can not or should not be exceeded by the object resource. The system of constraints from above has the form

$$r_i \leq B_{i\max}, \sum_{i=1}^{n} B_{i\max} \geq R, i \in [1, n]. \tag{4}$$

From (3) and (4) it follows that

$$B_{i\max} \geq r_i \geq B_{i\min}, i \in [1, n] \tag{5}$$

$$\sum_{i=1}^{n} B_{i\max} \geq R \geq \sum_{i=1}^{n} B_{i\min} . \tag{6}$$

In view of (5). expression (1) is transformed to the form

$$r \in X_r = \left\{ r \middle| B_{i\max} \geq r_i \geq B_{i\min}, i \in [1, n] \right\}. \tag{7}$$

Let us consider the polar (degenerate) cases of inequality (6). If $R = \sum_{i=1}^{n} B_{i\min}$, then the considered problem is reduced to such distribution of the global resource, for which every object obtains its minimum allowable individual resource: $r_i^* = B_{i\min}, i \in [1, n]$.

If the global resource can fully satisfy the needs of the objects, i.e., $R = \sum_{i=1}^{n} B_{i\max}$, then the problem is solved as $r_i^* = B_{i\max}, i \in [1, n]$.

Thus, in the polar cases of inequality (6) the considered problem has trivial solutions. And only if the expression (6) becomes a *strict* inequality

$$\sum_{i=1}^{n} B_{i\max} > R > \sum_{i=1}^{n} B_{i\min} , \tag{8}$$

the problem of optimizing distribution of limited resources gets the sense.

The problem is formulated: under the condition (8) to define such individual resources $r^* \in X_r$, for which requirement (2) is fulfilled and some objective function $Y(r)$, which type should be selected and justified, takes the extreme value.

METHOD OF SOLUTION

In the problem of optimizing the distribution of limited resources the limit $r_i \leq B_{i\max}, i \in [1, n]$ from above, is considered as a simple optimization constraint, the approaching to which does not threaten the system very much. Quite a different meaning has the limit $r_i \geq B_{i\min}, i \in [1, n]$ from below. The resource approaching this limitation threatens the very possibility of the appropriate object functioning. One can say, as in Voronin (2017) is said, that "the limitation from below is "criteria-forming" in the sense that the objective function must increase the difference between the individual resource and its limit from below".

Therefore, the expression of the desired objective function should: 1) include constraints from below in the explicit form, 2) penalize the system for the partial resources approaching these constraints, 3) be differentiable by its arguments. The simplest objective function, satisfying these requirements, is

$$Y(r) = \sum_{i=1}^{n} B_{i\min}(r_i - B_{i\min})^{-1}. \tag{9}$$

The analysis of formula (9) shows that this is nothing but an expression of the scalar convolution of the *maximized* individual criteria $r_i, i \in [1, n]$, by the nonlinear trade-off scheme (NTS) in the problem of multicriteria optimization (Voronin, 2014). Indeed, in the considered problem the resources $r_i, i \in [1, n]$, have a dual nature. On the one hand, they can be considered as independent variables, the *arguments of optimization* of the objective function $Y(r)$. On the other hand, for everyone of the objects it is logical the desire to maximize its individual resource, to go away as far as possible from the dangerous limit $B_{i\min}$ to improve the efficiency of its operation. From this point of view, the resources $r_i \geq B_{i\min}, i \in [1, n]$ can be regarded as individual quality *criteria* of operation of the corresponding objects. These criteria are subject to maximization, they are limited from below, nonnegative and contradictory (the increase of one resource is possible only at the expense of reducing the other).

The NTS concept is based on the principle "away from the constraints". It is assumed that the DM utility function estimates as preferable those solutions that give the greater remoteness of the criteria from hazardous constraints. The scalar convolution $Y(r)$ is a model of the utility function and includes in the explicit form the difference $r_i - B_{i\min}$, as a characteristic of tension of the decision making solution. This allows one to penalize the criteria for the approximation to their limits.

On the ground of the told above, the problem of vector optimization of limited resources, taking into account the isoperimetric constraint for arguments, becomes

$$r^* = \arg\min_{r \in X_r} Y(r) = \arg\min_{r \in X_r} \sum_{i=1}^{n} B_{i\min}(r_i - B_{i\min})^{-1}, \sum_{i=1}^{n} r_i = R. \tag{10}$$

Problem (10) can be solved both analytically, using the Lagrange method of multipliers, and by numerical methods, if analytical solution is difficult.

The analytical solution involves the construction of the Lagrange function in the form

$$L(r,\lambda) = Y(r) + \lambda\left(\sum_{i=1}^{n} r_i - R\right),$$

where λ is an indefinite Lagrange multiplier, and solving the system of equations

$$\frac{\partial L(r,\lambda)}{\partial r_i} = 0, i \in [1,n]$$
$$\frac{\partial L(r,\lambda)}{\partial \lambda} = \sum_{i=1}^{n} r_i - R = 0$$

For solving multicriteria problems by numerical methods, using the NTS concept and the constraints on the arguments and criteria, the algorithms are developed and the computer program is written (Voronin, 1999). For its use in practical calculations, it is necessary to reduce the initial multicriteria problem to a canonical form.

The NTS mechanism of the given program is designed for minimized criteria. To use it in our case, it is necessary to apply a monotone (Germeyer theorem) transformation, reducing maximized criteria $r_i, i \in [1,n]$, to the form of the minimized one. This transformation can be

$$y_i(r) = 1 / r_i, A_i = 1 / B_i, i \in [1,n].$$

It is clear, that the criteria $y_i(r)$ are bounded from above by $A_i, i \in [1,n]$. Then the objective function takes the canonical form of scalar convolution by the nonlinear trade-off scheme in a unified form for the minimized criteria (Voronin, Albert, 2017)

$$Z(r) = \sum_{i=1}^{n} A_i\left[A_i - y_i(r)\right]^{-1}.$$

The scalar convolution acts as a tool of composition of the criteria for the various alternatives $r \in X_r$, and the problem of vector optimization of distribution of limited resources, taking into account the isoperimetric constraints on the arguments, becomes

$$r^* = \arg\min_{r\in X_r} Z\left(r\right) = \arg\min_{r\in X_r} \sum_{i=1}^{n} A_i \left[A_i - y_i\left(r\right)\right]^{-1}, \sum_{i=1}^{n} r_i - R = 0\,.$$

This problem can be solved by means of the universal program of multicriteria optimization. Let us examine briefly some of its capabilities.

THE PROGRAM OF VECTOR OPTIMIZATION

For solving a wide range of optimization problems the vector optimization program TURBO-OPTIM is developed and described in Voronin (1999). The program is executed in language Borland C++3.1, using the Turbo Vision library, which provides the efficient use of computer resources, standardized and convenient environment for the user, the ease of modification and debugging.

For working with the program, the following steps are to be fulfilled:

- Select a set of individual criteria so that they all would take positive values and require minimization;
- Determine the admissible limit value for every criterion;
- Select a set of parameters (independent variables), on which the particular criteria depend;
- Determine the range of variation of every parameter (minimum, initial (starting) and maximum values);
- Set for the parameters the constraints in the form of the inequalities $g_j(r) \le 0, j \in [1,k]$, where k is a number of constraints;
- Determine the type of the dependence of the individual criteria upon the parameters.

The program allows solving the optimization problems for the following cases of connection of the individual criteria with the arguments of the optimization (parameters):

- The criteria are expressed through the parameters explicitly, analytical dependences are known;
- The criteria are some functionals, and for calculation of their values, the solution of the system differential equations is needed;
- The dependences of the criteria upon the parameters are not known, and for parameters determination the experiments are needed;
- The criteria values can be obtained by running the program written by a user;

- There is a table of the dependences of the individual criteria upon the parameters.

In every of the cited cases, the program gives a user the means of finding the minimum of the generalized criterion, built by the nonlinear trade-off scheme, by one of the methods of optimization: 1) the method of simplex planning in the Nelder-Mead modification and 2) the nonlocal method of nonlinear programming (dual optimization method, (Voronin, A.N., 1999)).

ILLUSTRATIVE EXAMPLES

Example 1

To perform two flights (n=2) the airport has fuel, totaling R=12 tons (figures are conditional). The minimum requirement of the first flight is $r_1 \geq B_{1\min}$ =2 tons, the second – $r_2 \geq B_{2\min}$ =5 tons. They are limits from below for the individual resources. The oil tanks capacity of the first aircraft is $B_{1\max}$ =7 tons, the second – $B_{2\max}$ =10 tons. They are limits from above.

Condition (8) as a strict inequality (dimensions are omitted)

$$B_{1\min} + B_{2\min} = 7 < R = 12 < B_{1\max} + B_{2\max} = 17$$

is observed. Hence, the problem of optimizing the distribution of limited resources can be posed and the solution will be nontrivial.

Problem 1

It is necessary to get the analytical solution of compromise-optimal distribution of fuel between the flights.

The Lagrangian function is built

$$L(r,\lambda) = B_{1\min}(r_1 - B_{1\min})^{-1} + B_{2\min}(r_2 - B_{2\min})^{-1} + \lambda(r_1 + r_2 - R)$$

The system of the equations is obtained

$$\frac{\partial L(r,\lambda)}{\partial r_1} = -B_{1\min}(r_1 - B_{1\min})^{-2} + \lambda = 0$$
$$\frac{\partial L(r,\lambda)}{\partial r_2} = -B_{2\min}(r_2 - B_{2\min})^{-2} + \lambda = 0$$
$$r_1 + r_2 - R = 0$$

Substituting the numerical data

$$-2(r_1 - 2)^{-2} + \lambda = 0$$
$$-5(r_2 - 5)^{-2} + \lambda = 0$$
$$r_1 + r_2 - 12 = 0$$

and solving this system by the Gauss method (successive elimination of variables), we obtain

$r_1* = 3{,}94$ tons, $r_2* = 8{,}06$ tons.

The posed problem is solved under assumption that the relative importance of both flights for DM is the same. Otherwise, the weighting coefficients α_1 and α_2, reflecting the individual DM preferences, are introduced in the objective function. These coefficients should be normalized and defined on the simplex:

$$\alpha_1, \alpha_2 \in X_\alpha = \left\{ \alpha_i \middle| \alpha_i \geq 0, \sum_{i=1}^{n=2} \alpha_i = 1, i \in [1;2] \right\}.$$

Example 2

In the design office the order for the design and manufacture of scaled-down prototypes of aircrafts of the three species (n=3): 1) passenger, 2) transport, 3) sport and training, is received. To fulfill the order, the financing of the total volume R =10 million UAH (hereinafter figures are conditional) is provided.

The complete budget for every project (limits from above) is calculated:

$r_1 \leq B_{1\max} = 7$ m UAH; $r_2 \leq B_{2\max} = 5$ m UAH; $r_3 \leq B_{3\max} = 4$ m UAH.

By means of economic calculations the minimum amounts of funding the individual projects, below which the design is not possible (limits from below), are determined:

$r_1 \geq B_{1\min}$ =2 m UAH; $r_2 \geq B_{2\min}$ =1 m UAH; $r_3 \geq B_{3\min}$ =0,5 m UAH.

Condition (8) is a strict inequality (dimensions are omitted)

$$\sum_{i=1}^{n} B_{i\max} = 16 > R = 10 > \sum_{i=1}^{n} B_{i\min} = 3,5\,,$$

so the above technique can be applied to non-trivial optimization of distribution of limited resources.

Problem 2

By using the vector optimization TURBO-OPTIM program, find the compromise-optimal values of the individual fundings r_1^*, r_2^* and r_3^* for the design and manufacture of the scaled-down prototypes of the passenger liner, transport aircraft and sport, respectively.

On the basis of the stages of work with the program, one sets: the "analysis" mode, method of "simplex-planning" optimization (default) and then enter the numerical data (the dimensions are omitted):

$$r_{1\min} = B_{1\min} = 2; r_{1start} = 3; r_{1\max} = B_{1\max} = 7$$
$$r_{2\min} = B_{2\min} = 1; r_{2start} = 3; r_{2\max} = B_{2\max} = 5$$
$$r_{3\min} = B_{3\min} = 0.5; r_{3start} = 3; r_{3\max} = B_{3\max} = 4$$
$$r_1 + r_2 + r_3 - 10 = 0$$
$$y_1 = 1 / r_1; y_2 = 1 / r_2; y_3 = 1 / r_3$$
$$y_{1\max} = A_1 = \frac{1}{B_{1\min}} = 0.5; y_{2\max} = A_2 = \frac{1}{B_{2\min}} = 1; y_{3\max} = A_3 = \frac{1}{B_{3\min}} = 2$$

After this, the command "execute" is given, and the program determines the desired values of the individual fundings of the projects:

r_1^*=4, 945 mUAH; r_2^*=3, 083 mUAH; r_3^*=1, 972 mUAH.

The obtained result corresponds to the unified version of the convolution by the nonlinear trade-off scheme, which is applied for the public use.

UNIFICATION

As noted above, the choice of a compromise scheme is the prerogative of a human, a reflection of his subjective utility function for solving specific multicriteria problem. Nevertheless, it was possible to identify some patterns and on this objective basis to construct a scalar convolution of criteria, the form of which is determined by the substantive views of essence of the studied phenomenon (NTS). The phenomenon of the individual preferences of the decision maker is formally represented by the presence of vector α in the structure of substantional model (11).

$$Y\left(a,y\right)=\sum_{i=1}^{n}a_iA_i[A_i-y_i]^{-1}\,. \tag{11}$$

There are various estimates of the role of subjective factors in solving multiobjective problems. Subjectivity is acceptable, and even desirable, if this problem is solved in the interests of a particular person. Indeed, if a human operator in ergatic system has the possibility to adjust the parameters of the workplace under his own individual characteristics, it improves the quality of the controlled process; suit made to measure in the customer's company, usually better than store-bought ready-made clothes, etc. Therefore, the mechanism of individual preferences is rather intensively used in the practice of multicriteria decision problems solution.

However, subjectivity in their decision is permissible and desirable only as long as the result is intended for a specific decision-makers or narrow groups of people with similar preferences. If it is intended for general use, it has to be completely objective, standardized. In these cases, the mechanism of the individual preferences of the methods of solution of multicriteria tasks should be excluded in order to avoid arbitrariness and ambiguity of the results of decisions. According to Gilbert, the overall task of science is to "deliver us from chance, bias personal sentiments and habits and protect against subjectivism". The formalization of qualitative concepts eliminates the inevitable in intuitive considering the ambiguity of interpretations, and, that is much more important, allows you to explore the phenomena by mathematical methods, that usually already at the first steps brings new important results.

When the result of the multicriteria problem decision is intended for general use, it is unified and individual preferences are leveled on statistics; becomes applicable principle of insufficient reason by Bernoulli-Laplace: if a priori probabilities of possible hypotheses are not known, they should be set equal, i.e., all hypotheses should be regarded as equally probable. As applied to multiobjective problem, this means that all the weighting coefficients α_i, $i\in[1,n]$ in the expression for the scalar convolution of criteria to be minimized must be equal unless there is no prior information about different values of criteria. Since in the formulation of the problem we considered the criteria equal in importance, with the unification we should take in (11) all the weights equal: $\alpha_i \equiv 1/n$, $\forall i \in [1,n]$. Then

$$Y(\alpha, y) = \frac{1}{n}\sum_{i=1}^{n}\left[A_i - y_i\right]^{-1}.$$

Taking into account that the multiplication by $1/n$ is a monotonic transformation, which, in Germeier theorem, does not alter the comparison of the results, we go to the unified expression for the scalar convolution of criteria

$$Y(y) = \sum_{i=1}^{n}\left[A_i - y_i\right]^{-1}. \tag{12}$$

This formula is recommended in all cases where the multicriteria problem is solved not in favor of any one particular decision-maker, but for general use.

In Voronin (2013) it is proposed to start a multicriteria decision *in all cases* using formula (12). The result and the corresponding values of the partial criteria are imposed to decision maker to assess. If the decision maker believes that the obtained solution does not satisfy him and the correction according to his personal preferences is required, then, the procedure for determining the weighting coefficients α_i, $i \in [1,n]$ is organized. To optimize the formula (11) is used. Turning to our analogy, we note that the store bought ready to wear a suit usually needs only a minor adjustment.

For taking into account the DM individual preferences, the above program contains the appropriate option.

In the case when the global resource is allocated between the objects not directly, but through intermediaries, the system becomes hierarchical (Prilutskiy 1996). The given approach can be applied also in this case.

CONCLUSION

The problem is solved of such the control system resource allocation between the individual elements (objects), which provide the most efficient operation of the system in the given circumstances. A nonlinear scheme of compromise approach is appropriate in the case (Voronin 2009).

REFERENCES

Prilutskiy, M. K. (1996). Multicriteria distribution of a uniform resource in hierarchical systems. Avtomatika i telemekhanika, 2, 24-29.

Voronin, A. N. (1999). *Vector optimization of dynamic systems*. Kiev: Tehnika.

Voronin, A. N. (2004). Vector optimization of hierarchical structures. Problems of control and informatics, 6, 26-34. doi:10.1615/JAutomatInfScien.v36.i11.40

Voronin, A. N. (2009). A nonlinear trade-off scheme in multicriteria evaluation and optimization problems. Cybernetics and systems analysis, 4, 106-114.

Voronin, A. N., & Ziatdinov, J. K. (2013). Theory and practice of multi-criteria decision: Models, methods, implementation. Lambert Academic Publishing.

Voronin, A. N. (2014). *Multicriteria Decision-Making: Systemic Approach*. Lambert Academic Publishing.

Voronin, A. N. (2017). *Multi-Criteria Decision Making for the Management of Complex Systems*. IGI Global. doi:10.4018/978-1-5225-2509-7

Chapter 8
Mathematical Modeling of Information Warfare in Techno-Social Environments

A. P. Mikhailov
Keldysh Institute of Applied Mathematics, Russia

G. B. Pronchev
Lomonosov Moscow State University, Russia

O. G. Proncheva
Keldysh Institute of Applied Mathematics, Russia & Moscow Institute of Physics and Technology, Russia

ABSTRACT

The chapter discusses a number of mathematical models of information battle in techno-social environments. Some models take into account such battle factors as the mass information media's incomplete coverage of the society, the individuals' acquisition of the information only after receiving it twice, the individuals' forgetting the information, a priori bias to support a party to the battle, and polarization of the society. For simpler models, the results are described in brief. For more complicated ones, mathematical research has been conducted with the sociological interpretation of the results.

INTRODUCTION

The value of information for both an individual and the society had been realized long before the very word emerged. Many technological achievements and inventions were adapted by people for storing or spreading the information in this way or another

DOI: 10.4018/978-1-5225-5586-5.ch008

while other inventions were designed directly for that. Nowadays it can be spoken about the united techno-social environment that encompasses both the individuals, technical means and carriers. The environment is a field for spreading the rumors, gossips, urban legends, commercial advertisement and political propaganda. In some cases, two antagonistic information streams are transmitted in the society, e.g. ones that carry the opposite evaluations of one and the same political event. In this case, one may talk of an information battle process. This chapter is dedicated to several models of the process.

BACKGROUND

A review of sociological literature on this area of focus could be a multi-volume edition itself, so here it is only the works of Herman and Chomsky (2006), DiFonzo and Bordia, (2005, 2007), Pronchev and Muraviov (2011) that will be mentioned. The authors by no means claim their review to be neither exhaustive nor representative but they rather proceed from their own preferences.

The first mathematical single rumor spreading models were suggested quite a long ago (Daley & Kendall, 1964; Maki & Thompson, 1973). In the most general terms, these models assume that at each time point some individuals from those making up a social group possess certain information and transmit it to other individuals. Thus, the information is propagated. The deterministic and stochastic models are distinguished, and in some cases - deterministic and stochastic variants of one and the same model. In this work it is only the deterministic models that are considered.

The mechanics of the Daley-Kendall model looks as follows. At each time point, each member of the society belongs to one of the three classes: ignorants, spreaders, or stiflers. Ignorants are not yet aware about the rumor; spreaders know the rumor and propagate it, while stiflers know it but do not spread it. Initially, one member of the society is a spreader, and all the other ones – ignorants. Contacts between the individuals are described in the molecular-kinetic terms: e.g., the frequency of meetings between ignorants and spreaders is proportional to the multiplication of the current quantities of these classes (certainly this implies the homogeneity of the society). The individuals can pass from one class to another in three cases: (i) if an ignorant meets a spreader, the ignorant also becomes a spreader, (ii) if two spreaders meet, then both of them become stiflers, and (iii) if a spreader meets a stifler, the spreader becomes a stifler too. Hereinafter the spreaders passing to the class of stiflers will be called the stifling effect.

The distinction of the Maki-Thompson model prerequisites consists in only one spreader turning into a stifler when two spreaders interact (the second one remains a spreader), i.e. in a more limited character of the stifling-effect.

These early works were developed under the influence of epidemiology models (however, the influence still remains fairly strong). So early as when introducing the notions of ignorants, spreaders and stiflers, Daley and Kendall specified that the classes are analogous to classes of "susceptibles", "infectious persons", and "removed cases" in epidemiology. Meanwhile, it is not only the transfer of ideas from one scientific branch to another one that is in question, but so is the search of differences. So, the same authors see the difference in the fact that in epidemiology models, transition from the infectious persons class to the removed cases one (i.e. recovery or isolation) occurs merely with the course of time, without being influenced by peers in the society. Meanwhile, in the rumor model developed by them the stifling-effect takes place due to encountering another spreader or stifler.

The main question of these two models is to determine the quantity of ignorants at the end of the process. The answer is as follows: if the initial quantity of spreaders equals one, then the finite (given an infinitely long time) quantity of ignorants in both models equals about 0,203 of the total number. In the works of Belen and Pearce (2004), and Belen (2008) for the Maki-Thompson model, the question of the final quantity of ignorants in the case when the initial quantity of spreaders is more than one was also studied. In particular, it has been shown that if at the initial point almost all individuals belong to the class of spreaders, then the class of ignorants at the end of the process makes up approximately 1/e of its initial number.

The sociological meaning of this result can be explained as follows. The daily experience prompts that when the circulation of a rumor is over in the society, then, as a rule, there remain rather numerous ignorants in it. Why does this happen? Why does the rumor fail to cover the entire society? The Daley-Kendall model and Maki-Thompson model explain it by all spreaders becoming stiflers due to communications between each other and the stiflers, thus having failed to transmit the rumor to the remaining ignorants.

The authors of this paper consider this explanation unsatisfactory, as it explains the rumor ceasing to circulate only by the communications system between the individuals, while completely ignoring the nature of the information message transmitted by means of the rumor. In other words, so each of the numerous rumors has to cover one and the same share of the population! In reality, some rumors are known to win a wider audience (and get spread much faster) than others. Moreover, certain rumors can cover almost all adult population of a country while many information messages cease to circulate so early as after the second or third spreader, i.e. they actually even fail to become rumors in the ordinary sense of the word. This confirms that the influence of the stifling-effect on the propagation of information in the society is in fact fairly small and it can be neglected. For this reason, the models discussed in this paper do not contain the stifling-effect.

Nevertheless, it cannot but be acknowledged that the works of Daley-Kendall and Maki-Thompson have given birth to an important scientific area of focus. Today, it includes a vast bibliography and has mainly been developing as a section of mathematics, in a certain way isolated from social sciences.

Now, some other fields of study in this area will be outlined in brief. Numerous works deal with studying the processes of information propagation in social networks – Nekovee et al. (2007) and Gubanov et al. (2010), can be cited as an example. A fairly rare example of modeling the propagation of rumors relying on the certain social mechanism is presented in the paper of Shvedovskiy (1981). In it, the information propagation model is built with an emphasis on the mechanism " learned something at work – retold it in the family, learned something in the family – retold it at work". The competing rumors models are much less known although they were also created quite long ago, at least, in the work of Osei ansd Thompson, (1977). Among the recent works, for instance, Kaligotla et al. (2015) and Escalante and Odehnal (2017) can be pointed out.

The above works deal with the propagation of rumors. In other words, in these models, the information message is only transmitted from person to person, i.e. exclusively through interpersonal communications.

In real life, it is mass media that also play quite a part in information streams propagation.

As an empirical example showing the combination of the information being propagated via mass media and via rumors, the work of Yanagizawa-Drott (2014) can be mentioned; it is dedicated to studying the influence of the violence promoting RTLM radio station on 1994 genocide in Rwanda. In the work, it has been demonstrated that the most intensive ethnic cleansing took place in villages that received the calls for hatred from the radio station as well as in the villages neighboring them (that got the same calls as retold by their neighbors).

If two sources send out different information streams contradicting each other via their affiliated mass media, then it is already not the propagation of rumors but an information warfare process or a propaganda battle that is in question (Mikhailov et al., 2017). Each of the streams is then propagated in one and the same society through interpersonal communications. The winning "party" of the warfare is considered to be the one that has more spreaders at the end of the process, i.e. with quite large values of time (it should be reminded that there is no stifling-effect in the works discussed here, and therefore – no such class of individuals as stiflers).

This chapter sums up a number of the authors' results concerning the information battle modeling.

BASIC MODEL OF INFORMATION ATTACK

First the basic model of information attack is going to be discussed. It is analogous to single rumor models but it admits that an ignorant can receive it either from the mass media or through interpersonal communications from a spreader. Now, the process of the information spreading in a group of interacting individuals numbering N_0 is going to be considered.

Let $N(t)$ be the quantity of spreaders at time point t, $\alpha > 0$ - the intensity of information propagation via the mass media; βN - the intensity of information propagation through rumors ($\beta > 0$). If the initial quantity of spreaders equals zero, then the basic model is given by:

$$\frac{dN}{dt} = (\alpha + \beta N)(N_0 - N) \tag{1}$$

Solution of the problem (1) is written as follows:

$$N = N_0 \frac{\alpha \exp\left[(\alpha + \beta N_0)t\right] - \alpha}{\alpha \exp\left[(\alpha + \beta N_0)t\right] + \beta N_0}$$

It follows from simple analysis that it is always positive, except time point $t = 0$, it grows monotonously as time passes and tends from below to value N_0 with the course of time. Thus, ultimately (formally under $t \rightarrow \infty$) all members of the group go to the class of spreaders.

A subtler gradation of information propagation modes is obtained by analyzing the speed of information threat escalation depending on the parameters of the model. It can be easily shown that when meeting the condition

$$N_g = \frac{1}{2}\left(N_0 - \frac{\alpha}{\beta}\right) > 0 \tag{2}$$

there is time point t_{cr}, when the maximum speed of recruitment is achieved. Here $N_{cr} = N(t_{cr})$ is the number of members recruited at time point t_{cr}. Let it be called the maximum "stir" point (it exists not for any values of the model parameters).

It follows from the analysis (2) that depending on the proportions between the model parameters three information propagation modes are possible:

1. The intensity of mass media broadcasting is higher than the intensity of rumors: $\alpha > \beta N_0$. In this case $N_{cr} < 0$, $t_{cr} < 0$, i.e. the speed of ignorants turning into spreaders is reduced with the course of time.
2. $\alpha = \beta N_0$: here $N_{cr} = 0$, which means that the speed of turning into spreaders is the maximum possible one at the initial time point $t = 0$, and it is reduced under $t > 0$.
3. $\alpha < \beta N_0$: the speed of turning into spreaders under $t < t_{cr}$ goes up, being maximum under $t = t_{cr}$, and goes down under $t > t_{cr}$. Meanwhile, the stir maximum is achieved with the number of followers equaling N_g.

EXPANDED MODEL OF INFORMATION ATTACK

The following superstructures for the basic model have been suggested.

Mass Information Media Having an Incomplete Coverage of the Society

Let the population under consideration consist of two homogeneous subgroups numbering N_1, N_2. The members of the first subgroup can receive the information both from the mass media and through rumors while the members of the second one do not use the mass media so they only receive the information through rumors. There is no passing of individuals from one subgroup into the other, and they do not make any distinctions when transmitting the rumors as for who belongs to which subgroup.

Let the quantity of spreaders of the *i*-th subgroup at time point t be called $X_i(t)$. Ignorants of the first subgroup receive the information both from the mass media and from $X_1 + X_2$ spreaders while the second subgroup ignorants – from spreaders only, thus

$$\frac{dX_1}{dt} = \left[\alpha + \beta\left(X_1 + X_2\right)\right]\left(N_1 - X_1\right)$$

$$\frac{dX_2}{dt} = \beta\left(X_1 + X_2\right)\left(N_2 - X_2\right)$$

Two-Step Information Acquisition

Practice shows the information action is effective if it is conducted as a campaign during which the information message is repeated consistently. Within this variant of the model, it is assumed that an ignorant becomes a spreader within two steps. Those receiving the information only once do not spread it on. Such individuals are called pre-spreaders; let the number thereof be denoted as $n(t)$. With spreaders being recruited from pre-spreaders, and the latter – from ignorants, the model is given by

$$\frac{dn}{dt} = (N_0 - N - 2n)(\alpha + \beta N)$$

$$\frac{dN}{dt} = n(\alpha + \beta N)$$

Forgetting the Information

Let it be supposed that contrary to the model the reverse transition from spreaders to ignorants is possible, i.e. that the spreaders can forget the information. Then the model equation is written as

$$\frac{dN}{dt} = (N_0 - N)(\alpha + \beta N) - \gamma N .$$

Here the parameter $\gamma > 0$ characterizes the intensity of spreaders' forgetting the information.

Expanded Model

Now, let the model be built taking into account all the three factors described above. The population consists of two subgroups numbering N_1, N_2. The members of the first subgroup receive the information both from the mass media and through rumors while the members of the second one – through rumors only. There is no passing of individuals from one subgroup into the other. The numbers of spreaders and pre-spreaders in the *i*-th are equal to $X_i(t), x_i(t)$, respectively. As for forgetting, let it be assumed that pre-spreaders forget at intensity δ and come back to the class of ignorants, while spreaders forget at intensity γ and become pre-spreaders. With these assumptions, the model is written as follows:

$$\frac{dX_1}{dt} = x_1\left(\alpha + \beta\left[X_1 + X_2\right]\right) - \gamma X_1$$

$$\frac{dX_2}{dt} = \beta x_2\left[X_1 + X_2\right] - \gamma X_2$$

$$\frac{dx_1}{dt} = \left(\alpha + \beta\left[X_1 + X_2\right]\right)\left[N_1 - 2x_1 - X_1\right] - \delta x_1 + \gamma X_1$$

$$\frac{dx_2}{dt} = \beta\left[X_1 + X_2\right]\left[N_2 - 2x_2 - X_2\right] - \delta x_2 + \gamma X_2$$

$$x_1\left(0\right) = x_2\left(0\right) = X_1\left(0\right) = X_2\left(0\right) = 0 \tag{3}$$

BASIC MODEL OF THE INFORMATION BATTLE

Now, let the population numbering N_0, in which two media sources sending out two messages that are antagonistic to a certain extent at intensities α_1, α_2, be considered. These messages are retold by individuals at intensities β_1, β_2, thus generating two competing rumors and two parties amounting to $X\left(t\right)$ and $Y\left(t\right)$ spreaders. This process is called the information battle. The party having a larger quantity of spreaders under $t \to \infty$ is considered to be the winner of the battle. In this model, it is assumed that a spreader belonging to one party is insensitive to the message of the opposing party.

The mechanics of the model is generally similar to the single message models discussed above. Given the quantity of ignorants equaling $N_0 - X(t) - Y(t)$, the basic model of the information battle is obtained (Mikhailov, & Marevtseva, 2011):

$$\frac{dX}{dt} = \left(\alpha_1 + \beta_1 X\right)\left(N_0 - X - Y\right), \quad X\left(0\right) = 0,$$
$$\frac{dY}{dt} = \left(\alpha_2 + \beta_2 Y\right)\left(N_0 - X - Y\right), \quad Y\left(0\right) = 0 \tag{4}$$

For this model, the question about the winner of the battle was studied. In the work of (Mikhailov, A.P.& Marevtseva, N.A., 2011), it has been proven that the necessary and sufficient condition for the first party victory (i.e. the condition for $\lim X\left(t\right) > \lim Y\left(t\right)$ under $t \to \infty$) is given by

$$\frac{\beta_1}{\ln\left(1 + \beta_1 N_0 / \left(2\alpha_1\right)\right)} > \frac{\beta_2}{\ln\left(1 + \beta_2 N_0 / \left(2\alpha_2\right)\right)}. \tag{5}$$

Accordingly, the opposite sign inequality means the victory of the second party and the equality – a "draw".

The same work generalizes this model for the situation of battle between not two but arbitrary quantity M of mutually antagonistic parties. In this case, the model is written as a system of M non-linear ordinary differential equations:

$$\frac{dN_i}{dt} = \left(\alpha_i + \beta_i N_i\right)\left(N_0 - \sum_{i=1}^{M} N_i\right), N_i(0) = 0, i = 1,.., M \tag{6}$$

EXPANDED MODEL OF THE INFORMATION BATTLE

The model taking into account all additional factors introduced for the information attack model is given by Mikhailov et al. (2014)

$$\begin{aligned}
\frac{dX_1}{dt} &= x_1\left(\alpha_1 + \beta_1\left(X_1 + X_2\right)\right) - \gamma_1 X_1 \\
\frac{dX_2}{dt} &= \beta_1 x_2\left(X_1 + X_2\right) - \gamma_1 X_2 \\
\frac{dY_1}{dt} &= y_1\left(\alpha_2 + \beta_2\left(Y_1 + Y_2\right)\right) - \gamma_2 Y_1 \\
\frac{dY_2}{dt} &= \beta_2 y_2\left(Y_1 + Y_2\right) - \gamma_2 Y_2 \\
\frac{dx_1}{dt} &= \left(\alpha_1 + \beta_1\left(X_1 + X_2\right)\right)\left(N_1 - X_1 - Y_1 - 2x_1 - y_1\right) + \gamma_1 X_1 - \delta_1 x_1 \\
\frac{dx_2}{dt} &= \beta_1\left(X_1 + X_2\right)\left(N_2 - X_2 - Y_2 - 2x_2 - y_2\right) + \gamma_1 X_2 - \delta_1 x_2 \\
\frac{dy_1}{dt} &= \left(\alpha_2 + \beta_2\left(Y_1 + Y_2\right)\right)\left(N_1 - X_1 - Y_1 - x_1 - 2y_1\right) + \gamma_2 Y_1 - \delta_2 y_1 \\
\frac{dy_2}{dt} &= \beta_2\left(Y_1 + Y_2\right)\left(N_2 - X_2 - Y_2 - x_2 - 2y_2\right) + \gamma_2 Y_2 - \delta_2 y_2
\end{aligned} \tag{7}$$

Here x_i, y_i is the quantity of pre-spreaders of parties X, Y in the i-th group; X_i, Y_i is the quantity of spreaders. The numerical investigation of this model has been conducted, with a special focus on the case when a party has a stronger propaganda via the mass media while the other one has a more "viral" information, that is, $\alpha_1 > \alpha_2, \beta_2 > \beta_1$.

The results of numerical experiments show that for each group, in general terms, the dynamics is as follows: first of all, the number of pre-followers increases and reaches the maximum, next it decreases, with the number of followers growing. Figure 1 and Figure 2 show the dynamics of the number of followers and pre-followers from both groups for the experiment adopting the following parameter values:

$$\begin{aligned}
&N_1 = 100, N_2 = 200, \gamma_1 = 0,01, \gamma_2 = 0,3, \delta_1 = 0,1, \\
&\delta_2 = 0,02, \alpha_1 = 0,13, \alpha_2 = 0,06, \beta_1 = 0,04, \beta_2 = 0,1.
\end{aligned}$$

Figure 1 and 2 show that the majority of the first group members (i.e. most individuals using the mass media) are covered by the first source (i.e. $X_1(t) > Y_1(t)$ under quite large t values), and most second group members (i.e. ones not using the mass media) – by the second source (i.e. $X_2(t) < Y_2(t)$ under quite large t values). However, while for the first group the "superiority" of the first source is minor, in the second group, the gap between ones covered by the first source and those believing the second one is much larger. This happens because of the "viral"

Figure 1. Dynamics of followers and pre-followers number for group 1; The solid line stands for x(t) and X(t), respectively; the dotted line – y(t) and Y(t)

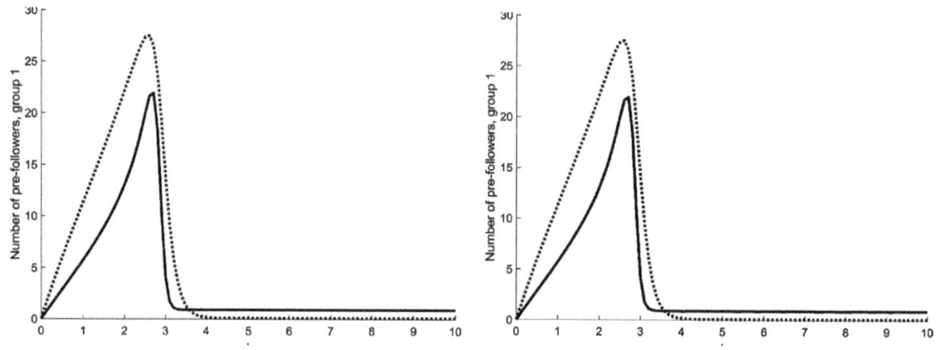

Figure 2. Dynamics of followers and pre-followers number for group 2; The solid line stands for x(t) and X(t), respectively; the dotted line – y(t) and Y(t)

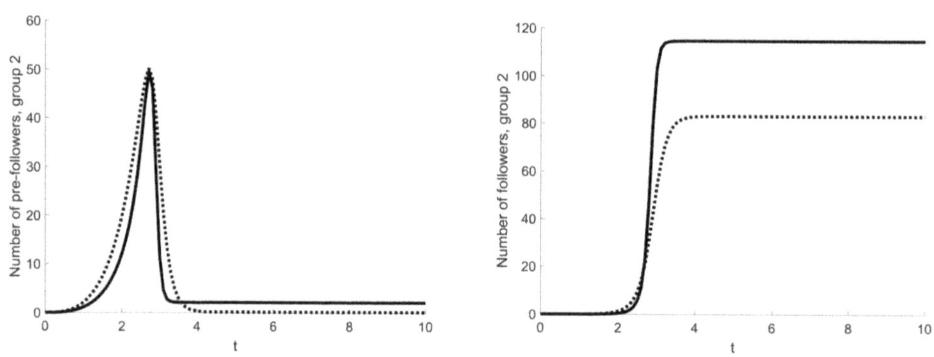

character of the information from the second source producing a great influence on both groups (as the individuals from different groups communicate with each other), with the first source having the advantage for the first group only.

If the values of coefficients α_1 and β_2 increase, the complete "takeover" of the second group by the second source is observed as well as the first group people prevailing who are covered by the first source. Meanwhile, larger information forgetting coefficients result in the shift of stationary distribution toward the second source. The reason of this consists in the fact that the individuals who "have forgotten" are recruited by the second source to a greater extent than by the first one.

CONSIDERATION OF DESTABILIZING EFFECT

Let the initial model of the information battle (2) be considered for the case of a periodic destabilizing effect. In particular, let one more component – a periodic one – be added to the "background" constant intensity of propaganda of one of the parties. Thus, the parameter characterizing the intensity of the first party information propagation via the mass media is given by a periodic piecewise constant function of time:

$$\alpha_1(t) = \begin{cases} \alpha_1^*, t \in [iT; iT + t_{sw}) \\ \alpha_1^* + h, t \in [iT + t_{sw}; iT + T) \end{cases}, i \in 0 \cup \mathbb{N} \tag{8}$$

where $\alpha_1^* > 0, h > 0$. Let it also be assumed that the intensity of propagation through interpersonal communications is one and the same for the information of parties considered, with the intensity being small.

Thus, the system of equations (4) is studied under $\beta_1 = \beta_2 = \beta << 1$, constant parameter $\alpha_2 > 0$, and the $\alpha_1(t)$ function given by the above expression (8).

Preliminary Change of Variables and Zeroth-Order Asymptotics

Let the following change be made to system (4):

$$\begin{aligned} X &= -u + \alpha_1^* v \\ Y &= u + \alpha_2 v \end{aligned} \tag{9}$$

The objective of the change consists in diagonalizing the matrix that expresses the recurrent relation between the values of the functions sought at various time points within interval $[kT; kT + t_{sw})$ - see below, proportion (14).

As a result of the change, Cauchy problem is obtained from (4):

$$\begin{aligned} \frac{du}{dt} &= \frac{1}{\alpha_1^* + \alpha_2}\left(\alpha_2\alpha_1^* - \alpha_1(t)\alpha_2 + \beta(\alpha_1^* + \alpha_2)v\right)\left(N - (\alpha_1^* + \alpha_2)v\right) \\ \frac{dv}{dt} &= \frac{1}{\alpha_1^* + \alpha_2}\left(\alpha_1(t) + \alpha_2 + \beta(\alpha_1^* + \alpha_2)v\right)\left(N - (\alpha_1^* + \alpha_2)v\right) \\ u(0) &= u^0, v(0) = v^0 \end{aligned} \tag{10}$$

where $u^0 = \left(-\alpha_2 X^0 + \alpha_1^* Y^0\right) / \left(\alpha_1^* + \alpha_2\right)$, $v^0 = \left(X^0 + Y^0\right) / \left(\alpha_1^* + \alpha_2\right)$. The solution of system (10) will be looked for as asymptotics:

$$\begin{aligned} u(t) &= u_0(t) + \beta u_1(t) + o(\beta) \\ v(t) &= v_0(t) + \beta v_1(t) + o(\beta) \end{aligned} \tag{11}$$

By applying expansions (11) to system (10) and equalizing the coefficients in front of equal degrees β, the equations for the zeroth and first approximations of functions $u(t)$ and $v(t)$ are obtained.

This is what is obtained in the zeroth approximation:

$$\begin{aligned} \frac{du_0}{dt} &= \frac{1}{\alpha_1^* + \alpha_2}\left(\alpha_2 \alpha_1^* - \alpha_1(t)\alpha_2\right)\left(N - \left(\alpha_1^* + \alpha_2\right)v_0\right) \\ \frac{dv_0}{dt} &= \frac{1}{\alpha_1^* + \alpha_2}\left(\alpha_1(t) + \alpha_2\right)\left(N - \left(\alpha_1^* + \alpha_2\right)v_0\right) \\ u_0(0) &= u_0,\ v_0(0) = v_0 \end{aligned} \tag{12}$$

The nearest objective consists in finding the recurrent relations between the values of functions $u_0(t), v_0(t)$ at time points kT and $kT + T$. This will allow finding the stationary solution to system (12).

Let it be considered over interval $\left[kT; kT + t_{sw}\right)$

$$\begin{aligned} du_0 / dt &= 0 \\ dv_0 / dt &= N - \left(\alpha_1^* + \alpha_2\right)v_0 \end{aligned} \tag{13}$$

Here it is assumed that the values of $u_0(kT), v_0(kT)$ are known. It is obtained by solving system (13)

$$\begin{pmatrix} u_0(t) \\ v_0(t) \end{pmatrix} = P(t - kT)\begin{pmatrix} u_0(kT) \\ v_0(kT) \end{pmatrix} + D_0(t - kT),\ kT < t < kT + t_{sw} \tag{14}$$

where

$$P(t)=\begin{pmatrix}1 & 0\\ 0 & e^{-(\alpha_1^*+\alpha_2)t}\end{pmatrix},\ D(t)=\begin{pmatrix}0\\ \dfrac{N}{\alpha_1^*+\alpha_2}\left(1-e^{-(\alpha_1^*+\alpha_2)t}\right)\end{pmatrix} \tag{15}$$

Therefore, at point $kT+t_{sw}$, functions $u_0(t), v_0(t)$ have values

$$\begin{pmatrix}u_0(kT+t_{sw})\\ v_0(kT+t_{sw})\end{pmatrix}=P(t_{sw})\begin{pmatrix}u_0(kT)\\ v_0(kT)\end{pmatrix}+D_0(t_{sw}) \tag{16}$$

Now, let half-interval $[Tk+t_{sw};Tk+T)$ be considered. Within it, system (12) is as follows:

$$\begin{aligned}\frac{du_0}{dt}&=h\alpha_2 v_0-\frac{h\alpha_2 N}{\alpha_1^*+\alpha_2}\\ \frac{dv_0}{dt}&=-(\alpha_1^*+h+\alpha_2)v_0+\frac{(\alpha_1^*+h+\alpha_2)N}{\alpha_1^*+\alpha_2}\end{aligned} \tag{17}$$

Solving system (12) within the given span with initial conditions (16), the following is obtained:

$$\begin{aligned}&\begin{pmatrix}u_0(t)\\ v_0(t)\end{pmatrix}=Q(t-t_{sw}-kT)\begin{pmatrix}u_0(kT+t_{sw})\\ v_0(kT+t_{sw})\end{pmatrix}\\ &+G_0(t-t_{sw}-kT), kT+t_{sw}\le t<kT+T\end{aligned} \tag{18}$$

where

$$\begin{aligned}Q(t)&=\begin{pmatrix}1 & \dfrac{h\alpha_2}{\alpha_1^*+h+\alpha_2}\left(1-e^{-(\alpha_1^*+h+\alpha_2)t}\right)\\ 0 & e^{-(\alpha_1^*+h+\alpha_2)t}\end{pmatrix},\\ G_0(t)&=\frac{N}{\alpha_1^*+\alpha_2}\left(1-e^{-(\alpha_1^*+h+\alpha_2)t}\right)\begin{pmatrix}\dfrac{-h\alpha_2}{\alpha_1^*+h+\alpha_2}\\ 1\end{pmatrix}\end{aligned} \tag{19}$$

It is quite easy to obtain the values of function $u^0(t), v^0(t)$ at point $kT+T$ from (18), and with (16) taken into account, to derive the sought recurrent relation for them:

$$\begin{pmatrix} u_0(kT+T) \\ v_0(kT+T) \end{pmatrix} =$$

$$Q(T-t_{sw})P(t_{sw})\begin{pmatrix} u_0(kT) \\ v_0(kT) \end{pmatrix} + Q(T-t_{sw})D_0(t_{sw}) + G_0(T-t_{sw}) \tag{20}$$

Thus, the zeroth approximation of solution of system (10) has been found and, using the reverse change for (9), the zeroth approximation of solution of system (4) can be found.

Let the way of finding the stationary solution for system (10) be described in brief. Eigenvalues λ_1 and λ_2 and eigenvectors ψ_1, ψ_2 of matrix $Q(T-t_{sw})P(t_{sw})$ corresponding to them have to be found. Expansions of the columns are performed in the basis

$$\begin{pmatrix} u^0 \\ v^0 \end{pmatrix} = A_1\psi_1 + A_2\psi_2, Q(T-t_{sw})D_0(t_{sw}) + G_0(T-t_{sw}) = B_1\psi_1 + B_2\psi_2 \tag{21}$$

where coefficients A_1, A_2, B_1, B_2 may be quite cumbersome but they are determined unambiguously. Next, it is not difficult to obtain it from (20) and (21) that

$$\begin{pmatrix} u_0(kT) \\ v_0(kT) \end{pmatrix} = A_1\lambda_1^k\psi_1 + A_2\lambda_2^k\psi_2 + B_1\psi_1\sum_{i=0}^{k-1}\lambda_1^i + B_2\psi_2\sum_{i=0}^{k-1}\lambda_2^i \tag{22}$$

By passing to the limit under $k \to \infty$ in this expression, it is obtained:

$$\begin{pmatrix} u_0^s \\ v_0^s \end{pmatrix} = A_1\begin{pmatrix} 1 \\ 0 \end{pmatrix} - \frac{N}{\left(1 - e^{-(\alpha_1^*+\alpha_2)t_{sw} - (\alpha_1^*+h+\alpha_2)(T-t_{sw})}\right)}\psi_2 \tag{23}$$

After substitution of previously found A_1, ψ_2 in this expression and change (9), the stationary values of initial variables X_0^s, Y_0^s are obtained. In particular, they have property $X_0^s + Y_0^s = N$. Thus, under $t \to \infty$ all members of the society are distributed between the rival parties.

Terms of the First Order Asymptotics

Let the substitution of asymptotic expansions (11) into system (10) be discussed on. Cauchy problem for the first approximation functions is obtained by equalizing the coefficient under the first degree of small parameter β. Just like in the case with the zero approximation, the general strategy consists in finding the recurrent relation between the values of functions of the first approximation at time points kT and $kT + T$.

Within span $\left[kT; kT + t_{sw}\right)$, the equations for functions $u_1\left(t\right), v_1\left(t\right)$ are given by

$$\begin{aligned} &\frac{du_1}{dt} = u_0\left(kT\right)\left(N - \left(\alpha_1^* + \alpha_2\right)v_0\left(kT\right)\right)e^{-\left(\alpha_1^*+\alpha_2\right)\left(t-kT\right)} \\ &\frac{dv_1}{dt} = -\left(\alpha_1^* + \alpha_2\right)v_1 + \frac{N\left(N - \left(\alpha_1^* + \alpha_2\right)v_0\left(kT\right)\right)}{\alpha_1^* + \alpha_2}e^{-\left(\alpha_1^*+\alpha_2\right)\left(t-kT\right)} \\ &+\left(v_0\left(kT\right) - \frac{N}{\alpha_1^* + \alpha_2}\right)\left(N - \left(\alpha_1^* + \alpha_2\right)v_0\left(kT\right)\right) \end{aligned} \tag{24}$$

The solution of system (24) is written as

$$\begin{pmatrix} u_1\left(t\right) \\ v_1\left(t\right) \end{pmatrix} = P\left(t - kT\right)\begin{pmatrix} u_1\left(kT\right) \\ v_1\left(kT\right) \end{pmatrix} + D_1\left(t - kT\right),\ kT < t < kT + t_{sw}$$

where vector $D_1\left(t\right)$ is explicitly expressed through the zeroth approximation functions found above. Then, it is obtained at the end of this interval:

$$\begin{pmatrix} u_1\left(kT + t_{sw}\right) \\ v_1\left(kT + t_{sw}\right) \end{pmatrix} = P\left(t_{sw}\right)\begin{pmatrix} u_1\left(kT\right) \\ v_1\left(kT\right) \end{pmatrix} + D_1\left(t_{sw}\right) \tag{25}$$

The system of equations for functions $u_1(t), v_1(t)$ within interval $[kT + t_{sw}; kT + T)$ is given by

$$\frac{du_1}{dt} = h\alpha_2 v_1 + u_0\left(N - \left(\alpha_1^* + \alpha_2\right)v_0\right)$$
$$\frac{dv_1}{dt} = -\left(\alpha_1^* + h + \alpha_2\right)v_1 + v_0\left(N - \left(\alpha_1^* + \alpha_2\right)v_0\right)$$

Its solution is written as

$$\begin{pmatrix} u_1(t) \\ v_1(t) \end{pmatrix} =$$
$$Q\left(t - kT - t_{sw}\right)\begin{pmatrix} u_1\left(kT + t_{sw}\right) \\ v_1\left(kT + t_{sw}\right) \end{pmatrix} + G_1\left(t - kT - t_{sw}\right), kT + t_{sw} \le t \le kT + T$$

where vector $G_1(t)$ is explicitly expressed through the zeroth approximation functions found above. Then, it is obtained at the end of this interval:

$$\begin{pmatrix} u_1(kT + T) \\ v_1(kT + T) \end{pmatrix} = Q\left(T - t_{sw}\right)\begin{pmatrix} u_1\left(kT + t_{sw}\right) \\ v_1\left(kT + t_{sw}\right) \end{pmatrix} + G_1\left(T - t_{sw}\right) \tag{26}$$

The sought recurrent relation is obtained from (25) and (26):

$$\begin{pmatrix} u_1(kT + T) \\ v_1(kT + T) \end{pmatrix} =$$
$$Q\left(T - t_{sw}\right)P\left(t_{sw}\right)\begin{pmatrix} u_1(kT) \\ v_1(kT) \end{pmatrix} + Q\left(T - t_{sw}\right)D_1\left(t_{sw}\right) + G_1\left(T - t_{sw}\right)$$

Just like in the zeroth approximation, the recurrent relation has been obtained. Thus, the values of functions $u_1(t), v_1(t)$ at each time point $t > 0$ can be found.

Numerical Example

This section discusses the numerical example of solving system (4). The objective is to demonstrate the qualitative properties of the solution as well as to evaluate the quality of the asymptotics constructed. Let it be assumed that

$\alpha_1^* = 0,06;\ h = 0,11;\ \alpha_2 = 0,1;\ t_{sw} = 1,5;\ T = 3;\ \beta_1 = \beta_2 = 0,002;\ N = 100$.

and in particular, the information propagation mechanisms are comparable under these parameter values.

In the work of Petrov and Proncheva (2015) it has been obtained that for a certain individual who is not yet aware of the information of none of the parties, probability p_α of receiving the information from the mass media for unit time is related to parameter α by relation $\alpha = \ln\left(1 - p_\alpha\right)^{-1}$. Thus, $\alpha_2 = 0,1$ corresponds to probability of $p_2 = 0,095$. For the mass media of the first party: values $\alpha_1^* = 0,06$ and $\alpha_1^* + h = 0,17$ corresponds to probabilities of 0,058 and 0,156.

Similarly, for an unaware individual, probability p_β of receiving the information from another individual for unit time is related to parameter β by relation $\beta = \ln\left(1 - p_\beta\right)^{-1}$. Value $\beta_1 = 0,002$ corresponds to probability of $p_\beta = 0,001998$. Therefore, if, for example, at some given time point the information of the first party is propagated by 20 individuals while the information of the second type – 50 individuals (exactly one half of the group considered), then for each of 30 individuals who are not covered yet, the probability to receive the information of the first party through interpersonal communications equals $1 - \left(1 - p_2\right)^{20} = 0,039$, and the information of the second party: $1 - \left(1 - p_2\right)^{50} = 0,095$.

Notably, parameter β is a small one in its conceptual meaning, as in the actual society, an individual has the opportunity to receive the information through interpersonal communications from a small quantity of individuals only, while model (4) implies the homogeneity of the society, thus performing the implicit averaging on all individuals.

Figure 2 gives an obtained numerically graph of Cauchy problem solution (4) for the given parameter values. On the whole, the progress of the battle can be described as follows: under $0 < t < 1,5$ the lag of the first party is formed and increases, under $1,5 < t < 3$ it is reduced almost to zero, under $3 < t < 4,5$ it increases again, after which the first party not only bridges the gap but also steps up. The numbers of party followers achieved under great time values are as follows: $X^s = 50,1$, $Y^s = 49,9$.

Experiments with other values of β show that with this parameter increased, the oscillations of curve $X\left(t\right)$ around its main trend become less abrupt. The conceptual reason of that consists in the fact that β increasing results in a greater quantity of individuals receiving the information through interpersonal communications and a smaller one – from the mass media; thus, the oscillations of the mass media broadcasting intensity play a less important part.

In Figure 4, the constructed asymptotics is compared to the numerically obtained solution. The curves are evidently quite close to each other, with the asymptotics (even the zeroth-order one) describing the qualitative properties of the solution correctly.

Figure 3. Solid line: $X(t)$; dotted line: $Y(t)$

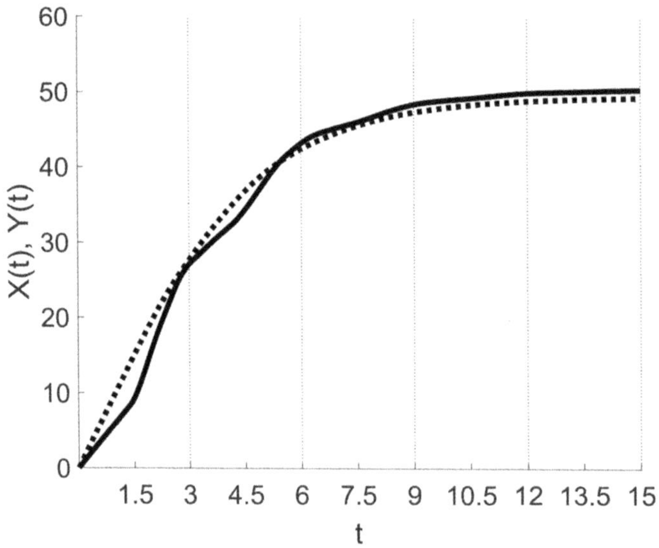

Figure 4. Solid bold line – numerically obtained solution, solid thin line – zeroth-order asymptotics, dotted line – first-order asymptotics

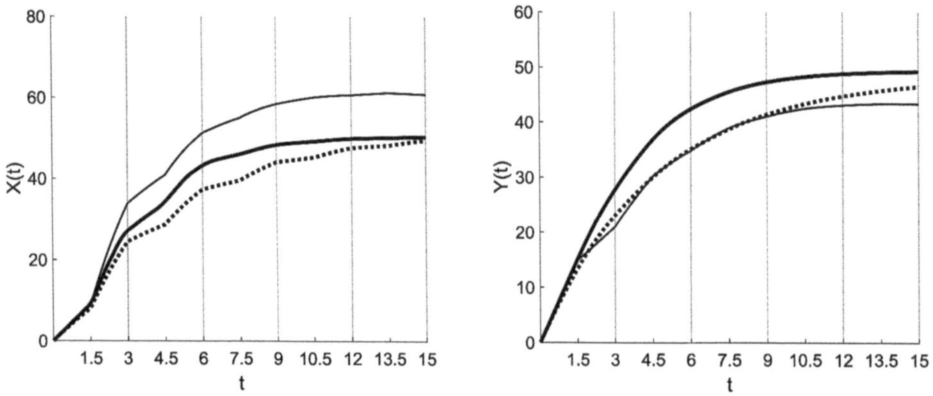

THE MODEL OF INDIVIDUALS CHOOSING STANDPOINTS IN THE INFORMATION BATTLE

The model of individuals choosing their standpoints in the information battle developed in the work of Petrov et al. (2016) that focuses on the process of an individual adopting one of two viewpoints offered to the individual can be referred to another type of models. The model has been developed on the basis of Rashevskiy neurological pattern (Rashevskiy, 1933).

In this model, each individual is characterized by scalar value φ describing the individual's internal inclination to support this or that party of the battle. If $\varphi > 0$, then without the external incentives, the individual supports party X, if $\varphi < 0$ - party Y. Thus, value φ can be interpreted as a value reflecting the fundamental (and deemed unchangeable for the time span considered) political beliefs of the individual.

Each individual is characterized by his own value of variable φ, and N_0 individuals making up the society are distributed at density $N(\varphi)$ in such a way, that $\int_{\varphi_1}^{\varphi_2} N(\varphi)\,d\varphi$ has the meaning of the quantity of individuals for which the values of variable φ lie within the range from φ_1 to φ_2. With regard to this, the evident equality $\int_{-\infty}^{\infty} N(\varphi)\,d\varphi = N_0$ is true. At each time point each individual is a spreader of this or that party. With the course of time, the individual can change his standpoint under the effect of the mass media and contacts with other individuals.

Intensities $b_1(t)$ and $b_2(t)$ of propaganda, respectively, for the first and second parties are given exogenously. They may be determined by the quantity of information messages in the mass media per unit time. These values are the same for all individuals due to the general coverage of the society by the mass media. The model is given by the equation for function $\psi(t)$ through which the numbers of spreaders of the first and second parties are expressed:

$$X(t) = \int_{-\psi(t)}^{\infty} N(\varphi)\,d\varphi, \quad Y(t) = \int_{-\infty}^{-\psi(t)} N(\varphi)\,d\varphi \tag{27}$$

This equation is written as

$$\frac{d\psi}{dt}\left[1-2A\alpha DN\left(-\psi\right)\right]=A\alpha\left[C\left(2\int_{-\psi(t)}^{\infty}N\left(\varphi\right)d\varphi-N_0\right)+b_1-b_2\right]-a\psi \qquad (28)$$

Here positive parameters A, α, C, D characterize the psychological features of the individuals and are considered in detail in the work of Petrov et al. (2006).

Initial condition $\psi\left(0\right)$ that is essential for determining $\psi\left(t\right)$ unambiguously is found from the distribution of spreaders at time point $t=0$ and is given by:

$$X\left(0\right)=\int_{-\psi(0)}^{\infty}N\left(\varphi\right)d\varphi \qquad (29)$$

or, which is the same, by $Y\left(0\right)=\int_{-\infty}^{-\psi(0)}N\left(\varphi\right)d\varphi$.

So, function $\psi\left(t\right)$ is found as the solution of initial problem (28),(29) for the integral-differential equation (11). In order to obtain the conceptual conclusions about the system under study, after finding function $\psi\left(t\right)$, numbers $X\left(t\right)$ and $Y\left(t\right)$ of individuals can also be obtained using (27) that show responses R_1 and R_2, respectively (and, therefore, they also show the shares of such individuals $X\left(t\right)/\left[X\left(t\right)+Y\left(t\right)\right]$, $Y\left(t\right)/\left[X\left(t\right)+Y\left(t\right)\right]$), as well as other conceptual characteristics of the process.

For the initial analysis of model, the simplest case is considered – when the imitative mechanism only works toward the current quantity of individuals (but no to the speed of change thereof) and there is no propaganda. Thus,

$$D=0,\ b_1\left(t\right)=b_2\left(t\right)=0 \qquad (30)$$

In which case, equation (28) is written as

$$\frac{d\psi}{dt}=A\alpha C\left(2\int_{-\psi(t)}^{\infty}N\left(\varphi\right)d\varphi-N_0\right)-a\psi \qquad (31)$$

The corresponding stationary equation

$$A\alpha C\left(2\int_{-\psi(t)}^{\infty} N\left(\varphi\right)d\varphi - N_0\right) - a\psi = 0 \tag{32}$$

represents a traditional imitative behavior model (Rashevsky, 1933). It is known that if function $N\left(\varphi\right)$ is given by

$$N\left(\varphi\right) = \frac{1}{\sqrt{2\pi}}\exp\left[-\frac{\varphi^2}{2}\right], \tag{33}$$

then the quantity and nature of stationary solutions of equation (31) are determined by the value of systemic parameter $\gamma = a / \left(A\alpha C\right)$. Particularly, if $\gamma > \gamma_{cr} = 2 / \sqrt{2\pi} \approx 0,7979$, then there is one stationary solution $\psi = 0$ which is asymptotically stable. Meanwhile, if $\gamma < \gamma_{cr}$, then equation (31) has three stationary solutions $\psi_i, i = 1,2,3$, with $\psi_1 < \psi_2 = 0 < \psi_3$. Solutions ψ_1, ψ_3 are asymptotically stable and solution $\psi_2 = 0$ is unstable.

In order to study the process of transition from the initial condition to the relevant stationary situation, let a series of numerical experiments with the model be conducted. For this, let it be changed $t' = A\alpha Ct$. The following equation is obtained from (31):

$$\frac{d\psi}{dt'} = 2\int_{-\psi}^{\infty} N\left(\varphi\right)d\varphi - N_0 - \gamma\psi \tag{34}$$

Let the individuals number measuring unit be selected so as $N_0 = 1$. Without losing generality, making the input model data more precise for the numerical experiment, let the initial condition $\psi\left(0\right) = 1$ and function $N\left(\varphi\right)$ of type (33) be adopted. According to formula (29), this initial condition means that

$$X\left(0\right) = \int_{-1}^{\infty} N\left(\varphi\right)d\varphi = \frac{1}{2} + \int_{-1}^{0} N\left(\varphi\right)d\varphi > \frac{1}{2} \tag{35}$$

$Y\left(0\right) = 1 - X\left(0\right) < \frac{1}{2}$, i.e. at time point $t = 0$ over half of the individuals are spreaders of the first party.

The solution of equation (34) is a monotonous function; it goes down to zero under quite large values γ in such a way that $\lim_{t\to\infty} \psi\left(t\right) = 0$ (which corresponds to the case of asymptotic stability of stationary solution $\psi = 0$), and under small ones – it approaches the positive stationary values depending on γ (which corresponds to the case of asymptotic stability of non-zero stationary solutions ψ_1 and ψ_3).

From the conceptual standpoint, this means that it depends on the value of systemic parameter γ what proportion between the followers of parties at battle will be established with the course of time. For example, let it be $\gamma > \gamma_{cr}$. Then $\lim_{t\to\infty} \psi\left(t\right) = 0$ and, according to formula (27), the following is obtained for quantity $X\left(t\right)$ of individuals who express response R_1:

$$\lim_{t\to\infty} X\left(t\right) = \lim_{t\to\infty} \int_{-\psi(t)}^{\infty} N\left(\varphi\right) d\varphi = \int_{0}^{\infty} N\left(\varphi\right) d\varphi = \frac{1}{2}$$

Similarly, it is obtained that $\lim_{t\to\infty} Y\left(t\right) = 1/2$. So, if value γ is rather high, there will be equality established with the course of time – the parties will have equal quantities of spreaders despite one party prevailing initially. Therefore, the imitation effect is in this case less important that the own (internal) preferences of the individuals the distribution of which is described by function $N\left(\varphi\right)$.

However, if $\gamma < \gamma_{cr}$, then under the said initial conditions it is obtained $\lim_{t\to\infty} \psi\left(t\right) = \psi_3 > 0$, and the following is obtained from (27):

$$\lim_{t\to\infty} X\left(t\right) = \lim_{t\to\infty} \int_{-\psi(t)}^{\infty} N\left(\varphi\right) d\varphi = \int_{-\psi_3}^{\infty} N\left(\varphi\right) d\varphi = \frac{1}{2} + \int_{-\psi_3}^{0} N\left(\varphi\right) d\varphi > \frac{1}{2}$$

Thus, if value γ is small enough (and at the initial time point the spreaders of party X were the majority), then with the course of time there will be a stationary situation established in which over the half of the group members will be spreaders of party X.

If the initial value of function $\psi\left(t\right)$ is negative: $\psi\left(0\right) < 0$ (which corresponds to relation $X\left(0\right) < Y\left(0\right)$)), then with the course of time there will be a stationary situation established in which over the half of the group members will be spreaders of party Y, i.e. $\lim_{t\to\infty} \psi\left(t\right) = \psi_1 < 0$ and $\lim_{t\to\infty} X\left(t\right) < 1/2$.

Figure 5. Function graph $N(\varphi)$

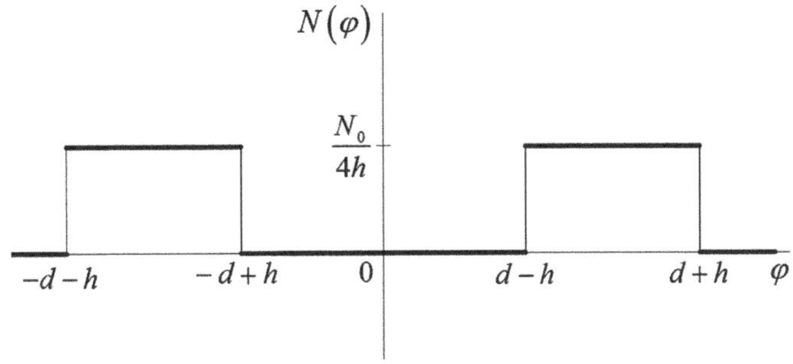

THE INFLUENCE OF POLARIZATION OF THE SOCIETY ON THE INFORMATION BATTLE OUTCOME

This section deals with the distribution written as follows:

$$N(\varphi) = \begin{cases} 0, & \varphi < -d - h \\ \frac{N_0}{4h}, & -d - h \le \varphi \le -d + h \\ 0, & -d + h < \varphi < d - h \\ \frac{N_0}{4h}, & d - h \le \varphi \le d + h \\ 0, & \varphi > d + h \end{cases}. \tag{36}$$

Here $d > h > 0$. The conceptual meaning of this type of distribution is as follows. The society is assumed to consist of two groups, each of them having the inclination to support "their" source of information. Parameter d characterizes the extent of polarization of the society, i.e. how radical the moods of each group are. Parameter h characterizes the extent of inconsistency of each group, i.e. how similarly the members of the group are inclined to support the selected information source, without other factors.

Figure 5 shows the graph of function $N(\varphi)$.

Let it be denoted as

$$f(\psi) = A\alpha\left[C\left(2\int_{-\psi(t)}^{\infty} N(\varphi)\,d\varphi - N_0\right) + b_1 - b_2\right].$$

For finding the stationary solutions of equation (1), all possible ways of function graphs intersection have to be considered:

$$f(\psi)=\begin{cases} A\alpha\left[-N_0C+b_1-b_2\right], & \psi\le -d-h \\ A\alpha\left[\dfrac{CN_0}{2h}\left(\psi+\left(d-h\right)\right)+b_1-b_2\right], & -d-h<\psi\le -d+h \\ A\alpha\left(b_1-b_2\right), & -d+h<\psi\le d-h \\ A\alpha\left[\dfrac{N_0C}{2h}\left(\psi+\left(h-d\right)\right)+b_1-b_2\right], & d-h<\psi\le d+h \\ A\alpha\left[CN_0+b_1-b_2\right], & \psi>d+h \end{cases} \tag{37}$$

and $a\psi$.

Let designations $P=\dfrac{A\alpha\left(b_1-b_2\right)}{a}$, $Q=\dfrac{A\alpha CN_0}{a}$ be introduced. The mutual configuration of straight line $a\psi$ and polygonal line $f\left(\psi\right)$ depends on the relation between four numbers: $P+h$, $Q-P-h$, $Q+P-h$ and d. The relations between the first three numbers can be ordered according to the value of parameter h.

For each of the listed cases, various sub-cases are considered in the order corresponding to higher polarization of the society d. With regard to this, it is borne in mind (see comment after formula (5)) that $d>h$.

Depending on the parameter values, from 1 to 5 equilibrium positions are possible for which the following designations are introduced:

$$\psi^1=P+Q>0,$$

$$\psi^2=\frac{Q\left(-d-h\right)+2hP}{2h-Q}>0,$$

$$\psi^3=P>0,$$

$$\psi^4=\frac{Q\left(d-h\right)+2hP}{2h-Q}<0,$$

$\psi^5 = -Q + P < 0$.

Under $t \to \infty$ equilibrium position ψ^1 can only be achieved with such parameter values under which $\psi^1 > d + h$. Then, if under the relevant initial conditions the equilibrium position is achieved, then

$$\lim_{t\to\infty} X(t) = \int_{-\psi^1}^{\infty} N(\varphi)\,d\varphi = \int_{-\infty}^{\infty} N(\varphi)\,d\varphi = N_0,\ \lim_{t\to\infty} Y(t) = \int_{-\infty}^{-\psi^1} N(\varphi)\,d\varphi = 0,$$

which means the total victory of the first source (it is supported by all individuals). Achievement of ψ^2 is only possible with such parameter values under which $d - h < \psi^2 < d + h$, this is why

$$\frac{N_0}{2} = \int_{-d+h}^{\infty} N(\varphi)\,d\varphi < \lim_{t\to\infty} X(t) = \int_{-\psi^2}^{\infty} N(\varphi)\,d\varphi < \int_{-d-h}^{\infty} N(\varphi)\,d\varphi = N_0 ,$$

$$0 < \lim_{t\to\infty} Y(t) < \frac{N_0}{2},$$

which means a partial victory of the first source (the number of its supporters is larger than that of the second source, but the first source is supported by a part of the individuals only). ψ^3 can be achieved with such parameter values under which $0 < \psi^3 < d - h$, hence

$$\lim_{t\to\infty} X(t) = \int_{-\psi^3}^{\infty} N(\varphi)\,d\varphi = \int_{0}^{\infty} N(\varphi)\,d\varphi = \frac{N_0}{2},\ \lim_{t\to\infty} Y(t) = \frac{N_0}{2},$$

which means a draw. ψ^5 can be achieved with such parameters under which $\psi^5 < -d - h$, with

$$\lim_{t\to\infty} Y(t) = \int_{-\infty}^{-\psi^5} N(\varphi)\,d\varphi = \int_{-\infty}^{+\infty} N(\varphi)\,d\varphi = N_0, \lim_{t\to\infty} X(t) = 0,$$

which means the total victory of the second source. In case ψ^2 and ψ^3 coincide, it is the first source that is the outright winner.

In Figure 6, the results of analysis in case inequality $h < Q / 2 - P$ is fulfilled are given. For each value of polarization *d* and initial condition $\psi(0)$, the outcome of the battle is given: the total victory of this or that party or a draw. If polarization is small enough (i.e. $h < d < Q - P - h$), then they have equal chances to win, although party X has an advantage in the intensity of propaganda. Meanwhile, draw is also possible. Hereinafter the "chances to win" are understood in terms of initial distribution of individuals between parties, as it is shown in the figure. As polarization grows within these limits, chances of each party to win decrease while chances for a draw go up. As soon as polarization exceeds the value of $Q - P - h$, party Y loses any chances to win, i.e. the only possible options are either the victory of party X or a draw. With regard to this, as polarization increases further, the chances of party X to win are reduced. Finally, under $d > Q + P - h$, it is only a draw that is possible.

Condition $h < Q / 2 - P$ and Figure 6 associated with it do not exhaust all possible cases as for problem (27). Figure 7 shows graphs for two other ones (of six cases). Meanwhile, the situation given in Figure 7b is degenerate in a certain sense: a party having less intensive propaganda cannot win, regardless of the initial conditions.

The graphs presented show that in all cases if polarization of the society is quite high, an advantage in propaganda becomes insufficient, i.e. a party having a

Figure 6. Dependence of battle outcome on the initial condition and polarization extent when condition (6) is met.

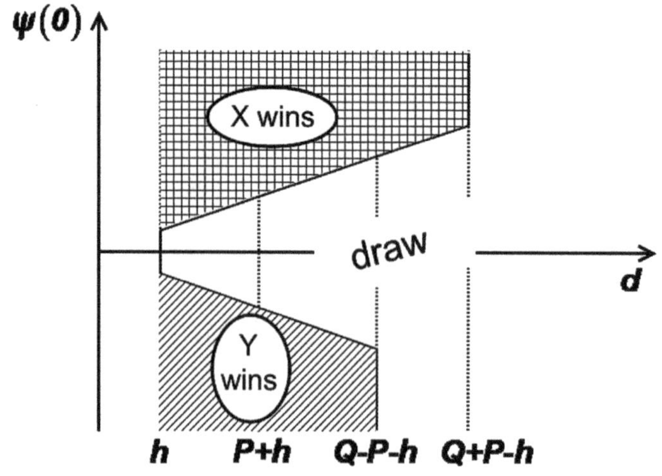

Figure 7. Dependence of the information battle outcome on the initial condition and polarization extent; (a) case $0.5Q - P < h < 0.5(Q - P)$, *(b): case* $0.5Q < h < 0.5(Q + P)$

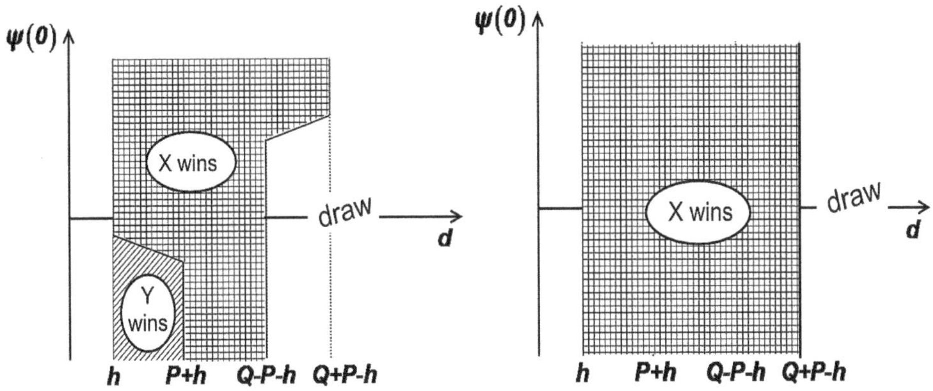

stronger propaganda cannot win, no matter what the initial condition may be. Another conclusion is that a moderate polarization is as a rule more favorable for this party (and in all cases it is not less favorable) than a low polarization.

THE PROCESS OF SLOW POLARIZATION OF THE SOCIETY

In the previous section, polarization of the society was assumed to be a constant. Now the case is considered when it increases linearly with the course of time. Such processes are associated with fundamental change in the structure of the society, so they are quite slow (as compared to the processes of information battle over certain issues). Due to this, let the polarization increase speed be assumed as a small one:

$$d(t) = d_0 + \varepsilon t, \tag{38}$$

where $\varepsilon << 1$. Numerical experiments show that the solutions of problem (27) have an internal transition layer (Figure 8). Such solutions are called contrast structures (Vasilieva et al., 1994, 1995). The objective of this section is to construct asymptotics of solutions of this type. With regard to this, condition (6) will still be assumed to be fulfilled.

By changing variable $\theta = \varepsilon t$ in (27), it is obtained:

Figure 8. On the left: numerical solution of equation (27) with the following parameters: $a = 200$, $\alpha = 1$, $A = 4$, $N_0 = 100$, $C = 0.065$, $b_1 = 3$, $b_2 = 1$, $h = 0.02$, $d = 0.05$, $\varepsilon = 1$. *On the right: the number of supporters of party* X *(dotted line) and that of party* Y *(solid line) with the same parameters*

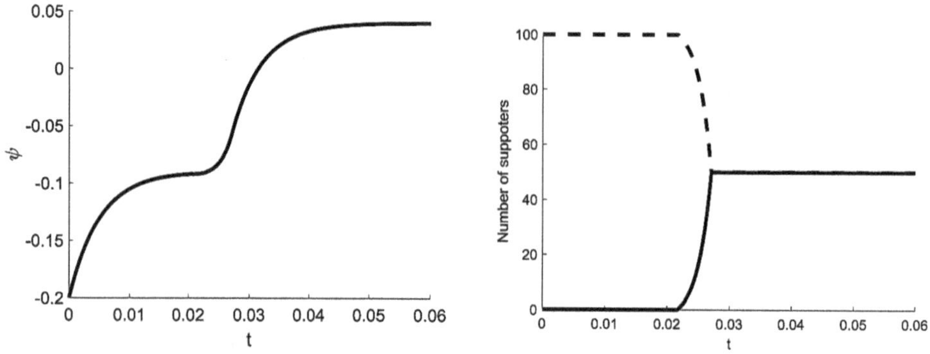

$$\varepsilon \frac{d\psi}{d\theta} = f\left(\psi, \theta\right) - a\psi, \tag{39}$$

$$X\left(0\right) = \int_{-\psi(0)}^{\infty} N\left(\varphi\right) d\varphi . \tag{40}$$

Here

$$f\left(\psi,\theta\right) = \begin{cases} A\alpha\left[-CN_0 + b_1 - b_2\right], & \psi \le -d_0 - \theta - h \\ A\alpha\left[\dfrac{CN_0}{2h}\left(\psi + \left(d_0 + \theta - h\right)\right) + b_1 - b_2\right], & -d_0 - \theta - h < \psi \le -d_0 - \theta + h \\ A\alpha\left(b_1 - b_2\right), & -d_0 - \theta + h < \psi \le d_0 + \theta - h \\ A\alpha\left[\dfrac{CN_0}{2h}\left(\psi + \left(h - d_0 - \theta\right)\right) + b_1 - b_2\right], & d_0 + \theta - h < \psi \le d_0 + \theta + h \\ A\alpha\left[CN_0 + b_1 - b_2\right], & \psi > d_0 + \theta + h \end{cases} . \tag{41}$$

Concerning the initial condition, let it be assumed for certainty that it is the most conceptual case that takes place in which the society passes through all conditions viewed in section 3 and the solution of problem (39), (40) has the greatest quantity of transition layers possible. In particular, let it be assumed

$$h < d_0 < P + h\,,\ \psi(0) < -Q + P\,. \tag{42}$$

According to the boundary functions method (Vasil'eva et al, 1995), asymptotics of the solution of problem (39)-(41) is written as

$$\psi(\theta,\varepsilon) = \\ \psi_0(\theta) + \Pi_0\left(\frac{\theta}{\varepsilon}\right) + \Omega_0\left(\frac{\theta-\theta_0}{\varepsilon}\right) + \varepsilon\left[\psi_1(\theta) + \Pi_1\left(\frac{\theta}{\varepsilon}\right) + \Omega_1\left(\frac{\theta-\theta_0}{\varepsilon}\right)\right] + \ldots \tag{43}$$

Here θ_0 is the contrast structure localization point (relevant value of $t_0 = \theta_0 / \varepsilon$ is marked in Figure 8), $\Pi_i(\theta / \varepsilon)$ and $\Omega_i\left((\theta - \theta_0)/\varepsilon\right)$ are functions describing the boundary layer in the neighborhood of point $\theta = 0$ and the transition layer in the neighborhood of point $\theta = \theta_0$, respectively; and $\psi_i(\theta)$ are regular members of asymptotics ($i = 0,1,2,\ldots$).

Let only the zeroth-order asymptotics be constructed, after which the obtained result be compared to the solution obtained by numerical methods.

The degenerate equation corresponding to (39) is given by

$$f(\psi,\theta) - a\psi = 0\,. \tag{44}$$

Under small enough θ, the equation has three roots: ψ^1, ψ^4, ψ^5 – with ψ^1 and ψ^5 being stable ones and ψ^4 – the unstable one. When conditions (42) are met, the initial condition is found in the area of influence of root ψ^5. Hence, $\psi_0(\theta) = \psi^5$ under $\theta < \theta_0$.

Value θ_0 is determined by root ψ^5 ceasing to exist. This happens under $d(t) = Q - P - h$. Therefore, the following is obtained for θ_0:

$$\theta_0 = Q - P - h - d_0\,. \tag{45}$$

Under $\theta > \theta_0$ and quite small difference $\theta - \theta_0$, degenerate equation (44) has three roots: ψ^1, ψ^2 and $\psi^3 = P$ – with ψ^1 and ψ^3 being stable ones and ψ^2 – the unstable one. Under $\theta \to \theta_0 - 0$ the solution of problem (39)-(41) is found in the neighborhood of root ψ^5, i.e. under $\theta \to \theta_0 + 0$ it falls within the area of influence of root ψ^3. Meanwhile, due to root ψ^3 existing and being stable under all $\theta > \theta_0$, then $\psi_0(\theta) = \psi^3$ under all $\theta > \theta_0$.

So,

$$\psi_0(\theta) = \begin{cases} -Q + P, & 0 \le \theta \le \theta_0 \\ P, & \theta > \theta_0 \end{cases}, \tag{46}$$

where θ_0 is determined by expression (45). Therefore, the regular part of the zeroth approximation asymptotics has been constructed.

Now, let boundary function $\Pi_0(\theta / \varepsilon)$ be constructed. Bearing in mind that $\theta / \varepsilon = t$, the equation for $\Pi_0(t)$ is obtained from (39)-(41) with (46) considered:

$$d\Pi_0 / dt = \Phi(\Pi_0) = \\ = \begin{cases} -a\Pi_0, & \Pi_0 \le Q - P - d_0 - h \\ a\left[\frac{Q}{2h}\left(-Q + P + \Pi_0 + (d_0 - h)\right) + Q - \Pi_0\right], & -d_0 - h + Q - P < \Pi_0 \le -d_0 + h + Q - P \\ -a(-Q + \Pi_0), & -d_0 + h + Q - P < \Pi_0 \le d_0 - h + Q - P \\ a\left[\frac{Q}{2h}\left(-Q + P + \Pi_0 + (h - d_0)\right) + Q - \Pi_0\right], & d_0 - h + Q - P < \Pi_0 \le d_0 + h + Q - P \\ a(2Q - \Pi_0), & \Pi_0 > d_0 + h + Q - P \end{cases}. \tag{47}$$

The initial condition for function $\Pi_0(t)$ is determined from the condition as follows:

$$\psi_0(0) + \Pi_0(0) = \psi(0). \tag{48}$$

Hence it is obtained:

$$\Pi_0(0) = \psi(0) + Q - P. \tag{49}$$

It follows from condition (48) that $\Pi_0(0) < 0$. In order to determine the formula for function $\Phi(\Pi_0)$, it should be pointed out that

$$\Pi_0(0) - Q + P < -Q + P < -P - 2h < -d_0 - h$$

Therefore, in a certain right semi-neighborhood of point $\theta = 0$ equation $\Phi(\Pi_0) = -a\Pi_0$ takes place, and so equation (47) is given by

$$\frac{d\Pi_0}{dt} = -a\Pi_0 . \tag{50}$$

By solving it with initial condition (49), the following is obtained:

$$\Pi_0\left(t\right) = \left(\psi^0 + Q - P\right)e^{-at} . \tag{51}$$

This function takes on values within half-interval $\left[\psi^0 + Q - P; 0\right)$. Thus, for all values $t > 0$ there is $\Pi_0\left(t\right) - Q + P \le -d_0 - h$, and hence, due to (47), it is obtained that $\Phi\left(\Pi_0\right) = -a\Pi_0$. Therefore, equation (50) and representation (51) following from it hold true under all $t > 0$.

Now, let internal transition layer function $\Omega_0\left(\left(\theta - \theta_0\right)/\varepsilon\right)$ be constructed. Let variable $\tau = \left(\theta - \theta_0\right)/\varepsilon$ be introduced; moreover, an additional expansion in the neighborhood of point $\theta_0 : \theta = \theta_0 + \varepsilon\tau$ will be performed. From (39)-(41), equation for $\Omega_0\left(\tau\right)$ is obtained as follows:

$$d\Omega_0 / d\tau = \Psi\left(\tau\right) =$$
$$= \begin{cases} a\left(-Q - \Omega_0\right), & \Omega_0 \le -Q \\ a\left[\dfrac{Q}{2h}\left(\Omega_0 + Q - 2h + \varepsilon\tau\right) - \Omega_0\right], & -Q < \Omega_0 \le -Q + 2h \\ -a\Omega_0, & -Q + 2h < \Omega_0 \le Q - 2P - 2h \\ a\left[\dfrac{Q}{2h}\left(2P + 2h + \Omega_0 - Q\right) - \Omega_0\right], & Q - 2P - 2h < \Omega_0 \le Q - 2P \\ a\left(Q - \Omega_0\right), & \Omega_0 > Q - 2P \end{cases} \tag{52}$$

The initial condition for function $\Omega_0\left(t\right)$ can be determined from condition

$$\psi_0\left(\theta_0\right) + \Omega_0\left(0\right) = \psi\left(\theta_0\right).$$

Hence it is obtained that

$$\Omega_0\left(0\right) = -Q . \tag{53}$$

Therefore, equation (52) is written as follows in a certain right semi-neighborhood of point $\theta = \theta_0$:

$$\frac{d\Omega_0}{d\tau} = a\left[\frac{Q}{2h}\left(\Omega_0 + Q - 2h + \varepsilon\tau\right) - \Omega_0\right].$$

By solving this equation with initial condition (53), it is found that

$$\Omega_0\left(\tau\right) = \frac{2Q\varepsilon h}{a\left(Q-2h\right)^2} e^{\frac{a}{2h}(Q-2h)\tau} - \frac{Q\varepsilon}{Q-2h}\tau - \frac{2Q\varepsilon h}{a\left(Q-2h\right)^2} - Q.$$

The solution will be given by this up to time point τ_1 which is found from condition:

$$\frac{2Q\varepsilon h}{a\left(Q-2h\right)^2} e^{\frac{a}{2h}(Q-2h)\tau} - \frac{Q\varepsilon}{Q-2h}\tau - \frac{2Q\varepsilon h}{a\left(Q-2h\right)^2} = 2h.$$

Under $\tau > \tau_1$, equation (52) will be written as

$$\frac{d\Omega_0}{d\tau} = -a\Omega_0.$$

By solving this equation with the initial condition

$$\Omega_0\left(\tau_1\right) = -Q + 2h,$$

the result is obtained:

$$\Omega_0\left(\tau\right) = \left(-Q + 2h\right)e^{a\tau_1}e^{-a\tau}. \tag{54}$$

As $\left(-Q+2h\right)e^{a\tau_1}e^{-a\tau} < \left(-Q+2h\right)e^{a\tau_1} < -2Pe^{a\tau_1} < 0 < Q - 2P - 2h$, representation (54) is true under all $\tau > \tau_1$.

So, the zeroth approximation of function $\psi\left(\theta\right)$ is given by

$$\psi(t) = \begin{cases} -Q + P + \left(\psi(0) + Q - P\right)e^{-at} + o(\varepsilon), & t \leq \dfrac{\theta_0}{\varepsilon}, \\ \left(\psi(0) + Q - P\right)e^{-at} + \dfrac{2Q\varepsilon h}{a\left(Q-2h\right)^2} e^{\frac{a}{2h}\left(Q-2h\right)\left(t-\theta_0/\varepsilon\right)} - & \\ -\dfrac{Q}{Q-2h}\left(\varepsilon t - \theta_0\right) - \dfrac{2Q\varepsilon h}{a\left(Q-2h\right)^2} - Q + P + o(\varepsilon), & \dfrac{\theta_0}{\varepsilon} < t \leq \tau_1 + \dfrac{\theta_0}{\varepsilon}, \\ P + \left(\psi^0 + Q - P\right)e^{-at} + & \\ +\left(-Q + 2h\right)e^{a\tau_1}e^{-a\left(t-\theta_0/\varepsilon\right)} + o(\varepsilon), & \theta > \varepsilon\tau_1 + \dfrac{\theta_0}{\varepsilon}. \end{cases} \tag{55}$$

This asymptotics yields a high precision of approximation to the solution even with values of small parameter ε that are close to unity. Figure 9 shows a comparison of zeroth approximation (55) and the numerically obtained solution.

Figure 9. Comparison of the solution obtained by numerical methods and the zeroth approximation under the following parameters: $a = 200$, $\alpha = 1$, $A = 4$, $N_0 = 100$, $C = 0.065$, $b_1 = 3$, $b_2 = 1$, $h = 0.02$, $d = 0.05$, $\varepsilon = 1$, $\theta_0 = 0.2$, $\tau_1 = 0.0062$. *Here the solid line stands for solution obtained by numerical methods and the dotted line – for the zeroth approximation.*

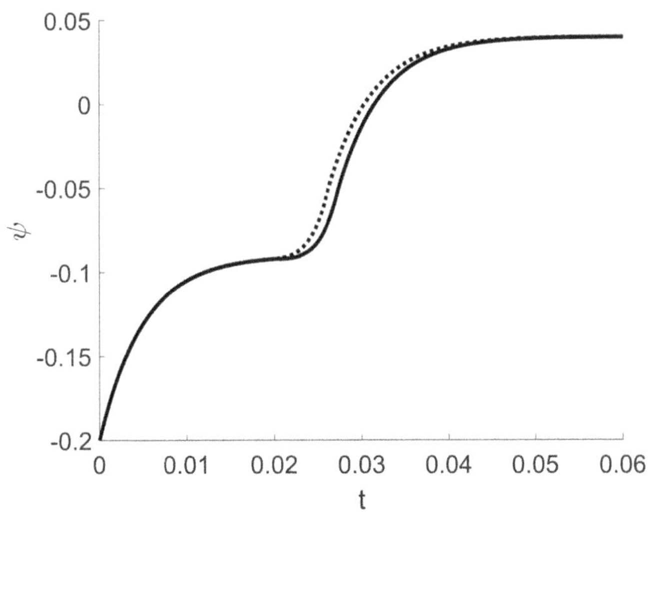

CONCLUSION

In this chapter we consider a set of models of information attack and information warfare in a society, taking into account both information dissemination in the interpersonal communication and propaganda through the media. The process of confrontation is that two sources spread information in a society so that each individual can become a spreader of either one or the other (depending on the kind of information she received first); also there are two opposing media in the system and the information of both sources can be spread through rumors. An spreader disseminates information of her "party", and she is impervious to the opposite information course. The winner of the confrontation is the source which has a larger number of spreaders to a particular point t (for example, to t tending to infinity).

The methods of mathematical formalization of such factors of the spread of information as information forgetting by individuals, non-coverage of a society by the media and the two-step adoption and forgetting of the information by individuals are developed.

We created mathematical model of information warfare in a society by adding three factors listed above to the basic model. Our model has the form of the Cauchy problem for nonlinear system of eight ordinary differential equations. The series of numerical experiments was carried out, the meager attention was paid to the case when one source has more intensive media propaganda, but the information from the other source more rapidly spreads through interpersonal communication (i.e. in the system there are two large parameters of the same order). It was found that in the part of the society that receives information both through the media and interpersonal communication, a steady ratio between the number of spreaders of both sides establishes over time, and these numbers have the same order (with above parameters proportional tend to infinity). At the same time, in the part of the society that receives the information only through interpersonal communication, the number of spreaders was established the stationary level at which the number of spreaders of the second source are much greater then numbers of spreaders of the first source.

Also this chapter considers modeling a situation that has never been studied before, i.e., information warfare during the destabilizing effect. The model was studied analytically and numerically. It was shown that a short-term increase in the propaganda intensity doesn't significantly influences the result of the information warfare if the increase takes place at the very beginning of this process. In the real information war, this case may occur depending on the particular situation.

The final part of the chapter is devoted to the model of making choice by individuals. This model is based on the model built on Rashevsky's neurological scheme and has a form of integro-differential equation. The model is applied to the study of the question of how the level of political polarization affects the outcome of the propaganda battle. The model has been investigated analytically and numerically. It is shown that moderate political polarization favors the side that runs more intensive propaganda. However, the advantage of stronger propaganda is impaired if the polarization is great enough, because neither media nor individuals can reassure their radical opponents.

ACKNOWLEDGMENT

This research was supported by the Russian Foundation for Basic research (projects 16-01-00306 and 17-01-00390).

REFERENCES

Belen, S. (2008). *The behaviour of stochastic rumours* (PhD Thesis). The University of Adelaide.

Belen, S., & Pearce, C. E. M. (2004). Rumours with general initial conditions. *The ANZIAM Journal*, *4*(03), 393–400. doi:10.1017/S1446181100013444

Bordia, P. & DiFonzo, N. (2005). Psychological motivations in rumor spread. *Rumor mills: The social impact of rumor and legend*, 87-101.

Daley, D. J., & Kendall, D. G. (1964). Stochastic Rumors. *Journal of the Institute of Mathematics and Its Applications*, *1*(1), 42–55. doi:10.1093/imamat/1.1.42

DiFonzo, N., & Bordia, P. (2007). Rumor, gossip and urban legends. *Diogenes*, *54*(1), 19–35. doi:10.1177/0392192107073433

Escalante, R., & Odehnal, M. (n.d.). *A deterministic mathematical model for the spread of two rumors*. arXiv:1709.01726

Gubanov, D. A., Novikov, D. A., & Chkhartishvili, A. G. (2010). *Sotsialnye seti modeli informatsionnogo vliyaniya upravleniya i protivoborstva [*Social networks of the model of information influence, management and battle]. Fizmatlit.

Herman, E., & Chomsky, N. (2006). *A propaganda model*. Media and Cultural Studies.

Kaligotla, C., Yücesan, E., & Chick, S. E. (2015). An agent based model of spread of competing rumors through online interactions on social media. In *Proceedings of the 2015 Winter Simulation Conference* (pp. 3985-3996). IEEE Press. 10.1109/WSC.2015.7408553

Maki, D. P., & Thompson, M. (1973). *Mathematical Models and Applications*. Englewood Cliffs, NJ: Prentice-Hall.

Mikhailov, A. P., Petrov, A. P., Marevtseva, N. A., & Tretiakova, I. V. (2014). Development of a Model of Information Dissemination in Society. *Mathematical Models and Computer Simulations*, *6*(5), 535–541. doi:10.1134/S2070048214050093

Mikhailov, A. P., Petrov, A. P., & Proncheva, O. G. (2017). Modeling the effect of political polarization on the outcome of propaganda battle. Computational Mathematics and Information Technologies, 1, 65–81.

Nekovee, M., Moreno, Y., Bianconi, G., & Marsili, M. (2007). Theory of Rumor Spreading in Complex Social Networks. *Physica A*, *374*(1), 457–470. doi:10.1016/j.physa.2006.07.017

Osei, G. K., & Thompson, J. W. (1977). The supersession of one rumour by another. *Journal of Applied Probability*, *14*(01), 127–134. doi:10.2307/3213265

Petrov, A. P., Maslov, A. I., & Tsaplin, N. A. (2016). Modeling Position Selection by Individuals during Information Warfare in Society. *Mathematical Models and Computer Simulations*, *8*(4), 401–408. doi:10.1134/S2070048216040141

Pronchev, G.B., & Muraviev, V.I. (n.d.). Sotsialnye seti kak faktor perekhoda Rossii k innovatsionnomu razvitiyu [Social networks as a factor of Russia's transition to innovation development]. *Sotsiologhiya* [Sociology], *3*, 36-56.

Rashevsky, N. (1933). Outline of a Physico-mathematical Theory of Excitation and Inhibition. *Protoplasma*, *20*(1), 42–56. doi:10.1007/BF02674811

Samarskiy, A. A., & Mikhailov, A. P. (2001). *Principles of Mathematical Modelling: Ideas, Methods, Examples*. CRC Press.

Shvedovskiy, V A. (1981). Modelirovanie rasprostraneniya informatsii v smezhnykh sotsialnykh gruppakh [Modeling of the information spreading in adjacent social groups]. *Matematicheskie metody v sotsiologhicheskom issledovanii* [Mathematical methods in sociological research], 207-214.

Yanagizawa-Drott, D. (2014). Propaganda and Conflict: Evidence from the Rwandan Genocide. *The Quarterly Journal of Economics*, *129*(4), 1947–1994. doi:10.1093/qje/qju020

Chapter 9
A Framework for Analyzing the Impact of Data Analytics and the Internet of Things on Digital Marketing

Dimitris K. Kardaras
Athens University of Economics and Business, Greece

Bill Karakostas
VLTN BBVA, Belgium

Stavroula G. Barbounaki
Merchant Marine Academy of Aspropyrgos, Greece

Stavros Kaperonis
Panteion University of Social and Political Sciences, Greece

ABSTRACT

The proliferation of the internet of things will open up new opportunities for implementing the digital transformation of businesses. Available data is expected to rise in unprecedented levels of quantity with the IoT playing an important role towards that end. Data analytics techniques will provide businesses with refined pieces of information in almost all aspects in both B2C and B2B context, thus refining services design and customization with more flexibility and options that focus right at the heart of consumers' needs. Digital marketing depends on these developments. This chapter aims at proposing a framework for analyzing the implications of data analytics and IoT on digital marketing.

DOI: 10.4018/978-1-5225-5586-5.ch009

INTRODUCTION

Customers are increasingly using digital media to communicate and interact with companies. Most of such interactions take place on the Web, thus generating vast amounts of data, which analysis reveals valuable insights pertaining to customer preferences, behaviour patterns, etc. As a result, companies have already started showing interest in Web analytics, in order to understand online customers' behaviour, preferences and improve their experience, while getting insights on how to increase business revenues (Chaffey, & Patron, 2012). Web Analytics are used by more than 60% of the top 10 million most popular websites around the world (Web Technology Surveys, 2014). Digital marketing is a strategy to promote products and brands through the internet or digital media. It helps in developing and maintaining customer relationships through online activities. There are a number of tools that can be used such as Customer Relationship Management (CRM), social CRM, email software, e-commerce software, marketing automation software and Web analytics (TechNavio, 2017). The Digital Marketing Institute (DMI) refers to digital marketing as "The use of digital technologies to create an integrated, targeted and measurable communication which helps to acquire and retain customers while building deeper relationships with them" (Royle, & Laing, 2014). The importance of Digital Marketing is already been confirmed in a study by IBM consisting of interviews with CMOs (IBM Institute for Business Value, 2011). These CMOs highlighted the following four biggest challenges: (1) explosion of data (i.e. big data), (2) social media, (3) proliferation of channels, and (4) shifting consumer demographics. Customer behaviour changes and technological developments, justify the IBM study. The computer screen has obviously been the most popular display of Web content, but things have changed. Recent market statistics show the dramatic proliferation of smartphones since 2005, and the profound customers' shift towards mobile marketing. Indeed, more than 50% of searches are carried out on mobile, 91% of Facebook usage, Daily Active users, is on mobile, 80% of Facebook advertising revenue is on mobile, 90% of mobile media time is spent in mobile apps (Digital marketing Megatrends, 2017).

Now, data analytics techniques can be, more than ever, used to analyse the masses of data that users generate on the Web. The proliferation of devices such as computers, laptops, smart TVs and smartphones established new communication channels between customers and businesses. In the coming years the proliferation of the Internet of Things (IoT) is expected to further expand the number of ways that companies contact customers and vice versa. Therefore, consumers navigate and proceed to purchases on the Internet through various channels, revealing their preferences. They write reviews and share their experiences with other consumers, thus providing valuable data for their likes and dislikes as well as they comment on the quality level of the services they consume. The use of data analysis techniques such as statistics, multi-criteria analysis methods and recently Artificial Intelligence (AI) and machine learning can provide solutions to e.g. attract, engage, persuade customers and create value for companies. Discovering customer behaviour patterns, designing customised services, redesigning business processes that bring customer experience to the next level, interacting in a personalised manner, are but a few examples. New services, such as the Chat bots are expected to change customer experience in a B2C context by utilising data analysis and AI and providing personalised interactive communication (Digital marketing Megatrends, 2017). Social media also play an important role in the new digital environment. Research results show (Leeflang, et al., 2014) that more than 90% of all customers read online product reviews before they proceed to purchasing and that 67% of all consumers' decisions to but are based on user-generated content (UGC). Consumers, before making up their mind what product to buy, they read at least four product reviews (Godes & Silva, 2012; Kee, 2008). The consultation of the reviews is being found to be very influential (Godes & Silva, 2012; Kee, 2008). Thus, social media creates content that allows customers to interact with each other, exchange opinions, and experiences. Interestingly, that content may be more influential than advertising. The demographics also have changed. Consumers between 18 and 35 years of age, i.e. the Millennials have established their careers, homes and families. This is now the largest living generation; it spends collectively $600 billion a year. Brands will grow digital investment in order to connect with these digital natives (Forbes, 2017a).

Business in line with these developments and expectations increase their spending on digital marketing. Market statistics and projections show that digital advertising spending globally which accounting for desktops and laptops as well as mobile devices is estimated to reach a total of 335 billion U.S. dollars by 2020. With respect to mobile internet advertising, which is a heavily invested sub-sector of the digital advertising industry, is estimated to reach over 247 billion U.S. dollars in 2020 (Digital Advertising, 2015). More market statistics show that due to the increasing use of smartphones and the availability of cheap internet services more than 30% of businesses are planning to spend around 75% of their advertising expenditures on digital marketing within the next five years (TechNavio, 2017). According to (Forbes, 2017a), the US spending in paid search, display advertising, social media advertising, online video advertising and email marketing will reach $120 billion by 2021, and it is expected to account for the 46% of all advertising in five years.

This chapter aims to propose a framework for analysing the implications of data analytics and IoT on digital marketing. It suggests that IoT based smart devices will provide the means to collect data across communication channels as well as along value chain between customers and businesses. This chapter draws on the Virtual Value Chain (VVC) (Rayport & Sviokla, 1995) and the Customer Service Life Cycle frameworks. Business process modelling is used to capture the information flow along the value chain. The use of data analysis provides valuable insights for consumers' preferences. This chapter shows how DEMATEL can be used to investigate the interrelationships between customer related data, with digital media characteristics and business processes in order to facilitate the development of personalised digital marketing campaigns.

BACKGROUND

Introduction to Internet of Things (IoT)

The IoT represents a significant technological field with enormous implications for both consumers and businesses. The pace of the IoT market development reflects its importance. Gartner (2017) forecasts suggest that 8.4 billion IoT connected devices will be in use worldwide in 2017, up 31 percent from 2016, and is expected to reach 20.4 billion by 2020. Total spending on endpoints and services will reach almost $2 trillion in 2017. China, North America and Western Europe are the leading areas in using of IoT devices and the three regions together will represent 67% of the global number of IoT devices in 2017 (Gartner, 2017). IoT services are central to the rise in IoT devices, with their spending to reach $273 billion in 2017. According to (Forbes, 2017b), B2B spending on IoT technologies, apps and solutions will reach $267 billion by 2020. The 50% of the total IoT investment will target discrete manufacturing, transportation and logistics, and utilities. IoT Analytics spending is predicted to generate $21.4 billion by 2020. Finally, spending on IoT applications is expected to generate $64.1 billion by 2020.

What Is IoT?

The term IoT was coined in the late 1990s, however many of the technologies that underpin IoT such as semiconductors and wireless networks have predated that by several decades. The IoT is created by the convergence of hardware, software and communication technologies. The hardware consists of the connected devices – which range from simple sensors to smartphones and wearable devices – and the networks that link them, such as 4G LTE (as well as the forthcoming 5G) and wireless technologies such as Wi-Fi and Bluetooth. Software components include applications and platforms that store and process IoT generated data. The combination of such components makes possible the creation of services that create value for businesses and consumers.

IoT has great potential for all business sectors, including marketing, retailing and supply chain processes. However, for the IoT premise to become a reality there are several enablers both technical and organisational that need to be realised, as well as several obstacles that need to be overcome. These are discussed in the following sections.

IoT Standardisation

For IoT to flourish, interoperability of the various systems and technologies that comprise it must be achieved. Ongoing standardization efforts involve harmonizing Internet protocols for a wireless IoT networks. Adoption of these protocols and standards involves collaboration among government standards institutes like ETSI, organizations like IETF/IAB, and alliances like ZigBee.

IoT as a Service

A parallel activity towards making IoT widely available to businesses and customers is the concept of IoT as service that is similar to other online IT services, such as cloud and storage services.

IoT as a service builds upon the effect of economies of scale, the scope of sharing IoT assets, and the ubiquity of Internet connectivity. It also relies on industry wide standardization and interconnectivity. The unique value proposition of IoT as a service may come from combining IoT architectural components such as physical objects, network, data storage, and applications to providing customized services to businesses on a pay-as-you-go basis (Lee, 2017). IoT as a service has complementarity to Cloud processing and Big Data analytics on the Cloud services.

IoT Platforms

An IoT platform is a type of middleware that helps to connect IoT devices, data and applications, and thus overcome interoperability problems. IoT platforms facilitate easy connectivity of devices to the platform and can reduce the complexity of IoT application development. Additionally, IoT platforms can provide integrated data analytics and machine learning services for automating the analysis of IoT data.

Intelligent/Cognitive IoT

Cognitive technologies can analyse the massive amounts of unstructured data generated by IoT to identify hidden trends and patterns and to mine profitable business knowledge. In the retail sector, for example such intelligent analysis of IoT generated data can be used to better understand consumer behaviours and deliver differentiated, individualized shopping experience at any point in time (IBM, 2011).

IoT Technical Enablers

Efficient IoT Device Management

The IoT is an ambitious paradigm that significantly increases the scale of connected devices. To manage the complexity of such a scale, interworking solutions that can reuse pre-existing technologies seamlessly with newer and more efficient technologies is a necessity.

Controlled Data Transmissions and Context Awareness

Due to the tremendous volumes of data generated by IoT it is not always feasible to process all the streaming data available to those devices. The concept of context aware data processing refers to the ability of sensors and devices to use context specific information such as location, temperature, and the availability of a certain device, to decide what types of data to collect and interpret to provide relevant information for decision-making. For example, context-aware data processing can deliver relevant information to a consumer by knowing the consumer's current location.

IoT Adoption Inhibitors

Security

IoT security standards are required protect against cybercrime and national security threats, and help to ensure that the system is trustworthy and trusted (UK Government Chief Scientific Adviser, 2014). *The Internet of Things: making the most of the Second Digital Revolution].* As IoT is built on top of the Internet, security issues pertaining to the Internet also apply in IoT (Lee, 2017). As the number of connected IoT devices increases, the number of the end-to-end connection points increases exponentially and the number of potential security holes increases in proportion. Protecting the IoT is however, a complex and difficult task. The number of attack vectors available to malicious attackers might increase exponentially, due to global connectivity ("access anyone") and accessibility ("access anyhow, anytime") of the IoT (Lee, 2017). IoT data and devices must therefore have security built-in by default.

Energy Efficiency

IoT devices should support energy efficiency, as this will help increase the range of potential applications and manage the burden on energy supply generated by the potential billions of IoT devices.

Data Quality

The quality of data obtained from the IoT is crucial, in order to gain user engagement and acceptance of the IoT paradigm (Lee, 2017). If data quality is poor, trust in the decision based on the data will be low and the adoption of IoT technologies can be hindered. When data collection cost is high and the quality of the data is low, the value of the IoT decreases rapidly.

Lack of IoT Specific Business Models

To realize the potential benefits, firms need an appropriate measure in order to properly assess the risks and rewards of the technology (Lee, 2017). Many IoT projects have unclear problem definitions and are using emerging technologies, thus causing a higher risk of project failure than traditional technology projects.

As with the Internet originally, applications of the Internet of Things are developing organically, with experimentation in every sector. The first source of uncertainty is in the relatively few established business models for achieving profitability. Until these become clear, it is reasonable to expect caution from businesses developing and buying IoT technologies. Early developments come from industry giants with economies of scale that mean large investments for incremental benefits are viable. However, the existing information technology capability of many organisations is likely to be insufficient to harness the volume and variety of data generated by the Internet of Things [UK Government Chief Scientific Adviser (2014). *The Internet of Things: making the most of the Second Digital Revolution*]. Disruptive new firms therefore have already emerged to break into existing markets or create new ones through innovative new ideas.

Potential of IoT for Businesses

Across many industries, the potential of IoT has started to be realised. For example, data harvested from IoT sensors and devices can be used to enhance the customer experience, optimize store operations and improve inventory and supply chain management. IoT is driving innovation and new opportunities by bringing every object, consumer, process and service into the digital realm (Gregory, 2015). The proliferation of connected devices coupled with improved technology platforms and adoption of common standards is expected to drive the rapid growth of IoT-enabled capabilities across industries.

IoT in Retail

Analysts predict the IoT retail market to grow 20 percent to $35 billion in the next five years (Forbes, 2017c). The IoT can have a disruptive impact on the retail industry. Retailers are already experimenting with ways to use intelligent, connected devices to offer new services, reshape experiences and enter new markets. This trend is expected to accelerate (IBM, 2016)

According to (Forbes, 2017c):

- *78% of retailers acknowledge the importance of integrating online and store customer experience*
- *87% of retailers plan to deploy mobile POS devices in their stores allowing their customers to self-scan and pay for products by 2021.*
- *90% of retailers plan to implement 'buy online-pay in store' services by 2021.*

Using IoT sensors to automate many of the labour-intensive operations in stores and warehouses, such as tracking inventory or changing prices on individual items, frees staff to spend more time interacting with customers and thus improving their levels of satisfaction. IoT also, makes it possible for managers to adjust pricing in real-time, using smart tags to lower prices on promotional or low-turnover items or increase pricing on higher-demand items (IBM, 2016). A fully integrated pricing system would help retailers improve synchronization of prices between the shelves and the cash tills/registers and also across all retail channels, to verify prices are consistent between online and brick and mortar stores.

Inside the store, IoT devices can control environment conditions and reduce cost. For example, IoT-enabled sensors can control lighting and temperature to both improve customer comfort and to support more cost-effective energy usage.

IoT in Marketing

According to MARKETO (2017) 51% of the world's top global marketers expect that IoT will revolutionize the marketing landscape by 2020. The IoT through the inherent interconnectivity of digital devices provides endless opportunities for brands to listen and respond to the needs of their customers – with the right message, at the right time. Marketers can extract data from IoT devices in the customers' environments (places where they spend their leisure time, shop etc) an interpret them to shape trends and tailor contact approach with the consumer. The Internet of Things can impact customer experience, by collecting and analysing more and more diverse consumer data to gain better customer insight. Thus, combined with Big Data analytics, IoT can be used to [MARKETO] (2017):

- *Analyse customer buying habits across different platforms and channels.*
- *Gather previously unavailable knowledge about how consumers actually interact with products.*
- *Gain a deeper insight as to the stage of the buying process a consumer is at each time.*
- *Provide point of sale (POS) tailored information and advice, such as targeted advertisements.*
- *Quickly resolve any issues the consumer may have that stop the closing of the sale.*
- *Thus, thanks to IoT marketing can become real time and data driven.*

The Virtual Value Chain

The VVC was introduced by Rayport and Sviokla, (1995) as a model to assist in identifying the value of information and deriving information strategies. The physical value chain (Porter, 1985), identifies the primary and the support activities as a series of actions that convert inputs to outputs and produce value for businesses and customers. Information technology however, has changed the way modern organizations operate to create value. The shift now is on information management. The VVC model suggests five stages, as a way to identify the potential value of information.

1. **Gather Information:** The advances of the Information and Communication Technology (ICT) over the years made digitization of information possible. The anticipated proliferation of the IoT devices will further expand the capabilities of collecting data that could capture almost all human and business activities along both the VVC and the physical value chain. For example, smart product

labels, using printed electronics technology, will be able to capture data that can track product identity, identify products' location and usage from factory floor to high street, to living room to the recycling back and finally of products' decomposition into their components' materials. Information many also be collected via different sources, such as internal organizational sources, i.e. corporate databases, or external sources, such as the Internet, and IoT devices. Thus, issues pertaining to protocols and information integration across technological platforms need to be addressed.

2. **Organise Information:** Information may be gathered in the form of videos, images, sounds, texts, numbers, etc. Big Data are characterized by large Volumes, High Velocity and Volatility as well as of their unstructured nature. All this data and information needs to put in place and stored in a structured way in databases. This is a challenge, but challenges are to be tackled through technological advances.
3. **Select Information:** The aim of organisations is to provide quality services to customers in a profitable manner. The VVC in its third stage suggests that businesses should select and analyse information that is valuable already, or can be used to create value. Businesses need to identify what information is potentially valuable from the masses of data and information that is collected and made available in their databases. Data analytics techniques play an important role in identifying the valuable pieces of information and analysing them. Advances in artificial intelligence would make it possible for algorithms to dig in large data sets and surface the important bits of information. However, what is valuable, to whom and when is subject to various circumstances, personal choices and subjectivity and luck. Data analytics should be used to analyse the value of information in the light customers' personal subjectivity as well as by taking into consideration the dynamic and constantly changing business and social environment. For example, the fact that a customer's preference is identified and it is now known to a company, does not guarantee that the customer will not react to a competitor's advertisement positively and change his/her preferences for at least once. Data mining and machine learning can identify that a customer is possibly willing to change so a company act in a pre-emptive way, even before the competitor's message was sent. That is not always possible though. Machine learning techniques need training. However, sudden changes in customers' behaviour do not give enough time to reassess his or her preferences. Companies rely on real time data that IoT connected devices can capture. Thus, when the competitor's advertisement message was sent to the customer a company will have to opportunity to analyse the new set of data and then react promptly.

4. **Synthesise Information:** Data analysis results should be combined in way that they form a service, which in turn is expected to be delivered to the customer. Following the example presented in stage 3, assume there are three sets of relevant information that need to be combined so that and their synthesis would result valuable decisions, actions and services for both the company and its customers. First, the competitor's advertisement carries information pertaining to product and to customer. Then, data analysis results provide information that indicates the possibility of the customer to switch to the competitor. Finally, a third set of information pertaining to how a company should react to retain its customer is synthesised so a company knows when to react, how and towards which customer.
5. **Distribute Information:** The results of the synthesis should be delivered to the customer, who is probably using a variety of devices such as a smartphone, smartwatch, smart tooth brush, smart refrigerator, to name just a few of the billions of IoT smart devices that will be available in the coming years. The messages should reach the customer in the desired format, at the right place and time. Thus, no surprise that one of the major trends is to develop technologies that allow adaptive web design, thus providing more tailored customer experiences from different devices (Digital Marketing Megatrends, 2017).

A study by Bhatt and Emdad (2001) indicates how the VVC can be used to uncover competitive advantage opportunities along the physical value chain, by considering the 4P's (Product, Place, Price, Promotion) marketing model. Indeed, with respect to product information, smart labelling may allow a firm to obtain information from its suppliers electronically, which then it can be automatically delivered to the customers' IoT devices upon customer request. Moreover, the VVC provides the possibility of quick customisation of products and services, by allowing personalisation depending on the products features a customer wishes to activate, the pay and delivery methods of their products, etc. With regard to the place, just-in-time access to the products and services implies that customers can consume fulfil their needs at the right time and place, i.e. exactly when a service is need. Different pricing schemes can also be designed depending on the situation and circumstances under which a customer demand is expressed or identified by a company. Assume that smart IoT devices (e.g. a smartwatch, or smart glasses communicate with the smart label of a competitor's product. This event can be interpreted as the customer showing interest for the particular product. Then, advertisement messages from other suppliers can come through the customers IoT devices combined with competitive price offers. The VVC can promote products and services by collecting valuable information across the value chain, combine it and deliver it to the customer.

Information related to supplementary or competitive products, their components, ingredients, origins and methods of production, are examples of such promotion messages, which can be delivered as mentioned previously at the right time and place, when the customer exhibited an interest for the product or a competitor took an initiative to address the customer. With the proliferation of the IoT people and businesses will be strongly connected with each other, thus providing almost full information of each other activities and intentions.

The Customer Service Life Cycle (CSLC) Model

Earlier versions were introduced by Burnstine (1980) and by IBM's Business Systems Planning process (IBM Corporation, 1981). They included the following four stages: *requirement*, *acquisition*, *ownership* and *retirement*. The CSLC was extended by Ives and Learmonth (1984) and Learmonth (1986) to a 13-stage model that can assist businesses to specify customer oriented strategic opportunities for IS. Revisions of the CSLC have been proposed by Ives and Mason, (1990) and Piccoli et al., (2001) and Lightner (2004). The CSLC is originally found in the literature as "customer resource life cycle" since the terms "resource" and "service" are used interchangeably (Piccoli et al., 2001; Lightner, 2004). According to Ives and Learmonth,(1984), the stages represent a life cycle which customers follow when acquiring their products. The 13 stages of the CSLC are:

Establish requirements of how much of a product/service is required, Specify the attributes of the product, Select sources where the customer can buy the product, Order the product, Authorise and Pay, Acquire, Test and Accept that the acquired product meets customer's specifications, Integrate with other products in an inventory, Monitor the use of the product so that unauthorised use is prohibited, Upgrade the product, Maintain and Repair if needed, Transfer or Dispose, i.e. return, or dispose of the product inventory if necessary and Account for much is spent on the product (Ives & Learmonth, 1984).

Websites and IoT devices that provide services, which successfully assist customers in satisfying their needs through the various stages of the CSLC, improve both customer satisfaction and businesses improve their financial performance (Lightner, 2004; Wade & Nevo, 2005-6; Hoekstra et al., 2015). The CSLC is adopted in the current study since it provides a suitable framework that can be used in order to investigate customer oriented services in a systematic way. This chapter uses the VVC in combination with the CSLC. The VVC is considered in all stages of the CSCL, in searching valuable information that can be targeted and selected by using IoT devices. The selected information will indicate what content to promote in digital campaigns.

The *Customer Journey Map*, is been proposed in digital marketing (Johnston, 2015) as a template to assist in content management. It suggests an approach to systematically approach the question "what content to create?" i.e. to specify what content should be sent to the customers. The customer journey is defined by Johnston (2015), as the "things that people want to accomplish as they interact with a brand". Then, content the right content is mapped to customers' goals. The aim of the *first step* in the customer journey mapping is to decide the most important customers or market segments to focus on depending to the business goals. The *second step*, suggests that the customer state should be clarified, i.e. knowing information about the customer *who* and *where* they are, what are they *preferences* and *needs*. This information may be available when the customer uses an application or a service on a connected device. During the *third step*, the goals of the customer are specified. The question that needs to be answered is "what are the goals of the customer, when interacting with the company?" Step three, breaks down the goals into tasks that can be mapped to information needs. *Step four* specifies, which communication channels customers would probably use, thus customising the content and their interaction according to the characteristics of the digital media, e.g. type and features of smartphone, smart label, interactive TV, wearables, etc. Finally, in *step five* content and tasks along the customer journeys should be matched to the appropriate channels and formats that are likely to work best.

The Decision Making and Trial Evaluation Laboratory (DEMATEL) Method

This chapter suggests that multi-criteria techniques can be used, among other data analytics techniques such as statistics, machine learning, etc., in order to model business priorities expressed in terms of the Key Performance Indicators (KPIs). Multi-criteria methods can be utilised within the context of the digital marketing for they can model and investigate the knowledge as well as the subjective views and perceptions of businesses decision makers as well as their customers. There are several multi-criteria methods such as the Analytic Hierarchy Process (AHP), and its fuzzy variation (Fuzzy AHP), the DEMATEL, etc.

The DEMATEL method was developed by the Battelle Geneva Institute (Fontela & Gabus, 1976). DEMATEL is a multi-criteria method which is used to model and analyze complex relationships among factors pertaining to a particular domain. DEMATEL is used to calculate the importance of criteria pertaining to a problem domain. The method is also applied to real life problems in order to investigate the interactions among important criteria and examine how interrelated factors affect each other. The method can equally handle qualitative and quantitative factors. The

DEMATEL causal models provide the means to simulate and evaluate alternative actions and policies.

The DEMATEL method has been extensively used in MCDM problems such as in formulating marketing strategies, evaluating e-learning services, developing control systems, dealing with safety problems, examining environment watershed plans, etc. (Chang & Chen, 2008, 2009; Chen et al., 2010; Hori & Shimizu, 1999; Lin et al., 2010a, 2010b; Lin & Tzeng, 2009; Liou et al., 2007; Ou Yang et al., 2008; Tzeng et al., 2007). The DEMATEL is implemented as follows:

1. Generate the Direct Relation Matrix. The direct relation matrix is calculated usually based on experts' responses. However, data can be collected regarding customers' behaviour, preferences, etc. Data that is collected (e.g. experts' views) indicate the level of influence that a factor exerts on another by using the following scale: 0 for no influence, 1 for somewhat influence, 2 for medium influence, 3 for high influence and 4 for very high influence. The direct relation matrix $A = [a_{i,j}]$ is a nxn matrix, where $a_{i,j}$ indicates the degree to which factor (i) affects factor (j). In the case of a group of experts, all responses are averaged to produce the average matrix Z, where $Z = \left[z_{i,j}\right]$, with i,j indicating performance criteria.
2. Calculate the normalized initial Direct- relation matrix D. The Matrix D is calculated using the following formulas.

$$D = \lambda * Z,$$

where

$$\lambda = \min\left[\frac{1}{\max\sum_{j=1}^{n}\left(z_{i,j}\right)}, \frac{1}{\max\sum_{i=1}^{n}\left(z_{i,j}\right)}\right],$$

where $1 \leq i \leq n \, and \, 1 \leq j \leq n$.

3. Derive the Total relation matrix T, where $T = D\left(I - D\right)^{-1}$.
4. Calculate the sums of rows and columns of matrix T. The sum of rows is calculated by $r = r_i\left[i, j\right]_{nx1} = \sum_{j=1}^{n} t\left(i, j\right)$ and the Sum of columns is calculated

by $c = c_j\left[i, j\right]_{1xn} = \sum_{i=1}^{n} t\left(i, j\right)$. The value of r(i) indicates the total effect given by criterion (i) both directly and indirectly. The value of c(j) shows the total effect received by criterion (j) both directly and indirectly. If (j = i), the value of (ri+ci) represents the total effects both given and received by factor (i), while the value of (ri-ci) shows the net contribution by factor (i) on the system. If (ri-ci) is positive, factor (i) is a net cause, while If (ri-ci) is negative, factor (i) is a net receiver.

5. 5. Set a threshold value (α). The threshold is calculated with the formula,

$a = \frac{\sum_{i=1}^{n}\left(t_{i,j}\right)\sum_{j=1}^{n}\left(t_{i,j}\right)}{n^2}$, where n is the number of criteria. The threshold is used to cut-off the most important criteria, which will be included in the DEMATEL causal model.

6. Build the DEMATEL causal model. A cause and effect relationship diagram, by mapping all coordinate sets of $\left(r_i + c_i, r_i - c_i\right)$. The causal model indicates the importance of the most important criteria, i.e. those above the threshold and the degree of influence among criteria.

A Framework for Analysing the Impact of IoT on Digital Marketing

Assume that IoT devices when connected with each other constitute a graph where the graph nodes represent variables carrying data and information that reflect important aspects of human and business every day activities. The CSLC provides a structured way to identify the customer data and the customer activities with business interest. The IoT connected devices can be used (if they exist already, or new IoT devices can be designed and developed), in order to collect the required customer data. Subsequently, businesses within the digital marketing context can decide how to approach the customer in a customised way, i.e. *what content to advertise, when, where, through which devices, with the appropriate digital media mix*. The arcs that connect the nodes represent how variables interact with each other. The anticipated proliferation of the IoT will expand the IoT devices graph, thus expanding the network of information sources, across time, space, activities, personal priorities and business policies.

Figure 1 shows, that the "smart heating device" communicates with other IoT devices, collects the necessary data and then optimises the heating parameters, by

Figure 1. The smart watch, smart meteo and the smart heating devices connected constitute an IoT graph

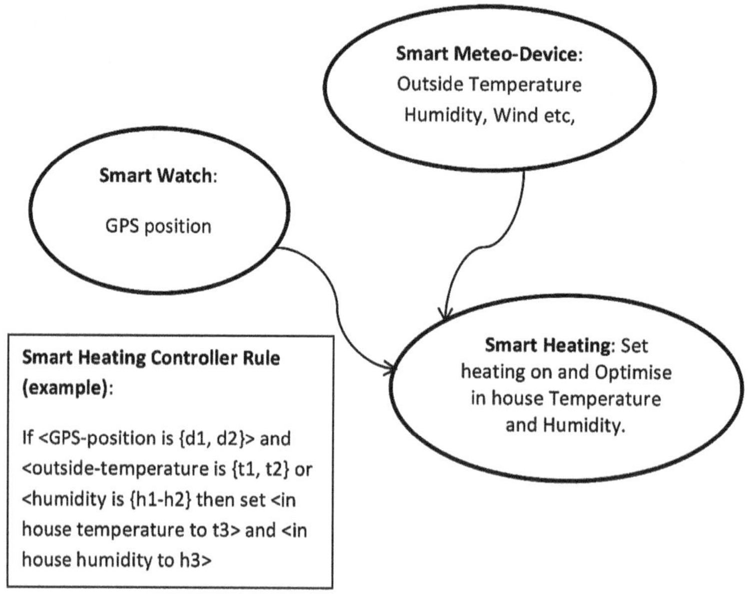

applying some rules that reflect personal preferences regarding the heating settings. Considering the vast quantities and the volatile nature of big data, it is a difficult task to identify what is perceived as valuable data and what is not. Distinguishing what data is valuable and what is not, is to some extent a subjective matter that depends on personal customer choices or on different business priorities in a commercial setting. Therefore, in the context of digital marketing, where information and knowledge regarding customer's needs and preferences is of paramount importance, a framework needs to cater for identifying what is significant, when, where to whom and under which circumstances. The paths across the IoT graph constitute alternative VVC (Rayport & Sviokla, 1995). Alternative paths imply that several VVC may be hidden but yet still to be identified. Such VVC are formed and depend on the possibilities for information dissemination across customers, suppliers, intermediaries, etc. Some VVC may be long lasting some other may last for some time depending on the circumstances, e.g. the amount of value they create, the period of time they are conceived as useful, etc. Data that is collected along the VVC should be analysed. This data is classified as relevant to one or more stages of the CSLC model, thus specifying the customer need. It is important to know the aims of the customer, for the digital message can be better focused when targeting customer related KPIs more effectively. Thus, the proposed framework in this chapter, suggests that data analytics techniques should be utilized in order to identify pieces of information that are valuable along both the VVC and the CSLC and to measure how valuable such data is for a customer or a business. The plethora of possible VVC that can be created and identified within the IoT graph and the potential of data analytics can provide fast and effective means of data management in order to be able to answer questions such as: Who are the potential customers? When is the right time for each of the customers? The data analysis results will lead to the design, implementation and distribution of e-services across the VVC that are offered to targeted customers that are really interested. Such e-services should be made available at the right time and place, along the VVC. In the context of the digital marketing an e-service consumer is a potential customer who is receiving advertising messages through electronic means, most probable but not necessarily, through the internet. An e-service provider is the digital marketing agent whose interest is to identify the potential customer, at the right time, when the customer is more than ready to find the advertisement interesting and proceed with purchasing the promoted services or the goods.

Thus, the proposed framework suggests that the CSLC and the VVC are used to identify the "*what*" should be offered to a customer. Process modelling, indicates the "*where*" and "*when*", i.e. the place and time a service is made available to a customer. Process modelling is applied in order to capture the operational aspects that link e-service providers and service consumers as well as to investigate the potential of the IoT devices. Data analytics techniques are used to unravel and evaluate the value that is generated for the customer.

As Figure 2 shows, the proposed framework suggests that the IoT provides the means for data collection across VVC. Use cases reflect the value propositions, i.e. the outcome that customers, suppliers or other participants would anticipate from the VVC. Business processes modelling is utilized to capture the functionality across each VVC. It reflects the information flow that consists of a series of potentially useful information elements, as well as it shows the operations that take place in space and time so that the required information will be collected and analysed in order to produce the requested use cases. Data analytics techniques will be utilized to analyse and manage the available data and help identify which customer or supplier to focus on, where and when to act and deliver an e-service, e.g. an advertising message. The evaluation of the advertising value has been the focus of several research works. This study considers digital marketing KPIs, draws on Ducoffe (1995) and Martins et al. (2017) that suggest *informativeness*, *irritation* and *entertainment* as the antecedents of the advertising value. The informativeness, refers to the ability provide the customers with information related to products. The irritation implies techniques that employed by advertisers that annoy, or manipulate consumers. Consequently, such techniques are perceived as unwanted. Next, the entertainment refers to pleasant

Figure 2. Depicts the proposed framework for utilizing IoT and data analytics in digital marketing

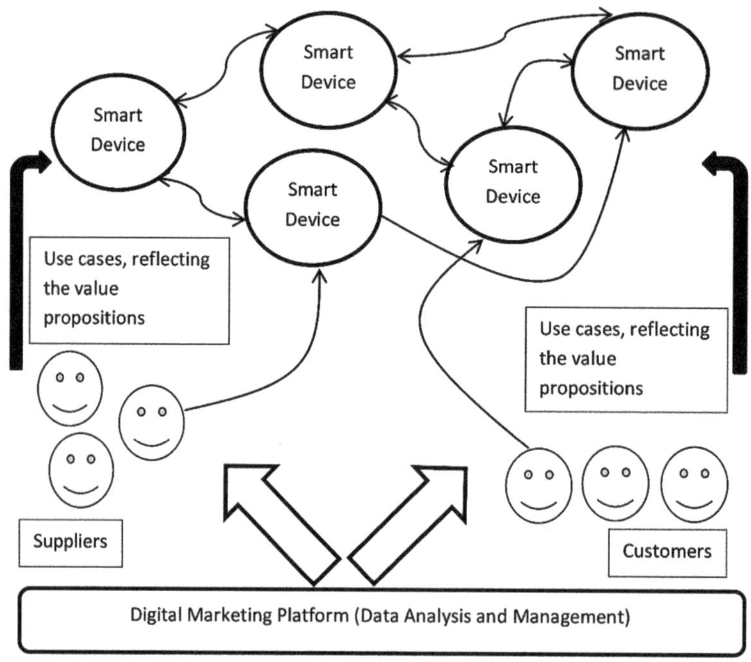

advertising, which results to positive impacts on brands. The proposed framework suggests that the following steps should be implemented.

Step 1: *Define the digital marketing KPIs*. Successful advertising depends on its ability to persuade the customer, present relevant information and invoke reasoning and emphasis (Sheehan, 2014). Although the establishment of KPIs is highly subjective depending on the strategy and vision of each company, measures such as *purchase intention, customer retention, customer experience*, as top priorities. Digital marketing specific KPIs typically include the *number of clicks, conversion rate, click through rate (CTR)*, etc.

Step 2: *Specify Uses Case(s)*. The uses cases indicate the customer requirements, in terms of quantity and quality. Uses cases may involve tasks such as purchasing a product, consuming a service, seeking information or advice for a product, completing a task. Use cases represent the informativeness antecedent according to Ducoffe (1995) and Martins et al. (2017), by specifying what are the important data elements that customers want to know. The successful implementation of each use case depends among others on the accessibility and processing of the available information that pertain to the use case. Thus, this framework defines a uses case in terms of the data elements that are necessary for the successful completion of the uses case. Thus, $UC_i = \left[UCde_{i1}, UCde_{i2}, ...UCde_{in}\right]$, where UC_i represents the use case, and $UCde_{in}$ represent the *n-th* data element required for the UC_i completion. For example, the use case "*want to buy a theatre ticket*", involves several tasks and requires the processing of several data elements that can be identified by using the CSLC stages. Therefore, one or more CSLC stages, such as "specify the number of the tickets, "specify the seat in the theatre, "select which theatre to go", etc., may be part of the implementation of the theatre ticket use case. Each one of the stages requires a number of data elements, such as ticket price, availability of seats, theatre play reviews, theatre location, etc.

Step 3: *Identify Digital Media and digital Formats for transmitting the Advertising messages.* In the IoT era the plethora of smart devices will make it easier to find a communication channel, but perhaps more demanding to identify the most effective one. Therefore, digital messages can be transmitted through various channels e.g. smartphones, smartwatches, smart cars and smart devices of any kind. Messages can be sent in a number of formats, such as text, video, sound, image. There are five groups of factors that can influence the selection of the most suitable digital media (Bunt et al., 2007): *User-specific features*, refer to users' representation preferences, e.g. a customer may prefer video to image interfaces. Next are the *Information features*, which suggest that digital media exhibit different levels of suitability for displaying data elements. For example, a restaurant menu is more appropriate to be shown with a video than with an image or sound. *Contextual information* pertains to where a customer is located when a message arrives. Environmental conditions such as noise, light, weather, speed, etc. may deter the quality of the advertising message. *Media constraints* imply that a single digital media may not be enough but instead a combination of media would more effectively deliver the advertising message to the customer. Finally, *Limitations of technical resources* refer to device limitations such as screen size, bandwidth, etc. Each combination of digital media and digital formats is most appropriate for different data elements, under different circumstances. For example, a voice message would be more appropriate than a video or text when driving. Thus, by taking into consideration the information features, and the limitations of smart devices, advertising messages can be defined as

$$AdvMsg = [M_{device1}^{text}, M_{device1}^{video}, M_{device1}^{sound}, M_{device1}^{image}, ..., M_{device(k)}^{format}],$$

where "device" indicate a smart IoT device, which is used to transmit the message by using the selected format.

Step 4: *Apply DEMATEL.* Although various data analytics techniques can be used, this chapter illustrates how DEMATEL can be used to analyse data and use the analysis results in digital marketing. Its application returns the importance weights and the ranking of what data elements to advertise, how to advertise in terms of the most appropriate devices and formats to use. Since used cases are associated with CSLC stages, it would also be possible to identify the "when" to advertise, even before a customer proceeds to an action. In fact, IoT devices transmit data on real time, so that an advertising agent would know when a customer is starting a specific task. However, with the use of CSLC and predictive analytics it would be possible to predict the next most probable action of the customer and deliver advertising messages pre-emptively. A different DEMATEL model can be used for each Use case and each Customer. Data collected through IoT devices are fed back to the model so it identifies any changes in customer priorities and behavioural aspects.

Step 5: Utilise the DEMATEL causal model to develop scenarios. The causal model indicates how concepts considered in DEMATEL affect each other. It provides therefore the means for evaluating alternative scenarios, for different customers, circumstances, business priorities, etc.

Illustrative Example

Assume a customer use case "*customer wants to drink coffee*". The use of the CSLC in order to investigate further the use case, identifies a number of subsequent tasks and decisions related to the use case. Their successful implementation depends on identifying, selecting and analysing relevant data. The use of the CSLC specifies a number of requirements. For simplicity reasons, Table 1 shows, only the first three stages of the CSLC. Thus, drawing on the 1st CSLC stage, Table 1 shows, that a customer needs to specify the quality, i.e. the number of cups of coffee he or she would like to consume, as part of the fulfilment of the above-mentioned use case. Subsequently, opportunities for digital marketing messages that relate to the 1st stage of the CSLC are specified. Such messages may refer to alternative coffee brands, drinks, etc. Whether advertising is worth the effort or not is a decision that depends on relevant data analysis. Such data elements may include coffee consumption, coffee brand, time of having coffee, etc. This data can be collected from potentially thousands and millions of customers by using IoT devices such as customers' smart coffee machines, smart labelling on coffee packages, etc. The data and the results of its analysis may be used to update the customers' profile, in a Customer

Table 1. Linking use cases and the CSLC with digital advertising

Use Case	CSLC Stages	Digital Advertising Opportunity	Data Elements Involved	Digital Media
"Customer wants to drink coffee"	How many cups to consume? Specify quantity (Stage 1 in CSLC)	• Advertise: • Alternative coffee brands; • Alternative drinks; • Supplementary goods to coffee	Quantity of coffee consumed per week	• Mobile phone • Smart coffee machine • Smart car
	Where to drink the coffee? (Stage 2 in CSLC)	• Advertise: • Alternative coffee shops; • Alternative ways of transportation, e.g. taxi firms; • Parking places	• Services offered in alternative coffee shops (music, view, etc; • User reviews for shops • Visits per shop • Time spent in shop, etc	• Mobile phone • Smart coffee machine • Smart car
	How would the customer like the coffee (Stage 3 in CSLC)	• Advertise: • Alternative coffee flavours; types of coffee.	Quantity of coffee consumed per week/type of drink	• Mobile phone • Smart coffee machine

Relationship Management (CRM) system in real time manner, and help identify the customers who would most likely respond to an advertising message. Furthermore, tracking changes in the customers' habits and behaviour would be made possible, by collecting and analysing real time data with the use of IoT connected devices. Finally, the advertising message will be delivered to the target customers via IoT devices e.g. smart phones, smart coffee machines, smart cars, etc. as shown in Table 1. More data then can be collected as feedback, in order to assess the effectiveness of advertising on different IoT devices, the response of customers, etc.

Assume a company considers *purchase intention*, *customer retention*, *conversion rate* and *CTR* as its major digital marketing KPIs. A digital marketing agent is employed to advertise alternative coffee shops (see stage 2, in Table 1), drawing on data such as *quantity of coffee consumption*, *music* and *view quality* of alternative shops. Customers' *smart phones* and *smart watches* will be used to deliver *sound* or *text* advertising messages.

The application of the DEMATEL calculates the inter-relationships among the digital media and data elements shown in Table 1, as well as with digital marketing KPIs that reflect the business priorities. After performing the DEMATEL calculations, in step3, the T-matrix is produced as shown in Table 2. For simplicity reasons not all digital media, or data elements etc., as shown. The threshold value (a=0,08) is calculated, using the formula in DEMATEL step5. The T-matrix shows how the concepts used in DEMATEL interact and affect each other. Values shadowed in green are below threshold thus are omitted from further consideration. According to DEMATEL, values below the threshold are not considered as important. Table 2

Table 2. The T-matrix

T Matrix	Purchase Intention	Customer Retention	Conversion Rate	CTR	Quantity of coffee	Music played in shop-1	View in shop-1	Smartphone sound	Smartwatch image
Purchase Intention	0	0	0	0	0	0	0	0	0
Customer Retention	0,232110883	0,07897679	0,228167064	0,203215	0	0	0	0	0
Convertion Rate	0,147175846	0,183861516	0,038880486	0,034629	0	0	0	0	0
CTR	0,187468883	0,244222943	0,222048472	0,045997	0	0	0	0	0
Quantity of coffee per week	0,231819822	0,308683281	0,305176323	0,255447	0	0	0	0	0
Music played in shop-1	0,253428575	0,303620398	0,299860804	0,264749	0,188341	0	0	0	0
View in shop-1	0,163255931	0,170273624	0,183123221	0,164467	0,125561	0	0	0	0
Smartphone sound	0,248567176	0,245875978	0,234937451	0,224451	0,163969	0,013452915	0	0	0
Smartwatch image	0,138667418	0,098024796	0,115353619	0,118184	0,045969	0	0,00896861	0	0

shows, that "Purchase Intention" does not affect any of the other variables, but it is affected by all others. The T-matrix shows that customer retention affects purchase intention, conversion rate and CTR almost equally. From the digital marketing agent's point of view, the question is what to advertise and which digital media to use. The T-matrix shows that displaying an image on customer's smart watch has no impact on customers' perception regarding the music played in shop-1. So, it is considered as a media of no advertising interest in this case. Instead, it could possibly be used as an advertising means for increasing coffee consumption or improving customers' appreciation of shop's 1 view. However, since its value of impact is below the threshold (a), this slight impact is considered as not important. Thus, displaying an image on the customers' smart watch it does not look like a good option in this case. Smart phone instead, exhibits some impact (although above threshold, still not very strong) for increasing weekly coffee consumption. Thus, the suggestion that advertising on smart phone by delivering a sound message to the customer is a preferable way to increase coffee consumption. The results also show that increasing the coffee consumption will result into improvements in all digital marketing KPIs. Additionally, although there is some indication that using a smart phone to send a sound advertising message will have a positive effect on promoting shop's 1music collection, this is below threshold. Thus, other IoT devices and digital means could also be considered to advertise the music or view, etc. Indeed, by expanding the DEMATEL Z matrix more KPIs, digital media and data elements will be considered thus, covering more CSLC stages and more aspects related to the use case in focus. Looking further into in data analysis, by calculating the (ri+ci) in DEMATEL step4 results in Table 3, show that the most important KPI to consider is the customer retention, which has the highest value, followed by purchase intention and CTR.

Similarly, by comparing the digital media, the findings indicate the higher importance of sending sound message on customers' smart phones. However, not all customers have the same requirements, even for the same use case. Customer priorities can be modelled as a vector, considering the same concepts as in the DEMATEL matrix. Assume that a customer is particularly interested in music. So, in terms of advertising promoting music to that customer is a priority. Suppose the following vector, in Table 4, represents customer's requirements. A higher priority for music than the view is shown with the corresponding degrees of interest.

To deal with such a situation, the multiplication of the customer's vector with the transposed T-matrix, will indicate what advertising actions should be taken.

The multiplication result is shown in Table 5.

Table 3. Ranking of KPIs and Digital Media

	R+C	R-C
Purchase Intention	1,602494536	-1,602494536
Customer Retention	2,376009423	-0,891069228
Convertion Rate	2,032093915	-1,223000967
CTR	2,010876612	-0,611401722
Quantity of coffee per week	1,62496571	0,577287293
Music played in shop-1	1,323452612	1,296546783
View in shop-1	0,815648991	0,797711771
Smartphone sound	1,131253464	1,131253464
Smartwatch image	0,525167142	0,525167142

Table 4. Customer's Vector show higher interest in shop's-1 music than in view

Purchase Intention	Customer Retention	Conversion Rate	CTR	Quantity of coffee per week	Music played in shop-1	View in shop-1	Smartphone sound	Smartwatch image
0	0	0	0	0	3	1	0	0

Table 5. What advertising actions to take

Purchase Intention	Customer Retention	Conversion Rate	CTR	Quantity of coffee per week	Music played in shop-1	View in shop-1	Smartphone sound	Smartwatch image
0	0	0	0	0	0	0	0,040358744	0,00896861

Results indicate that smartphone sound message should be sent to the customer in order to promote the music and an image to the customer's smartwatch to promote the view. However, both suggestion have a low (0,04) and (0,008) degrees of impact, indicating that other media should be explored. Similarly, several scenarios can be examined that involve customers with different priorities, a variety of digital media, various formats and different sets of KPIs.

Therefore, this chapter suggests that the use of IoT can provide the means for collecting real time data regarding customers' and other digital marketing stakeholders. Data analytics, such as the application of DEMATEL, allow agents to reach useful conclusions regarding the planning and evaluating different scenarios of the advertising mix, digital media and customer targets.

FUTURE RESEARCH DIRECTIONS

The digital transformation appears on many lists of strategic priorities. It requires though profound changes from the foundation of business processes, up to changing the mentality, and vision. Digital marketing is an important and flourishing business area, which attracts increasing attention in both academia and in businesses. Future research may focus on investigating how different types of customers react to digital advertising. As the IoT will be tracking human activities it would interesting to examine issues pertaining to how to judge and interpret customers' experience and mood. Time consideration also includes topics of interest since VVCs evolve and change over time. It is important to be able to predict such changes and translate them into stage models, such as the CSLC, that can more accurately predict the next actions of customers. The combination of data analytics and IoT could redefine the KPIs currently in use and lead to the development of performance models that can improve marketing accountability and assist in evaluating advertising investments.

CONCLUSION

By exploiting the (loT) technologies, more and more devices will be able to collect data regarding human activities; this data can be stored with cloud services and share it among other IoT smart devices. Data analytics can be used to dig in selected data, analyse it and shed light in to the problem domains, produce reports and create results. There is a wide range of domains and applications where IoT can be used. This chapter focus on digital marketing.

The IoT era is expected to revolutionise the way marketing and in particular digital marketing is approaching the customer. The development (IoT) technologies and services provide the means for integrating information gathering and processing across the value chain of digital marketing. The collection of valuable information pertaining to all stakeholders (customers, suppliers, and digital marketing agencies), will facilitate the development of new bread (e)services that allow stakeholders to communicate with each other more by understanding each other's needs more timely and effectively.

Analysis of data collected from IoT devices will be key to any company's successful IoT strategy. Early research has already shown that IoT success relies on strategic sharing of data and quick analysis of its implications (Borowski, 2017). By 2020, IoT devices will outnumber humans with a ratio of 4-to-1, creating new dynamics for marketing, sales and customer service" (Borowski, 2017). Digital marketing agents, already have access to data platforms that track clicks, impressions, many other metrics related to web analytics. The IoT though, will turn almost every device into a smart device with sensors collecting and transmitting data, smart labels, communicating with other smart devices. The vast amount of data that will be made available to businesses hide numerous VVCs that need to be identified activate them. Data analytics advances are already in places to materialise and monetise investments in IoT and data analysis. IoT and data analytics will usher digital marketing into realising the untapped potential of data.

The purpose of this chapter is to explore the role of IoT in digital marketing, and to propose a framework that can be used to analyse IoT uses, opportunities and challenges in a systematic and quantify its impact. The proposed framework suggests that KPIs should be defined and integrated into VVCs and business processes, so that special and time related information about the customers' requirements is collected and used for advertising purposed and beyond, such as in services design, customisation, etc. The combination of the DEMATEL within the context of the CSLC and the concept of VVCs, provides an approach to digital marketing that allows agents to identify what product and services features attract customers attention more and start collecting data about these features by utilising the IoT. The proposed approach allows digital marketing agents to assess the effectiveness of their actions and plans in terms of KPIs, such customer retention, purchase intention, etc., in a way that the KPIs reflect their needs and their strategic priorities.

This study illustrates how MCDM methods such as the DEMATEL, can be used in order to utilise the potential of the IoT. Such techniques allow the decision makers to define their own priorities and evaluate alternatives. The integration of recent advances in other data analytics fields such as the machine learning, data mining, etc. with MCDM methods can provide digital marketing agents with powerful tools to analyse customer trends, plan for their digital marketing mix and assess their business strategies in the light of real time information flows. Further, AI and machine learning can feed MCDM methods with detailed and up-to-date customer patterns and establish a process of data collection, analysis and assessment with real time data.

REFERENCES

Bhatt, G. D., & Emdad, A. F. (2001). An analysis of the virtual value chain in electronic commerce. *Logistics Information Management*, *14*(1/2), 78–85. doi:10.1108/09576050110362465

Borowski, C. (2017). *How to prepare for IoT changing customer service*. Retrieved November 15, 2017, from https://www.softwareadvice.com/resources/iot-customer-service/

Bunt, A., Carenini, G., & Conati, C. (2007). Adaptive content presentation for the web. In P. Brusilovsky, A. Kobsa, & W. Nejdl (Eds.), Lecture notes in computer science: Vol. 4321. *The adaptive web* (pp. 409–432). Berlin: Springer. doi:10.1007/978-3-540-72079-9_13

Burnstine, D. C. (1980). *BIAIT: an emerging management engineering discipline*. Petersburg, NY: BIAIT Int., Inc.

Chaffey, D., & Patron, M. (2012). From web analytics to digital marketing optimization: Increasing the commercial value of digital analytics. *Journal of Direct Data and Digital Marketing Practice*, *14*(1), 30–45. doi:10.1057/dddmp.2012.20

Chang, H. H., & Chen, S. W. (2008). The impact of online store environment cues on purchase intention: Trust and perceived risk as a mediator. *Online Information Review, 32*(6), 818–841. doi:10.1108/14684520810923953

Chang, H. H., & Chen, S. W. (2009). Consumer perception of interface quality, security, and loyalty in electronic commerce. *Information & Management, 46*(7), 411–417. doi:10.1016/j.im.2009.08.002

Chen, V. Y., Lien, H. P., Liu, C. H., Liou, J. J., Tzeng, G. H., & Yang, L. S. (2011). Fuzzy MCDM approach for selecting the best environment-watershed plan. *Applied Soft Computing, 11*(1), 265–275. doi:10.1016/j.asoc.2009.11.017

IBM Corporation. (1981). *Business Systems Planning: Information systems planning guide.* GE20-0527-3. IBM Corp.

Digital Advertising. (2015). Retrieved October 11, 2017, from https://www.statista.com/statistics/237974/online-advertising-spending-worldwide/

Digital marketing Megatrends. (2017). *Digital marketing Megatrends.* Retrieved November 9, 2017, from https://www.smartinsights.com/managing-digital-marketing/marketing-innovation/digital-marketing-trends-2016-2017/

Ducoffe, R. (1995). How consumers assess the value of advertising. *Journal of Current Issues and Research in Advertising, 17*(1), 1–18. doi:10.1080/10641734.1995.10505022

Fontela, E., & Gabus A. (1976). *The DEMATEL observer.* Academic Press.

Forbes. (2017a). *US Digital Marketing Spend Will Near $120 Billion By 2021.* Retrieved November 9, 2017, from https://www.forbes.com/sites/forrester/2017/01/26/us-digital-marketing-spend-will-near-120-billion-by-2021/ - 401bc054278b

Forbes. (2017b). *Internet of Things Market to Reach $267B by 2020.* Retrieved November 9, 2017, from https://www.forbes.com/sites/louiscolumbus/2017/01/29/internet-of-things-market-to-reach-267b-by-2020/ - 210fc901609b.

Forbes. (2017c). *Internet of Things will revolutionize retail.* Retrieved March 19, 2017, from https://www.forbes.com/sites/louiscolumbus/2017/03/19/internet-of-things-will-revolutionize-retail/#72ee42cc5e58

Gartner. (2017). Retrieved November 9, 2017, from https://www.gartner.com/newsroom/id/3598917

Godes, D., & Silva, J. C. (2012). Sequential and temporal dynamics of online opinion. *Marketing Science, 31*(3), 448–473. doi:10.1287/mksc.1110.0653

Gregory, J. (2015). *The Internet of Things: revolutionizing the retail industry*. Accenture Strategy.

Hoekstra, J. C., Huizingh, E. K., Bijmolt, T. H., & Krawczyk, A. C. (2015). Providing Information and Enabling Transactions: Which Website Function Is More Important for Success? *Journal of Electronic Commerce Research, 16*(2), 81–94.

Hori, S., & Shimizu, Y. (1999). Designing methods of human interface for supervisory control systems. *Control Engineering Practice, 7*(11), 1413–1419. doi:10.1016/S0967-0661(99)00112-4

IBM. (2016). *The Future of Retail is Consumer-Connected and Cognitive*. IBM Report.

IBM Institute for Business Value. (2011). *From stretched to strengthened – Insights from the Global Chief Marketing Officer Study*. IBM CMO C-suite Studies.

Ives, B., & Learmonth, G. P. (1984). The information system as a competitive weapon. *Communications of the ACM, 27*(12), 1193–1201. doi:10.1145/2135.2137

Ives, B., & Mason, R. O. (1990). Can information technology revitalize your customer service? *The Executive, 4*(4), 52–69. doi:10.5465/AME.1990.4277208

Johnston, M. R. (2015). *Wonder What Content to Create? Try a Customer-Journey Map*. Retrieved November 9, 2017, from http://contentmarketinginstitute.com/2015/11/customer-journey-map-template/

Kee, R. (2008). The sufficiency of product and variable costs for production-related decisions when economies of scope are present. *International Journal of Production Economics, 114*(2), 682–696. doi:10.1016/j.ijpe.2008.03.003

Kumar, R., Balaji, M. S., Sadeque, S., Nguyen, B., & Melevar, T. (2017). Constituents and consequences of smart customer experience in retailing. *Technological Forecasting and Social Change, 124*, 257–270. doi:10.1016/j.techfore.2016.09.022

Learmonth, G. P. (1986). Information system technology can improve customer service. *ACM SIGMIS Database, 18*(2), 6–10. doi:10.1145/24673.24674

Lee, I. (Ed.). (2017). The Internet of Things in the Modern Business Environment. IGI Global. doi:10.4018/978-1-5225-2104-4

Leeflang, P., Verhoef, P., Dahlström, P., & Freundt, T. (2014). Challenges and solutions for marketing in a digital era. *European Management Journal, 32*(1), 1–12. doi:10.1016/j.emj.2013.12.001

Lightner, N. (2004). Evaluating e-commerce functionality with a focus on customer service. *Communications of the ACM, 47*(10), 88–92. doi:10.1145/1022594.1022599

Lin, C. L., Chen, C. W., & Tzeng, G. H. (2010a). Planning the development strategy for the mobile communication package based on consumers' choice preferences. *Expert Systems with Applications*, *37*(7), 4749–4760. doi:10.1016/j.eswa.2009.11.009

Lin, C. L., Hsieh, M. S., & Tzeng, G. H. (2010b). Evaluating vehicle telematics system by using a novel MCDM techniques with dependence and feedback. *Expert Systems with Applications*, *37*(10), 6723–6736. doi:10.1016/j.eswa.2010.01.014

Lin, C. L., & Tzeng, G. H. (2009). A value-created system of science (technology) park by using DEMATEL. *Expert Systems with Applications*, *36*(6), 9683–9697. doi:10.1016/j.eswa.2008.11.040

Liou, J. J. H., Tzeng, G. H., & Chang, H. C. (2007). Airline safety measurement using a hybrid model. *Journal of Air Transport Management*, *13*(4), 243–249. doi:10.1016/j.jairtraman.2007.04.008

MARKETO. (2017). *The Marketing Power of the Internet of Things.* Retrieved November 9, 2017, from https://uk.marketo.com/infographics/the-marketing-power-of-the-internet-of-things/

Martins, J., Costa, C., Oliveira, T., Gonçalves, R., & Branco, F. (in press). How smartphone advertising influences consumers' purchase intention. *Journal of Business Research.*

Ou Yang, Y. P., Shieh, H. M., Leu, J. D., & Tzeng, G. H. (2008). A novel hybrid MCDM model combined with DEMATEL and ANP with applications. *International Journal of Operations Research*, *5*(3), 160–168.

Piccoli, G., Spalding, B. R., & Ives, B. (2001). The Customer Resource Life Cycle: A framework for improving customer service through information technology. *The Cornell Hotel and Restaurant Administration Quarterly*, *42*(38), 38–45.

Porter, M. (1985). *Competitive Advantage*. New York: The Free Press.

Rayport, J. F., & Sviokla, J. (1995). *Exploiting the Virtual Value Chain.* Harvard Business Review, November–December.

Royle, J., & Laing, A. (2014). The digital marketing skills gap: Developing a Digital Marketer Model for the communication industries. *International Journal of Information Management*, *34*(2), 65–73. doi:10.1016/j.ijinfomgt.2013.11.008

Sheehan, K. B. (2014). *Controversies in contemporary advertising* (2nd ed.). Thousand Oaks, CA: Sage Publications.

TechNavio. (2017). *Global Digital Marketing Software Market 2015-2019.* Retrieved November 9, 2017, from https://www.technavio.com/report/global-digital-marketing-software-market-2015-2019

Tzeng, G. H., Chiang, C. H., & Li, C. W. (2007). Evaluating intertwined effects in e-learning programs: A novel hybrid MCDM model based on factor analysis and DEMATEL. *Expert Systems with Applications*, *32*(4), 1028–1044. doi:10.1016/j.eswa.2006.02.004

UK Government Chief Scientific Adviser. (2014). The Internet of Things: Making the most of the Second Digital Revolution. A report by the UK Government Chief Scientific Adviser.

Wade, M. R., & Nevo, S. (2005). Development and Validation of a Perceptual Instrument to Measure E-Commerce Performance. *International Journal of Electronic Commerce*, *10*(2), 123–146.

Web Technology Surveys. (2014). *Usage of traffic analysis tools for websites.* Retrieved November 9, 2017, from http://w3techs.com/technologies/overview/traffic_analysis/all

Chapter 10
Enabling Small-Scale Actors to Operate on Markets of Energy and Ancillary Services

Mikhail Simonov
Instituto Superiore Boella (ISMB), Italy & European Commission, Italy

Luisa Tibiletti
Universita di Torino, Italy

ABSTRACT

Widespread renewable energy alters infrastructures and business by changing a way to balance between the demand and the offer. In customer-centered model, flexible economic behavior of small-scaled energy actors mitigates variability and uncertainty in flows of power and energy. Flexible cooperative behavior of many intraday market participants has a potential to reduce uncertainty in renewable energy flows. However, owners of small-scale renewable energy plants play limited market role. This chapter presents changed socio-economic and technology contexts and attracts attention to new challenges. New ICT enabler activates role of small-scale renewable energy actors by complementing their physical energy by structured information about the capacity and flexibility. In new market scenario, unpredictability of renewable energy is reduced by adding knowledge and exploiting better flexible behavior. Main conclusion is about using the information about flexibility to activate small-scale actors on real-time markets while improving ecological sustainability.

DOI: 10.4018/978-1-5225-5586-5.ch010

INTRODUCTION

In any business scenario, the *producer* of a good plays certain well-defined role during all the steps of product lifecycle. In most of known business scenarios, there is a visible time gap between the instant of time when the product is created and offered to commerce, and the time instant when the product is sold (consumed). As a result, the producer's role appears segmented in time. At the beginning of the lifecycle, the producer warrants the availability of the amount over certain time, the quality of a product, and the homogeneity of the quality. During the remaining stages of the product lifecycle, the producer warrants the availability of the product and parts of it for the replacements and reparations. Moreover, during the product distribution and commercialization stage, the producer warrants the non-deterioration of quality during certain duration of time. Usually consumers purchasing a good, they desire to know the name of producer and the brand because of reputation aspects.

In electric energy business example that uses storage-less power distribution systems, no gap appears between the time instants when an energy product is being produced and when it is being consumed. In effect, the electricity being produced (measured in kWh) is immediately consumed or lost. Because the electricity product is standardised, all kilowatt-hours appears identical. For this reason, the brands can remain unknown. Because energy consumer deals with the power distribution companies, the role of energy producers acting on energy markets has certain peculiarity. In the current energy business scenario (Sioshansi, 2013), large-scale energy companies bid directly on the energy markets, while the owners of small-scale power plants cannot operate in the same way. In other words, Small-Scale Actors (SSA) play passive market role, so there is a need to include them in energy markets by offering them new empowering tools.

The market of energy products and services is comprised of distinct day-ahead and real-time *processes* organized in such a way to meet reliability needs and serve loads. Main energy product on the Day-Ahead Market (DAM) is represented by an *amount of electricity* (expressed in kWh but priced in monetary units after the conversion rate $/kWh) that is delivered daily to the consumer in the form of a *flow of capacity*. In the *demand-led* model, the forward market establishes the generation (laggard) required to meet *forecast demand* (leader). Flow aspects can be described by the *rate* (expressed in units/s) that can be constant or time-varying and by the timescale (expressed in units of time) associated with the use of the reserved capacity (expressed in units). In this scenario, consumer has a complete freedom to transform said capacity into a work by expending energy at *any rate* $\partial E \,/\, \partial t$ (expressed in kWh/s) being agreed between the parts at any time. The maximum contractual threshold can be defined sharply (for example X kW max) or softly (for example up to X kW at any time, but more than X kW for less than Y seconds once at a time).

Because the maximum capacity is infrequently demanded, the demand-led business scenario imposes throttling energy plants at different rates (levels) to diminish loses and to maximize the sold amounts of energy. Energy producers appreciate and incentive the kind of demand that remains almost stable in time $E_{Demand}(t) \approx const.$ Energy consumers expend energy at very variable rates that range between zero and the $E_{Max}/\Delta t$. Hence, it makes sense defining a collateral energy product that expends energy after *well-defined levels of power* by stepping (ramping) between said levels after well-specified ordering function R(t), for example the $\frac{\partial}{\partial t}\left(\frac{\partial}{\partial t}E\right)$.

Since the *energy product* is standardized, there is substantial difference between the market roles played by large- and small-scale actors. To include actively small-scale actors in energy markets, there is a need to define new energy product they can offer. Power systems all around the world are dramatically changing because of the role of different business drivers that act towards a modernization of the grid infrastructure (a) and a revolution in operating conditions (b). One of the most important drivers is the scaling up Renewable Energy Sources (RES). In the recent history, the advent of RES occurred by exploring decentralized ubiquitous form of energy generation in the Low Voltage (LV) grid segments. At that time, the widespread of RES was stimulated by policy actions, while the economic incentives were largely explored by citizens to newly install small-scale RES plants. An effect of this activity is the creation of the very well-diversified Generation Portfolio (GP) and the change in the requirements for the monitoring, automation, and control in the power infrastructure.

For an extremely long while, power grids were *load-driven* after a system model that assumed loads *being* well-predictable. In this assumption, the throttling between different levels of power generation being scheduled for a next - usually day-ahead - period can be planned based on the *statistical* prediction. However, any known kind of statistical prediction is imperfect. As such, the oscillations between the expected values and the real ones are compensated at run-time (Van der Veen, 2016) because of the assumption that the loads are fully controllable and possible concentrated in large-scale power plants governable directly after the top-down controlling paradigm. New energy business scenario dominated by pervasive RES becomes *generation-driven* and *prosumption-driven* because uncertain ubiquitous generation leads an uncertain consumption being affected by unknown factors of flexibility in social behaviour. Since the rest of power system must follow said relationship between the production (the capacity) and the demand, the balancing procedure should be as quick as possible. However, the RES model cannot follow the legacy assumptions because of the different adaptability of RES with respect to the Traditional Energy Sources (TES). For this reason authors rethink the role of small-scale actors in consumer-centred energy system.

BACKGROUND

Climate change dramatically impacted by changing uncertainties associated with the Rates Of Change (ROC) in energy/power production and consumption, $RoCoE = \frac{\partial E}{\partial t}$ and $RoCoP = \frac{\partial P}{\partial t}$ respectively. In traditional energy networks, the balance between the demand for power/energy and the offer of power/energy was managed by increasing *the amount* of commodity or by shedding certain interruptible load flows. The past question of interest was about equating the corresponding amounts of the demand and the supply in technical and/or market perspectives (Bruninx et al., 2016). In newest scenario, the question of interest is about the *time* and *timescales* available to decide about balancing the *amounts* of demand and of supply, scheduling *accumulations* of reserves over time, or optimizing the curtailments in the case of insufficient time to decide an alternative management technique. The use of RES instead of using TES manifests substantial difference between the allowed ROCs associated with the uncertainty about achieving upper limits of scalability during the time in prospect (Mancarella, 2017). It imposes substantial changes on the intraday markets. In the current energy business scenario, both the flexibility and ancillary services are provided by qualified (e.g. large-scale mainly) actors. In a far ahead scenario, customer-centred grid emerges new paradigm about changing economic behaviour of small- and medium- scaled energy actors instead of varying the amounts of commodity that is called flexibility. Flexible *cooperative* behaviour of many small-scale energy actors participating in market might optimize energy. At the same time, flexible behaviour of many actors might over-concentrate unbalances in time up to destabilize power system. This aspect describes substantial difference that exists between the large-scale and the small-scale RES actors (Panteli, 2015). In addition to offering an amount of intermittent energy being modulated after the laws of Nature, these actors can adjust said modulation of power levels by using flexibility. Small-scale actors can offer well-modulated set of levels of powers after the flexible behaviour in addition to the amount of energy. In other words, the human behaviour of many RES actors might be explored in order to transform random crowd behaviour in an optimized cooperative flexible flow of actions on energy markets.

Given the above-mentioned aspects, this chapter focuses on the exploitation of *flexibility at ubiquitously distributed (demand) side* as an enabler that includes small-scale RES energy actors in markets. Authors discusses about how to quantify their flexibility by measurements, how to support knowledgeable decisions about trading energy products and ancillary (balancing) services, and how to connect new actors to the Business Information Systems (BIS) to allow them to formulate offers and to be paid for. This chapter is intended to explain the main issues concerning the participation in the energy markets of small-scale actors. The intended readers are students, industrial researchers, investors in innovative businesses, and other categories of readers.

ISSUES, CONTROVERSIES, PROBLEMS

Market Issues

An electricity market is a system and a collection of processes enabling *economic operations* with energy product *E(t)*. Offers to sell and offers to buy (an amount) use supply and demand principles to set the price. From economic point of view, both electric power (expressed as \$/s) and electric energy (expressed as \$) represent an energy-containing commodity that can be traded on the markets. Power (measured in megawatts, MW) is the metered net electrical transfer *rate* at any given *instant of time*. Energy (measured in megawatt-hours, MWh) is an *amount* of electricity that flows through a metered point for a given *period of time*. There are three main kinds of market operations with electricity. On the Day-Ahead Market (DAM), the *forecasted amounts* of electricity (E_1, …, E_k, all expressed in MWh) are committed. The *price in hourly timescale* is determined by matching offers from generators to bids from consumers at each node. This way, a classic supply and demand equilibrium price is calculated by considering the transmission constrains for each region after the operator's load flow model. In Intraday Market (IM), fine tuning of equilibrated amounts over time (E_1, …, E_{24}, hourly periods in the example) is operated. In order to ensure system reliability, the Balancing and Ancillary Services Markets (BASM) at fine-grained timescale consider procurement for services, such as kinds of reserves, kinds of regulation, and installed capacity. In this way the room for *variability* E_k+/-x% for each time slot k is planned and reserved. Three markets represent three different needs: to ensure the *availability* of required amounts (1), to distribute dynamically amounts over time periods (2), and to ensure the *fast control response* at run-time (3). Small-scale actors indirectly participate in the DAM by selling their amounts to Aggregators, but they do not have tools to define and to sell any ancillary service in real-time. The main issues stay in how these actors can measure the amounts and the rate of energy while doing other business, how the flow of electricity is expressed in monetary terms, how many small flows of RES electricity can be controlled, and how a set of Service Level Agreements (SLA) can be set and verified for many small-scale actors.

Energy/Power Economics

Energy resources can be viewed as renewable or depletable (non-renewable). Some Renewable Energy Resources (RES) can be stored, while others are not storable. The advent of renewable resources of energy forces new market relationships, especially those concerning numerous small-scale energy actors because this category of actors is not actively included in the markets. Human utilization of energy resources and energy commodities and the consequences of that utilization stay in the field of energy economics. Energy amounts embodied in all energy commodities/resources offer the ability to perform work. Energy is a peculiar good because of the *capacity for doing work.* In this definition energy is a product that satisfies the *need of acting* because energy commodities being purchased e.g., electricity, gas, gasoline, or diesel fuel – can be used to provide energy services for human activities, such as lighting, heating, cooking, lifting objects, accelerating a process, but also motive power, electronic activity, and so on. Energy resources of any kind needs to be harvested in one form, needs to be converted in the desired form, and needs to be delivered at right time to the right users in right places.

In typical human activities using energy, energy actors never create or destroy energy, but they perform energy conversion between its various forms. In daily life, humans routinely materialize complex sequences of energy conversion processes to provide desired services. Therefore, energy E is materialized in the form of a flow $E(t)$ that exists and varies in time (Figure 1). However, the energy amounts being expended in one timescale (milliseconds) are billed in another coarser-grained timescale (months).

Small- or large- scaled energy actor owning energy conversion plant can exploit the production capacity in full or partially during the whole lifetime of the plant or during certain shorter periods of time. By running the energy conversion plant at

Figure 1. The flow of power and the flow of energy in time

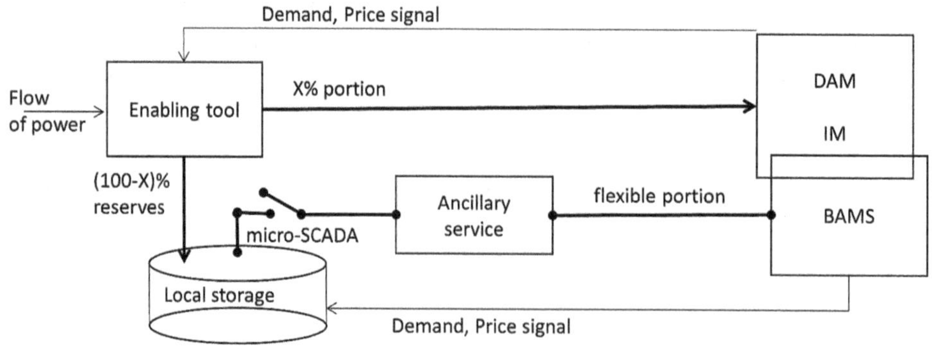

the maximum capacity during all the possible time (e.g. *lifetime*), the corresponding flow of power can materialize work at the only condition of being delivered to the end-users, being used, and being paid for. In all other cases the flow of energy will be never expended and/or paid for. As such, the amount of marketable energy heavily depends on the demand for power that exists at *exactly the same time*. Because of peculiar use of energy in storage-less energy distribution grids, the flow of energy production $\frac{\partial E_p}{\partial t}$ and the flow of demand $\frac{\partial E_d}{\partial t}$ are necessarily simultaneously equated in time $\frac{\partial E_p}{\partial t} = \frac{\partial E_d}{\partial t}$. For this reason, the terms *demand* (flow seen by the consumer) and *response* (flow seen by the producer) represent the same semantic concept, e.g. the effective Rate of Work that expends the flow of energy/power at that well-specified time. The demand-response dualism has two important implications: the energy flow (expressed in kWh/s), seen as an energy-containing commodity (valued in \$), has certain price (expressed in \$·s/s) and the availability at any time of a flow of any entity, seen as a networked service, has another price. Given that, an abstract amount of accumulated energy is a good, while the flow of electricity being modulated in time is a service.

Demand for energy on the market is primarily derived from the energy requirements of desired services. As such, energy demand represents the demand for desired services. Consumers purchase electricity to perform functions using electricity *at the time they desire them*, e.g. artificial lighting is mainly operated in evening and night time, refrigeration is operated all the time, space heating is operated mainly in winter time, air conditioning is mainly operated in summer time, while washing/drying closes/dishes, heating water, operating electronic equipment depend on individual preferences. When the energy is being demanded by end-users (which is simultaneous with the production process), they convert it in yet other forms after certain *conversion pattern* that can be *measured analytically* because it is a composition in time-space of several processes. For example, the transformation of electric- to mechanic- form is driven by motors in appliances such as refrigerators, air-conditioning units, or vacuum cleaners that might work in parallel of sequentially in time. At the same or different time, electric- to thermal- conversion is driven by space heating, clothes dryers, or water heating. In a household or at an industrial site, electric- to radiation- conversion is driven by the stock of lighting, televisions, computers, and monitors. The *expected changes* in the load/generation appear graphically in the form of ramps (Figure 2). Photovoltaic RES production (in the Figure 2 example) presents an upward ramp in morning time followed by a downward ramp in the afternoon time. To measure analytically the time-varying flow of electricity in the form of ramps, specific demand-oriented energy meter is

Figure 2. Time-varying flow of RES electricity

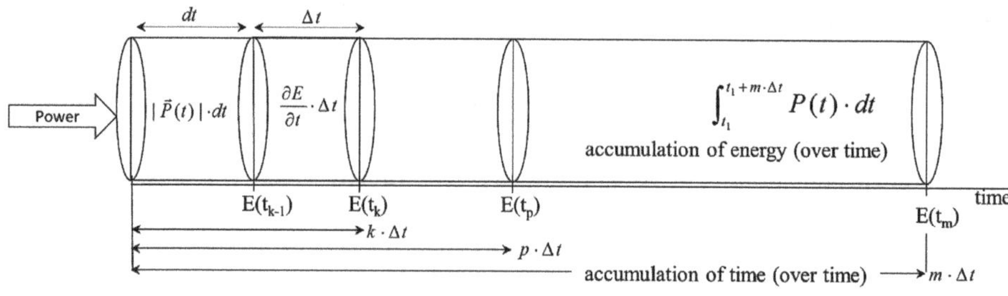

required. In addition to cumulative daily amounts that can be computed immediately based on the hourly figures, analytical accounting of electricity adds information about demanded quantities over time plus the information about both the variability and the uncertainty, which computation is much more sophisticated and relies on extra information.

The explicit and well-measurable *electricity demand* is derived from the hidden and less traceable demand for the underlying services. Real-life process that expends generation capacity of one or more large- or small-scaled plants becomes electricity demand realized by one or more energy consumers. Energy conversion efficiency directly determines energy demand. Market actors can choose among various conversion efficiency alternatives by selecting appliances of energy efficiency classes C, B, …, A+++ to significantly influence energy demand. To the extent that actors understand their conversion efficiencies, expectations of future energy prices can influence choices of equipment. When the gas prices become too high, household actors can decide to invest money in home insulation. In general, increased energy prices reduce demand by reducing use of energy services and motivating selection of higher conversion efficiency equipment.

The flow of electric energy is often considered in economics (Kneese, 1993) as an *essential good* because almost any human activity is energy-dependent. For an essential good, the demand remains positive at any high price (limitless) because consumers allocate all their income to purchase it. Therefore, any energy flow – any amount structured appears marketable. *Particular kind of* energy appears not essential because one form of energy can be converted into another one. Any aggregate of purchased kinds of energy appears not essential because extremely energy-efficient houses, like Zero Energy Buildings (ZEB), might require relatively little energy. High enough prices can reduce the demand for purchased energy up to zero because a percentage of consumers can decide to install RES plant to warrant the electricity at constant and known a-priori price for heating and/or for cooking. Likewise, consumers can adopt bicycles to reduce their fuel expenses (for traveling). This kind of changed behavior transforms ex-consumers into new small-scale prosumers. In this likely scenario, *purchased energy* loses qualities of an essential good. Moreover, the lack of preference in terms of purchasing shares for the energy mix from small- and/or large- scale energy actors uncovers the need of specific enablement tool for small-scale energy actors to allow them competing in the fair market conditions with the large-scale actors.

The *expected profitability* of any newly installed (RES) energy plant is computed over its whole lifetime in MWh·lifetime. The nominal capacity of a plant might vary over long years by decaying slowly. Likewise, the peak power being generated during *certain time slots* might vary depending on the weather conditions. Additionally, the revenues expressed in monetary terms depend on how/when the amounts are being sold due to the time-varying market prices and depend on the capability to sell up to 100% of the production. By moving to the daily timescale (0-24h), the rental (overnight) capacity of the plant is expressed as a simple percentage of the lifetime production. The profitability is variable because it depends on the choice of energy-conversion technology. In real-time dimension (timescale in milliseconds), the effective RES generation is unknown a-priori. For this reason, the electricity flow should be measured analytically in both electricity- and monetary- units (kWh/s and $/s respectively).

Measuring Demand for Power

The flow of electricity can be expressed either in units of electricity kWh/s or in units of money $/s. By definition, a product is anything *capable of* satisfying a need that can be offered to a market to satisfy that need. In addition, products also include essentially intangible services which are activities or benefits that do not result in the ownership of anything. The time-varying Demand for Power (DfP) that *explores randomly* the capacity of the grid imposes the use of grid monitoring and Energy Management System (EMS) tools. The DfP being modulated in certain desired fashion has a potential to act as an equivalent of a Balancing Service (BS). Since the re-modulated DfP can satisfy a specific balancing need of Smart Grid, it can be exploited on the BASM. For this reason, the structured succession of terms $\{(q_1,\Delta t_1),\ldots, (q_k,\Delta t_k),\ldots\}$ built in such a way that satisfies needs of main energy actors can be seen as a new marketable ancillary service. This exercise takes *any unexpected* ramp of supply levels and replaces it by an *expected* ramp. In other terms, the functions f and g exist such as $q_k=f(q_{k-1})$ and $\Delta t_k=g(\Delta t_{k-1})$. The above-mentioned transform takes *unexpected* periods of time in which electrical power is being provided and replaces them by an *expected* succession of time intervals. The added value comes from the uncertainty being reduced.

In order to compare two differently modulated in time DFPs, a metrics needs to be defined. The DFP is measured by using demand-oriented meters called also as the Demand Measurement Unit (DMU). While known Smart Meters (SM) start from a signal of power P - being digitally sampled in time t -, newer DMUs start from the signal of flexibility R - being sampled in time τ. The accumulation in time t of the flow of commodity being expended in time τ is governed by the business analytics investigating the variability of $R(\tau)$.

In the current demand-led Smart Grid (SG) scenario, smart meters measuring energy at sub-hour time resolution play a role of the main technology enabler because offering two-way connectivity with the centralized Industrial Control Systems (ICS/ SCADA). Unfortunately, known cumulative energy meters cannot offer true demand figures. Enabling Demand-Response Management (DRM) function requires new and additional ICT framework. After the advent of diffused generation from RES, differently scaled RES actors were introduced in the energy business scenario. The main known issue is the discrepancy between the business operations that any-scale energy actor can potentially perform with the energy product and the limited operations effectively allowed to small-scale actors. Apparently, there is no substantial difference between a flow of power/energy being injected into smart grid by one 10 MWh_P plant and a flow received form 1,000 smaller-scale 10 kWh_P plants running simultaneously. Likewise, there appears no substantial difference between energy being drawn from smart grid by one 10 MWh_D consumer and the demand operated by 1,000 smaller-scale 10 kWh_D consumers. In order to allow small-scale actors in the same fashion the large-scale actors do, the Aggregator role was introduced. However, the composition of several many small-scale actors introduces both the advantages in terms of averaging and disadvantages, for example in terms of amplification of effects (reader thinks about the simultaneity of drop-outs of power or energy). The main challenge explored in this chapter is the transformation of the role of small-scale actors to emerge new contributions in the improved energy efficiency and robustness/reliability/resilience of Smart Grid.

Modelling Load And Demand

In a power system, the *behavior of* a load in time is modeled by a *function of power* P(t)=V(t)xI(t) plotted graphically in the form of Load Shape (LS). At longer run, the load flow P(t) accumulates an amount of energy E(t) expressed as an integral $E(t) = \int_{t_1}^{t_2} P(t)dt$. Two different loads can behave very differently during certain amount of time $[t_1,t_2]$, but both of them can accumulate the same amount of energy over certain time $E(t)= P_1\cdot[t_i,t_j] =P_2\cdot[t_k,t_p]$, while the durations $\|t_i,t_j\|$ and $\|t_k,t_p\|$ might be any (the same or not the same). To measure *how* different loads do accumulate energy in time, ad hoc parameters were proposed. The *load factor* $f_c(t) = \frac{P_{Avg}(t)}{P_{Max}(t)}$ defined as a ratio between the average- and the maximum- loads gives raw idea about the variability between the P_{Avg} and the P_{Max}. However, the linear model $P_{Avg}(t) = f_c(t) \cdot P_{Max}(t)$ is insufficient in the presence of accelerations.

Given a signal of power P(t) and its digital measurements $\{P(t_1), P(t_2), \ldots, P(t_k), \ldots\}$ in time $\{t_1, t_2, \ldots, t_k, \ldots\}$, part of behavioural information is encoded in *amplitudes* $P(t_j)$. When the power remains unchanged over two intervals of time of the same duration, the ratio $\frac{P(t_k)}{\left\|t_k - t_{k-1}\right\|} = \frac{P(t_{k+p})}{\left\|t_{k+p} - t_{k+p-1}\right\|}$ is an invariant. In this assumption, the equivalence

$$\left(k \cdot P(t_k)\right) \cdot \left\|t_k - t_{k-1}\right\|^{-1} = P\left(t_{k+p}\right) \cdot \left(k \cdot \left\|t_{k+p} - t_{k+p-1}\right\|^{-1}\right)$$

explains how information can be encoded in frequencies. When timers are uniform, the variability appears in magnitudes of power. When the levels of power are fixed, the variability appears in frequencies. Therefore, the frequencies $\{\|t_1-t_0\|^{-1}, \|t_2-t_1\|^{-1}, \ldots, \|t_k-t_{k-1}\|^{-1}, \ldots\}$ and $\{\|t_1-t_0\|^{-1}, \|t_2-t_0\|^{-1}, \ldots, \|t_k-t_0\|^{-1}, \ldots\}$ bring information about the partition of time in a set of periods during which the *Rate of Change of Power* (RoCoP) remains nearly unchanged.

Compared with the random *powers* $\{P_1, \ldots, P_k\}$, the structured *demand* is described by the Quantities Demanded (QD). For each interval of time, the variability of electricity that runs at variable rates of flow can be synthetically described by the levels of power P_{Min}, P_{Max}, $P_{Average}$, $P_{Shortest}$, $P_{Longest}$, $P_{Predominant}$, and analytically by the $R(t) = \frac{\partial P(t)}{\partial t}$, and by the $R'(t)$. On demand-billed energy service, Charges for Power (CfP) and Charges for Demand (CfD) are separate. In the example, suppose user operates a miscellaneous electric equipment of 10 kW of loads. During a month, a relay switches it on at 8:00AM of every day and leaves it working *for 6 minutes* only. At the *end of month*, user pays for 30 kW of *accumulated* power only. However, this actor used the right of keeping operating full load of 10 kW at *any time of any day*. This *freedom to make randomly the peaks* suggests a charge for demand because of the commitment to provide the response. For this reason, the price of power is proportional to each *amount of power being used*. The price criteria for demand-based billing do exploit the Time Of Use (ToU) concept. Demand billing does not end *until after* the periodic energy exchange *has been less than* X kWh for Y *consecutive periods of time*. The *demand-oriented measurements* accumulate over time units expressed in kW·h, while the *demand estimators* (Berrisford 1990) derive a stepwise structure labeled by *different factors*. Small-scale actor willing to sell its energy product needs a technical tool that represents the *dynamics of* DfP in time.

The *Demand Factor* (DF, or f_{demand}) is a measure defined as a fractional amount of some quantity *being effectively used* relative to the maximum amount that *could be potentially used* by the same system $f_{demand} = \dfrac{Demand(t_k)}{Demand_{max}}$. In real life energy-transforming system the DF(t)≤1 for ∀ t and the DRM targets to maximize it by DF(t)→1. The DF function of time is of our interest because it describes *how* the amount of demand *varies in the selected timescale*. In the above example with daily timescale, the f_{demand}(30 days) is [10kW·(6min. ·30 times)] / [10kW·(1440min. ·30 times)] = 30kW/7,200 kW = 0.004 and it generically suggests an optimization. The *realized value* depends on the energy being expended by the customer (1st factor) but also on the *choice criteria* for time period (2nd factor). Let authors vary a sliding window by choosing 1440, 60, 15, or 6 minutes of every day. The DF time series *realized for the same demand* unhide an interesting behavioral information: the hourly DF is almost zero except the slot [8:00,9:00], the DF([8:00, 8:15])=0.4, but the DF([8:00, 8:06])=1. Even if the timescale is conventionally fixed, an *intelligent choice of time windowing* can *uncover the behavior* of electric equipment operated by this customer. Because the DF(t)=1 when the *duration of observational period* equates the ToU of energy, authors customize the measurement observer in order to *trace the succession of peaks of accumulated work* until isolating periods of time such as (DF([t_{k-Tk},t_k])→Max) AND (|t_{k-Tk}-t_k|→Max). In other words, instead of stepping by 15 minutes of *natural time*, the authors count the *time of energy use* at each possible rate of flow. Measurement observer (digital tool) reports about non-ignorable changes in the form of events then.

The easiest way to choose the time windowing is by following the market time slots (hourly, every 30 minutes, every 15 minutes, and so on). Making the optimal choice of above time windowing – in order to emerge the durations of steadily flowing energy commodity - is non-trivial issue. Since each energy user expends energy in unpredictable manner and it never declares peaks in advance, the only a-posteriori *data-driven choice* seems feasible. Technically, a solver gets time series representing the work and tries finding the best averaging of peak(s) over a large sliding window. The deadlock comes from the current definition of the demand factor assumed to be *time independent quantity* where the numerator is taken as the maximum demand in the *specified time period*. To unlock, authors change the definition of the demand- and load- factors and the ways to calculate them digitally. New approach requires *exact or colored-noise measurement* of time-varying AC periodicity $T_k(\xi)$, of the interval energy gauged to the ends of AC periods E(t_{j-Tk},t_j), ad-hoc filter specialized to shape process-activity-oriented units of "almost the same" work, and neural coding and approach to knowledge elicitation.

Energy systems are designed to meet both the Energy Demand [ED, expressed in units of energy and time] and the Load Demand [LD, expressed in units of power and time] at different scales of time ranging from the DAM up to the real-time control. Energy demand can be quantified through the realized values of Cumulative Energy (CE) supplied by smart meters (SM). The demand has more complex structure because it depends on several factors such as the customer's type (household, commercial, industry, etc.), the customer's equipment, the climate conditions (outdoor temperature, light), and so-called Human Factors (HF, e.g. consumption patterns, inhabits, etc.). The energy demand during specific period of time might be rather stable. Conversely, the load demand might vary substantially within a given period. For this reason, true LD figures cannot be estimated based on the ED data reported by smart meters. Demand for Power (DfP) can be treated as the Quantity Demanded (QD), an economic category that describes the total amount of commodity demanded at *any* given point in time. Additionally, the QD depends directly on the price of a commodity. The degree to which the QD changes with respect to price is called the elasticity of demand. However, the DAM price of a commodity is associated with the amounts of energy only. Instead, BAMS operations with the variability and uncertainty of power flows are materialized in the form of ancillary services. As a result, operating with the *prices of power* becomes tricky.

The *Demand for Energy* (DfE) is an economic principle that describes the utility for a good (energy) and associated services (delivery of energy, commitment, and so on) of an economic agent. The demand for an energy product, or an energy service, or for the association of both of them, is an enumeration (e.g. a list) of quantities demanded at each possible price. In contrast to demand, quantity demanded is the exact quantity demanded at a certain well-defined price. The DfE expresses a consumer's *desire and willingness to pay* certain price for a commodity of specific kind and for the delivery service. Holding all other factors constant, the price of energy signal that varies *once-at-a-time* (OaT) can be used to modulate the demand for energy in amplitude, by increasing or by decreasing it. Until the *desire to pay for energy* is not materialized by an actor, the Imaginary Demand (ID) indicates an *amount that could be used* by the system. It is a kind that equates *energy*. Once the purchase is recorded, the *Amount of Demand* (AoD) becomes real. It is a kind that equates *work*. Therefore, the amount of demand is a *time-dependent quantity* that can be described by a kind of factor. The term *Demand Factor* (DF) refers to the fractional amount of some quantity *being effectively used* relative to the maximum amount that *could be used* by the same system. In this case, the DF is a ratio between the effective amount of demand and the possible imaginary demand, e.g. DF = AoD/ID.

Individual Demand refers to the demand of a particular consumer. Individual energy-transforming work is conditioned by several circumstances and factors that vary in type and degree. *Aggregate Demand* refers to the overall or average demand of many market participants. Overall, it is affected by the same factors, but the way they affect the aggregated demand is different compared with a way they affect the individual one. For example, a particular demand is influenced by a personal income, but it does not significantly affect aggregate demand in a large energy system. For this reason, supply- and demand- factors *appear unique* for a given product or service. A *Demand Profile* (DP) is usually plotted as a graph that shows slopes moving from left to right on a demand-supply chart. Compared with a Load Profile (LP) that plots *amounts* of power that vary in naturally ordered *time*, such a graph expresses the dependency between the monetary *amount* (price) and the demanded or supplied *amount*s. This specific aspect makes a chart "timeless". Depending on how the price signal changes, a demand/supply curve slopes upward or downwards because an increase in price usually corresponds to a lower demand/provision of energy. In other words, an *increase in demand* moves right-side the demand curve. In this case, the curves of the demand and the supply *intersect at a higher price* and consumers pay more for the energy. At long run, competitive markets tend to push prices toward the equilibrium. However, equilibrium prices float because several many factors affecting demand/supply are time-varying.

Enablement Technology

For a long while, energy users have infrequently interacted with meters when reading data (monthly). The advent and the widespread of small-scale renewable energy plants follows the common and well-known innovation *pattern* that includes an initial period *x* in which the RES is not used, before technology for using the RES is completely developed. In this stage, actors install two separate smart meters to account the cumulative amounts of production and consumption, sell the produced energy to their Distribution Service Operator (DSO) at one price, and buy the energy being consumed at differently modulated price, while RES generators are not exchanging information with the Industrial Control Systems (ICS). In that initial stage, no specific technology enablers are offered to small-scale actors.

The rates of RES availability rise over time more- or less- rapidly as that technology develops and RES demand increase. In this stage, the prices of the energy mix with certain percentage of RES start changing in intraday timescale. The RES energy appears cheaper because there is no need to purchase fuel to operate power plants. However, the RES might require more sophisticated, so more expensive, balancing. Therefore, RES actors start adopting demand-oriented measurement devices to compute analytically their quantities being demanded / offered. In this intermediate stage, specific technology enabler, namely the Demand-response Measurement Units (DMU), appears. The complexity of measurement data increases exponentially. The DMU measures the accumulation, divides it into ramp-like objects, makes a guess about a customer group from a defined geographical area that goes to purchase our energy/power product/service in a defined time period in a defined marketing environment under a defined marketing program. In addition to cumulative amounts of energy from smart meters, small-scale actors start collecting structured information about the Levels of Powers (LoP) and Time of Use (ToU) of their flows in real time. The natural modulation of RES power flows after the forces of Nature remains unchanged. However, small-scale actors acquire familiarity with the real-time aspects of their power flows and learn the importance of modulating them after certain criteria, for example the coordinated stepwise changes between levels of power. In the absence of economic incentives, RES plants lack remotely-operated relays that can materialize throttling between different levels.

At longer run, when RES energy is widely spread over the power networks, RES commodity prices fall after the mean-reversion model. At certain time *y*, depletion of the non-renewable resource results in rising costs, while the extraction rate declines. The coexistence of RES and non-RES lasts until all the stocks being depleted. At that point *z*, the consumers of the depletable resource must replace means of satisfying their energy service demand by considering 100% RES scenario with low inertia and very fast timing up to frequency instability and possible blackout. At that time, all small-scale actors will be completely included in the market scenario by using new technology enablers. The DMU, the remotely operated ICS/SCADA, and the automated/fast energy trading framework exemplify the set of technology enablers being required in this stage.

The requirement of enabling the inclusion of small-scale energy actors in markets is timely because it accompanies the transition from 100% non-RES and mixed RES with non-RES scenario up to the 100%-RES one. The availability of analytical tools to account the levels of energy flows is not sufficient because, in the current energy market regulation, small-scale actors are not allowed to act directly on the Intraday and BASM markets. They role is restricted to be passive only because Distribution System Operators (DSO) or their equivalent Aggregators do acquire all amounts of their energy at the price that does not dependent on how the flow is modulated over time. Main energy product (amount of energy) is valued after the simplified formula $\Pi(E,t) = AoE(t_k) \cdot UP$, where the AoE denotes the cumulative amount of energy being sold and the UP denotes the standard unitary price. After the introduction of variable price that changes in real time as UP(t), the structure of demand-response can be valued differently after the formula $\Pi(E,t) = \sum_{k=1}^{k=n} AoE(t_k) \cdot UP(t_k)$ (Figure

3), where the AoE indicates the amount of energy being accumulated over sub-period Δt compatible with the market timescale, and the UP(t) denotes the unitary price associated with the same interval of time Δt.

Quantifying Capacity and Production

With renewable energy projects, a major area of risk is quantifying the expected energy production and uncertainty. One of the drivers of this risk is the uncertainty in solar irradiance and/or wind intensity data. For this reason, the collection of on-site measurements can be used to mitigate some risks of using modelled data to estimate energy and cash flows. Commonly, a single system level time series of renewable energy production is derived by summing total system historical production for each well-defined time interval (for example an hour) and dividing by total installed capacity to yield a normalized value for each time interval. In this approach, there is no analytical information about the variability and uncertainty in the data inside each timescale. This suggests that use of a single system level time series is not a valid approach when an accurate information about constraint levels are required. The single time series did not consider differences between the amounts of capacity and the time-varying flow of its effective use.

In the load-driven model, the load being leading P is assumed to be *any*, while the generation being following is assumed to be changing stepwise between different *possible levels* of capacity C_k in order to meet *any* random composition of *any* random number of *any* random DfP. In this model, consumers pay for the demand for power *after* an energy being consumed over certain interval of time (1) independently on *how* the power was used. The variability between the maximum- and the minimum-levels of demand for power can be controlled by setting up the contractual limits P_{max}=const for certain percentage of population and by adopting the demand-based billing to the remaining percentage of population. When the contractual limits are impractical, the demand factor is being measured (2) and used in billing. Demand-

Figure 3. The flow of power expressed in monetary terms

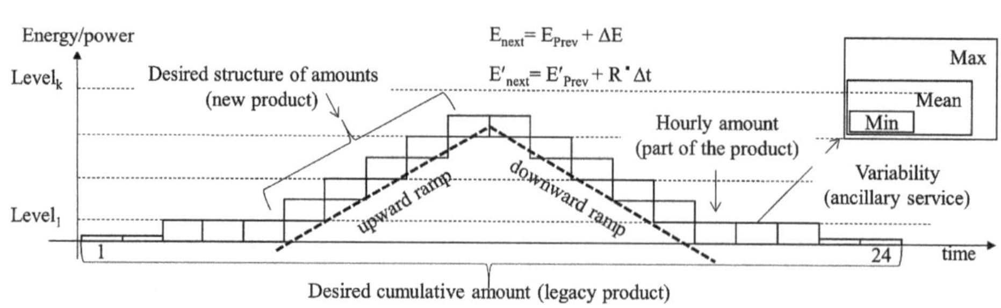

billed customers pay after the energy being effectively used (1) and after the capacities being structurally explored during the billing period.

$$\forall P \rightarrow C(t) \in \{C_1, C_2, \ldots, C_k, \ldots\} \tag{1}$$

$$AoL(t) = \int_{t_1}^{t_2} P(t)dt \tag{2}$$

$$f_c(t) = \frac{P_{Avg}(t)}{P_{Max}(t)} \tag{3}$$

$$\mathrm{Cos}\,t(t) = AoL(t) \cdot up_E(t) + \sum f_c(t) \cdot up_C(t) \tag{4}$$

$$P(t) \in \{P_1, P_2, \ldots, P_k, \ldots\} \tag{5}$$

In the generation-driven model, the generation being leading G is assumed to be *any*, while the DfP being following is assumed to be changing stepwise between different *allowed levels* of DfP_k in order to meet *any* random composition of *any* random number of *any* random generation capacity. In new model, consumers pay after *how* they demanded the power in time. On other words, the price is associated with the demand's structure in time (1) and with discrepancy between the *allowed stepwise changes* and the effective ones (2). The variability between the maximum- and the minimum- levels of generation capacity can be controlled by adopting the demand-based billing as the default option (1) and by setting up the structured information about the QD being allowed contractually (x) for certain percentage of (baseline) population, and by accepting the anticipatory structured information about the flexible Changes of Quantities Demanded (CoQD) with respect to the allowed QD (x) for other percentage of flexible portion. When the contractual limits are impractical, the demand factor is being measured (2') and used in billing. Demand-billed customers pay after the energy being effectively used (1') and after the capacities being structurally explored during the billing period.

$$\forall G \rightarrow DfP(t) \in \{DfP_1, DfP_2, \ldots, DfP_k, \ldots\} \text{ (1')}$$

$$AoD(t) = \int_{g_{Acc}(t_1)}^{g_{Acc}(t_2)} DfP(t)dt \text{ (2')}$$

$$f_{Load}(t) = \frac{P_{Avg}([t_k, t_p])}{P_{Max}([t_k, t_p])}, \; f_{Demand}(t) = \frac{DfP_{Max}([t_k, t_p])}{DfP_{Max}(\forall t)} \quad (3')$$

$$\mathrm{Cos}\, t(t) = AoL(t) \cdot up_E(t) + \sum f_c(t) \cdot up_C(t) \quad (4')$$

$$P(t) \in \{P_1, P_2, ..., P_k, ...\} \quad (5')$$

Quantifying Generation

For several practical reasons, many generators installed in large power systems do not operate at their full capacity all the time. A generator's output may vary according to conditions at the power plant, fuel costs, as instructed by the electric power grid operator, or because of the unfavorable weather conditions in the case of renewable energy sources. It represents a different set of uncertainties. Knowing the amount of Energy Generation (EG) being effectively produced might be insufficient to figure out *how* the energy product is being fabricated. In order to describe the production process in better detail, the Electricity Generation Capacity (EGC) and the Time of Use (ToU) might be useful. The difference $Var(EG) = EGC \cdot ToU - EG$ might inform about running at lower capacity all the time, about keeping reserves, about renting full capacity during less working hours, or about any mixed scenario. The exact analytical information about the *production process* is encoded in all the effective levels of capacity (EGC_{eff}) combined with the partitioning of time in respective effective ToU_{eff} at each generation level. In the current scenario, this information is not of the consumer's interest. However, this kind of information is currently unavailable to small-scale energy actors. The Event-Driven Energy Metering method (EDM) has materialized the above-mentioned accounting modality (Simonov, 2013). Nowadays, installing the EDMs at the premises of small-scale energy producers is possible. This operation releases the exact structure of the generation. The EDMs were designed to be used in networked modality in order to support a multi-agent system in controlling the grid in decentralized fashion. Once the analytical information about the effective generation is available, it can be compared with the demand figures. Likewise, installing the EDMs at the premises of small-scale energy consumers releases the exact structure of the demand. The comparison between the time series of demand and generation emerges the figures explaining the balancing actions. Given that, the DMU functionality can be obtained by modifying the EDMs.

MAIN FOCUS OF THE CHAPTER

This Chapter focuses on the inclusion of small-scale energy actors – Producers, Consumers, and Prosumers – in energy markets. In order to enable the desired operation, authors discuss about the peculiar marketable product coming from small-scale RES actors, which is the physical electric energy from the legacy scenario being accompanied by the certification of the ecology-friendly aspects and by the detailed information about the structure of energy flow in time. To define such a complex product, authors propose new analytic measurement tool that quantifies both the amounts and the rates of energy over desired timescale. are measured, how the flow of electricity is expressed in monetary terms, how the flow of RES electricity can be controlled, and how the Service Level Agreements (SLA) are set and verified.

Consequently, authors focus on making analytic the measurement of effective capacity/demand figures. Given the availability of new kind of information, authors discuss about the modalities of its use. One of the challenges is making more flexible the flow of demand/capacity. Authors analyses new flexibility product in terms of the need, the ownership, the price, and the ways to operate with the flexibility. Once the detailed information is added to the physical flow of power, authors discuss about exploiting new knowledge in consumer-centered smart grid.

Methodology Approach

The research issue under investigation is the enabling role of the flexibility R(t) at both demand and supply sides, the Transactive Energy Control (TEC) approach, and the way to widespread its use at a scale (Figure 4).

Figure 4. The role of the demand flexibility in achieving the climate objectives by containing the energy amounts being expended over time

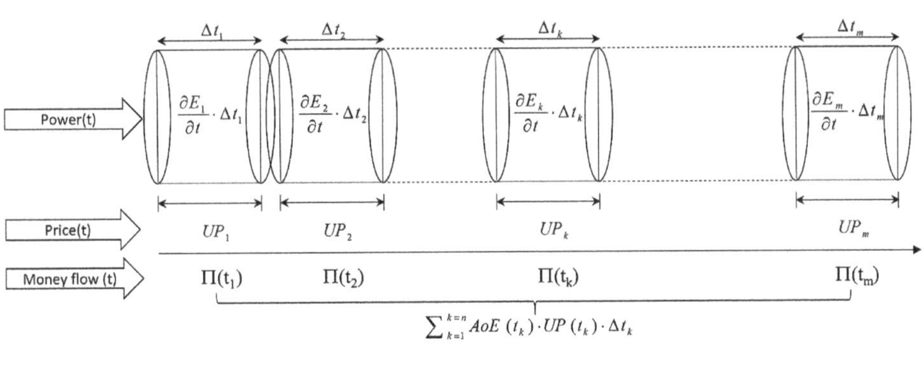

This issue appears important because it indicates sustainable way to contain steadily growing demand for newly generated energy amounts by shaping intelligently the patterns of demand – instead of or in addition to the amounts of demand - based on the mutual knowledge about the time-varying changes in the capacity/availability of the energy resource. The outcome appears highly impacting. The research outcome allows preserving the average energy consumption in any geographic area by differently apportioning the,available richness over time instead of insisting on the amounts and/or different re-distribution over population. All the population worldwide of small-scale RES owners can get direct benefit from the DSF by splitting the energy production in two complementary parts. The main part forms the legacy energy product (X%), while the remaining portion is directed to the local storage in order to make reserves for fast actuating of ancillary services whenever needed. In this way, newly added storage operated by web-enabled mini-SCADA converts the standalone capacity in the networked demand-response action optimally distributed over time.

This work started from the specialized literature review in order to establish the availability of components dealing with the DSF. The most difficult and less researched issues appear to be the analytic measurement of the population that originates the DSF and the real-time measurement of the change in demand figures they originate.

In order to acquire information about the shapes of demand-response, the observational study was considered. In the known state of the art, demand-oriented energy meters are not deployed to small-scale actors. Authors explored the Event-Driven Meters being deployed by the PowerIntellimeter project to several users in Northern Italy because it allowed acquiring the QD. In the examples, authors used anonymized time series of *real life data* from some industrial and residential users. Newly acquired individual- (a) and aggregated in groups- (b) data emerged a possibility to define new metrics and to build useful indicators. Given the experimental data, business analytics were derived by using state of the art statistical, descriptive, and sensitivity analysis tools. In order to materialize new functionalities depicted in this chapter, the EDM prototype was reworked then.

Metamodeling and Drivers for Inclusion

Since any energy amount coming from any actor can be easily negotiated on the market, the differentiation of the energy products should be found in various aspects, specifically in those unrelated with the *cumulative daily quantities*. In one perspective, an increase in energy production from renewables increased the need for *generation-side scheduling flexibility*. Therefore, cheaper generation side flexibility will be absorbed by the energy markets. In another perspective, *high variability over time* of the electricity price challenges offering energy amounts during well-defined peak periods. Therefore, new ancillary services that support short-term operations during above-mentioned time slots will be demanded. Because the two broad categories of decision-makers in an energy economy are consumers/users and suppliers/firms, one possible driver for active inclusion of small-scale actors in market operations emerges from the *optimality of consumer choice* (Chugh 2015). Each actor in each of these groups makes its decisions in order to achieve some goal, for example to maximize a satisfaction or a profit. However, *human behavioral issues* and the *policy responses* have not been deeply explored in the available literature. For this reason, the following discussion reflects the authors' viewpoint. Major difference between small-scale RES and large-scale non-RES plants stays in the limited Environmental Impact (EI) in the Energy Mix (EM). In non-RES operations, costs of many important environmental damages are not visibly incorporated into purchase prices for energy. As a result, non-RES energy purchase price *appears identical* to the RES purchase price. Energy and environmental economists differently assign fair monetary valuation of the ecological impacts of energy operations. Ecological economics reject the idea that a monetary value could equate environmental impacts. In the author's belief, consumers privilege RES energy because it is better ecologically sustainable and because it contains raising prices of other energy vectors. This kind of driver requires a kind of Environmental Certification (EC) that informs consumers about the added value being incorporated in the energy flow coming from small-scale RES actors.

Another driver is associated with the requirement for reserves in power systems. Reader know that system generation must be as close as possible to the system load and electrical losses to ensure that system frequency is maintained at or very close to nominal levels. In the actual energy business scenario, the ancillary balancing services are offered by the generation plants. In other words, sufficient ramp capacities are reserved at generation side only to respond to the *expected changes* in both the user-dependent loads and intermittent user-independent generation plus certain reserves are made to cover certain proportion of their uncertainties due to *unexpected changes*. The provision of ramps is a service negotiated on the intraday energy markets up to near-real time. Balancing service is completely described by the starting instant of time, the duration of lead-in period (initial latency), the time required for changing the level of power from the previous value up to the new one, and the Rate of Change of Power (Figure 5). The materialization of this service requires an energy amount $E^{upward}(t)$ being modulated in well-specific fashion after the flexibility R(t)=const. In economic perspective, the provider of the upward ramp service that expends $E^{upward}(t)$ to reach new higher generation capacity level should receive extra money to cover the fuel expenses $E^{downward}(t)$ while reverting its generation system back to the previous power level. It explains the price difference between the upward – $R(t)>0$ - and downward – $R(t)<0$ - balancing services. Recently, flexible ramp capability products for generation-side operations were defined (Wang, 2014).

Figure 5. Ancillary balancing services, upward and downward

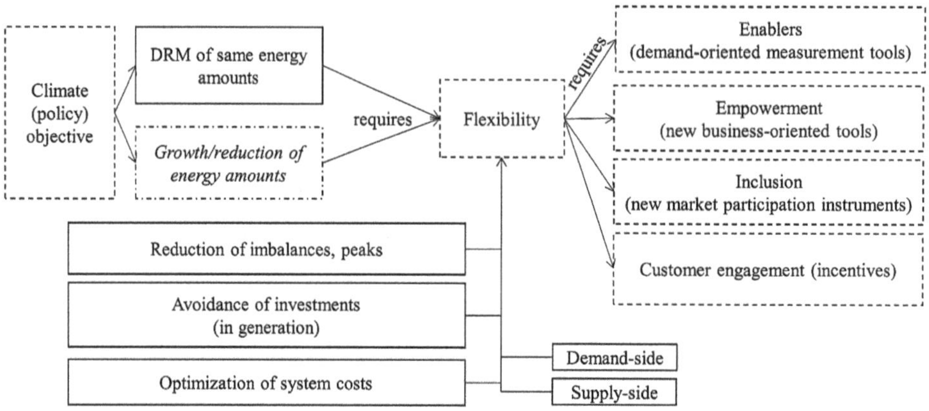

Since the flexi ramping products are mainly procured in real-time markets, the fact represents a driver for inclusion.

In the current situation, flexible ramping services are provided only by conventional generation units. In the case of an unbalance $\Delta P(t) = P_k(t) - P_j(t)$, there is no conceptual difference between *increasing the generation* from the level of power $P_j(t)$ up to the level $P_k(t)$ and *decreasing the demand* from the power level $P_k(t)$ up to the power level $P_j(t)$. This simple consideration opens to the inclusion of small-scale actors in the market scenario. By definition, the flexible ramping service reserves flexibility in a *specific time slot* for future use when the forecasted load changes plus some unexpected load changes will happen.

In effect, small-scale actors can provide flexible ramping services at the demand side in order to diminish the requirement for flexible ramping services at the generation side. The difficulty stays in the respecting the appropriate timescale of operations, e.g. in timely triggering of a control condition and in the actuation of an immediate reaction by re-modulating the levels of demand at the premises of a sufficient number of customers. Therefore, the inclusion operation depends on the technology framework that acquires *analytical information* about the amount of RES energy (1), about the distribution in time of the effective capacity (ramp-like shape), e.g. about the quantities being demanded or not demanded (2), about the equivalent savings that can be achieved by privileging the purchase of energy from this well-specified small-scale actor instead of purchasing form the generic mix (3), and about the effective commerce on the market (4).

The inclusion issue can be split into separate but complementary components: the analytical accounting of RES amounts and the rates of flows (a), the measurement of the effects of the choice that varies expending non-RES by replacing them by

RES (b), the cooperation ICT platform that exchanges analytical information about RES flows of small-scale actors and decides the usages of such better ecologically sustainable energy (c), and the marketplace software that allows selling new eco-friendly energy product or the equivalent ancillary service operated at the demand side on the market in real-time timescale (d).

One component of the added value for optimization is represented by the additional knowledge unavailable from large-scale actors. Several components of the power system's conditions cannot be easily predicted because the load levels, the RES outputs, and the transmission capacity's availability depend on both poorly predictable and highly variable customer behavior (a kind of operational risk). In this scenario, small-scale actor can negotiate the compliancy with the desired variability and can reduce uncertainty. Instead of reserving *additional generation capacity* in the form of an upward ancillary service and reserving *additional generation flexibility* in the form of a downward ancillary service, small-scale user can offer the *responsive demand availability* above or below the required level to meet actual system's resilience constraints. The materialization requires technology enabler for operating on-line so that this actor can be called on to mitigate the RES generation decreases due to unpredictability or variability of the external conditions by diminishing the demand. Likewise, on-line *flexible demand capacity* will be called on to mitigate the case of generation increases by increasing the demand. This *flexible demand-response capacity* can be referred to as *equivalent operating reserve*. In order to offer different shapes and sizes of flexibility, small-scale actors can act in groups.

Another component of added value in price terms is represented by lowered environmental impact and by improved energy efficiency of energy-conversion plants. The effective inclusion is warranted by using the automated fast trading platform that emerges and makes explicit the peculiar characteristics of the energy product from small-scale actors.

There are three different electricity market segments: Day-Ahead Market, Intraday Market, and Market of Balancing Services (DAM, IM, MBS respectively). Small-scale actors play no role at the DAM. The Intraday segment gains importance after strong raise in renewable – intermittent by nature and poorly predictable in the various hourly slots of the day - energy production because the scheduled RES production negotiated in the DAM auction presents non-ignorable margin of error. The IM offers the possibility to optimize the distribution of RES energy amounts in time after more precise information becoming available closer to actual production time. Ideally, the owners of small-scale RES power plants would benefit from trading up to less the one hour before energy delivering. However, this kind of self-balancing activity is currently unavailable because network balancing is managed by different actors. In longer electricity market perspective, RES integration with its generation-led philosophy will dominate because of the balancing issues in inertia-less context.

Variability and uncertainty are the *expected- and the unexpected- changes* (respectively) in quantities demanded (Figure 6). The power system-level variability and uncertainty cause the requirement for reserves. When variability occurs at remote nodes of the network at shorter time resolutions that actual scheduling resolutions of centralized Energy Management Systems (EMS) are not configured for, the reserves or their equivalent (qualified flexibility) are required because frequency/voltage deviation is an effect of insufficiently timely managed unbalances in power flows. In the multi-scaled example, an *hourly scheduled market* call for reserves for variability that occurs at *any sub-hour resolution*. Should the reserves be materialized by the 15-minute scheduling program to ensure balance of supply and demand at that timescale, other reserves are required to mitigate the variability at sub-minute resolutions. Under uncertainty, flexibility is reserved for selecting a different supply-demand profile than the previously scheduled one.

SOLUTIONS AND RECOMMENDATIONS

Demand-Side Flexibility

In physical terms, the *flexibility* has a meaning of time derivative, e.g. a rate of change in a power flow $R(t) = \frac{\partial}{\partial t} P(t)$. After this definition, the flexibility is expressed in W/s.

The R(t) represents changes in load(s). Instead of *varying the quantity* of a commodity being offered on the market at a given time, an attempt to *piloting the dynamics* of the demand for power was recently proposed in the context of TEC

Figure 6. The variability and the uncertainty in the figures of energy and flexibility

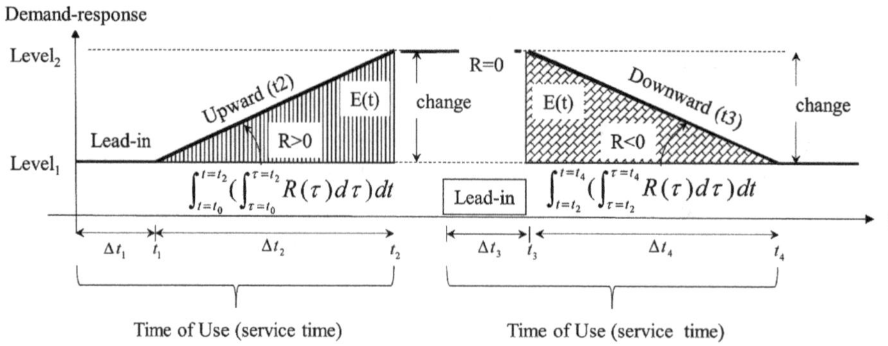

framework defined as a system of economic and control mechanisms that allows the dynamic balance of supply and demand across the entire electrical infrastructure using value as a key operational parameter. This new concept is currently known as the *flexibility of demand* for power associated with the key concept of value (CEER, 2016). By definition, the Demand-Side Flexibility (DSF) is a *capacity to change* energy usage process by end-use customers (including different types of energy users, residential or non-residential ones) from their "normal" or current consumption patterns in response to market signals, such as time-variable electricity prices or other incentive payments, or in response to acceptance of the consumer's bid, alone or through aggregation, to sell demand reduction/increase at a price in electricity markets or for internal portfolio optimization (Allcott, 2011). While the Supply Side Flexibility (SSF) can be observed directly as a simple change in Power, the Demand Side Flexibility (DSF) is a more complex object since it represents a temporal change *with respect to* a baseline profile. Once a change in demand has occurred, the former baseline can no longer be observed. Reader pays attention that the demand-led power system is a fast-slow system that runs at two different velocities in which the variation-in-demand $\frac{\partial}{\partial t}Demand(t)$ is equilibrated by the variation-in-supply $\frac{\partial}{\partial t}Supply(t)$. Therefore, making the measurement of flexibility statistically is a complex task.

Legacy associates generically the *demand* with the *value* Value=f(Demand), without specifying the *structure of* QD. New multi-scale interpretation associates each *Change in Demand* (CiD) with the *Value being Modulated* (VbM) through one or more economic signals Value=g($Signal_j$, ChangeInDemand). On an individual level (derived from Eurelectric 2014), flexibility is the *modification of prosumption patterns* in reaction to an external signal in order to provide an ancillary service within any multi-energy system. In this interpretation, the ancillary (balancing) service is represented by flexible ramps modeled by piece-wise linear functions of time. The flexibility becomes measurable through the parameters such as the Amount of Demand (AoD) being modulated, the Duration of Flexibility (DoF), the Pattern of Demand (PoD) being modulated, the Rates of Change (RoC) in the pattern, the Response Time (RT) or the latency of the action, and the geo-location of the node. In other words, the flexibility R(t) can be generically described by a *pattern*. New realized demand pattern comes from the input PoD after the action RoC expected to last (DoF-RT) in time. On an aggregated level in multi-scale representation, the DSF can be materialized by collective cooperative behaviour of a (big) group of people (small-scale actors) that decide to change their demand-response behaviour in order to achieve the shared prosperity in terms of sustainable use of energy-containing commodities. The above transformation represents a societal challenge.

The exemplified pattern of demand (Figure 7) partly annotated as being flexible and/or non-flexible indicates a flexibility potential. In this graphical representation, each vertical segment combines an Amount of Demand with the corresponding Time of Use. Better detailed explanation is given in the subsequent paragraphs.

Value of Flexibility

The relationship between Energy E(t), Power P(t), and Flexibility R(t) in physical terms is one of simple derivatives, e.g. R(t)=P′(t)=E′′(t). Reader knows that the flow of electricity is associated with a flow of monetary units. Since the flexibility can be seen as a derivative, a monetary equivalent can be assigned to this category by pricing each rate of flow at each amount of time. In order to sell the flexibility R(t) - from the demand and/or from the supply side - periodically, its value needs to be determined by an energy actor. Until the pattern of demand *is being changing*, the flexibility concept is represented by a $\frac{\partial}{\partial t}P(t)$. When more power is required, generators flexibly offer a ramping up service. In a simple ramping up service, the R(t)=const>0. As the need for power reduces, flexibility is required again, this time to ramp down power. In a simple ramping down service, the R(t)=const<0. The rate at which power changes in time is proportional to the scale of flexibility required. When an actor decides that the previously known pattern of demand is discontinued because it *is changed enough*, the flexibility becomes the $\frac{\partial}{\partial t}Demand(t)\cdot$ The DSF appears to be a good that is very similar to the additional generation capacity, but it is CO_2 and particulate matter emission-less. The DSF is an energy-equivalent being collectively produced by certain group of people that is immediately expended by the totality of consumers, so it is an extremely short-living good. However, the *expected* DSF is supposed to be known in advance, so it appears predictable.

Figure 7. The pattern of demand of industrial customer annotated as being locally flexible

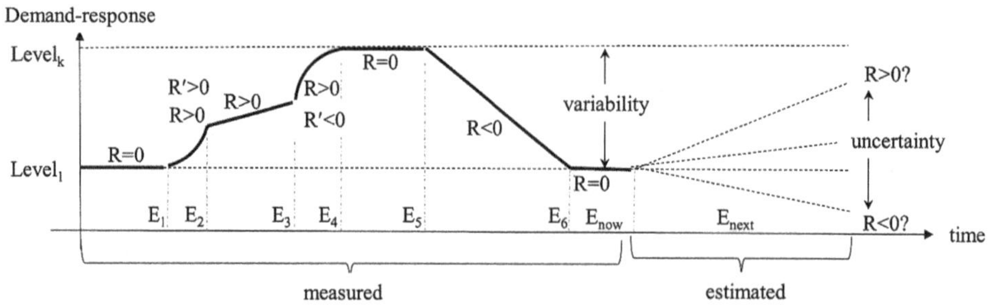

Therefore, the expected DSF should have a market price similar to- or higher than- the price of energy offered by power plants that use peak generators only. For example, ten percent DSF being effectively realized on a real intraday market during an over-crowded time slot between 9:00 and 11:00 AM has a specific size (10% of the traded volume) and a specific price (averaged spot price during the today's time slot 9.00-10.00 AM). However, the DSF is not a tangible asset that belongs to certain well-known energy producer, but a virtual product that depends on the collective behavior of many actors. In this example, the incentive-driven collective behavior of energy-efficiency oriented users materializes the desired amount of the expected DSF. Thus, the DSF belongs to the community of energy users and it can be traded by someone on behalf of them. Most likely, the price of the DSF is cleared by utility. Moreover, the incentive (reward) that can be offered to end users cannot exceed the variable cost of energy production by peak generators. For this reason, the determination of the market price of DSF is not a trivial task.

Measuring Perception of Energy Efficiency

The concept of flexibility can be associated with the concept of economic utility. In this specific context, a utility function could be used to measure the *level of satisfaction* that a consumer obtains from consuming *energy product* and/or *energy service*. A common way to aggregate the consumer preferences in energy efficiency is to use suitable utility functions (Jehle, 2001). A utility function may have any number of arguments (Mount & Reiter, 1976). However, the overall consumer's satisfaction level depends on two macro-groups of factors positively and negatively affecting the decision to consume a product. The electric energy is a product that has a price Π_E (in \$) associated with a total amount of energy E (in kWh). However, two main factors affecting the decision to consume energy and keep limited the bill are the ongoing level of Demand for Power c_1 (in \$) and the effective Time of Use of electricity c_2 (in \$) that happens at that specific level. In other words, the $E_\$=AoD_\$\cdot ToU_\$=c_1\cdot c_2$ (in \$). Users do attempt optimizing the *iso-level* of money Π_E (in \$) by increasing the rate of work (in kW) but reducing the working time (in seconds), or by increasing the working time (in seconds) but by reducing the rate of work (in kW). In the ramping service example - as on the Figure 5 -, the rate of change of the rate of work is constant (in kW/s), so the rate of work (in kW) is constantly changing over service time (in seconds).

A common utility function used to measure the energy efficiency (Jehle, 2001) is given by $u(c_1,c_2)=\left[\alpha\cdot c_1^{\frac{\sigma-1}{\sigma}}+\beta\cdot c_1^{\frac{\sigma-1}{\sigma}}\right]^{\frac{\sigma}{\sigma-1}}$ where σ represents the elasticity of substitution between the two goods c_1 and c_2. According to Cobb-Douglas model, the utility function appears in the form $u(c_1,c_2) = A \cdot c_1^{\alpha} \cdot c_1^{\beta}$. Here, the c_1 and c_2 are two different components of the energy product, where the desired demand for power is c_1 (in \$) and the required use time is c_2 (in \$). Both elements c_1 and c_2 participate in determining the market price of electricity because the $Energy_\$ = (Power_\$ * Time_\$)$ after the market-based definition of time-varying unitary price $up_\$$. Authors consider the trade-off that a consumer faces when making consumption decision reflected in the choice of 2-argument model. In the example, authors considered symmetric square root utility functions in three dimensions $u(c_1,c_2) = \alpha \cdot \left(\sqrt{c_1} + \sqrt{c_2}\right)$, $u(c_1,c_2) = \alpha \cdot \left(\sqrt{c_1} \cdot \sqrt{c_2}\right)$, and $u(c_1,c_2) = \beta \cdot \sqrt{(c_1)^2 + (c_2)^2}$ (Figure 8). The interpretation of the role of unitary price $up^\$$ is not unique because

$$(Power \cdot Time) \cdot up^{\$}_{tenergy} = Power \cdot (Time \cdot up^{\$}_{time}) = (Power \cdot up^{\$}_{tpower}) \cdot Time\,.$$

In order to keep limited the monetary flow associated with the flow of energy $\frac{Energy_\$}{\Delta t} = \frac{Power_\$}{\Delta t} \cdot \frac{TimeOfUse_\$}{\Delta t}$, economic agent tries shortening periods of time when the power is high but reduces attention when low energy flow is expended over longer use period.

Our utility function contains two inputs c_1 and c_2. By holding constant the consumption of the energy product $u(c_1,c_2)$, an increase in the consumption of one input (c_1) is associated with the decrease in the consumption of another input (c_2) and symmetrically vice-versa. In other terms, the total response (utility) surface appears associated with ever-decreasing rates. Graphically, variations in marginal utility become visible in the slopes of the utility function with respect to each of its argumentsinisolation.Giventhat,authorsusethefunctional $u(c_1,c_2) = I \cdot \sqrt{(c_1)^2 + (c_2)^2}$

Figure 8. Utility function that accounts the value of the Powers and the Time of Use. The c_1 stands for the power, the c_2 stands for the time

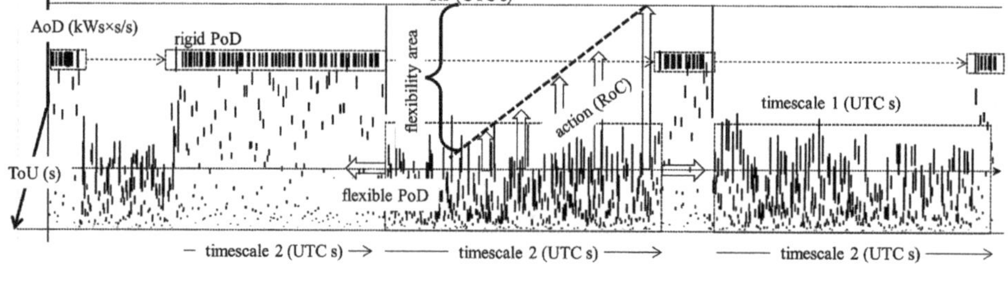

as a kind of metric to *perform ordering* of demand figures and to measure their evolution in time (Figure 8). In the previous picture (Figure 7), each vertical line plotted in the form of $\sqrt{(c_1)^2 + (c_2)^2}$ makes emphasis on a particular iso-*level (extent) of utility*. That means the same amount of money paid for certain energy product/service may appear differently on the above-mentioned shape. In other words, the set of all combinations of function arguments that yield some well-specified monetary value will appear graphically as a kind of motion, a kind of trajectory, or a kind of contour that represents the flexibility concept. From the dimensional analysis viewpoint, the function u appears as $\sqrt{[\$]^2 + [\$]^2} = [\$]$. The u should not be interpreted as a mix of energy and time of use units because both the terms are converted to monetary equivalents by using the unitary price factors. Geometrically, given the pair (c_1,c_2) plotted on the Cartesian plane as (x,y), the $u(c_1, c_2) = \sqrt{(c_1)^2 + (c_2)^2}$ represents the diagonal after the Phitagorean theorem. The functional I can be used to map said diagonal to any other desired plane surface.

Now, let authors taking the same fixed amount of $(c_1 \cdot c_2)$ and let authors explore *all the combinations* $(n \cdot c_1, n^{-1} \cdot c_2)$ obtained after the once-at-a-time variation of the n = {1,2,...,k,...}. Next, let authors continue by taking the same fixed amount of money and let authors explore *all the combinations* $u(c_1, c_2) = \sqrt{(n \cdot c_1)^2 + (n \cdot c_2)^2}$ obtained after the once-at-a-time variation of the n = {1,2,...,k,...}. At the end of the above-described experiment, two traces of u are being plotted on the chart (Figure 8). The $Trace(n \cdot c_1, n^{-1} \cdot c_2)$ appears on top of each rectangle $c_1 \times c_2$. The $Trace\left(\sqrt{(n \cdot c_1)^2 + (n^{-1} \cdot c_2)^2}\right)$ appears lower that the upper bounds of each rectangle $c_1 \times c_2$. In both cases, the form of the trace appears unchanged. A possible interpretation of newly obtained digital trace is the expectation of the correlation between the demanded quantities and the time of use. All combinations (c_1, c_2) staying above the higher shape (dotted red line) represent extra spendings for electricity. All combinations (c_1, c_2) staying below the lower shape (dashed green line) represent extra savings. The combinations (c_1, c_2) staying between the lines (red and green lines) represent the most likely, elastic, behaviour of the demand for electricity. This concept will be used to define boundaries separating the expected changes in the demand figures (variability) from the random ones (uncertainty).

The picture might be evolved by considering time-varying unitary price associated with the levels of the demand $up_\$(c_1)$ and the time-varying unitary price associated with the time of use $up_\$(c_2)$.

In other designs, the possible expressions are

$$Energy_{\$} = \alpha \cdot \left[(Power \cdot u_p) + (Time \cdot u_t)\right],$$

the

$$u(c_1, c_2) = I \cdot \sqrt{(Power \cdot u_p)^2 + (Time \cdot u_t)^2},$$

and more.

Quantitative Assessment of Flexibility

The consumer expends energy to perform real life activities. Each performed activity leaves the trace in the form of an amount of demand for energy and the respective time of use. That is, every pair (AoD, ToU) represents both the consumer choice/ preference and the activity driving toward a goal. Because achieving a goal represents certain value for the user, the energy equivalent (AoD, ToU) expresses implicitly the same value. However, achieving a goal could be associated with a sequence of quantities demanded over time. Since the amount of demand [expressed in kW·h] alone is not sufficient to inform about the rates of work [expressed in kW·h/s], the pre-requisite for DSF estimation is the analytical acquisition of the *structure of* the AoD [expressed in kWh/s, and units of time in another timescale, e.g. seconds, minutes, fractions of hour, hours, days, years, or lifetime] from real life by measurements (Figure 9). The relationship between two timescales is dictated by the granularity of the ToU concept, which is gauged to the intervals of time associated with the same price and/or the granularity of the demand-billed levels of powers.

Figure 9. New smart meter enriched by the real-time demand-measurement function starts supplying the structure of the Quantities Demanded

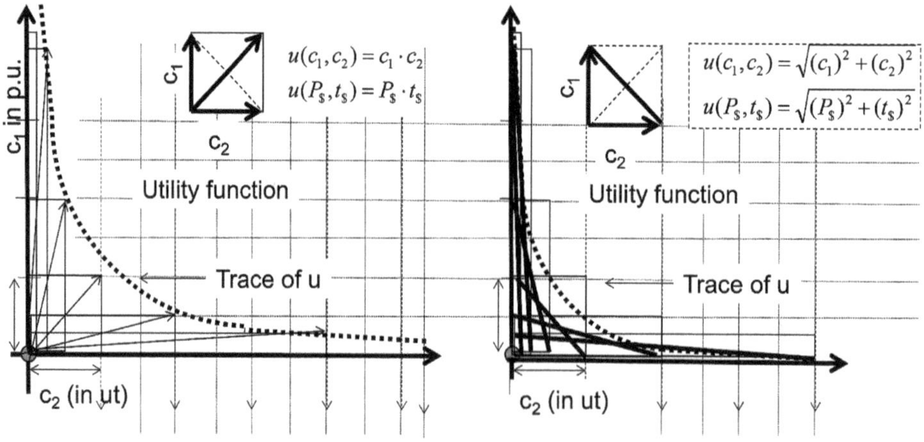

In other terms, the DMU measures the $\frac{\partial}{\partial t}P(t)$ [expressed in kW/s] and obtains the $\frac{\partial}{\partial t}P(t)\cdot p_{\$}(t)$ [expressed in \$/s]. Newly obtained sequence of monetary values is analyzed then.

New DMU collects a variety of data going to be displayed, analyzed, and used to make a decision about splitting the amount of energy into parts and selling them on the DAM, IM, and BASM markets. For each day, the DMU collects time series of the demand figures. At regular time intervals, the DMU computes the conserved values (averages by regression analysis), and measures the variability and its evolution over time. In the presence of price signal, the DMU compares newer time series with time series recorded before said signal. This function materializes the verification procedure for the Demand-Response Management (DRM) program. The Customer Baseline (CBL) is a sequence of QD [expressed in kW·h/s] effectively expended during well-defined ToU [expressed in s_{use}] at certain well-specified Rate of Work (RoW) [expressed in (kW·h)/s] by certain customer or a group of. The CBL is computed starting from the demand-oriented time series. The structured PoD is exemplified on the ad-hoc developed visual form (Figure 1) by plotting the diagonals A_jC_j from the Figure 3 appearing in the form of vertical strobes $\sqrt{AoD^2+ToU^2}$ [expressed in digital units interpreted semantically as an economic utility function only] that are sequenced in non-uniform frequency domain after time wrapping factors $||t_j-t_{j-1}||^{-1}$: 1^{-1} in order to make ad-hoc timers appearing virtually as unitary ones[1]. After this definition, the realized DSF is a difference between two time series and namely the CBL_j in the baseline scenario hypothesis and the CBL_k after the signal being issued and being considered by customer(s).

The valuation of DSF can be done either explicitly or implicitly. Since DSF appears explicitly on the market, it can be sold as a product/service on a power market. Therefore it requires a specific control that traces the CBLs and other parameters used in the Demand-Response Management (DRM) actions.

The DSF is produced by a well-defined group of actors that makes certain percentage *x* of the total population of energy users *y*. For each member of the DSF-making group x_j, the CBL is analytically measured by using the real-time demand-oriented EDM metering device (Simonov et al., 2017) that produces the Quantities Demanded. More precisely, the input data includes the Amounts of Energy, the Time of Use of energy, the demand factors, and similar values. Given the CBL ordered in natural time, the Load Duration Curve (LDC) is being produced by computations of true levels of load and re-ordering of newly established data then. As an effect, the $DSF=CBL_k-CBL_j$ becomes measurable at multi-levels, for an individual customer *x* and/or for any *individual group* G_y of *y* customers being scaled from $y<N$ up to the

entire portfolio G_N that counts *N* customers, but also for any arbitrary composition $\{G_i \oplus \ldots \oplus G_j \oplus \ldots\}$ that combines said groups of DSF-makers. Additionally, since the DSF is also associated with the duration of action, the multi-scale timing should be adopted (viola time arrows on Figure 1) for measuring the DSF resulting from single incentive or from a series of. Therefore, the ensemble of flexibility-making actors populates the sample space modeled after the N·T-cube with the effective dimensions drawing form the size of portfolio N [expressed in scalars] and the upper bound of the *duration* [expressed in seconds of natural time] of flexibility action T gauged to *timers* [expressed as a partition of time-arrow].

The information contained in the CBLs is consumed by small-scaled RES actors in order to realize the *decision variables* that will be used to support (possibly automated) decisions to trade the DSF or not to trade at given market price. A kind of composite indicator is required to realize the decision-making values associated with the DSF as a market good. Here, the DSF-index receives time series of numeric estimates of the structure of QD [expressed in kWh/s and hours and/or in $/s and hours] and the estimate of risk/uncertainty associated with the crowd behavior. To complete the model, new index of responsiveness is being computed as a percentage change in one variable (the Change In Value, CIV) with respect to the percentage change in another variable (the Change in Risk, CIR). The DSF operation appears useful until this index $\varepsilon_{civ|cir}=(\Delta CIV/CIV)/(\Delta CIR/CIR)$ remains greater than 1, e.g. in all cases when the added values appears higher compared with the increase in risks.

On the other hand, the DSF is implicit because it does not need such a process. In effect, the DSF is produced by *x*, but it is never sold by individual to anyone. The DSF remains for the benefit of the universality of final consumers *y* and for the corresponding retailer or for the Balance Responsible Party (BRP) as an optimization respectively of its sourcing costs or imbalances (CEER, 2016). In this assumption, the DSF value is already embedded - as part of - in any Intraday amount $AoE(t_k)$ and it can be expressed as a percentage and as a set of percentage changes. The DSF tool extracts and makes explicit the flexibility. By assuming that the value for the day *j* is $DSF(t_j)$, the DSF can be recursively evolved after the formula $DSF(t_j)=DSF(t_{j-1})+/-\Delta DSF(t_j)$, where the delta term is driven by the ratio between the $AoE(t_k)$ and the $AoE(t_{k-1})$. More accurate description of the process requires deeper discussion in a separate work.

Real Life Application That Exploits Flexibility

All social activities actuated by humans have a time-based order. The timescale over which the DSF is required follows broad ranges of *durations* because load profiles have differently scaled shorter- and longer- lasting seasonal components. There are daily, weekly, monthly, and annually changing patterns of demand. Additionally, some responsiveness should be quick enough to cope with a failure of a generator.

In demand-led power systems, the capacity to generate new energy is used at different rates of time by throttling between the levels of power. By fixing the total daily amount of energy expressed either in kWh or in monetary units, its distribution over time in storage-less system is variable because of time-varying demand and physical laws imposing to consume the total of produced energy in *exactly the same timescale*. As such, the daily amount of capacity can be decomposed in the daily amount of demand plus the corresponding amount of reserves/inertia. Currently, the ratio between the capacity and the reserves is computed empirically based on the past statistical estimates. When the power system is running at the highest capacity, or it is low-inertia or inertia-less, the DSF becomes a tool that can govern the security of supply. For this reason it is important to estimate the extent of flexibility/elasticity in the network.

Being flexible with how and when end-users consume and small-scale plants produce energy means increasing certainty that the power generated and delivered matches the amount being used at exactly that the same time. The DSF as a service provision to power system appears on the power market after when modifying generation and/or consumption patterns in reaction to an external signal, for example a change in price, becomes measurable (Ilic et al., 2013). Once the DSF is quantified, it can be expended. In the Customer-Centered Smart Grid (CCSG) new paradigm called flexibility appears. It is about changing economic behavior of small- and medium- scaled energy users instead of varying the amounts of commodity. This behavioral aspect cannot be ignored because the cooperative behavior of many such actors participating in liberalized intraday market can mitigate poorly predictable energy production from renewable sources. It has several implications on power markets in terms prices. At the same time, new scenario has multiple implications on the technology side of country-wide critical infrastructure such as Smart Grid (Karnouskos, 2011). In the past, investments were concentrated on large scale generators and their running. In new scenario, the investments come to smaller decentralized PV-, Wind-, and Bio- plants. New data-driven cooperative modality requires different ICT equipment and complex software (Lamparter et al., 2010). It moves to the software markets and markets of internet-enabled services. It enables a generational change that moves decision making from few control rooms to the democratic neighborhood of the web. In the RES context with limited availability of resources and/or in the context with limited interconnectivity, this concept could offer additional benefits because applicable at different scales, for example at the microgrid level. In the example, let authors assume that an individual runs its own nano-generator in order to compensate temporary unavailability of the commodity from the distribution grid. To improve resilience of the local distribution topology, several individuals – a group of x – decide running higher-scaled generators in shifts lasting up to 24/x hours each. Since the individual demand levels are not constant in time but the production rate of generators is constant, the cost of the expended fuel between members of the group was compensated mutually (choice 1). However, the changes in amount of expended energy can be measured and the demand-oriented billing (choice 2) can be introduced. The cost repartitioning after metering figures can emerge a benefit because of the possibility to run shorter or longer shifts (choice 3) or because of the opportunity to sell extra energy to the external network (choice 4). At this point the market-based choice 4 can be exploited through the DSF.

Market and Security Aspects

Market competition is a balance in the supply of wholesale electricity, including generation and demand response, where there is an ideal harmony between provider profits and consumer savings. The current generation of market management systems has made significant technological strides to facilitate various market rules and designs towards competition. The aggregation of this functionality has helped ensure sufficient amount of transmission capacity in the market, as well as the elasticity of demand with respect to price. For energy trading to be realized, the necessary tools as well as timely information exchange between all stakeholders need to be provided. Part of it is also the actual smart metering i.e. the high granularity of metering data acquisition. Through better resolution of the production and consumption (prosumption) data and effective analysis, any market participant is able to monitor and even predict his energy behavior. Data-driven real time smart meter technology, as well as the necessary energy services, prosumers will be able to offer and purchase electricity.

Going back to the example, self-generation is a tool to mitigate a-posteriori chronic unavailability of the commodity from distribution network. The DSF can mitigate exactly the same issue based on the information about programmable unavailability (by shifting in time the demand) and/or about programmed availability (by deciding flexible and better elastic shares in the prosperity) of the commodity (Suvak, 2010). It becomes clear why the DSF can be used to adapt urban environments to climate change (Carter et al., 2015).

Un-Hiding Structure of Demand

In real life, the measurements of magnitudes of power/energy being produced or consumed are any. After the DF definition, the ratio between the levels of power can be expressed in both the angle- and the percentage- like forms, which might suggest the partitioning of maximal contractual thresholds in something similar to a set of percentiles. The structure of demand/capacity appears in a form of levels, which suggests the information re-encoding after Lebesgue. Many mapping options exist. In the (Simonov, 2015), authors suggested the mapping between the domain of real numbers (R) and the domain of discrete levels (C) based on the transform f(P)=Round(Log(Abs(E(t)) / 16 ; 2) ; 0) that inherits from common musical notation as illustrated on Figure 10. This scheme has an advantage to allow very compact and intuitive visual music-like representation.

Once the flow of production/consumption is gauged to a set of pre-defined levels, the staves C_0,C_1,... in the example, the persistence of the same level of production/demand is being measured as the ToU. After the DMU, the analytic information about the process appears. It is a new knowledge asset being created in order to empower small-scale energy actors to understand their operations (processes). New knowledge representation concentrates focus on the longer-lasting operations performed at the same level of Rate of Work (RoW) as illustrated on Figure 11. In this representation, small-scale actor can discriminate between usual and unusual levels/patterns of work and can recognize repetitive and non-repetitive activities. In this example, the operations occur at 4 levels of power by ranging between the levels C_5 and C_8. During the period of observations, the load factor f_{load} moves between C_5/C_8, C_6/C_8, C_7/C_8, and C_8/C_8. This representation simplifies the state space $C=\{C_0,C_1,...,C_k,...\}$ by narrowing it to the only set $\{C_5,C_6,C_7,C_8\}$.

Modeling Variability in Demand

In digital systems, any measurement outcome z(x) is intrinsically imprecise because of the limited precision of the observational process. Because of this, any observation z(x) of real-life process h(x) that results in the demand for energy/power contains errors ε(t). In other terms, the observed stocks fill in the surrounding area $h(x) \in \left[z(t) - Max(\varepsilon(t), z(t) + Max(\varepsilon(t))\right]$ plotted around the apparent trajectory

Figure 10. Mapping between the domain of real numbers and the set of discrete levels (of demand-response)

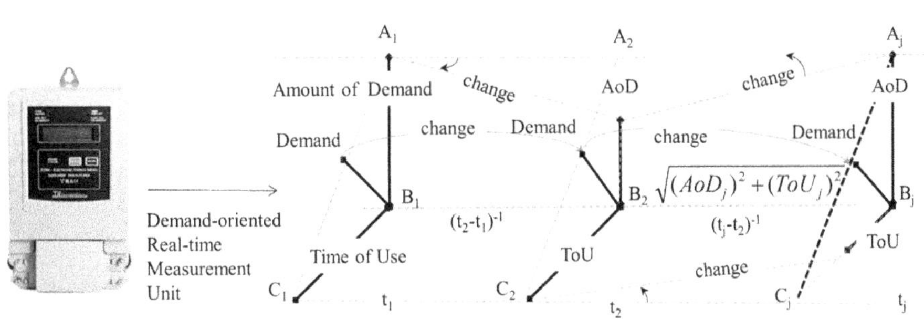

Figure 11. Visual representation of energy operations raising attention of small-scale users

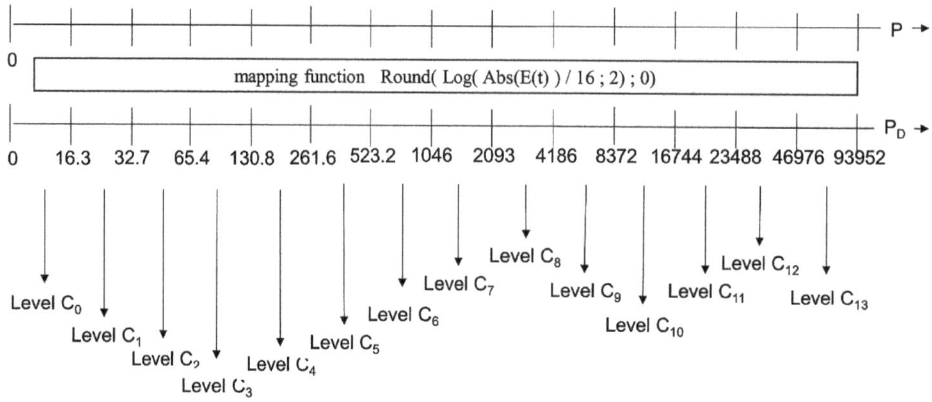

of z (Figure 12). For the same reason, the comparison between two time series of observed demand figures $z_1(x)$ and $z_2(x)$ is never sharp. To filter small fluctuations but to capture the essence of being near the same specific level of demand, threshold-based rules are used. In the example, if $(DfP_i\text{-}DfP_k)<\Delta_1$ then let $(DfP_i=DfP_k)$, where the Δ_1 can be set either empirically or set to the $\mathrm{Max}(\varepsilon(t))$ if the last one term is known.

The Demand for power is a time-varying *flow* that can keep a steady state $\frac{\partial DfP}{\partial t}=0$ for certain while (Figure 12), or it can change the speed at any accelerated fashion after the $\frac{\partial^2 DfP}{\partial t \partial t}=any$. The most frequent case is represented by the on-off events that represent stepwise level changes $(DfP_i,[t_{i\text{-}k},t_i])\rightarrow(DfP_j,[t_j,t_{indefinite}])$.

Figure 12. Linear modeling of variability in demand figures

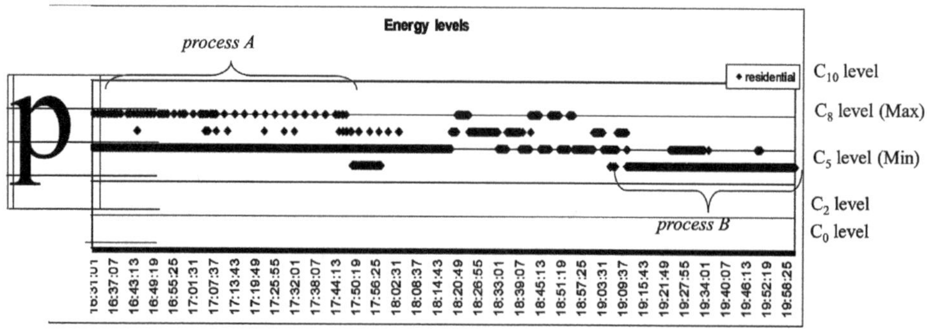

Other kinds of changes between the levels of demand can be accompanied by the constant acceleration $\frac{\partial DfP}{\partial t} = const$, by the acceleration being non-linear $\frac{\partial DfP}{\partial t} \neq const$, and/or by a series of stepwise changes or ramps described by sets of Rates of Flow (RoF) and by sets of Rates of Change of a Rate of Flow (RoCoRoF).

Since the flow of demand for energy is expressed in kWh/s, the variability, in terms of acceleration/deceleration, it is expressed in kWh/s^2. Likewise, the variability in the flow of demand for power being expressed in kW/s, it is expressed in kW/s^2. Comparing two random but stepwise ramps is computationally expensive. To simplify the comparison process, ramp-like objects can be approximated by the linear model $r(t) = DfP(t_0) + \frac{\partial DfP}{\partial t} \cdot ToU$ where the rate of flow DfP and its derivative draw from the past knowledge, while the r(t) refers to the uncertain next time (Figure 12).

From system's control perspective, an efficient tracking mechanism has to assess holistically the signal of demand DfP(t) as a flow against the entire ramps represented as flows instead of operating with the individual stocks that make a ramp. In this modeling, the triplet (t_0, RoF_0, RoCoRoF) is sufficient to enable any agent to compute the r(t) is the form RoF_0+RoCoRoF·(now-t_0). Likewise, the next occurrence of the level-crossing in the demand can be computed after the analytic formula. By using the above-mentioned logarithmic level-gauging function f(P)=Round(Log(Abs(E (t))/16;2);0), the threshold Δ_1 becomes level-dependent, e.g. the Δ_1=h(f(P)). By using the derivatives in the finite form, the linear tracking model becomes

$$r(t_k) = DfP(t_{k-1}) + \Delta DfP(t_{k-1}) \cdot (t_k - t_{k-1}),$$

or recursively

$$r(t_k) = DfP(t_0) + \Delta DfP(t_0) \cdot ToU,$$

where $ToU(t_k) = t_k - t_0$. In our interpretation, the ramp-like demand behaviour that continues matching previously established ancillary (balancing) service does not require any further attention, while any deviation from the above-mentioned ramp model needs to be detected and managed.

In short, unexpected jumps between two pre-programmed levels of demand $(r(t_k) - DfP(t_{k-1})) > \delta_1$ expressed in kWh/s and unexpected accumulations of fluctuations over time deviating from the expected trendline (the ramp) needs to be triggered and can be detected by using the above-mentioned computational processes.

Using Laplace Transform

New observational process established by the DMUs moves information from the physical world to the differently conceptualized abstraction.

In the legacy *load-driven model*, the load P being leading is assumed to be *any*. For this reason known smart meters perform *uniform* time-sampling of the signals of voltages and currents in order to compute the energy being accumulated over *any* time t. Given *any* timer Δt set to the same constant, the signal of power is being represented in the form (6) for any t_j. As an effect, the interval energy can always be computed after the computation (7), while the accumulated energy can always be computed after the formula (8). In this conceptualization the flexibility can be computed after the operator (9).

$$P(t_j + n \cdot \Delta t) = V(t_j + n \cdot \Delta t) \times I(t_j + n \cdot \Delta t) \tag{6}$$

$$E(t) = \int_{t_j + n \cdot \Delta t}^{t_j + (n+1) \cdot \Delta t} P(t) dt \tag{7}$$

$$E(t) = \int_0^{n \cdot \Delta t} P(t) dt \tag{8}$$

$$R(t) = \frac{\partial}{dt} P(t) \tag{9}$$

In the current practice, the P is being measured. The R is being estimated through the derivative of P. The E is being estimated through the anti-derivative of P. The information is being encoded in three independent variables R, P, and E.

In the generation-driven model, the signal of energy E becomes a (causal) leader. The load P becomes a laggard with respect to natural time. Compared with a former signal of power, any energy has a peculiarity because it is discrete. In alternate current, the minimal quanta of energy are always gauged to the ends of the AC periods or to their halves. Reader knows that in real life power systems the AC periodicity is never sharp (50 or 60 Hz nominal frequency). Another peculiarity is the energy accumulation over time that occurs in any fashion, which requires fine-grained spectral resolution when sampling after Shannon. Alternatively, the sampling approach might go beyond Shannon. In data-driven compressive sensing, an on-going measure of AC periodicity dictates minimal quantum of AC energy, which becomes (10). In this approach, the AC cycle-wide average powers are derived by using the formula (11). Because the laggard P becomes discrete, the flexibility R is computed after the formula (12) because it depends on the averaged P only. Since the computation of R requires two terms of P, obtaining the R being gauged to the ends of AC cycle has an important implication since the E needs to be measured for each half of the AC cycle.

$$E(\pi) = \int_{t_j}^{t_j+T_j} P(t)dt \rightarrow H(\pi) \tag{10}$$

$$P(\pi) = \frac{E(\pi)}{T_j} \tag{11}$$

$$R(\pi) = \frac{P(\pi_j) - P(\pi_{j-1})}{T_j} \rightarrow \delta(\pi) \tag{12}$$

To sum up, the periodicity T - e.g. the frequency T^{-1} - is being measured by tracing the P first. The E is being measured then. The R is being estimated through the derivative of P. The finest granularity of the R is one AC cycle. The finest granularity of the E and of the P is half-cycle. For practical reasons, authors gauge the flows R, P, and E to the ends of AC cycles. The *information* is being encoded in an neuromorphic Action Potential (AP) being formed by using the Laplace transform (δ(π),H(π)). In other words, every *stepping* AC cycle is represented by the corresponding *stateless* term (13), while any succession of sub-sequent AC cycles accumulates information in a *stateful* term (14).

$$[t_j, t_j + T_j] \rightarrow \left(\delta(t_j), H\left([t_j, t_j + T_j]\right)\right) \tag{13}$$

$$[0, \sum_{j=1}^{j=n} T_j] \rightarrow \left(\delta\left(n \cdot T_j\right), H\left(\left[0, \sum_{j=1}^{j=n} T_j\right]\right)\right) \tag{14}$$

Reader notes that newly designed computational framework for the inclusion of small-scale actors do not use the reference frame of time being gauged to the exact UTC timers. In other words, given the Δt timer set to 20ms for a 50Hz system, the outcome of the Boolean trigger (15) depends on the effect of aperiodicity of the AC signal being accumulated up to now.

$$IF\left(n \cdot \Delta t = \sum_{j=1}^{j=n} T_j\right) \tag{15}$$

Inclusion of Small-Scale Actors: Creating Awareness (Step 1)

First of all, small-scale energy actors should acquire better awareness about their *operations with energy*. In generation-led scenario, they do not need information about the powers but the flexibility only. In current scenario, energy producers know about *daily amounts* of energy and about their breakdown in 15-minutes intervals, mainly because of smart metering. Given the afore-mentioned discussion, UTC timers gauged to every 15 minutes appear less relevant. Unlikely our actors trace the relationship between the weather conditions (cloudiness index in the case of photovoltaic generation) and the reduced amount of energy compared with the nominal productivity of the plant. In order to create better awareness about the structure of the effective production and the relation with the nominal capacity, this class of actors should receive the DMU equipment. In this assumption, small-scale actors gets energy/flexibility figures in the form of (δ,H) being graphically displayed as a succession of vertical strobes $\sqrt{(AoD)^2 + (ToU)^2}$ as illustrated by the Figure 7.

The price of electricity on the markets is time-varying. Because the unitary price UP(t) of electricity can vary in time at any timescale, total amounts of energy – the cumulative sums -, are valued differently by changing time slots. To inform the small-scale actor about the expected market value of their energy product/ service, authors deploy the DMU connected to the stock exchange data feeder. New electronic device accesses real time unitary prices, gets amounts of energy and its rates over time, and values the monetaray flow in terms of the expected and real figures. Users get access to the flowing information expressed in the form $/time. Newly computed information is used to illustrate the real-time *market aspects* of RES flow to the small-scale actor, which is novel. Compared with the past scenario when metering equipment was connected to the utility's side for billing purposes, newly deployed measuremet equipment empowers small-scale actors by offering them the live connection to the markets in real time (Figure 13). At this stage the web connectivity to the remote data feeder is used in read-only modality in order to create awareness about the product and its possible value. Authors assumed that this information flow is costless.

Once new equipment is installed at their premises, small-scale actors receive new stream of real-time information about their productivity and about energy drop-outs. Reader notes that this information flow is relatively slow because it reports about significant deviations from the steady conditions. In simpler words, until the energy

Figure 13. Logical system architecture that connects small-scale actors to the (energy) stock exchange data feeder

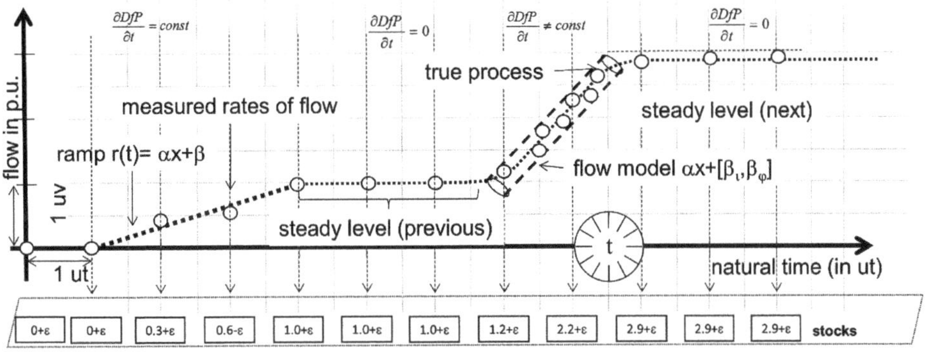

production pattern remains unchanged, no newer information is fed. This information can be consumed locally or conveyed to their Agent (Broker, Aggregator) in order to be commercially exploited on the markets.

Inclusion of Small-Scale Actors: Monitoring SLA (Step 2)

The intermittent RES energy is poorly predictable. In generation-led scenario it can happen that the rate of flow unexpectedly drops down. Given the pre-existing metering equipment reporting about the interval-energy data (cumulative sums) only, unlikely small-scale energy actors can ensure the adherence to the Service Level Agreement (SLA) which associates penalties with power drop-outs. To get awareness about the volatility and the uncertainty in RES production, we deploy to small-scale actors new functionality that detects and counts energy and power drop-outs in the flow that exceed well-defined thresholds ($delta_1$ expressed in MW/s and $delta_2$ expressed in MWh/s). In simpler words, when the energy expending pattern is heavily affected by price being changing or by the quantities being varying too much, new event is delivered to the user.

After the roll-out of low-cost DMU to the premises of small-scale actors, they start directly consuming local data in order to estimate the adherence to the SLA. Alternatively, small-scale actors can convey said data to their Agent, Broker, or Aggregator in order to delegate them monitoring the adherence to the contracted SLA. In this stage, the adherence to the SLA is measured a-posteriori without an ambition to control it. The government in real-time of the variability and the uncertainty of RES flows is subject of the next step.

Inclusion of Small-Scale Actors: Local Control (Step 3)

In this stage, small-scale actors acquire tools allowing them to control locally the changes in energy flows. In the case of need, small-scale actors can mitigate eventual discrepancies with the committed SLA. Once the DMU measurement equipment un-hides discrepancy with the contracted SLA, the imbalance in terms of energy needs to be repaired. In real-time scenario, small-scale actor has no possibility to react promptly because usually this kind of actors is running very different primary business. In such a case, small-scale actors consider installing a kind of low-cost Industrial Control System (ICS) that can operate Supervisory Control and Data Acquisition (SCADA) operations. In order to mitigate short-lasting power drop-outs, the installation of local storage in any form (Figure 14) appears advantageous. It can be a battery, a number of connected batteries, an electric vehicle being attached to the network, and so on. Based on the local information about insufficient generation compared with the ongoing level specified by the SLA, newly added ICS can addition the flow of power coming from the storage in order to compensate deficiency. Once this architecture is materialized and small-scale actors become familiar with planning correctly their dispatch operations, they can start offering valuable ancillary services at low risks because of the reserves and reduced (mitigated) RES uncertainty.

Inclusion of Small-Scale Actors: Enabling Market Operations (Step 4)

Individually, small-scale actor has no possibility to directly act on the markets because it lacks information allowing real time control of the process (a) and a tool allowing interaction with other actors (b). In the example, small-scale RES generator sells all the energy to the utility. In new scenario, many small-scale actors start using the demand/capacity measurement units (DMU) in order to describe their respective Customer Base Lines (CBLs) in terms of generation and/or demand. Given an ensemble of time series, an agent (in the MAS) computes the cumulative CBL for

Figure 14. Small-scale actors start offering the energy product on the day-ahead market and the ancillary (balancing) service on the real-time markets

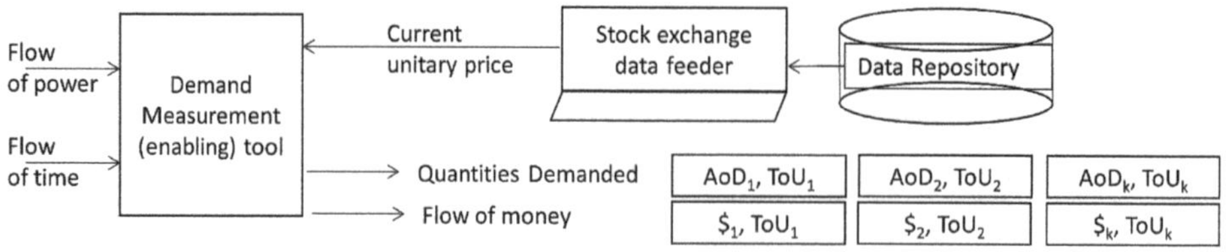

an aggregation. New Framework allows recording flexibility incentive signals. Given the knowledge about the timing of the signal, the changed CBL is directly associated with the flexibility action. At this point the aggregating agent has the information about the flexibility of the group of small-scale actors. New collectively owned product might be offered at the Intraday Market because the flexibility can be used to balance between the production and the demand.

Research Findings

Authors found that the Demand-Side Flexibility (DSF) is a *new energy service (product)* enabled by Digital Energy Technology-social (DET) framework because it exploits the convergence of technologies, policies, and financial drivers in an active liberalized market as analyzed in (Lim et al., 2014). In other words, the legacy energy product conceptualized as a simple accumulation of electricity over time in a stock, now it is redesigned as an amount of energy-containing resources being well-modulated ramp-like in a flow with desired behaviour.

Authors extended the legacy concept of *energy product* represented by an accumulation E(t) by adding the ancillary *ramping service* being materialized through the use of the flexibility R(t). In modernized conceptualization, the legacy energy product, e.g. an amount negotiated at the day-ahead market, is being coupled with the ancillary balancing service, e.g. flexible ramping negotiated intraday on the market. It generates two implications. At one side, it connects two separate transactions on the day-ahead- and on the intraday- markets in a singleton. In new context, two isolated markets are being merged. At another side, the flexibility of any actor in Smart Grid can be used to provide ancillary services because *more flexible behavior* with respect to the previous *more rigid behavior* reduces uncertainty in operational risks and increases the predictability of the operations. In new context, balancing contribution received from a qualified legacy actor and any-scale actor is exactly the same.

From fundamental research perspective, the pair of relationships between the Power and the Flexibility, and between the Energy and the Power can be explored mathematically in the context of newly established Laplace-transform-based computational framework. In effect, the $R_1(P,R)\rightarrow\delta$ has a meaning of *derivative*, while the $R_2(P,E)\rightarrow H$ has a meaning of *anti-derivative*. In other words, the *dot product* (VxI), where the term V denotes voltages and the term I represent currents, is being mapped to the pair of Dirac- and Heaviside- functions (δ,H) written in/for different frame of reference.

From applied research perspective, the resulting pair of functions (δ,H) being newly combined into a (Haar) wavelet, it can be used to encode better efficiently the same information carried out by the legacy triplet (R,P,E). In other words, the observational framework for a three-timescale system (t,τ,ξ) can be reduced to a two-scale fast-slow system (π,τ) because of integro-differential ties that exist between the time variables t, τ, and ξ from the original reference frame. This observation has a number of deeper implications that allow further simplification of the computational framework for demand-side flexibility, to be discussed in a separate research work.

The DSF operations are based on the anticipatory information about the amount/percentage of the limited resource/commodity that is-, can be-, or will be- unavailable to meet the demand. Authors adhere to more specific definition of the Transactive Energy (TE) as a software-based grid management of grid reliability and resilience driven through a kind of incentives. In this conceptualization, artificial intelligence software applications use economic signals and timely operational information to value the DSF as an indicator used to manage production and consumption of energy.

Authors defined the *measurable indicators* of DSF by using real time demand-oriented energy measurement tools (Simonov et al., 2017). Authors found that the known state of the art lacks tools including small-scale energy producers in the intraday markets (Liu et al., 2017), which is a major obstacle in any geographic context.

Authors project that the DSF will cause a *societal change* because it materializes a kind of collectively-owned (social) energy. In the past, the energy was seen as a *commodity being distributed* over distribution network. The DSF-based approach uses the information and *knowledge being shared* in order to sensitize people about the change in amount of prosperity that needs to be apportioned in optimal, fair, or other required fashion.

From the small-scale plant owner's viewpoint, the DSF is a knowledge-based *enabling tool* that includes them in the market. In addition to the anonymized AoE being available from any actor, the pattern of flexibility R(t) is individual and specific. From the ecology-friendly consumer's viewpoint, the DSF is a *driver* of the behavioral change that keeps sustainable the exploitation of natural energy-containing resources by humans. From the societal viewpoint, the DSF is a *democracy and policy tool* that elastically re-shapes the energy markets in a hybrid way.

Authors found that in the context of very different developing countries (World Bank, 2011), the DSF framework could be particularly beneficial to manage *fair access* to energy because of raising awareness and informing about energy needs, variations in demand figures, and ways to share the resource in knowledge-grounded fashion.

Finally, authors found applicable the Global Sensitivity Analysis (GSA) with respective sensitivity indices to behavioral tracking of certain group of flexibility-makers with respect to the action realized by other group(s). All renewable energy projects are sensitive to the (electrical) input parameters because of the constraints which hamper the financial analysis of the business operations. Hence, this investigation has to continue in the future work in order to express compositions of flexibility actions in nested- or differently organized models.

FUTURE RESEARCH DIRECTIONS

Further research is required because the transition from demand-led modality of management of Smart Grid to the generation-led modality has many implications. It implies the transition from the centralised control approach to the fully decentralized one. As stated previously, the wavelet (δ,H) encodes with different efficiency the information about the (VxI) construct. It suggests some further research on comparison between the computational framework grounded on a three-timescale system (t,τ,ξ) and a two-scale framework (π,τ) that explores integro-differential ties between time variables from the original reference frame.

The most important system-wide changes are illustrated in the Table 1. Here, authors depicted the change and the technology enabler required to activate the role

Table 1. Transition from demand-led energy business scenario to the Generation-led scenario

	Demand-Led Scenario	Generation-Led Scenario
Design pattern	• Top-down • Centralized high-inertia generation, HV transmission, MV, and LV distribution topologies	• Bottom up • Ubiquitous injection of powers in LV segments • Direct withdrawal from LV segments • Producers, Consumers, Prosumers
Control modality	• Centralized control model with ICS/ SCADA • Physical power plants • Physical inertia • Physical reserves (generation)	• Decentralized cooperative multi-agent control model with mini-SCADA • Microgrids • Virtual power plants • Virtual inertia & reserves
Demand-Response	DRM actions at the production side only	DRM actions at the production side, at the demand side, at both the production and the demand sides
Market	Large-scale and qualified actors only	All differently scaled actors acts on the market
Online	• PMU and PDC vs. WAMS (synchronized) • Smart meters vs. AMI (pull) • RTU vs. ICS/SCADA (pull/push)	• Smart meters vs. Cloud/Fog (push and pull) • Extended sensorial devices with demand-, phasor-, and power quality orientation vs. decentralized power- and energy- management systems (push) • Live events (publish-subscribe)
Offline	always allowed for metering equipment	in system fault conditions only
Accounting modality	• Cumulative sums of energy only • Variable tariffs modulated as a combination of in-peak and off-peak components	• Analytical accounting of energy flow • Analytical accounting of monetary flow • Demand-oriented billing • Observations, Accounting, and Control at the same fine-grained timescale compatible with real-time variability

of small-scale RES actors in the market-based business ties. In short, the disappearing centralized SSF option that throttles TES generators it will be progressively replaced by the decentralised multi-agent control system that exploits the DSF as a balancing service grid-wide.

The work described in this chapter originates further research going in two directions. One direction explores the governability of the flexibility of demand as a tool to *reduce the uncertainty* about the changes between demand levels. Another direction explores new role of small-scale RES generators in the transformation of the demand-led Smart Grid into the generation-led configuration by exploring the flexibility as a surrogate reserve and artificial inertia. There is a substantial difference between two above-mentioned roles, but the effects on containing or amplifying the imbalances in the system are identical. The discrepancy between the demand-for-power and the offer-of-power can be managed by varying the demand (1), the offer (2), or both components at the same time (3).

In the present chapter, authors detailed the design and the use of the demand measurement unit, of the inclusion framework that interacts with the market feeders in order to inform small-scale actors about the ongoing stocks of market prices and allow them to sell amounts of qualified RES energy (main energy product) and/or the well-specified uncertainty-less structure of demand (derivative energy product), and/or the flexibility of demand-response (ancillary balancing service or reserve).

An emerging trend is represented by the widespread of renewable energy grid-wide up to the theoretical limit of 100% intermittent RES. Under this low-inertia and high-uncertainty operational condition, the vulnerability of the system becomes very high. As a result, the changes in the roles of energy business actors are unavoidable. An important contribution to the system stability could be obtained by including many small-scale RES actors (prosumers) in the decentralized grid control scenario. The evolution of the depicted ICT tools will denote the future evolutionary scenario depicted by the authors of this chapter.

CONCLUSION

Climate change is a new reality that impacted on the structure of fossil- and nuclear-based energy businesses. To reduce CO_2 pollutants, energy business adopted environmental-friendly power plants from renewable energy sources. It increased the complexity of power systems and increased the cost of balancing services. The intermittent RES production by small-scale actors has several peculiarities requiring technology enablers to govern poorly predictable, weather-dependent, and inertia-less aspects. This chapter discussed about main drivers for inclusion of small-scale RES actors in the markets based on their capability to equate the structure of quantities demanded and the structure of the offer. To actuate new function, this chapter discussed about the measurement-, the comparison-, and the trading- frameworks. In terms of physics, the balance between the electric power being offered and the electric power being demanded at each instant over time is analytically accounted in terms of both the power and the rate of power. In power market terms, the quantities being traded are valued in real time by the corresponding marginal prices in terms of both the money and the rate of money. In the inertia-less RES scenario, the time to take economic decisions in order to safeguard the stability of the supply in the case of unexpected production drop-outs is explored locally by distributing computations ubiquitously. Because of the universality, new approach has an advantage to be transferable between different multi-energy domains. It can be used to optimize limited resources of the water, the oil, or any other kind of energy-containing substance.

Authors presented new ICT Framework for the inclusion of owners of small-scale renewable energy plants in the markets. In the past, investments were concentrated on large scale generators and their running. In newer scenario, the investments come to smaller decentralized PV-, Wind-, and Bio- plants. However, no investments in infrastructure are needed to materialize additional amounts of flexible energy. To support the addition of flexibility to power networks, new Framework is proposed. It includes the Measurement and Verification tools that create new knowledge about the presumption (a) and the Aggregator of Flexibility (b). Small-scale users receive new tool to determine the customer baseline, its change, and the effective price of the change. In market perspective, many small-scale users receive data-driven cooperation equipment and sophisticated software product in order to produce new knowledge about the structures of capacity and demand. Authors introduced new internet-enabled service for the inclusion of small-scale actors in the market.

Authors discussed about a new environmental-friendly energy product/service called DSF. In the past, investments were concentrated on large scale generators and their running in order to obtain *scalable amounts* (of energy). In newer scenario, the investments come to smaller decentralized PV-, Wind-, and Bio- plants in order to emerge *locally flowing QDs*. However, no investments at all in generators (Figure 2) are needed to *differently concentrate* the flows in after the flexibility. Instead, the investment goes to the cyber (information, software) assets. By introducing the DSF in power networks, new demand measurement and verification tools are required in order to determine the previous CBL, the new CBL, the effective amount of the DSF that can be used, and the correct price associated with the DSF. For this reason, the use of the DSF implies new data-driven cooperation between many users that should be supported by new ICT equipment and sophisticated software products. Therefore, it evolves software markets and enriches markets of internet-enabled services by introducing new high-tech products and services.

The advent of the flexible behavior on energy markets depends on the investment made in the knowledge sharing infrastructure (DSF Framework) that allows knowledge-based decisions, in the tools for inclusion as market participants (Participatory Framework) that allows operations, and in mentality changing practice (Framework of Operations) that scales up the size of the group of DSF-makers.

ACKNOWLEDGMENT

This research received no specific grant from any funding agency in the public, commercial, or not-for-profit sectors.

REFERENCES

Allcott, H. (2011). Rethinking real-time electricity pricing. *Resource and Energy Economics, 33*(4), 820-842.

Avila, N., Carvallo, J. P., Shaw, B., & Kammen, D. M. (2017). *The energy challenge in sub-Saharan Africa: A guide for advocates and policy makers: Part 1: Generating energy for sustainable and equitable development.* Oxfam Research Backgrounder series 2017. Retrieved from https://www.oxfamamerica.org/static/media/files/oxfam-RAEL-energySSA-pt1.pdf

Berrisford, A. J. (1990). *Statistical maximum demand measurement.* Sixth International Conference on Metering Apparatus and Tariffs for Electricity Supply 1990, Manchester, UK.

Bruninx, K. (2016). *Determining the impact of renewable energy on balancing costs, back up costs, grid costs and subsidies*. KU Leuven. Available online at http://www.creg.info/pdf/ARCC/161019-KULeuven.pdf

Carter, J. G., Cavan, G., Connelly, A., Guy, S., Handley, J., & Kazmierczak, A. (2015). Climate change and city: Building capacity for urban adaptation. *Progress in Planning, 95*, 1–66. doi:10.1016/j.progress.2013.08.001

CEER. (2016). *Scoping of flexible response, CEER discussion paper.* Ref: C16-FTF-08-04.

Chugh, S. K. (2015). *Modern Macroeconomics.* MIT Press.

Eurelectric (2014). *Flexibility and Aggregation (report).* Available online at http://www.eurelectric.org/media/115877/tf_balagr_report_final_je_as-2014-030-0026-01-e.pdf

Houghton, J. T., Meira Filho, L. G., Callander, B. A., Harris, N., Kattenberg, A., & Maskell, K. (Eds.). (1995). *The Science of Climate Change*. Cambridge University Press. Online at https://www.ipcc.ch/ipccreports/sar/wg_I/ipcc_sar_wg_I_full_report.pdf

Ilic, D., Goncalves Da Silva, P., Karnouskos, S., & Griesemer, M. (2013). An energy market for trading electricity in smart grid neighbourhoods. In *Proceedings of 6th IEEE International Conference on Digital Ecosystem Technologies-Complex Environment Engineering (IEEE DEST-CEE)*. IEEE. DOI 10.1109/dest.2012.6227918

Jehle, G. A., & Reny, P. J. (2001). *Advanced microeconomic theory*. Boston: Addison-Wesley.

Karnouskos, S. (2011). Demand side management via prosumer interactions in a smart city energy marketplace. *Proc. of IEEE International Conference on Innovative Smart Grid Technologies (ISGT 2011)*. 10.1109/ISGTEurope.2011.6162818

Kneese, A. V., & Sweeney, J. L. (1993). *Handbook of Natural Resource and Energy Economics*. North Holland.

Lamparter, S., Becher, S., & Fischer, J. G. (2010). An agent-based market platform for smart grids, In *Proceedings of the 9th International Conference on Autonomous Agents and Multiagent Systems: Industry track*. Richland, SC: International Foundation for Autonomous Agents and Multiagent Systems.

Lim, B., Spanger-Siegfried, E., Burton, I., Malone, E., & Huq, S. (2014). *Adaptation policy frameworks for climate change: developing strategies, policies and measures*. Cambridge, UK: Cambridge University Press.

Liu, Z., Wu, Q., Huang, S., & Zhao, H. (2017). Transactive Energy: A Review of State of The Art and Implementation. 2017 IEEE Manchester PowerTech, 1-6.

Mancarella, P. (2017). Power system security assessment of the future National Electricity Market. Report in support of the “Finkel Review”.

Mount, K., & Reiter, S. (1976). Construction of a continuous utility function for a class of preferences. *Journal of Mathematical Economics*, *3*(3), 227–245. doi:10.1016/0304-4068(76)90010-0

Panteli, M., & Mancarella, P. (2015, May). The Grid: Stronger, Bigger, Smarter? Presenting a conceptual framework of power system resilience. *IEEE Power & Energy Magazine*, *13*(3), 58–66. doi:10.1109/MPE.2015.2397334

Parry, M. L., Canziani, O. F., Palutikof, J. P., Van Der Linden, P. J., & Hanson, C. E. (Eds.). (2007). *Climate Change 2007: Impacts, Adaptation and Vulnerability. Contribution of Working Group II to the Fourth Assessment Report of the Intergovernmental Panel on Climate Change*. Cambridge, UK: Cambridge University Press.

Simonov, M., Chicco, G., & Zanetto, G. (2017). Event-Driven Energy Metering - Principles and applications. *IEEE Transactions on Industry Applications*, *53*(4), 3217–3227. doi:10.1109/TIA.2017.2679680

Sioshansi, F. (2013). *Evolution of Global Electricity Markets. New paradigms, new challenges, new approaches*. Elsevier.

Suvak, A. (2010). Integrated urban development strategies- comparing European and Hungarian approaches. *Review of Landscape Studies*, *3*, 139–146.

Van der Veen, R. A. C., & Hakvoort, R. A. (2016). The electricity balancing market: Exploring the design challenge. *Utilities Policy*, *43*, 186–194. doi:10.1016/j.jup.2016.10.008

Wang, B., & Hobbs, B. F. (2014). A flexible ramping product: Can it help real-time dispatch markets approach the stochastic dispatch ideal? *Electric Power Systems Research*, *109*, 128–140. doi:10.1016/j.epsr.2013.12.009

World Bank. (2011). *Guide to Adapting to Climate Change in Cities*. Online at https://collaboration.worldbank.org/servlet/JiveServlet/downloadBody/3212-102-1-3497/GuideToClimateChangeAdaptationInCities_102711.pdf

World Bank. (2016). *Climate Action Plan*. Online at https://openknowledge.worldbank. org/handle/10986/24451

KEY TERMS AND DEFINITIONS

Balancing and Ancillary Services Market (BASM): The institutional arrangement that establishes market-based balance management in an unbundled electricity market. This market deals with the balancing of electricity demand and supply in near real time after other energy markets have closed.

Change in Demand (CiD): Difference between two demand figures measured at different stocks or flows of time.

Customer-Centered Smart Grid (CCSG): A system that follows the demand-led paradigm (e.g., any detected variation in demand [causing agent] is equated by a variation in supply [effect]).

Day-Ahead Market (DAM): The main venue for trading power. On this market, sellers and buyers set the price and agree the trade for the delivery of power the following day. The DAM matches the demand with the offer but remains subject to network security and other constraints, whereby energy is co-optimized with ancillary services and other rules.

Demand Factor (DF): The fractional amount of some quantity, for example the demand for power/energy, being effectively used relative to the maximum amount of same quantity that could be used by the same system.

Demand for Energy (DfE): An abstract multi-scale object that represents the pair of values, the peak demand and a period of time in which electric energy is expected to be provided for a sustained period at a significantly higher than average supply level.

Demand for Power (DfP): An abstract multi-scale object that represents the pair of values, the peak demand (on-peak load), and a period of time in which electric power is expected to be provided for a sustained period at a significantly higher than average supply level.

Demand Profile (DP): A (graphical) representation of the variation in the electrical demand versus time.

Demand Response (DR): Is a temporal change in the power consumption of a customer to better match the demand for power with the supply.

Demand-Response Management System (DRMS): A software system that manages several aspects of DR programs.

Demand-Response Measurement Unit (DMU): An electronic measurement device with embedded computer that measures/estimates the market demand for a product by assessing the total volume that would be bought by a defined customer group in a defined geographical area in a defined time period in a defined marketing environment under a defined marketing program.

Distribution System Operator (DSO): Means an energy actor responsible for operating, ensuring the maintenance of and, if necessary, developing the distribution system in a given area and, where applicable, its interconnections with other systems and for ensuring the long term ability of the system to meet reasonable demands for the distribution of electricity (2007/72/EC) or gas (2007/73/EC).

Effective Generation Capacity (EGC): The electric output [kW_p] an electricity generator is effectively producing under current operational conditions during well-defined period of time.

Elasticity of Demand (ED): The degree to which the quantity demanded changes with respect to price.

Electric Consumption (EC_{kWh}): The measurement of total electricity used for a period of time expressed in kiloWatt hour [kWh].

Electric Demand (ED): The maximum amount of electrical energy measured in both kilowatts [kW_d] and kilovolt amperes [kVA] that is being consumed at a given time. The difference between the two terms is power factor.

Electricity Cost ($EC_\$$): An amount of monetary units that equates both Consumption [in kWh] and Demand [in kW_d or kVA].

Electricity Generation (EG): The amount of electricity [kWh] a generator produces over a specific period of time.

Electricity Generation Capacity: The maximum electric output [kW_p] an electricity generator can produce under specific conditions.

Energy Management System (EMS): A suite of power network and the generation monitoring, control and scheduling computer-aided applications used to optimize the aspects of performance of the power/energy system. EMS can also be referred to as SCADA/EMS or EMS/SCADA. Decentralized EMS includes monitoring, measurement (metering and sub-metering), and control functions across multiple locations plus the data and insights for better informed decision making about energy activities across sites.

Flexibility (F): In physical terms the flexibility has a meaning of time derivative (e.g., a rate of change in a power flow dP/dt). The supply side flexibility (SSF) can be observed directly as a change in power. The demand side flexibility (DSF) is a temporal change with respect to a baseline profile.

Generation-Centered Smart Grid (GCSG): A system that follows the generation-led paradigm (e.g., any *detected* variation in RES generation [causing agent] is equated by a variation in demand [effect] in the *same* timescale).

Industrial Control System (ICS): A collective but industry-dependent term used to describe different types of control systems and tools used to automate and to operate industrial processes.

Intraday Market (IM): The continuous trading mechanism for exchanging power intraday. Products on this market allow market participants to match generation and demand for each 15-minute period so as to satisfy their balancing requirement.

Load Profile (LP): A (graphical) representation of the variation in the electrical load versus time.

Pattern (P): A digital representation of an object or of a composition of objects.

Pattern of Demand (PoD): A digital representation of the demand for power/ energy that varies in the pre-defined timescale.

Quantities Demanded (QDs): Different quantities demanded at different prices at each particular point of time that forms the demand curve (a graph).

Quantity Demanded (QD): The total quantity of goods or services (energy commodity) demanded by customers at a particular price at any well-specified point in time. The QD depends on the price of a good or service in the marketplace, regardless of whether that market is in equilibrium.

Rate of Change (RoC): A rate that describes how one quantity (independent variable x) changes in relation to another quantity (dependent variable y), e.g. the RoC= (change in x) / (change in y). ROC is often used when speaking about momentum. When the y has a meaning of time, the RoC is the speed at which a variable x changes over a specific period of time t.

Renewable Energy Source (RES): Energy from a source that is not depleted when used.

Screening Curve (SC): A tradeoff method that combines simplified representations of generation costs for each energy-converting technology and system load projections (points) in order to determine/approximate the most cost-effective mix of generating technologies in operating regimes.

Service Level Agreement (SLA): A contract between a service provider and the end user that defines the level of service expected from the service provider. SLA defines what the customer will receive without defining how the service will be provided.

Small-Scale Actor (SSA): An owner of renewable energy plant being classified as "small-scale". This definition is country-specific and threshold-based. Limits are imposed in terms of capacity (less than X kW) and in terms of total annual electricity output (less than Y MWh).

Smart Grid (SG): Is a semantic label assigned to represent the cyber-physical system with ICT tools and modern electrical grid that gathers kinds of data and acts on information about the behaviors of suppliers and consumers. Currently, there is no globally agreed definition but several ones.

Smart Meter (SM): An electronic device with bi-directional communication that records and reports production/consumption of electric energy in predefined time intervals.

Time of Use (ToU): A broad term applied to the resource usage over a timescale being expressed in well-determined blocks of time, for example minutes, fractions of an hour, hours, on- and off- peak periods, where the flow of resources has the constant price being assigned to each ToU period.

Traditional Energy Source (TES): Energy from a source that is depleted when used.

Transactive Energy Control (TEC): The economic and ubiquitous network-wide environment for distributed energy control used to manage the flow or exchange of energy within an existing electric power system in regards to economic and market based standard values of energy.

Value Being Modulated (VbM): A sequence of values of some quantity being generated after well-specified (desired) function. The VbM time series can be used to represent a ramp or a ramping service.

ENDNOTE

1 For the sake of simplicity, in this work authors omits lengthy and complex discussion about semantic and physical meaning of this artificial digital construct drawing from the combined use of transforms.

Chapter 11
Techno-Social Systems in the Internet as a Tool for Social Adaptation of the Visually Impaired

Gennadi B. Pronchev
Lomonosov Moscow State University, Russia

Inna V. Goncharova
Lomonosov Moscow State University, Russia

Nadezhda G. Proncheva
Keldysh Institute of Applied Mathematics, Russia

Danila N. Monakhov
Lomonosov Moscow State University, Russia

Irina V. Vasenina
Lomonosov Moscow State University, Russia

Oksana G. Zubova
Lomonosov Moscow State University, Russia

ABSTRACT

The chapter deals with issues related to social adaptation of the visually impaired in techno-social systems of the internet. The current legislation providing access for visually impaired people to such techno-social systems is analyzed, as well as the way the legislation is implemented. Traditions and innovations in the field of accessibility of techno-social systems for visually impaired people in Russia are discussed. The opportunities of the electronic banking system of the European Union and Great Britain for the visually impaired are analyzed.

DOI: 10.4018/978-1-5225-5586-5.ch011

INTRODUCTION

In today's Russian society, the issue of social inequality is extremely crucial (Sushko et al., 2016b). Social inequality leads to stratification of the society into various levels of quality of life (Moser & Robin, 2006; Sushko et al., 2016a). One of the most important kinds of inequality is currently that of access to the information (Monakhov & Pronchev, 2015; Khodakova, 2009). It is not only the welfare of man but also his physical survival that depend on the opportunity of access to the relevant information (Goncharova & Pronchev, 2016; Pronchev et al., 2013).

This is especially urgent for people with health limitations (Goncharova & Pronchev, 2015). The current limited condition of social opportunities of the disabled persons urges finding the new ways for socially adapting the disabled into life of the civic society which by default is the "society of the healthy". The authors believe the problem will keep its relevance also in case the disabled persons make up the majority of the society or even if it all consists only of the disabled (Muravjov et al., 2013).

Techno-social systems created on the basis of multimedia Internet technologies can become a quite efficient means for leveling out the information inequality (Pronchev et al., 2016; Pronchev & Goncharova, 2016). Using the Internet services currently available, various social groups can if not overcome the inequality of access to the relevant information completely but anyway advance in this direction considerably (Pronchev, G.B. et al., 2016). Thus, prerequisites are built up for the disabled to adapt to ordinary life and for so-called barrier-free environment to be created.

The rapidly developing network technologies for processing big data arrays, the Big Data, also open up new opportunities in the sphere of social adaptation for people having health limitations. First of all, this is true for the ever growing volume of data and information sources. According to the forecast of the seventh annual research "IDC Digital Universe" (IDC, 2014), by the year 2020 the world volume of digital information will have grown up 10-fold, with 10% of the volume to be created by various gauges. In Russia, the growth tempo will be slower, so by 2020 the increase will have amounted to about 980 exabyte (2,2% of the world volume). Currently, the volume of information in Russia is estimated to be 155 exabyte (2,4% of the world volume). Researchers believe that the growth of information volume in Russia will be promoted by a higher number of the Internet users, people using social networks and smartphones, as well as by transition from analog television to the digital one.

The prospect for using the social data from techno-social systems opens up, including one to encompass the data from mobile devices into the Big Data. As a result, social workers will get broader opportunities for operational analysis of the new data streams and increasing the value of already accumulated data. The main changes are expected to occur at the level of structuring and the thread-specific data processing technique.

The information is accumulated from the most widespread data sources, such as the Internet (social networks, Internet stores, state services websites, gaming resources, mass media etc.), databases of the business sector and state services (utility services, healthcare, social insurance etc.), and readings of gauges and devices (RFID-labels), geographical positioning services (GPS and GLONASS).

The higher speed of enriching the Big Data arrays is promoted by mobile phones and smartphones the information from which is already being read continuously. There are currently studies of the "real time" Big Data processing. People with health limitations need continuous medical monitoring, and real-time monitoring of the organism for any diseases progressing frequently plays the decisive part. The "batch data processing" mode (when the data are processed in individual batches in a certain time) is applied when the time factor is not crucial. When doing social work, batch data processing can be used e.g. when the information about social and economic condition, quality of life of the disabled, spotting the problems in the communities of people having health limitations, particularities of economic behavior of the disabled and so on. The long-term data storage makes it possible to analyze the dynamics of different kinds of disease incidence, employment and education issues.

The Big Data technologies allow analyzing various sources of both structured and non-structured data. Currently the data may be received in different multimedia formats (digital letters, photographs, video, audio files etc.). The diversity of non-structured data results in difficulties with finding, storing and analyzing the data. One of the least structured data sources is the text data. The text analysis procedure is based on breaking down the phrases into the components. The investigation of the content of social networks is currently widely used in sociology for studying the opinion of the participants of social groups on various questions. The use of Big Data will allow taking into consideration the opinion of the disabled, analyzing the mood and attitude to various problems for a much larger number of users having health limitations, as well as getting a more versatile idea about them. There is also another important problem associated with confidentiality. Not all the data contained in the Big Data array can be used according to the ethical standards; moreover, these data can need special protection measures. According to the data of IDC, 40% of the world data and 49% of the data in Russia need various protection measures, up to the complete encryption. Meanwhile, as of today, it is so little as 20% of the total data volume that are actually protected (IDC, 2014).

The numerosity of the visually impaired – and this amounts to 285 million, including 39 millions of the blind in the world according to WHO estimate – calls for a special attention to this category of people (WHO, 2014). For people having total or partial loss of sight, the impairment means the impossibility to perceive information via the visual channel. Thus, the "conventional" virtual social environments based on the Internet technologies are unacceptable for this category of citizens and special environments have to be developed.

The currently available in the Russian Federation regulatory support of accessibility for the visually impaired to virtual social environments, on balance, allows solving the tasks the society faces (Goncharova et al., 2016).

In an earlier work by the authors (Goncharova & Pronchev, 2015), a review of virtual social environments used for the visually impaired was given. It should be pointed out that the existing techno-social systems are not numerous and are poorly standardized. The use of them requires special training for this category of citizens.

BACKGROUND

The UN Convention on the Rights of Persons with Disabilities provides the following definition: "disability is an evolving concept and that disability results from the interaction between persons with impairments and attitudinal and environmental barriers that hinders their full and effective participation in society on an equal basis with others". Thus, disability ceases to be considered as a defect of an individual but transforms into a serious issue of the society (WHO, 2014).

In the Russian Federation, the main legal instrument on protection of rights of the disabled persons is the Federal law "On social protection of the disabled in the Russian Federation" (Federal law, 1995). The law regulates the state principles of protection of the disabled persons in the social sphere and is a regulator of ensuring equal rights for the disabled in all spheres of life activity: political, economic and others, up to the Constitution of the Russian Federation and the principles and standards of the international law. According to this federal law, "a disabled person is a person having a deterioration of health accompanied by a persistent disorder of functions of the organism and conditioned by illnesses, consequences of injuries or defects which leads to limitation of the life activity and causes the necessity of social protection of the person" (Federal law, 1995).

The Russian Federation ratifying the Convention on the Rights of Persons with Disabilities in 2012 means recognizing the dramatic importance of persons with health limitations' entering the civic society as full-fledged members. It also implies reconsidering the notion "disability" as a result of the joint activity of a disabled person and the society as a whole (United Nations, 2006a, 2006b).

A healthy person obtains up to 80% of information via the visual channel, so for people having full or partial loss of sight, disability implies failure to be able to perceive information via the visual channel. Article 14 of the Federal law "On social protection of the disabled in the Russian Federation" stipulates the measures for ensuring the unhindered access of the visually impaired persons to the information: publishing the fine literature, scientific, educational and methodological, reference and information literature by the raised dots Braille font, acquiring the said literature for educational institutions and libraries (Federal law, 1995).

The crucially new typhlotechnic computer communication means open up vast opportunities for overcoming the information barrier and for social integration and adaptation of people having visual impairments: Braille font based keyboard, screen access software, speech synthesizers, typhloprinters etc. (Goncharova & Pronchev, 2015). One can learn to operate the PC of this kind both independently and in various training centers of the country, although they are not numerous today. For example, the most successful ones are the "Rehacomp" Institute of Rehabilitation of the All-Russian Society for the Blind (Rehacomp, 2017), and "Camerata" Center for Rehabilitation of the visually impaired (Camerata, 2017).

New multimedia technologies for interaction of visually impaired people and the PC emerging as well as the growing quantity of users from this category of citizens have yielded a change in the regulatory framework of Russia.

So, according to Federal law of the Russian Federation of December 1, 2014 No. 419-FZ "On making amendments to individual legislative acts of the Russian Federation on questions of social protection of the disabled due to ratification of the Convention on the Rights of Persons with Disabilities" (Federal law, 2014), Article 10 of Federal law of February 9, 2009 No. 8-FZ "On ensuring the access to the information about the activity of state agencies and local self-government authorities" (Federal law, 2009) was amended by part 6: "The procedure of ensuring the conditions of accessibility for the visually impaired persons of the official websites of the federal state agencies of the Russian Federation subjects and the local self-government authorities in the Internet network shall be established by the federal executive power agency authorized by the Government of the Russian Federation". The law became effective on January 1, 2016.

In Federal law of 24.11.1995 No. 181-FZ (as amd. on 29.12.2015) "On social protection of the disabled in the Russian Federation" (November 24, 1995), amendments on unacceptability of discrimination according to the attribute of disability (Article 3.1) and on ensuring an unhindered access of the disabled persons to the information were introduced (Article 14) (Federal law, 1995).

The letter of the Federal education and science supervision agency of March 25, 2015 No. 07-675 (Obrnadzor, 2015) instructs that "educational organizations shall ensure the availability of an alternative accessibility version of the educational organization official website in the Internet network for the low-sighted persons".

Accessibility versions located in the websites are prescribed by the legislatively consolidated right of access to the information for the visually impaired persons. Requirements for the accessibility version are detailed in the relevant standard GOST R 52872-2012 "The Internet resources. Requirements for accessibility to the visually impaired persons" (GOST, 2012). The main provisions of GOST stipulate the perceptibility, clearness, reliability and controllability of the Internet resources visited by the visually impaired people.

TECHNO-SOCIAL SYSTEMS FOR VISUALLY IMPAIRED PEOPLE IN RUSSIA

Traditions of Support of the Visually Impaired in the Russian Federation

Since the point the All-Russian Society for the Blind was founded in 1925 and for the entire Soviet period up to the collapse of the USSR, solid traditions had been formed for supporting the people having visual impairments in social, political, legal and economic spheres (VOS, 2017).

Social security and the size of disability allowance depended on the historical stages of development. In particular, one of the earliest decrees of November, 1917, was the resolution on the increased amount of disability pension. The constitution of 1936 consolidated the right of citizens for social benefits due to disability. During the Great Patriotic War, the urban and district commissions, departments of social security and mutual aid funds in the rural areas were active in taking care of the disabled persons. After the war, the functions of the Ministry of social security of the RSFSR were expanded considerably: alongside with its principal task of distributing the pension benefits, it was vested with the general management of the activity of the All-Russian Society for the Blind. Further drawing up of sizes of the social disability allowance was regulated by the USSR Law on state pensions (Goncharova & Pronchev, 2016).

The legal framework of supporting the low-sighted disabled persons relied on the international acts on protection of rights of the disabled, in particular: the Universal declaration of human rights of the disabled (1948), Declaration of social progress and development (1969), the International bill of human rights (1975), the Declaration on the rights of disabled persons (1975).

In the economic sphere, the main task of the state was employment of people having visual impairments. The All-Russian Society for the Blind conducted an active policy of constructing and organizing profitable enterprises in which specially equipped work places for the blind were organized, and in the 1970s, it achieved this objective.

It became possible for the low-sighted children to obtain the secondary education owing to organizing the specialized boarding schools.

The right for a higher education was consolidated by legislation owing to the efforts of the Society for the Blind in cooperation with the People's Commissariat of Education of the RSFSR back in the 1930s.

An achievement of the Soviet medical service system is the creation of medical and social assessment boards and the development of preventive measures promoting the rehabilitation of the low-sighted.

In the cultural and educational sphere, the work went along two directions, one of them being the explanatory policy by the mass media about the problems and actual side of life of the low-sighted persons among the country's population, and, consequently, forming a friendly attitude of the society to the visually impaired which promotes further integration of the latter into the civic society. On the other hand, specialized printed goods based on Braille font was published for people with visual impairments ("Life of the Blind", "Soviet School child", "Aid for the Cultural and Educational Worker", "Physical Culture and Sport", "Literature Reading", "In the World of Music", "Work of the Blind" and so on) (Goncharova & Pronchev, 2016).

The Fulfillment of the Right of Access to Virtual Social Environments for the Visually Impaired in the Russian Federation

The vast majority of the Internet resources of the state executive power structures at the federal level are equipped with the accessibility versions for the visually impaired that are up to the requirements of GOST R 52872-2012. For the visually impaired, the accessibility features of the Internet resources include the opportunities to increase the font size, to convert all colored graphic objects into black and white format, the option of turning off the graphic objects, with all of them being backed up by a verbal description. Alongside with this, the low-sighted can choose the page color, from white font on the black background up to the black font on the white background.

As a positive example, the following official websites can be quoted: that of the RF President (http://special.kremlin.ru/ events/president/news), of the Government of the Russian Federation (http://special. government.ru), state services portal of the Ministry of communication and media (http://www.gosuslugi.ru/ special), website of the Ministry of health of the Russian Federation (http://www.rosminzdrav.ru/ special), of the Federal agency for tourism (http://www.russiatourism.ru), of the Ministry of justice of the Russian Federation (http://minjust.ru/ru/ visuallimpaired), and of the Federal drug control service of the Russian Federation (http://fskn.gov.ru /special_fskn.shtml).

Nevertheless, the Federal agency for tourism (Rostourism) (http://www.russiatourism.ru) does not support an accessibility version for the visually impaired.

As for the legislative power at the federal level, the state structures also have the low-vision accessibility versions on their official websites. As an example, the Federal Assembly of the Russian Federation can be quoted: website of the State Duma (http://spec.duma.gov.ru,), that of the Federation Council (http://special.council.gov.ru).

The Internet portal of Moscow Region Duma (from http://moduma.ru) allows the low-sighted people to get all the required information. It has the features of changing the font size, contrast increase or change, and graphic object to text conversion.

However, not all official websites of the legislative power state structures at the regional level have got accessibility versions for the low-sighted. For instance, the official website of Kursk Region Duma (http://kurskduma.ru/index.php) has got no such function.

The General Prosecutor's Office has an accessibility version for the visually impaired persons on its Internet resource (http://www.genproc.gov.ru/special), with options of color scheme change and font size adjustment.

The most popular information search services are already in line with the developed standards of the Internet information presentation for the low-sighted people.

So, in May 2015, the main page of Yandex search engine became accessible both to the blind and to the low-sighted Internet users who work via the screen access software – JAWS, NVDA and VoiceOver. The main task of the portal is singling out the most critical information because a screen access software reads everything that is input. The blind users can also use the Mail and Yandex.Browser for Windows OS. Launching of the services was timed to coincide with the Global Accessibility Awareness Day dedicated to popularization in the IT-branch of accessibility ideas – i.e. of the interfaces accessibility to people with health limitations (Blog Yandex, 2014).

At the end of May, 2014, Google search engine launched a new free Google speech synthesizer (GoogleText-to-speech, 2014) that voices over the text in the device screen. This allows using the function "Read aloud" in Google Play Books, listening to the pronunciation of words in Google Translator, using TalkBack and other accessibility features (while all actions are voiced over). The following languages are supported: English (Great Britain, India, the USA), Indonesian, Spanish (Spain, the USA), Italian, Cantonese, Korean, Mandarin, German, Dutch, Polish, Portuguese (Brasil), Russian, Thai, Turkish, French, Hindi and Japanese.

However, not all official websites of socially important organizations currently support visual accessibility versions. According to the sociological survey conducted by FinPotrebSouz and the National Agency for Financial Studies (NAFI) on the verge of August and September 2015, "no website of 60 largest RF banks has got a "visual accessibility version" function which could have eliminated most of adaptive and psychological problems for people with reduced eyesight. A font that is twice as large than the main one used in the website is considered to be large, with one that is similar to the one used in the website (or slightly larger) being medium. So, 27 banks out of 60 have the medium font – while 13 remaining ones use the small one (smaller than the main font of the website text). Only 29 banks of the 60 have websites with a high contrast font which helps the partially sighted to read the information (FinPotrebSouz, 2015).

Thus, it can be stated that in Russia the mechanism for forming an accessible environment for people with health limitations, the visually impaired ones included, is being extensively institutionalized.

A true breakthrough in the accessibility policy was the federal target program "Accessible environment" adopted in 2011 that was designed for the years 2011 – 2015 but upon resolution of the Government has been extended up to 2020.

The set of measures taken is aimed at rendering the environment comfortable and convenient for all people. The consistent work is in progress that is aimed at social protection of the visually impaired as well as at active inclusion of them into interactions with various social institutes, with the opportunities for work and education, consumer services ensured, thus raising the income and improving the quality of life.

TECHNO-SOCIAL SYSTEMS FOR THE VISUALLY IMPAIRED IN THE EUROPEAN UNION

It seems interesting to compare the implementation of a barrier-free environment in Russia and in the European Union. According to the investigation conducted by the authors, it is in Great Britain that the advanced practice in this area of focus has been introduced.

Barrier-Free Environment in Great Britain

As estimated by Access Economics in 2009, there are almost two million people who live with a total or partial loss of sight in Great Britain. The community includes about 360000 people registered as the blind or the low-sighted who have serious and permanent losses of sight. The state policy of protection for the disabled is aimed at granting a broad social package: the weekly disability allowance ranges from GBP 33,6 to GBP 168 depending on the degree of disability (GOV UK, 2017). Alongside with that, there are various substantial benefits for buying medications, medical devices, wheelchairs etc. Housing and public utility services as well as maintenance of the residential buildings are partly paid for at the expense of the local municipal bodies.

An active part in creating a barrier-free environment with innovation products and digital communication means implemented is played by public organizations, foundations and libraries of Great Britain. The information about the most important organizations is given in Table 1.

Analysis and Evaluation of Websites of Great Britain's Banking System

Great Britain's banking sphere dates back to the 17th century and it is currently represented by several levels (see Figure 1). The top position is occupied by the Bank of England whose scope of activities includes the protection and provision of stability of the national currency as well as the development and consolidation of banking and financial systems. The second level is the domain of commercial banks that are under the external and internal control and of the securities accounting companies. The third level is occupied by building societies and credit unions. The main suppliers of credit resources are foreign-owned banks, which is the reason of their high presence.

Fierce competition and the necessity of profits maximizing force the banks to use all tools possible for attracting the customers. As a consequence, banks are in for the use of the latest developments in the area of information and communication technologies. Meanwhile, the low-sighted customers are ready to use the banking services via remote access. This is confirmed by the survey of the blind and low-sighted people using the electronic information services conducted at Robert Gordon University (Aberdeen Business School) back in 2004 (Lewis, 2004). The question of using the Internet in the banking sector was answered by 27,2% of the respondents in the positive and 9% of the respondents said they tried using them but found the websites inaccessible for usage.

For this study, the authors selected 56 banks of Great Britain from the existing lists (Bank of England, 2017; Swiftbic, 2017). Among the selected ones, there turned out to be 10 banks having the largest capital, 20 commercial banks, 5 banking enterprises of retail groups, and 21 British retail banking brands owned by the foreign banks (1 branch of the Russian bank included). The Internet addresses of the official websites of the banks under study are given in Table 2.

Assuming that the consumers of information and feedback sources are people with visual impairments, the following requirements were selected as the main parameters for evaluating the websites of Great Britain's banking system (Goncharova et. al., 2017):

Table 1. The information about the British organizations

Name and Website	Spheres of Activity
Guide Dogs for the Blind Association http://www.guidedogs.org.uk	Training of guide dogs; provision of guide dogs; other services increasing the mobility and independence of the blind and low-sighted people.
British Blind Sport organization http://www.britishblindsport.org.uk	A sports charity for the blind and low-sighted.
British computer association of the blind (BCAB) https://www.bcab.org.uk	An active group of the blind and low-sighted PC users, it offers training, discussion, creation of networks and assistance to all its members. Founded in 1969, it is the world's oldest computer association for the blind and low-sighted. The membership involves people of all qualification levels, interests and abilities.
The British Council for Prevention of Blindness http://www.bcpb.org	It was founded in 1976 as a charity for financing the scientific research in prevention of blindness and restoration of sight.
British Wireless for the Blind Fund http://www.blind.org.uk	It has been providing specially adapted radios for the low-sighted for 80 years.
Royal National Institute of Blind People (RNIB) http://www.rnib.org.uk	Itcoversallspheresoflifeactivityoftwomillionpeoplesufferingfromloss of sight.
The Royal Society for Blind Children http://rsbc.org.uk	It supports the blind and low-sighted children and young people aged 0-25 and their families, with financial assistance rendered too.
Knowsley Disability Concern http://www.kdc.org.uk	Initially founded in 1977 as a service for adults having learning limitations, KDC has evolved into a modern, insightful organization specializing in services for people with disabilities for them to be able to live in society independently.
International Glaucoma Association http://www.glaucoma-association.com	Its mission is to raise awareness about glaucoma, promote scientific research associated with early diagnosing and treatment, as well as to support the patients and ones looking after them.
Henshaws Society for Blind People https://www.henshaws.org.uk	One of the oldest charities in Great Britain, it renders expert support, counseling and training for all suffering from loss of sight to develop the skills and independence in daily life.
DeafblindUK http://deafblind.org.uk	The national specialized support service for the deafblind people
The helpline of Sightline Vision North West http://www.sightlinevnw.co.uk	Psychological assistance for people with health limitations
Action for Blind People https://actionforblindpeople.org.uk	Founded in 1857 as the Surrey Association for the General Welfare of the Blind, it was later reorganized into London Association for the Blind. Initially the main activities of the Association were teaching the blind reading and mastering the practical occupations, such as basket weaving. The organization currently encompasses all spheres of assistance to the visually impaired, including one in getting access to a number of technologies ranging from PCs to television and from smartphones and tablet PCs to video magnifiers.
Bradbury Fields http://www.bradburyfields.org.uk	A local charity for the low-sighted people living in the Merseyside area.
RNIB Library http://www.rniblibrary.com	The largest one in Europe, with 60 000 publications in the catalog. All services for the low-sighted are provided free of charge (audio format, Braille font, music). There is a real-time read out option on the website.
RNIB Newsagent's http://www.tnauk.org.uk	Free delivery of daily newspapers and periodicals in the Audio CD format or over USB. If there is a mobile phone or a PC, the daily newspaper or magazine can be received by e-mail or downloaded from the website.
SeeAbility https://www.seeability.org	The objective of SeeAbility is to encourage the people having a total or partial loss of sight and other numerous disabilities to completely fulfill their potential and improve quality of life. It was founded in the 18th century as the Royal school for the blind.
Sense https://www.sense.org.uk	The public organization offers high-quality various services throughout Great Britain for the deafblind, using the qualified personnel and a specialized network of volunteers and working with each person individually.
UCanDoIT http://www.ucandoit.org.uk	It has been active since 1998 in teaching people with health limitations to use the PC, with the focus on the Internet and e-mail skills. The training is individual and completely free of charge. By now, the team of 65 freelance teachers have conducted 50000 individual training sessions.

Figure 1. The UK banking system (percentage)

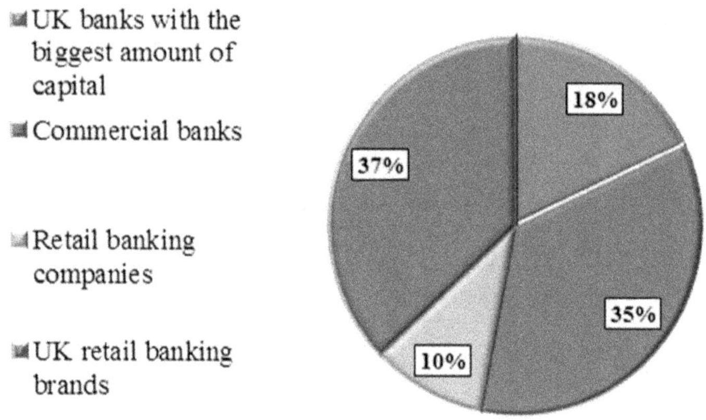

Table 2. The Internet addresses of the official websites of the banks under study

No.	Bank Name	Official Website
Banks of Great Britain Having the Largest Capital		
1	HSBC Holdings	http://www.hsbc.com
2	Barclays PLC	https://www.home.barclays
3	National Westminster Bank	http://personal.natwest.com
4	Midland Bank	https://www.midland.bank
5	Royal Bank of Scotland Group	http://www.rbs.com
6	Lloyds Banking Group	http://www.lloydsbankinggroup.com
7	Standard Chartered PLC	https://www.sc.com/en
8	TSB Bank	http://www.tsb.co.uk
9	Nationwide	http://www.nationwide.co.uk
10	Santander	http://www.santander.co.uk
Commercial Banks		
11	Airdrie Savings Bank	https://airdriesavingsbank.com
12	Aldermore	http://www.aldermore.co.uk
13	Arbuthnot Latham	http://www.arbuthnotlatham.co.uk
14	C. Hoare & Co	http://www.hoaresbank.co.uk
15	CAF Bank	https://www.cafonline.org
16	Charity Bank	https://charitybank.org
17	Close Brothers Group	http://www.closebrothers.com
18	CYBG plc	http://www.cybg.com
19	Coutts	https://www.coutts.com
20	Duncan Lawrie Bank	https://www.duncanlawrie.com

continued on following page

Table 2. Continued

No.	Bank Name	Official Website
21	Hampden & Co. PLC	https://www.hampdenandco.com
22	Julian Hodge Bank	http://www.julianhodgebank.com
23	Metro Bank	https://www.metrobankonline.co.uk
24	N M Rothschild & Sons	https://www.rothschild.com
25	Raphaels Bank	https://www.raphaelsbank.com
26	Secure Trust Bank	https://www.securetrustbank.com
27	Shawbrook Bank	https://www.shawbrook.co.uk
28	Unity Trust Bank	https://www.unity.co.uk
29	Virgin Money	http://uk.virginmoney.com
30	Weatherbys	https://www.weatherbys.co.uk
Banking Enterprises of Retail Groups		
31	Sainsbury's bank owned by Sainsbury, the British supermarket company	https://www.sainsburysbank.co.uk
32	Co-operative Bank	http://www.co-operativebank.co.uk
33	Harrods bank belonging to Harrods store in London	https://www.harrodsbank.co.uk
34	Post Office Money	http://www.postoffice.co.uk
35	Tesco Bank - Tesco supermarket company	http://www.tescobank.com
British Retail Banking Brands That Are Foreign-Owned		
36	Allied Irish Bank (GB), owned by AIB Group in Ireland	https://aibgb.co.uk
37	Axis Bank UK, India	http://www.axisbankuk.co.uk
38	Bank of Ceylon (UK), Sri Lanka	http://www.bankofceylon.co.uk
39	Bank of Baroda (UK), India	https://www.bankofbarodauk.com
40	Bank of China (UK), China	http://www.boc.cn/en/index.html
41	Bank of India (UK), India	http://www.bankofindia.uk.com/english/home_uk.aspx
42	Zenith Bank (UK), Nigeria	https://www.zenithbank.com
43	Bank of Ireland UK, Ireland	https://www.bankofireland.com
44	Citibank (UK), Citigroup in the USA	https://online.citi.com
45	ICBC (LONDON) PLC, China	http://www.icbc.com.cn/icbc/sy/default.htm
46	ICICI Bank(UK), India	http://www.icicibank.co.uk
47	Danske Bank, Denmark	http://www.danskebank.co.uk
48	Punjab National Bank (International), India	https://www.pnbint.com
49	SEB (UK), Sweden	http://sebgroup.com
50	Silicon Valley Bank UK, USA	http://www.svb.com
51	State Bank of India (UK), India	http://www.sbiuk.com
52	Svenska Handelsbanken, UK Branch, Sweden	http://www.handelsbanken.com
53	The Bank of East Asia, UK Branch, Hong Kong	http://www.hkbea.com
54	TSB Bank, Spain	http://www.tsb.co.uk
55	Union Bank of India (UK) Ltd, India	http://www.unionbankofindia.co.in
56	Alfa Capital Markets (Great Britain)	https://alfabank.ru/gbr

Source: (Bank of England, 2017; Swiftbic, 2017)

1. Text version available for any non-text content for its possible transformation into alternative forms that are convenient for various users (larger font, Braille font, text to speech).
2. A text version alternative for the media content available or an alternative audio recording available.
3. The option of content presentation in different appearances without loss of data or structure (adaptability), e.g. with a simpler page layout.
4. A text description explaining the pictures available for the graphic files.
5. Tables should not have too many cells and the nesting level of the table should be kept to the minimum.
6. The information presented in PDF format files as text has to be read out correctly in standard browsers for this file format using the screen accessibility software.
7. Complete navigation and control using the keyboard only, "hot keys" support.
8. The "accessibility" hyperlink available.
9. The "zoom in font", "contrast", and "audio version" hyperlinks available.
10. An alternative version of the website available for the visually impaired.
11. The maximum compatibility of the content with the current user applications and browsers, assistive technologies included, as well as with ones under development has to be ensured.

For the primary analysis, the simple "yes/no" visualization method was used: if the website has the said function, the parameter is given value 1, otherwise it is 0.

The results are brought down in Table 3.

Main results of the research

1. The greatest score according to 11-point scale was 9 points (81,8%). Structure presents in Figure 2. So many points were mainly awarded to banks supporting WCAG 2.0 standards. The parameters for which points were scored are as follows: 1, 2, 3, 4, 5, 6, 7, 8, 11. The category does not use the hyperlinks "alternative website version", "font zoom in", "contrast" and "audio version" explaining that by the fact that the website structure and content ensure a complete access for the people having sight limitations and using the relevant equipment, so additional hyperlinks are not necessary.
2. All websites of the British banks are compatible with the existing user applications and browsers (see Figure 3). Accessibility versions for the low-sighted can be accessed via the browser settings. There are combinations of keys for zooming in the text or for switching to keyboard-only mode of using the browser. E.g. in the Internet Explorer, Mozilla Firefox, Google Chrome, Opera browsers, the following combinations of keys are used: zoom in - Ctrl+ "+", zoom out - Ctrl+ "-". The Safari browser zooms in with Cmd + "+", and

Table 3. The results of the research

Banking System of Great Britain													
No.	**Bank Name**	**1**	**2**	**3**	**4**	**5**	**6**	**7**	**8**	**9**	**10**	**11**	**Score**
Banks of Great Britain Having the Largest Capital													
1	HSBC Holdings	1	1	1	1	1	1	1	1	0	0	1	9
2	Barclays PLC	1	1	1	1	1	1	1	1	0	0	1	9
3	National Westminster Bank	0	0	0	0	1	0	1	1	0	0	1	4
4	Midland Bank	0	0	0	0	1	0	0	0	0	0	1	2
5	Royal Bank of Scotland Group	0	0	0	0	1	0	1	1	0	0	1	4
6	Lloyds Banking Group	1	1	1	1	1	1	1	1	0	0	1	9
7	Standard Chartered PLC	0	0	0	0	1	0	0	0	0	0	1	2
8	TSB Bank	1	1	1	1	1	1	1	1	0	0	1	9
9	Nationwide	1	1	1	1	1	1	1	1	0	0	1	9
10	Santander	1	1	1	1	1	1	1	1	0	0	1	9
Commercial Banks													
11	Airdrie Savings Bank	0	0	0	0	1	0	0	1	0	0	1	3
12	Aldermore	0	0	0	0	1	0	0	0	0	0	1	2
13	Arbuthnot Latham	0	0	0	0	1	0	0	0	0	0	1	2
14	C. Hoare & Co	0	0	0	0	1	0	0	0	0	0	1	2
15	CAF Bank	1	0	0	0	1	0	0	1	1	0	1	5
16	Charity Bank	0	0	0	0	1	0	0	0	0	0	1	2
17	Close Brothers Group	1	1	1	1	1	1	1	1	0	0	1	9
18	CYBG PLC	0	0	0	0	0	0	0	1	1	0	1	3
19	Coutts	1	0	0	0	1	0	0	1	1	0	1	5
20	Duncan Lawrie Bank	0	0	0	0	0	0	0	0	0	0	1	1
21	Hampden & Co. PLC	0	0	0	0	0	0	0	0	0	0	1	1
22	Julian Hodge Bank	1	1	1	1	1	1	1	1	0	0	1	9
23	Metro Bank	1	0	0	0	1	0	0	1	0	0	1	4
24	N M Rothschild & Sons	1	0	0	0	0	0	0	0	0	0	1	1
25	Raphaels Bank	0	0	0	0	0	0	0	0	0	0	1	1
26	Secure Trust Bank	0	0	0	0	0	0	0	0	0	0	1	1
27	Shawbrook Bank	0	0	0	0	1	0	0	1	0	0	1	3
28	Unity Trust Bank	1	1	0	1	1	1	1	1	0	0	1	8
29	Virgin Money	0	0	0	0	0	0	0	1	0	0	1	2
30	Weatherbys	0	0	0	0	0	0	0	0	0	0	1	1
Banking Enterprises of Retail Groups													
31	Sainsbury's bank owned by Sainsbury, the British supermarket company	0	0	0	0	0	0	0	0	0	0	1	1
32	Co-operative Bank	1	1	1	0	1	1	1	1	0	0	1	8

continued on following page

Table 3. Continued

33	Harrods bank belonging to Harrods store in London	0	0	0	0	0	0	0	0	0	0	1	1
34	Post Office Money	1	1	1	1	1	1	1	1	0	0	1	9
35	Tesco Bank – Tesco supermarket company	1	0	0	0	1	0	1	1	0	0	1	5
British Retail Banking Brands That Are Foreign-Owned													
36	Allied Irish Bank (GB), owned by AIBGroup in the Republic of Ireland	1	1	1	1	1	1	1	1	0	0	1	9
37	Axis Bank UK, India	0	0	0	0	0	0	0	0	1	0	1	2
38	Bank of Ceylon (UK), Sri Lanka	0	0	0	0	0	0	0	0	0	0	1	1
39	Bank of Baroda (UK), India	0	0	0	0	0	0	0	0	0	0	1	1
40	Bank of China (UK), China	0	0	0	0	0	0	0	0	0	0	1	1
41	Bank of India (UK), India	0	0	0	0	0	0	0	0	0	0	1	1
42	Zenith Bank (UK), Nigeria	0	0	0	0	0	0	0	0	0	0	1	1
43	Bank of Ireland UK, Ireland	1	1	1	1	1	1	1	1	0	0	1	9
44	Citibank (UK), Citigroup in the USA	0	0	0	0	0	0	0	0	1	0	1	2
45	ICBC (LONDON) PLC, China	0	0	0	0	0	0	0	0	0	0	1	1
46	ICICI Bank (UK), India	0	0	0	0	0	0	0	0	0	0	1	1
47	Danske Bank, Denmark	0	0	0	0	0	0	0	0	1	0	1	2
48	Punjab National Bank (International), India	0	0	0	0	0	0	0	0	0	0	1	1
49	SEB (UK),Sweden	0	0	0	0	0	0	0	1	0	0	1	2
50	Silicon Valley Bank UK, USA	0	0	0	0	0	0	0	0	0	0	1	1
51	State Bank of India (UK), India	0	0	0	0	0	0	0	0	1	0	1	2
52	Svenska Handelsbanken, UK Branch, Sweden	0	0	0	0	0	0	0	0	0	0	1	1
53	The Bank of East Asia, UK Branch, Hong Kong	0	0	0	0	0	0	0	0	1	0	1	2
54	TSB Bank, Spain	1	1	1	1	1	1	1	1	0	0	1	9
55	Union Bank of India (UK) Ltd, India	0	0	0	0	0	0	0	0	0	0	1	1
Branches of the Russian Banks													
56	Alfa Capital Markets (Great Britain)	0	0	0	0	0	0	0	0	0	0	1	1

zooms out with Cmd + "-". So, according to the criterion of compatibility with applications and browsers, the minimum initial quantity of points scored by all bank websites is 1.

3. The distribution of indicators among all parameters has shown that most developers and service department managers kept to the condition of satisfying the minimum needs of the low-sighted users: 1, 2 points were scored by 59% of the websites (see Figure 4), and 16,2% of the bank websites meet 3 to 5 accessibility criteria (see Figure 5).

Figure 2. Structure of the UK banking system (maximum access to Websites)

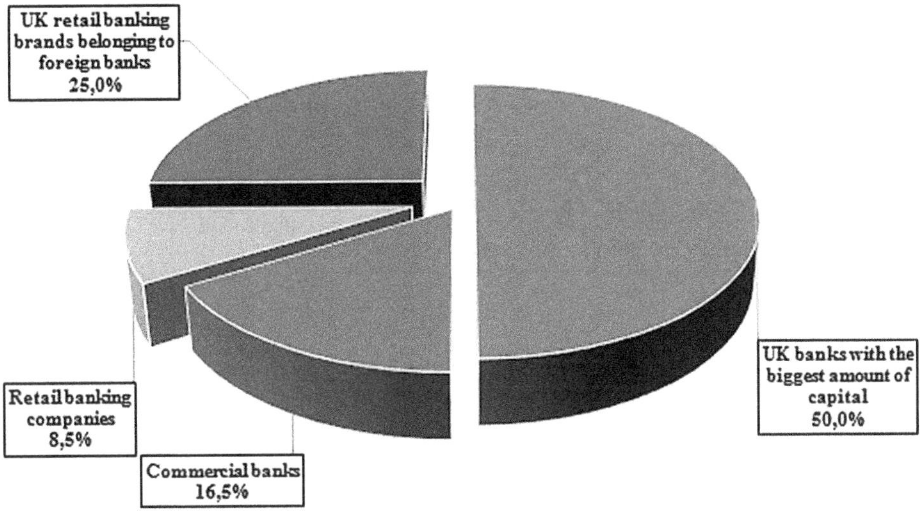

Figure 3. UK banks distribution according to parameter contents

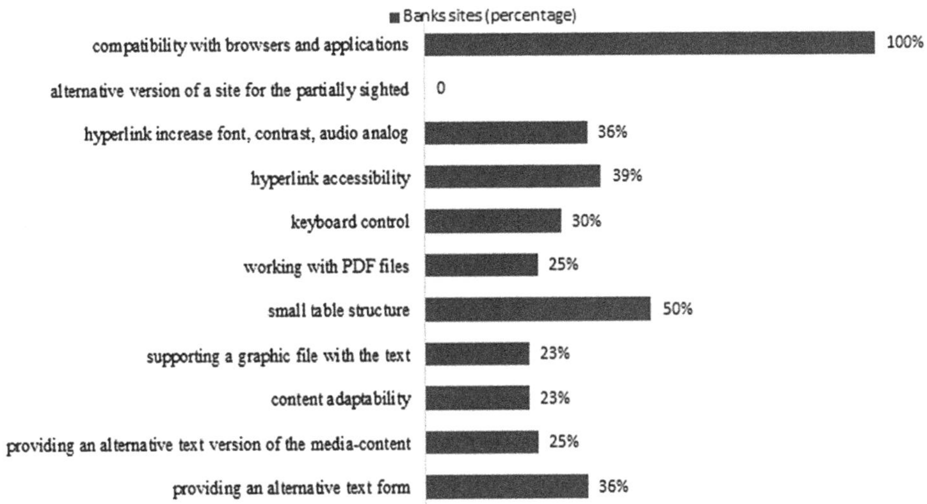

The research conducted reveals an emerging trend of changing the approaches in the indirect work with customers and with the traditionally formed image of a bank customer.

Figure 4. Minimum access level (1 or 2 points)

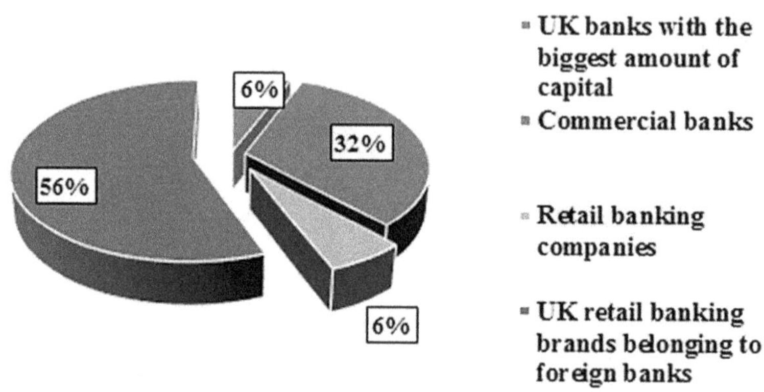

Figure 5. UK banks ranking by the number of parameters in primary points

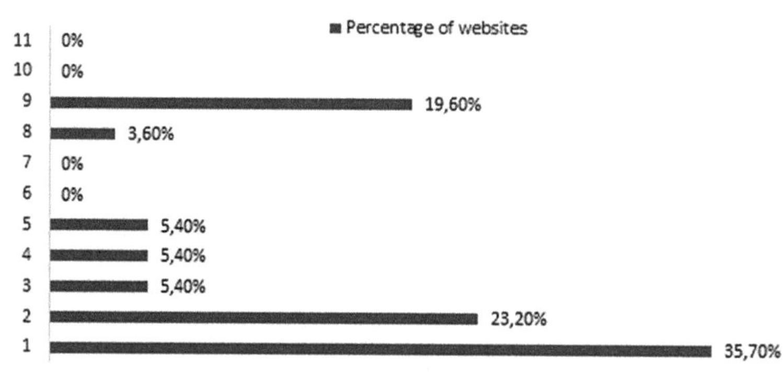

The analysis of the bank websites allows identifying the criteria for evaluating their activity from the standpoint of an accessible environment for the visually impaired and for checking the efficiency thereof in daily practices of such customers.

Countries of the European Union on the Whole

According to the estimates of the European Blind Union, in Europe there are about three million of the blind and low-sighted people (Euroblind, 2017), with the low-sighted numbering four times as much as the blind. The unemployment level among the visually impaired is over 75%, in particular, it is for women that it is much more difficult to find a suitable job. The older people aged 65 and over account for almost 90% of the low-sighted (Euroblind, 2017).

The European Union (EU) countries have approved the relevant laws according to which the Internet-resources of the government, state services or other websites providing widespread services of the general use (e.g. employment agencies, education, leisure organizations etc.) shall ensure accessibility for people with sight limitations.

As the guideline technical standard for ensuring the web content accessibility in the European area countries, the Web Content Accessibility Guidelines (WCAG 2.0, WCAG 1.0) are used. The Web Content Accessibility Guidelines (WCAG) are an integral part of documents created under the Web Accessibility Initiative (WAI) in the World Wide Web Consortium (W3C – the head organization of the international standards for the Internet) and ensuring the access to the Internet not only for the visually impaired but also for people with other physical disabilities. The current version, WCAG 2.0, was published in December 2008 and in October 2012 it got the status of an official international standard, ISO/IEC 40500: 2012.

The paper presents an analysis of the European experience of using the Internet-resources for the visually impaired. As the object of study, the Internet-resources of the EU banking system were selected. The authors believe this is a simple way to learn to what extent the recommendations of the regulators and public organizations are adhered to. Firstly, it is supervisors and controlling bodies, and secondly, it is fierce competition and an opportunity to increase profits that make the banks use all tools possible for attracting the customers.

The study covered 28 countries of the European Union. When choosing the banks, the authors were first of all interested in large national and state banks having a longstanding history.

The results presented below are quite characteristic.

- **Germany:** KFW bank (Kreditanstalt für Wiederaufbau, n.d.) is the German state bank, with 80% of shares owned by the federal government of Germany. The bank serves both individuals and legal entities. Accessibility for the visually impaired: there is a dialog box in the main page that allows changing the contrast; there is an "accessibility" (Barrierefreiheit) link at the bottom of the page; following the link lands one to a page containing a detailed manual for the low-sighted – how to zoom in font, to alter the color scheme, to work without the mouse, and to use the screen read out function.
- **France:** CIC bank (Crédit Industriel et Commercial, n.d.). The bank has over 5875 branches worldwide. Accessibility for the visually impaired: there is an "accessibility" (Accessibilité) link in the top right corner. There are such features as quick navigation of the menu in voice mode and keys combination for working without the mouse.
- **Austria:** HYPO Landesbank Vorarlberg bank (2017). Accessibility for the visually impaired: there is a font size zoom in option in the main page.

- **The Netherlands:** ABN AMRO Bank N.V. (2018). Accessibility for the visually impaired: there is a text to speech function; the telephone banking with speech recognition technology has been implemented; balance can be viewed using text messages; font size can be zoomed in.
- **Belgium:** Banque Degroof (n.d.) – the first private bank of Belgium. Accessibility for the visually impaired: font size zoom in option.
- **Italy:** Banca Piccolo Credito Valtellinese (n.d.). Accessibility for the visually impaired: font size zoom in option.

Issues, Controversies, Problems

The analysis of the banking sphere for accessibility of services to the visually impaired has shown that in some countries (Germany, France, the Netherlands etc.) favorable conditions are created for solving the required scope of tasks in the real time mode via the bank website: credits, deposit transactions, Internet-banking, payment for services and so on. The visually impaired users of such Internet-resources can scale the text, change the contrast, work without using the mouse, and listen to audio version of the online resource content.

Nevertheless, in a number of countries (e.g. in Bulgaria and Hungary), the Internet resources of banking system are not adapted for the visually impaired people to use. Here the pages browsed lack even the simplest function of font size zooming in.

Thus, when speaking about the European Union countries as a whole, it should be admitted that the technologies actually employed in the Internet banking are not completely up to the regulations that are current in the EU.

SOLUTIONS AND RECOMMENDATIONS

The program approach of forming an accessible environment for the visually impaired resulted in a higher interest on the part of the scientific community, various public and business organizations in the questions of research and creation of a barrier-free environment. In order to achieve the set goals, the standards on the accessible environment for the disabled have to be adjusted, and various services, agencies, organizations and the local communities have to cooperate in a consistent and meticulous manner. It is only through joint effort that a universal life environment can be created.

CONCLUSION

The modern world sees disability become a society-wide problem. The main task of the social policy of the state consists in ensuring an opportunity to extensively participate in all spheres of life activity of the society for the persons with disabilities by means of creating a barrier-free environment with techno-social systems implemented. In this process, it is not only the public organizations, foundations and libraries that can play the leading part but so can the banking system.

Studies have shown that the banking sector of Great Britain is interested in attracting the low-sighted customers when the profits obtained can completely compensate for the expenses incurred. Meanwhile, the majority of websites have the minimum accessibility level, which is especially true for foreign-owned banks. On the contrary, large banks having a lot of branches ensure a total access to the banking services on their websites. The leading part in this process belongs to the factor of the state support for the disabled people, the visually impaired ones including, as well as to the formed public opinion institute. However, the process is affected by the banking sector influence on the creation of a barrier-free environment with the modern digital technologies being understudied.

In order to organize the activity in more efficient forms, the work on website adaptation has to be continuous and it has to be carried out in joint cooperation with standard-developer companies, experts and public organizations of assistance for the disabled. This will allow not only promptly responding to any external change arising but also creating an effective organizational and functional diagnostics and analysis model.

ACKNOWLEDGMENT

This research was supported by the Russian Foundation for Humanities (grant number 15-03-00435-a) and Russian Foundation for Basic Research (grant number 16-01-00306-a).

REFERENCES

ABN AMRO Bank N.V. (2018). Retrieved March 11, 2017, from http://www.abnamro.nl

Banca Piccolo Credito Valtellinese. (n.d.). Retrieved March 11, 2017, from http://www.creval.it

Bank of England. (2017). *Banks of Great Britain*. Retrieved February 20, 2017, from http://www.bankofengland.co.uk/pra/Pages/ authorisations/banksbuildingsocietieslist.aspx

Banque Degroof. (n.d.). Retrieved March 11, 2017, from http://www.degroof.be

Blog Yandex. (2014). *New Yandex.Browser 14.12 became safer and more accessible*. Retrieved March 11, 2017, from http://clubs.ya.ru/yandexbrowser/ replies.xml?item_no=5105

Camerata. (2017). *Nizhny Novgorod Regional Center for Social, Labor and Psychological Rehabilitation of Visually Impaired Persons "Camerata"*. Retrieved March 11, 2017, from http://www.kamerata.org

Crédit Industriel et Commercial. (n.d.). Retrieved March 11, 2017, from http://www.cic.fr

Euroblind. (2017). *The European Blind Union*. Retrieved February 20, 2017, from http://www.euroblind.org

Federal law. (1995). *Federal law of the Russian Federation of 24.11.1995 No. 181-FZ (as amd. on 29.12.2015) "On social protection of the disabled in the Russian Federation"*. Retrieved March 11, 2017, from http://base.garant.ru/10164504

Federal law. (2009). *Federal law of the Russian Federation of February 9, 2009 No. 8-FZ "On ensuring the access to the information about the activity of state agencies and local self-government authorities" (as amended and modified)*. Retrieved March11, 2017, from http://base.garant.ru/194874/#ixzz3wgaEeIRs

Federal law. (2014). *Federal law of the Russian Federation of December 1, 2014 No. 419-FZ "On making amendments to individual legislative acts of the Russian Federation on questions of social protection of the disabled due to ratification of the Convention on the Rights of Persons with Disabilities"*. Retrieved March 11, 2017, from http://www.garant.ru/hotlaw/federal/586929

FinPotrebSouz. (2015). *Banks are not too friendly towards physically disabled people: the results of a joint research by FinPotrebSouz and National Agency for Financial Studies*. Retrieved March 11, 2017, from http://finpotrebsouz.ru/novosti

Goncharova, I. V., & Pronchev, G. B. (2015). Virtual social environment for people with visual impairments. *Politics & Society*, *5*, 586–590.

Goncharova, I. V., & Pronchev, G. B. (2016). On support of visually impaired people in modern Russian society. *Politics & Society*, *11*, 1479–1485.

Goncharova, I. V., Pronchev, G. B., & Krichever, E. I. (2016). On regulatory framework of virtual social networks accessibility for visually impaired people. *Modern Law*, *4*, 62–67.

Goncharova, I. V., Pronchev, G. B., Monakhov, D. N., Vasenina, I. V., & Zubova, O. G. (2017). Remote Banking Services for the Visually Impaired in Britain as a Tool for Creating Barrier-Free Environment. *Eurasian Journal of Analytical Chemistry*, *12*(7), 1405–1414. doi:10.12973/ejac.2017.00267a

Google Text-to-speech. (2014). *Google speech synthesizer*. Retrieved March 11, 2017, from https://play.google.com/store/apps/details? id=com.google.android.tts&hl=ru

GOST. (2012). *GOST R 52872-2012. The Internet resources. Requirements for accessibility to the visually impaired persons*. Retrieved March 11, 2017, from http://protect.gost.ru/v.aspx?control=8&baseC=-1&page=0&month=- 1&year=-1&search=&RegNum=1& DocOnPageCount=15&id=176157

GOVUK. (2017). *Financial help if you're disabled*. Retrieved August 20, 2017, from https://www.gov.uk/financial-help- disabled/disability-and-sickness-benefits

HYPO Landesbank Vorarlberg bank. (2017). Retrieved March 11, 2017, from http://www.hypovbg.at

IDC. (2014). *The Digital Universe of Opportunities: Rich Data and the increasing Value of the Internet of Things*. Retrieved March 11, 2017, from https://www.emc.com/leadership/ digital-universe/2014iview/index.htm

Kreditanstalt für Wiederaufbau. (n.d.). Retrieved March 11, 2017, from http://www.kfw.de

Lewis, A. (2004). A user survey of the experiences of blind and visually impaired people using electronic information services with regard to the practical implementation of these services in public libraries. MSc Information and Library Studies. The Robert Gordon University. Aberdeen Business School. Department of Information Management.

Monakhov, D. N., & Pronchev, G. B. (2015). Network technologies and cloud services as tool of achievement of digital equality among Russian citizens. *Representative power - 21st century: legislation, commentary, problems, 1-2*(136-137), 67-70.

Moser, G., & Robin, M. (2006). Environmental annoyances: An urban-specific threat to quality of life? *Revue Europenne de Psychologie Appliquée – European Review of Applied Psychology, 56*(1), 35–41. doi:10.1016/j.erap.2005.02.010

Muravyov, V. I., Pronchev, G. B., & Proncheva, N. G. (2013). Modern Internet technologies as an instrument of smoothing the social inequalities in the context of relationship between civil society and government. *Education and the Law, 12*(52), 77–85.

Obrnadzor. (2015). *Law of the Federal education and science supervision agency of March 25, 2015 No. 07-675*. Retrieved March 11, 2017, from http://www.obrnadzor.gov.ru/common/ upload/doc_list/07-675_pismo.pdf

OLEG. (2017). *The world statistics of the disabled*. Retrieved March 11, 2017, from http://vawilon.ru/statistika-invalidov-v-mire

Pronchev, G. B., & Goncharova, I. V. (2016a). About training of visually impaired people in work with the modern information-communication technologies. *Low and Education, 5*, 58–64.

Pronchev, G. B., & Goncharova, I. V. (2016b). The technology of EU Internet resources for people with visual impairments. *Bulletin of the Scientific Conferences, 3*(6), 88-89.

Pronchev, G. B., Goncharova, I. V., Elishev, S. O., & Khodakova, N. P. (2017). Accessibility of Virtual Social Environments for the Visually Impaired as a Means for Leveling Out Social Inequality in Russia. *Man in India, 97*(16), 107–116.

Pronchev, G. B., Monakhov, D. N., & Kovalchuk, V. K. (2016). Contemporary Internet as a Means for Leveling Social Inequality in the Context of Relationships between Civil Society and the State. *International Journal of Environmental and Science Education, 11*(17), 9959–9967.

Pronchev, G. B., Monakhov, D. N., Lontsov, V. V. (2013). Virtual Social Mediums Security in the Information Society. *Space and Time, 4*(14), 231-236.

Rehacomp. (2017). *Institute of Vocational Rehabilitation and Advanced Training of the Personnel of All-Russia public association of the disabled – All-Russia Society for the Blind (winner of the "Red Banner of Labor" award) "REHACOMP"*. Retrieved March11, 2017, from http://www.rehacomp.ru

Sushko, V. A., Pronchev, G. B., Proncheva, N. G., & Shisharina, E. V. (2016a). Emigration in Modern Russia. *Social Sciences, 11*, 6436–6439.

Sushko, V. A., Pronchev, G. B., Shisharina, E. V., & Zenkina, O. N. (2016b). Social and Economic Indices of Forming the Quality of Life. *International Journal of Environmental and Science Education, 11*(18), 10839–10849.

Swiftbic. (2017).*A list of banks of Great Britain*. Retrieved February 20, 2017, from http://www.swiftbic.com/banks-in- UNITED-KINGDOM.html

United Nations. (2006a). *Convention on the Rights of Persons with Disabilities. Resolution 61/106 adopted by the General Assembly of the United Nations on December 13, 2006*. Retrieved March11, 2017, from http://www.un.org/Docs/journal/asp/ ws.asp?m=A/RES/61/106

United Nations. (2006b). *UN Convention on the Rights of the disabled / Adopted by Resolution 61/106 of the General Assembly on December 13, 2006*. Retrieved March11, 2017, from http://www.un.org/ru/documents/decl_conv/ conventions/disability.shtml

VOS. (2017). *All-Russian Society for the Blind*. Retrieved March11, 2017, from http://www.vos.org.ru

WHO. (2014). *Visual impairment and blindness*. World Health Organization (WHO). Fact Sheet N 282, August 2014. Retrieved March11, 2017, from http://www.who.int/mediacentre/factsheets/fs282/en

Compilation of References

ABN AMRO Bank N.V. (2018). Retrieved March 11, 2017, from http://www.abnamro.nl

Allcott, H. (2011). Rethinking real-time electricity pricing. *Resource and Energy Economics, 33*(4), 820-842.

Anagnostopoulos, I. S., Zeadally, E., & Exposito, E. (2016, April). Handling big data: Research challenges and future directions. *The Journal of Supercomputing*, *72*(4), 1494–1516. doi:10.100711227-016-1677-z

Andreeva, V. A. (2013). Genres and types of a text in scientific and media discourses. In P. A. G. Orel (Ed.), Inter-U anthology of scientific works [Межвузовский сборник научных трудов] (pp. 283–287). Academic Press.

Andreeva, A. O. (2015). Manipulation in the Internet network. In Информационная безопасность и вопросы профилактики киберэкстремизма среди молодежи [Info safety and problems of preventing the cyber-extremism among youth] (pp. 21-28). Academic Press.

Ang, C. (2015). *Analyzing Financial Data and Implementing Financial Models Using R*. Springer. doi:10.1007/978-3-319-14075-9

Aranjelovic, O., Shakhnarovich, G., Fisher, J., Cippola, R., & Darrell, T. (2005). Face recognition with image sets using manifold density divergence. In *Proceedings of the Computer Vision and Pattern Recognition Conference* (pp. 581--588). Piscataway, NJ: IEEE.

Aski, A. S., & Sourati, N. K. (2016). Proposed efficient algorithm to filter spam using machine learning techniques. *Pacific Science Review A. Natural Science and Engineering*, *18*(2), 145–149.

Asmus, N. G. (2005). *Linguistic features of virtual communicative space.* PhD thesis abstract. Retrieved from http://www.lib.csu.ru/texts/diss/002160.pdf (in Russian)

Avila, N., Carvallo, J. P., Shaw, B., & Kammen, D. M. (2017). *The energy challenge in sub-Saharan Africa: A guide for advocates and policy makers: Part 1: Generating energy for sustainable and equitable development.* Oxfam Research Backgrounder series 2017. Retrieved from https://www.oxfamamerica.org/static/media/files/oxfam-RAEL-energySSA-pt1.pdf

Banca Piccolo Credito Valtellinese. (n.d.). Retrieved March 11, 2017, from http://www.creval.it

Bank of England. (2017). *Banks of Great Britain*. Retrieved February 20, 2017, from http://www.bankofengland.co.uk/pra/Pages/ authorisations/banksbuildingsocietieslist.aspx

Banque Degroof. (n.d.). Retrieved March 11, 2017, from http://www.degroof.be

Batura, T. V. (2012). Methods of social networks analysis. *Info Technologies*, *10*(4), 13–28. (in Russian)

Belen, S. (2008). *The behaviour of stochastic rumours* (PhD Thesis). The University of Adelaide.

Belen, S., & Pearce, C. E. M. (2004). Rumours with general initial conditions. *The ANZIAM Journal*, *4*(03), 393–400. doi:10.1017/S1446181100013444

Benesty, J., Chen, J., Huang, Y., & Cohen, I. (2009). *Pearson Correlation Coefficient*. Springer. doi:10.1007/978-3-642-00296-0_5

Berrisford, A. J. (1990). *Statistical maximum demand measurement*. Sixth International Conference on Metering Apparatus and Tariffs for Electricity Supply 1990, Manchester, UK.

Berry, M. W., & Kogan, J. (2010). *Text Mining: Applications and Theory*. Chichester, UK: Wiley. doi:10.1002/9780470689646

Bhatt, G. D., & Emdad, A. F. (2001). An analysis of the virtual value chain in electronic commerce. *Logistics Information Management*, *14*(1/2), 78–85. doi:10.1108/09576050110362465

Biuk, Z., & Loncaric, S. (2001). Face recognition from multi-pose image sequence. In *Proceedings of 2nd Int'l Symposium on Image and Signal Processing and Analysis* (pp. 319-324). Pula, Croatia: IEEE.

Blau, B. M., & Griffith, T. G. (2016). Price clustering and the stability of stock prices. *Journal of Business Research*, *69*(10), 3933–3942. doi:10.1016/j.jbusres.2016.06.008

Blog Yandex. (2014). *New Yandex.Browser 14.12 became safer and more accessible*. Retrieved March 11, 2017, from http://clubs.ya.ru/yandexbrowser/ replies.xml?item_no=5105

Bodyansky, E. V., & Rudenko, O. G. (2004). *Artificial neural networks: architecture, training and application*. Kharkov: TELETEH.

Bollen, J., Mao, H., & Zeng, X. (2011). Twitter mood predicts the stock market. *Journal of Computational Science*, *2*(1), 1–8. doi:10.1016/j.jocs.2010.12.007

Borch, K. (1963). *Price movements in the stock market. Econometric research program, research paper no. 7*. Princeton University. doi:10.21236/AD0407934

Bordia, P. & DiFonzo, N. (2005). Psychological motivations in rumor spread. *Rumor mills: The social impact of rumor and legend*, 87-101.

Borisov, V. S. (2007). Self-learning texts classifier in natural language. *Cybernetics and Systems Analysis*, (3): 169–176.

Borowski, C. (2017). *How to prepare for IoT changing customer service.* Retrieved November 15, 2017, from https://www.softwareadvice.com/resources/iot-customer-service/

Bray, T. (2014). *The JavaScript Object Notation (JSON) Data Interchange Format. Request for Comments: 7159, Internet Engineering Task Force.* IETF.

Breiman, L. (2001). Statistical modeling: The two cultures (with comments and a rejoinder by the author). *Statistical Science*, *16*(3), 199–231. doi:10.1214s/1009213726

Bruninx, K. (2016). *Determining the impact of renewable energy on balancing costs, back up costs, grid costs and subsidies*. KU Leuven. Available online at http://www.creg.info/pdf/ARCC/161019-KULeuven.pdf

Bukovina, J. (2016). Social media big data and capital markets – An overview. *Journal of Behavioral and Experimental Finance*, *11*, 18–26. doi:10.1016/j.jbef.2016.06.002

Bunt, A., Carenini, G., & Conati, C. (2007). Adaptive content presentation for the web. In P. Brusilovsky, A. Kobsa, & W. Nejdl (Eds.), Lecture notes in computer science: Vol. 4321. *The adaptive web* (pp. 409–432). Berlin: Springer. doi:10.1007/978-3-540-72079-9_13

Burnstine, D. C. (1980). *BIAIT: an emerging management engineering discipline*. Petersburg, NY: BIAIT Int., Inc.

Caltech. (2017). *Historical Stock Data — Caltech Quantitative Finance Group*. Retrieved October 1, 2017, from http://quant.caltech.edu/historical-stock-data.html

Camerata. (2017). *Nizhny Novgorod Regional Center for Social, Labor and Psychological Rehabilitation of Visually Impaired Persons "Camerata"*. Retrieved March 11, 2017, from http://www.kamerata.org

Carter, J. G., Cavan, G., Connelly, A., Guy, S., Handley, J., & Kazmierczak, A. (2015). Climate change and city: Building capacity for urban adaptation. *Progress in Planning*, *95*, 1–66. doi:10.1016/j.progress.2013.08.001

Carvalho, G., de Matos, D. M., & Rocio, V. (2007). Document retrieval for question answering: a quantitative evaluation of text preprocessing. In *Proceedings of the ACM first Ph. D. workshop in CIKM* (pp. 125-130). ACM. 10.1145/1316874.1316894

CEER. (2016). *Scoping of flexible response, CEER discussion paper*. Ref: C16-FTF-08-04.

Chaffey, D., & Patron, M. (2012). From web analytics to digital marketing optimization: Increasing the commercial value of digital analytics. *Journal of Direct Data and Digital Marketing Practice*, *14*(1), 30–45. doi:10.1057/dddmp.2012.20

Chang, H. H., & Chen, S. W. (2008). The impact of online store environment cues on purchase intention: Trust and perceived risk as a mediator. *Online Information Review*, *32*(6), 818–841. doi:10.1108/14684520810923953

Chang, H. H., & Chen, S. W. (2009). Consumer perception of interface quality, security, and loyalty in electronic commerce. *Information & Management*, *46*(7), 411–417. doi:10.1016/j.im.2009.08.002

Charnes, A., & Cooper, W. (1961). *Management models and industrial applications of linear programming*. New York: Wiley.

Chen, C., Su, X., & Lin, J. (2016). The role of information uncertainty in moving-average technical analysis: A study of individual stock-option issuance in Taiwan. *Finance Research Letters*, *18*, 263–272. doi:10.1016/j.frl.2016.04.026

Chen, V. Y., Lien, H. P., Liu, C. H., Liou, J. J., Tzeng, G. H., & Yang, L. S. (2011). Fuzzy MCDM approach for selecting the best environment-watershed plan. *Applied Soft Computing*, *11*(1), 265–275. doi:10.1016/j.asoc.2009.11.017

Chernyavskaya, V. E. (2013). Linguistics of text. Linguistic of discourse. PH Flinta. (in Russian)

Chisholm, E., & Kolda, T. G. (1999). *New term weighting formulas for the vector space method in information retrieval*. Computer Science and Mathematics Division, Oak Ridge National Laboratory. doi:10.2172/5698

Chugh, S. K. (2015). *Modern Macroeconomics*. MIT Press.

Chusavitina, G. N. (2015). Info safety and problems of preventing the cyber-extremism among youth. In Информационная безопасность и вопросы профилактики киберэкстремизма среди молодёжи [Materials of Intra-U conf.]. St. Tech. Univ.

Clark, E., & Araki, K. (2011). Text normalization in social media: Progress, problems and applications for a pre-processing system of casual English. *Procedia: Social and Behavioral Sciences*, *27*, 2–11. doi:10.1016/j.sbspro.2011.10.577

Conway, M. (2010, April 01). Mining a corpus of biographical texts using keywords. *Literary and Linguistic Computing*, *25*(1), 23–35. doi:10.1093/llc/fqp035

Crédit Industriel et Commercial. (n.d.). Retrieved March 11, 2017, from http://www.cic.fr

Daley, D. J., & Kendall, D. G. (1964). Stochastic Rumors. *Journal of the Institute of Mathematics and Its Applications*, *1*(1), 42–55. doi:10.1093/imamat/1.1.42

Danilova, V. A. (2016). *Influence of Social Networks Language upon Verbal and Witten Speaking of the pupils*. Retrieved from http://rodniki.asu.ru/wp-content/uploads/2016/02/Данилова.pdf (in Russian)

DiFonzo, N., & Bordia, P. (2007). Rumor, gossip and urban legends. *Diogenes*, *54*(1), 19–35. doi:10.1177/0392192107073433

Digital Advertising. (2015). Retrieved October 11, 2017, from https://www.statista.com/statistics/237974/online-advertising-spending-worldwide/

Digital marketing Megatrends. (2017). *Digital marketing Megatrends.* Retrieved November 9, 2017, from https://www.smartinsights.com/managing-digital-marketing/marketing-innovation/digital-marketing-trends-2016-2017/

Ducoffe, R. (1995). How consumers assess the value of advertising. *Journal of Current Issues and Research in Advertising*, *17*(1), 1–18. doi:10.1080/10641734.1995.10505022

Dunlap, R. (1997). The Golden Ratio and Fibonacci Numbers. World Scientific Publishing. doi:10.1142/3595

Eisenstein, J. (2017). Unsupervised Learning for Lexicon-Based Classification. In *Proceedings of the Thirty-First AAAI Conference on Artificial Intelligence* (pp. 3188-3194). Association for the Advancement of Artificial Intelligence.

Eldén, L. (2007). *Matrix Methods in Data Mining and Pattern Recognition*. Philadelphia: Society for Industrial and Applied Mathematics. doi:10.1137/1.9780898718867

Escalante, R., & Odehnal, M. (n.d.). *A deterministic mathematical model for the spread of two rumors*. arXiv:1709.01726

Estrada, E. (2018). *Applications of Networks to Real-World Problems*. Retrieved from http://www.estradalab.org/

Eurelectric (2014). *Flexibility and Aggregation (report)*. Available online at http://www.eurelectric.org/media/115877/tf_balagr_report_final_je_as-2014-030-0026-01-e.pdf

Euroblind. (2017). *The European Blind Union*. Retrieved February 20, 2017, from http://www.euroblind.org

Federal law. (1995). *Federal law of the Russian Federation of 24.11.1995 No. 181-FZ (as amd. on 29.12.2015) "On social protection of the disabled in the Russian Federation"*. Retrieved March 11, 2017, from http://base.garant.ru/10164504

Federal law. (2009). *Federal law of the Russian Federation of February 9, 2009 No. 8-FZ "On ensuring the access to the information about the activity of state agencies and local self-government authorities" (as amended and modified)*. Retrieved March11, 2017, from http://base.garant.ru/194874/#ixzz3wgaEeIRs

Federal law. (2014). *Federal law of the Russian Federation of December 1, 2014 No. 419-FZ "On making amendments to individual legislative acts of the Russian Federation on questions of social protection of the disabled due to ratification of the Convention on the Rights of Persons with Disabilities"*. Retrieved March 11, 2017, from http://www.garant.ru/hotlaw/federal/586929

Feldman, R., & Sanger, J. (2007). *The text mining handbook: advanced approaches in analyzing unstructured data*. Cambridge, UK: Cambridge University Press.

FinPotrebSouz. (2015). *Banks are not too friendly towards physically disabled people: the results of a joint research by FinPotrebSouz and National Agency for Financial Studies*. Retrieved March 11, 2017, from http://finpotrebsouz.ru/novosti

Fishburne, P. S. (1978). *Utility theory for decision making*. Moscow: Nauka.

Fontela, E., & Gabus A. (1976). *The DEMATEL observer.* Academic Press.

Forbes. (2017a). *US Digital Marketing Spend Will Near $120 Billion By 2021.* Retrieved November 9, 2017, from https://www.forbes.com/sites/forrester/2017/01/26/us-digital-marketing-spend-will-near-120-billion-by-2021/ - 401bc054278b

Forbes. (2017b). *Internet of Things Market to Reach $267B by 2020.* Retrieved November 9, 2017, from https://www.forbes.com/sites/louiscolumbus/2017/01/29/internet-of-things-market-to-reach-267b-by-2020/ - 210fc901609b.

Forbes. (2017c). *Internet of Things will revolutionize retail.* Retrieved March 19, 2017, from https://www.forbes.com/sites/louiscolumbus/2017/03/19/internet-of-things-will-revolutionize-retail/#72ee42cc5e58

Forum of Kommunarka settlement. (n.d.). Retrieved from http://new.msk.ru/

Forum of Pushkin Town. (n.d.). Retrieved from https://www.mypushkin.ru/

Forum of the City of Kashira. (n.d.). Retrieved from http://kashira.tv/forum/1

Forum of the City of Podolsk. (n.d.). Retrieved from http://www.informюpodolsk.ru

Forum of the Huajuapan de Leon town. (n.d.). Retrieved from http://foros.utm.mx/

Fukunaga, K. (1990). *Introduction to statistical pattern recognition*. Boston: Academic Press.

Gartner. (2017). Retrieved November 9, 2017, from https://www.gartner.com/newsroom/id/3598917

Gershkoff, A. (2014). *Interview: Amy Gershkoff, Director of Customer Analytics & Insights, eBay on How to Design Custom In-House BI Tools*. Retrieved from https://www.kdnuggets.com/2014/07/interview-amy-gershkoff-ebay-in-house-BI-tools.html

Giovannini, A. (1942). L'errore nelle matematiche. Periodico di Matematiche, 4(22), 57-65.

Go, A., Bhayani, R., & Huang, L. (2009). *Twitter Sentiment Classification using Distant Supervision*. Retrieved September 14, 2017, from http://s3.eddieoz.com/docs/sentiment_analysis/Twitter_Sentiment_Classification_using_Distant_Supervision.pdf

Godes, D., & Silva, J. C. (2012). Sequential and temporal dynamics of online opinion. *Marketing Science*, *31*(3), 448–473. doi:10.1287/mksc.1110.0653

Golovko, V. A. (2001). *Neural networks: education, organization and application*. Moscow: IPRZHR.

Goncharova, I. V., & Pronchev, G. B. (2015). Virtual social environment for people with visual impairments. *Politics & Society*, *5*, 586–590.

Goncharova, I. V., & Pronchev, G. B. (2016). On support of visually impaired people in modern Russian society. *Politics & Society, 11*, 1479–1485.

Goncharova, I. V., Pronchev, G. B., & Krichever, E. I. (2016). On regulatory framework of virtual social networks accessibility for visually impaired people. *Modern Law, 4*, 62–67.

Goncharova, I. V., Pronchev, G. B., Monakhov, D. N., Vasenina, I. V., & Zubova, O. G. (2017). Remote Banking Services for the Visually Impaired in Britain as a Tool for Creating Barrier-Free Environment. *Eurasian Journal of Analytical Chemistry, 12*(7), 1405–1414. doi:10.12973/ejac.2017.00267a

Google Text-to-speech. (2014). *Google speech synthesizer*. Retrieved March 11, 2017, from https://play.google.com/store/apps/details? id=com.google.android.tts&hl=ru

Goroshko & Polyakova. (2015). To assembly of genres typology in Social Media. *Speech Genres, 2*(12), 119-128. Retrieved from http://docplayer.ru/29050008- Internet-zhanry-udk-81-38-bbk-81-e-i-goroshko-t-l-polyakova-harkov-ukraina.html (in Russian)

GOST. (2012). *GOST R 52872-2012. The Internet resources. Requirements for accessibility to the visually impaired persons*. Retrieved March 11, 2017, from http://protect.gost.ru/v.aspx?control=8&baseC=-1&page=0&month=- 1&year=-1&search=&RegNum=1&DocOnPageCount=15&id=176157

Gottschlich, J., & Hinz, O. (2014, March). A decision support system for stock investment recommendations using collective wisdom. *Decision Support Systems, 59*, 52–62. doi:10.1016/j.dss.2013.10.005

GOVUK. (2017). *Financial help if you're disabled*. Retrieved August 20, 2017, from https://www.gov.uk/financial-help- disabled/disability-and-sickness-benefits

Granger, C. W. J. (1969). Investigating Causal Relations by Econometric Models and Cross-spectral Methods. *Econometrica, 37*(3), 424–438. doi:10.2307/1912791

Gregory, J. (2015). *The Internet of Things: revolutionizing the retail industry*. Accenture Strategy.

Groth, S. S., & Muntermann, J. (2011). An intraday market risk management approach based on textual analysis. *Decision Support Systems, 50*(4), 680–691. doi:10.1016/j.dss.2010.08.019

Gubanov, D. A., Novikov, D. A., & Chkhartishvili, A. G. (2010). *Sotsialnye seti modeli informatsionnogo vliyaniya upravleniya i protivoborstva* [Social networks of the model of information influence, management and battle]. Fizmatlit.

Guy, M., & Tonkin, E. (2006). Folksonomies Tidying up Tags? *D-Lib Magazine, 12*(1). Retrieved from https://cyberleninka.ru/article/ n/internet-memy-problema-tipologii

Haddi, E., Liu, X., & Shi, Y. (2013). The role of text pre-processing in sentiment analysis. *Procedia Computer Science, 17*, 26–32. doi:10.1016/j.procs.2013.05.005

Hagenau, M., Liebmann, M., & Neumann, D. (2013). Automated news reading: Stock price prediction based on financial news using context-capturing features. *Decision Support Systems*, *55*(3), 685–697. doi:10.1016/j.dss.2013.02.006

Herman, E., & Chomsky, N. (2006). *A propaganda model*. Media and Cultural Studies.

Hoekstra, J. C., Huizingh, E. K., Bijmolt, T. H., & Krawczyk, A. C. (2015). Providing Information and Enabling Transactions: Which Website Function Is More Important for Success? *Journal of Electronic Commerce Research*, *16*(2), 81–94.

Hori, S., & Shimizu, Y. (1999). Designing methods of human interface for supervisory control systems. *Control Engineering Practice*, *7*(11), 1413–1419. doi:10.1016/S0967-0661(99)00112-4

Houghton, J. T., Meira Filho, L. G., Callander, B. A., Harris, N., Kattenberg, A., & Maskell, K. (Eds.). (1995). *The Science of Climate Change*. Cambridge University Press. Online at https://www.ipcc.ch/ipccreports/sar/wg_I/ipcc_sar_wg_I_full_report.pdf

Huang, P., & Ni, Y. (2017). Board structure and stock price informativeness in terms of moving average rules. *The Quarterly Review of Economics and Finance*, *63*, 161–169. doi:10.1016/j.qref.2016.04.012

HYPO Landesbank Vorarlberg bank. (2017). Retrieved March 11, 2017, from http://www.hypovbg.at

IBM Corporation. (1981). *Business Systems Planning: Information systems planning guide*. GE20-0527-3. IBM Corp.

IBM Institute for Business Value. (2011). *From stretched to strengthened – Insights from the Global Chief Marketing Officer Study*. IBM CMO C-suite Studies.

IBM. (2016). *The Future of Retail is Consumer-Connected and Cognitive*. IBM Report.

IDC. (2014). *The Digital Universe of Opportunities: Rich Data and the increasing Value of the Internet of Things*. Retrieved March 11, 2017, from https://www.emc.com/leadership/ digital-universe/2014iview/index.htm

Ilic, D., Goncalves Da Silva, P., Karnouskos, S., & Griesemer, M. (2013). An energy market for trading electricity in smart grid neighbourhoods. In *Proceedings of 6th IEEE International Conference on Digital Ecosystem Technologies-Complex Environment Engineering (IEEE DEST-CEE)*. IEEE. DOI 10.1109/dest.2012.6227918

Ilvovsky, D., & Chernyak, E. (2014). Systems for automated text processing. Открытые системы. СУБД, 1. Retrieved from https://www. osp.ru/os/2014/01/13039687/

Ivakhnenko, A., & Stepashko, V. (1985). *Noise-immunity modeling*. Kiev: Naukova dumka. (in Russian)

Ives, B., & Learmonth, G. P. (1984). The information system as a competitive weapon. *Communications of the ACM*, *27*(12), 1193–1201. doi:10.1145/2135.2137

Ives, B., & Mason, R. O. (1990). Can information technology revitalize your customer service? *The Executive*, *4*(4), 52–69. doi:10.5465/AME.1990.4277208

Jehle, G. A., & Reny, P. J. (2001). *Advanced microeconomic theory*. Boston: Addison-Wesley.

Joachims, T. (2002). *Learning to classify text using support vector machines: Methods, theory and algorithms*. Kluwer Academic Publishers. doi:10.1007/978-1-4615-0907-3

Johnston, M. R. (2015). *Wonder What Content to Create? Try a Customer-Journey Map*. Retrieved November 9, 2017, from http://contentmarketinginstitute.com/2015/11/customer-journey-map-template/

Jun, Z., Ackerman, M., & Adamic, L. (2007). Expertise networks in online communities: structure and algorithms. In *Proceedings of the 16th Inter. Conference on World Wide Web (WWW '07)*. ACM.

Jung, S., & Qiao, X. (2014). A statistical approach to set classification by feature selection with applications to classification of histopathology images. *Biometrics*, *70*(3), 536–545. doi:10.1111/biom.12164 PMID:24588775

Kaligotla, C., Yücesan, E., & Chick, S. E. (2015). An agent based model of spread of competing rumors through online interactions on social media. In *Proceedings of the 2015 Winter Simulation Conference* (pp. 3985-3996). IEEE Press. 10.1109/WSC.2015.7408553

Karnouskos, S. (2011). Demand side management via prosumer interactions in a smart city energy marketplace. *Proc. of IEEE International Conference on Innovative Smart Grid Technologies (ISGT 2011)*. 10.1109/ISGTEurope.2011.6162818

Kearney, C., & Liu, S. (2014). Textual sentiment in finance: A survey of methods and models. *International Review of Financial Analysis*, *33*, 171–185. doi:10.1016/j.irfa.2014.02.006

Kee, R. (2008). The sufficiency of product and variable costs for production-related decisions when economies of scope are present. *International Journal of Production Economics*, *114*(2), 682–696. doi:10.1016/j.ijpe.2008.03.003

Kneese, A. V., & Sweeney, J. L. (1993). *Handbook of Natural Resource and Energy Economics*. North Holland.

Knyshov, G., Nastenko, I., Kondrashova, N., Nosovets, O., & Pavlov, V. (2014). Combinatorial algorithm for constructing a parametric feature space for the classification of multidimensional models. *Cybernetics and Systems Analysis*, *50*(4), 627–633. doi:10.100710559-014-9651-3

Kolokoltseva, T. N. (2012). Internet communication as new speech formation. In Интернет-коммуникация как новая речевая формация. PH Flinta.

Korshunov, A., Bekoborodov, I., Buzun, N., Avanesov, V., Pastukhov, R., Chikhraze, C., . . . Kuznetsov, S. (2014). Social networks analysis: methods and applications [Анализ социальных сетей: методы и приложения]. In *Transactions of the ISP RAS. Automatics & comp engineering* [Труды ИСП РАН. «Автоматика. Вычислительная техника»] (pp. 439-455). Academic Press. Retrieved from https://cyberleninka.ru/article/n/analiz-sotsialnyh-setey-metody-i-prilozheniya

Kotov, E. M., & Tselykh, A. N. (2004). Formation of info systems and search by similarity [Построение информационных систем и поиск по сходству.Автоматика]. *Вычислительная техника*. Retrieved from https://cyberleninka.ru/article/n/postroenie-informatsionno-poiskovyh-sistem-i-poisk-po-shodstvu

Koziev, E. (2010). *Normalization and lemmatization of the text using the thesaurus*. Retrieved from http://www.solarix.ru/for_developers/docs/text-normalization.shtml

Kreditanstalt für Wiederaufbau. (n.d.). Retrieved March 11, 2017, from http://www.kfw.de

Kubat, M., Holte, R. C., & Matwin, S. (1998). Machine learning for the detection of oil spills in satellite radar images. *Machine Learning*, *30*(2-3), 195–215. doi:10.1023/A:1007452223027

Kumar, R., Balaji, M. S., Sadeque, S., Nguyen, B., & Melevar, T. (2017). Constituents and consequences of smart customer experience in retailing. *Technological Forecasting and Social Change*, *124*, 257–270. doi:10.1016/j.techfore.2016.09.022

Lahat, D., Adali, T., & Jutten, C. (2014). Challenges in Multimodal Data Fusion. *22nd European Signal Processing Conference (EUSIPCO-2014)*, 101-105.

Lamparter, S., Becher, S., & Fischer, J. G. (2010). An agent-based market platform for smart grids, In *Proceedings of the 9th International Conference on Autonomous Agents and Multiagent Systems: Industry track*. Richland, SC: International Foundation for Autonomous Agents and Multiagent Systems.

Learmonth, G. P. (1986). Information system technology can improve customer service. *ACM SIGMIS Database*, *18*(2), 6–10. doi:10.1145/24673.24674

Lee, I. (Ed.). (2017). The Internet of Things in the Modern Business Environment. IGI Global. doi:10.4018/978-1-5225-2104-4

Leeflang, P., Verhoef, P., Dahlström, P., & Freundt, T. (2014). Challenges and solutions for marketing in a digital era. *European Management Journal*, *32*(1), 1–12. doi:10.1016/j.emj.2013.12.001

Lemmatizer in grammar dictionary. (2017). Retrieved from http://www.solarix.ru/for_developers/api/lemmatization.shtml

Lewis, A. (2004). A user survey of the experiences of blind and visually impaired people using electronic information services with regard to the practical implementation of these services in public libraries. MSc Information and Library Studies. The Robert Gordon University. Aberdeen Business School. Department of Information Management.

Lightner, N. (2004). Evaluating e-commerce functionality with a focus on customer service. *Communications of the ACM*, *47*(10), 88–92. doi:10.1145/1022594.1022599

Lim, B., Spanger-Siegfried, E., Burton, I., Malone, E., & Huq, S. (2014). *Adaptation policy frameworks for climate change: developing strategies, policies and measures*. Cambridge, UK: Cambridge University Press.

Lin, C. L., Chen, C. W., & Tzeng, G. H. (2010a). Planning the development strategy for the mobile communication package based on consumers' choice preferences. *Expert Systems with Applications*, *37*(7), 4749–4760. doi:10.1016/j.eswa.2009.11.009

Lin, C. L., Hsieh, M. S., & Tzeng, G. H. (2010b). Evaluating vehicle telematics system by using a novel MCDM techniques with dependence and feedback. *Expert Systems with Applications*, *37*(10), 6723–6736. doi:10.1016/j.eswa.2010.01.014

Lin, C. L., & Tzeng, G. H. (2009). A value-created system of science (technology) park by using DEMATEL. *Expert Systems with Applications*, *36*(6), 9683–9697. doi:10.1016/j.eswa.2008.11.040

Liou, J. J. H., Tzeng, G. H., & Chang, H. C. (2007). Airline safety measurement using a hybrid model. *Journal of Air Transport Management*, *13*(4), 243–249. doi:10.1016/j.jairtraman.2007.04.008

Liu, Z., Wu, Q., Huang, S., & Zhao, H. (2017). Transactive Energy: A Review of State of The Art and Implementation. 2017 IEEE Manchester PowerTech, 1-6.

Lorica, B. (2015). *Six reasons why I recommend scikit-learn*. Retrieved February 14, 2017, from https://www.oreilly.com/ideas/six-reasons-why-i-recommend-scikit-learn

Lukebuehler. (2013). *Source of historical stock data – Stack Overflow*. Retrieved September 16, 2017, from http://stackoverflow.com/a/17263126

Madala, H., & Ivakhnenko, A. (1994). *Inductive learning algorithms for complex systems modeling*. Boca Raton, FL: CRC Press.

Makagonov, P. (2015). Model of the Empirical Distribution Law for Syntactic and Link Words in Perfect Texts. . In Modern Computational Models of Semantic Discovery in Natural Language. IGI Global. doi:10.4018/978-1-4666-8690-8.ch002

Makagonov, P. (2015a). The evaluation of quality of a complex system based on the distribution of links between its objects. In The Modeling and Data Analysis (2015, N°1, pp. 27-40). Academic Press.

Makagonov, P. (2015b). Quality evaluation of texts on geosciences based on linguistic criteria. In X. I. I. Inter (Ed.), Conf. New ideas in Earth Sciences, S-XV, Numerical methods and mathematical modeling (pp. 280–281). Academic Press. Retrieved from https://cloud.mail.ru/public/ Vh7tiAF22PFz/eng.pdf

Makagonov, P. P., Dorado, R. M. V., & Espinoza, C. B. R. (2014). Measure of Mutual Influence among Members of a Social Network. In Modeling and Data Analysis [Моделирование и анализ данных] (2014, N°1, pp. 64-73). Academic Press.

Makagonov, P., Espinosa, S. Z., & Sboychakov, K. (2008). Application of document «search image» from digital library on museum site to simplify disclosing in Internet the document itself. In *XV Jubilee Intern. Conf. «Crimea 2008». — Libraries and Info resources in a contemporary world of science, culture, education and business*. Sudak.

Maki, D. P., & Thompson, M. (1973). *Mathematical Models and Applications*. Englewood Cliffs, NJ: Prentice-Hall.

Mancarella, P. (2017). Power system security assessment of the future National Electricity Market. Report in support of the "Finkel Review".

MARKETO. (2017). *The Marketing Power of the Internet of Things.* Retrieved November 9, 2017, from https://uk.marketo.com/infographics/the-marketing-power-of-the-internet-of-things/

Martins, J., Costa, C., Oliveira, T., Gonçalves, R., & Branco, F. (in press). How smartphone advertising influences consumers' purchase intention. *Journal of Business Research.*

Maruev, S. A. (2006). *A formal theory of labor technological competences and its applications.* PH of the Research Center on quality problems of human resource development. (in Russian)

Maruev, S., Stefanovsky, D., Frolov, A., Troussov, A., & Curry, J. (2014a). Deep Mining of Custom Declarations for Commercial Goods. *Procedia Economics and Finance, 12*, 397–402.

Maruev, S., Stefanovsky, D., Frolov, A., Troussov, A., & Curry, J. (2014b). Multidimensional Networks for Heterogeneous Data Modelling. *Proceedings of the International Conference on Intelligent Information and Engineering Systems INFOS 2014*, 67-77.

Maruev, S., Stefanovsky, D., & Troussov, A. (2015). Semantics of Techno-Social Spaces. In J. Zizka & F. Darena (Eds.), *Modern Computational Models of Semantic Discovery in Natural Language*. IGI Global. doi:10.4018/978-1-4666-8690-8.ch008

Matloff, N. (2017). *Statistical Regression and Classification: From Linear Models to Machine Learning*. Boca Raton, FL: CRC Press.

Mikhailov, A. P., Petrov, A. P., & Proncheva, O. G. (2017). Modeling the effect of political polarization on the outcome of propaganda battle. Computational Mathematics and Information Technologies, 1, 65–81.

Mikhailov, A. P., Petrov, A. P., Marevtseva, N. A., & Tretiakova, I. V. (2014). Development of a Model of Information Dissemination in Society. *Mathematical Models and Computer Simulations*, *6*(5), 535–541. doi:10.1134/S2070048214050093

Mitina, O. V., & Evdokimenko, A. S. (2010). *Methods of text analysis. Methodological cases and program realization* [Методы анализа текста и программная реализация]. Retrieved from https://psibook.com/articles/ metody-analiza-teksta-metodologicheskie-osnovaniya-i-programmnaya-realizatsiya.html

Mohammed, E. A., Far, B. H., & Naugler, C. (2016, April). Applications of the MapReduce programming framework to clinical big data analysis: Current landscape and future trends. *The Journal of Supercomputing*, *72*(4), 1–23.

Moiseev, M. V. (2011). Phraseologisation of precedent-related phenomena of the English Language [Фразеологизация прецедентных феноменов в английском языке]. In Gerald of the Omsk St. U, (2011. N° 3, pp. 262-268). Academic Press.

Moles, A. A. (2008). *Sociodynamics of culture*. PH BCG. (in Russian)

Monakhov, D. N., & Pronchev, G. B. (2015). Network technologies and cloud services as tool of achievement of digital equality among Russian citizens. *Representative power - 21st century: legislation, commentary, problems, 1-2*(136-137), 67-70.

Montemurro, M. (2001). Beyond the Zipf—Mandelbrot law in quantitative linguistics. Physica A 300, Statistical Mechanics and its Applications, 300(3), 567-578.

Moody, G., & Lehman, L. (2009). Predicting acute hypotensive episodes: the10th annual PhysioNet/ Computers in Cardiology Challenge. *Computers in Cardiology, 36*, 541–544. PMID:20842209

Moroslin, P. V. (2009). Internet language as object of linguistic researches [Язык Интернета как объект лингвистических исследований]. In Gerald of the Peoples' Friendship U of Russia (РУДН). Series Linguistics, (2009, No 3, pp. 10-17). Academic Press.

Moser, G., & Robin, M. (2006). Environmental annoyances: An urban-specific threat to quality of life? *Revue Europenne de Psychologie Appliquée – European Review of Applied Psychology, 56*(1), 35–41. doi:10.1016/j.erap.2005.02.010

Mostafa, M. M. (2013). More than words: Social networks' text mining for consumer brand sentiments. *Expert Systems with Applications, 40*(10), 4241–4251. doi:10.1016/j.eswa.2013.01.019

Mount, K., & Reiter, S. (1976). Construction of a continuous utility function for a class of preferences. *Journal of Mathematical Economics, 3*(3), 227–245. doi:10.1016/0304-4068(76)90010-0

Muravyov, V. I., Pronchev, G. B., & Proncheva, N. G. (2013). Modern Internet technologies as an instrument of smoothing the social inequalities in the context of relationship between civil society and government. *Education and the Law, 12*(52), 77–85.

Nastenko, Ie., Pavlov, V., & Nosovets, O. (2014). Modeling of differential diagnosis classifiers of pathological states of the cardiovascular system [in Russian]. *Eastern-European Journal of Enterprise Technologies, 6*(3), 30–35. doi:10.15587/1729-4061.2014.31079

Nastenko, Ie., Pavlov, V., & Nosovets, O. (2014). Synthesis classifiers differential diagnosis of the circulatory systems pathological conditions in a multidimensional space [in Russian]. *Inductive Modeling of Complex Systems, 6*, 105–122.

Nekovee, M., Moreno, Y., Bianconi, G., & Marsili, M. (2007). Theory of Rumor Spreading in Complex Social Networks. *Physica A, 374*(1), 457–470. doi:10.1016/j.physa.2006.07.017

Nelson, T. (1974). Computer Lib/Dream Machines. Self-Published.

Nezhura, E. A. (2012). New types of creolized texts in communicative space of the Internet [Новые типы креолизованных текстов в коммуникативном пространстве интернета]. Language Theory and Intercultural Communication [Теория языка и межкультурная коммуникация], 2, 47-52.

Ning, X., & Karypis, G. (2009). The set classification problem and solution methods. In *Proceedings of SIAM International Conference on Data Mining* (pp. 847-858). Springer. 10.1137/1.9781611972795.73

NIST/SEMATECH. (2016). *e-Handbook of Statistical Methods*. Retrieved December 14, 2016, from http://www.itl.nist.gov/div898/handbook/

Obrnadzor. (2015). *Law of the Federal education and science supervision agency of March 25, 2015 No. 07-675*. Retrieved March 11, 2017, from http://www.obrnadzor.gov.ru/common/upload/doc_list/07-675_pismo.pdf

OLEG. (2017). *The world statistics of the disabled*. Retrieved March 11, 2017, from http://vawilon.ru/statistika-invalidov-v-mire

Osei, G. K., & Thompson, J. W. (1977). The supersession of one rumour by another. *Journal of Applied Probability*, *14*(01), 127–134. doi:10.2307/3213265

Ou Yang, Y. P., Shieh, H. M., Leu, J. D., & Tzeng, G. H. (2008). A novel hybrid MCDM model combined with DEMATEL and ANP with applications. *International Journal of Operations Research*, *5*(3), 160–168.

Pang, B., Lee, L., & Vaithyanathan, S. (2002). Thumbs up?: sentiment classification using machine learning techniques. In *Proceedings of the ACL-02 conference on Empirical methods in natural language processing* (*vol. 10*, pp. 79-86). Academic Press. 10.3115/1118693.1118704

Panteli, M., & Mancarella, P. (2015, May). The Grid: Stronger, Bigger, Smarter? Presenting a conceptual framework of power system resilience. *IEEE Power & Energy Magazine*, *13*(3), 58–66. doi:10.1109/MPE.2015.2397334

Parry, M. L., Canziani, O. F., Palutikof, J. P., Van Der Linden, P. J., & Hanson, C. E. (Eds.). (2007). *Climate Change 2007: Impacts, Adaptation and Vulnerability. Contribution of Working Group II to the Fourth Assessment Report of the Intergovernmental Panel on Climate Change*. Cambridge, UK: Cambridge University Press.

Patel, J., Shah, S., Thakkar, P., & Kotecha, K. (2015). Predicting stock and stock price index movement using trend deterministic data preparation and machine learning techniques. *Expert Systems with Applications*, *42*(1), 259–268. doi:10.1016/j.eswa.2014.07.040

Paulus, T. M. (2007). Online but off-topic: establishing common ground in small learning groups. In *Proceedings of the 8th Inter. Conference on Computer supported Collaborative Learning (CSCL'07)*. Inter. Society of the Learning Sciences. 10.3115/1599600.1599710

Pavlikova, S. K. (2005). *Russian and English precedent sayings: Comparative analysis* [Русские и английские прецедентные высказывания: Сравнительный анализ] (thesis). Москва.

Pervushin. (2013). *Design and working up the program system for graphematic analysis of texts in Russian* [Проектирование и разработка программной системы графематического анализа текстов на русском языке] (Magister thesis).

Peters, I. (2006). Against folksonomies: Indexing blogs and podcasts for corporate knowledge management. *Preparing for Information 2.0. Online Information 2006. Proceedings*, 93-97.

Petrov, A. P., Maslov, A. I., & Tsaplin, N. A. (2016). Modeling Position Selection by Individuals during Information Warfare in Society. *Mathematical Models and Computer Simulations*, *8*(4), 401–408. doi:10.1134/S2070048216040141

Piccoli, G., Spalding, B. R., & Ives, B. (2001). The Customer Resource Life Cycle: A framework for improving customer service through information technology. *The Cornell Hotel and Restaurant Administration Quarterly*, *42*(38), 38–45.

Porter, M. (1985). *Competitive Advantage*. New York: The Free Press.

Potapova, R. K. (2005). New info technologies and linguistics [Новые информационные технологии и лингвистика] (4th ed.). PH KomKniga.

Press, G. (2015, July 20). Turing Award-Winner Stonebraker On The Future Of Taming Big Data Forbes. *Forbes*. Retrieved from https://www.forbes.com/sites/gilpress/2015/07/29/turing-award-winner-stonebraker-on-the-future-of-taming-big-data/2/#64779c7a19a7

Prilutskiy, M. K. (1996). Multicriteria distribution of a uniform resource in hierarchical systems. Avtomatika i telemekhanika, 2, 24-29.

Pronchev, G. B., & Goncharova, I. V. (2016b). The technology of EU Internet resources for people with visual impairments. *Bulletin of the Scientific Conferences, 3*(6), 88-89.

Pronchev, G. B., Monakhov, D. N., Lontsov, V. V. (2013). Virtual Social Mediums Security in the Information Society. *Space and Time, 4*(14), 231-236.

Pronchev, G.B., & Muraviev, V.I. (n.d.). Sotsialnye seti kak faktor perekhoda Rossii k innovatsionnomu razvitiyu [Social networks as a factor of Russia's transition to innovation development]. *Sotsiologhiya* [Sociology], *3*, 36-56.

Pronchev, G. B., & Goncharova, I. V. (2016a). About training of visually impaired people in work with the modern information-communication technologies. *Low and Education*, *5*, 58–64.

Pronchev, G. B., Goncharova, I. V., Elishev, S. O., & Khodakova, N. P. (2017). Accessibility of Virtual Social Environments for the Visually Impaired as a Means for Leveling Out Social Inequality in Russia. *Man in India*, *97*(16), 107–116.

Pronchev, G. B., Monakhov, D. N., & Kovalchuk, V. K. (2016). Contemporary Internet as a Means for Leveling Social Inequality in the Context of Relationships between Civil Society and the State. *International Journal of Environmental and Science Education*, *11*(17), 9959–9967.

Rao, T., & Srivastava, S. (2014). *Twitter sentiment analysis: How to hedge your bets in the stock markets. In State of the Art Applications of Social Network Analysis* (pp. 227–247). Springer.

Rashevsky, N. (1933). Outline of a Physico-mathematical Theory of Excitation and Inhibition. *Protoplasma*, *20*(1), 42–56. doi:10.1007/BF02674811

Rayport, J. F., & Sviokla, J. (1995). *Exploiting the Virtual Value Chain*. Harvard Business Review, November–December.

Rehacomp. (2017). *Institute of Vocational Rehabilitation and Advanced Training of the Personnel of All-Russia public association of the disabled – All-Russia Society for the Blind (winner of the "Red Banner of Labor" award) "REHACOMP"*. Retrieved March11, 2017, from http://www.rehacomp.ru

Reid, C. (1970). *Hilbert: With an appreciation of Hilbert's mathematical work by Hermann Weyl*. Springer-Verlag Berlin Heidelberg. doi:10.1007/978-3-662-28615-9

Richardson, L., & Ruby, S. (2007). *RESTful Web Services*. Sebastopol, CA: O'Reilly.

Rieh, S. Y. (2002). Judgment of information quality and cognitive authority in the Web. *Journal of the American Society for Information Science and Technology*, *53*(2), 145–161. doi:10.1002/asi.10017

Robertson, S. (2004). Understanding inverse document frequency: On theoretical arguments for IDF. *The Journal of Documentation*, *60*(5), 503–520. doi:10.1108/00220410410560582

Romashova, V. (2014). Pragma-stylistic features of Russian corps. Twitter-communication [Прагмастилистические особенности особенности Твиттер-коммуникации Российских корпораций]. In Communicative Studies [Коммуникативные исследования] (2014, N° 2. pp. 134-140). Academic Press.

Royle, J., & Laing, A. (2014). The digital marketing skills gap: Developing a Digital Marketer Model for the communication industries. *International Journal of Information Management*, *34*(2), 65–73. doi:10.1016/j.ijinfomgt.2013.11.008

Rubtsova, Y. V. (2015). Formation of texts corpus for tuning a tone classifier [Построение корпуса текстов для настройки тонового классификатора]. Software & Systems, 1(109).

Ruiz Figueroa, A., & Makagonov, P. P. (2007). Models of hard- and software advance based on the parallel computation study. *Interciencia, 32*(3), 160-166. (in Spanish)

Rusakova, O. F. (2007). Main variations of contemporary political discourse theories: background of classifications [Основные разновидности современных теорий политического дискурса: опыт классификаций]. Sci YB, the Institute of philosophy and law. Ural dept of RAS. —2007.

Ryazantseva, T. I. (2010). Hypertext and e-communication [Гипертекст и электронная коммуникация]. PH BCG (ЛКИ).

Sakr, S., Liu, A., & Fayoumi Ayman, G. (2014). The Family of MapReduce and Large Scale Data Processing Systems. *Journal ACM Computing Surveys, 46*(1). Retrieved July 22, 2014, from https://arxiv.org/pdf/1302.2966.pdf

Salton, G., & McGill, M. J. (1983). *Introduction to Modern Information Retrieval*. McGraw Hill.

Saluki Forum of South Illinois. (n.d.). Retrieved from http://www.salukination.net/forumlist.php

Samarskiy, A. A., & Mikhailov, A. P. (2001). *Principles of Mathematical Modelling: Ideas, Methods, Examples*. CRC Press.

Samorodova-Bogatskaya, L. (2015). Tradition and Innovation: Cyber-Landsgemeinde and Crowdsoursing as Modern Realization of Democratic Technologies. Int. J. of Applied and Fundamental Research, 2.

Samsudin, N., & Bradley, A. (2010). Nearest neighbour group-based classification. *Pattern Recognition*, *43*(10), 3458–3467. doi:10.1016/j.patcog.2010.05.010

Savva, Yu. B., & Davydova, Yu. V. (2015). About slang linguistic analysis problem in the task of automated searching for threats of dope habit dissemination in virtual social networks [О проблеме лингвистического анализа сленга в задаче автоматизированного поиска угроз распространения наркомании в виртуальных социальных сетях]. In Int. sci-tech. conf «Info systems and technologies».

Schumaker, R. P., & Chen, H. (2009). Textual analysis of stock market prediction using breaking financial news: The AZFin text system. *ACM Transactions on Information Systems*, 27.

Sedunov, A. A. (2007). A model of graphematic analysis in the system of natural language processing [Модель графематического анализа в системе обработки естественного языка]. In Gerald of VSU, Series System Analysis & Info Technologies. (2007, N° 2, pp. 69-77). Academic Press.

Seleznev, K., & Vladimirov, A. (2013). Linguistics and text processing [Лингвистика и обработка текстов]. In *Open Systems* [Открытые системы] (2013, N° 04). Retrieved from http://linter.ru/ru/press-center/detail/27/1660/

Shakhnarovich, G., Fisher, J., & Darrell, T. (2002). Face recognition from long-term observations. In *Proceedings of 7th European Conference on Computer Vision* (pp. 851-868). Copenhagen, Denmark: Springer.

Sheehan, K. B. (2014). *Controversies in contemporary advertising* (2nd ed.). Thousand Oaks, CA: Sage Publications.

Shevlyakov, G. L., & Oja, H. (2016). *Robust Correlation: Theory and Applications*. John Wiley & Sons. doi:10.1002/9781119264507

Shivnath Babu, S. (2010). Towards Automatic Optimization of MapReduce Programs Conference. *Proceedings of the 1st ACM Symposium on Cloud Computing*.

Shvedovskiy, V A. (1981). Modelirovanie rasprostraneniya informatsii v smezhnykh sotsialnykh gruppakh [Modeling of the information spreading in adjacent social groups]. *Matematicheskie metody v sotsiologhicheskom issledovanii* [Mathematical methods in sociological research], 207-214.

SIGMOD. (2014). *Proceedings of the 2014 ACM SIGMOD International Conference on Management of Data*. ACM.

Simonov, M., Chicco, G., & Zanetto, G. (2017). Event-Driven Energy Metering - Principles and applications. *IEEE Transactions on Industry Applications*, *53*(4), 3217–3227. doi:10.1109/TIA.2017.2679680

Singhal, A. K. (1997). *Term Weighting Revisite* (Doctoral dissertation). Faculty of the Graduate School of Cornell University.

Sioshansi, F. (2013). *Evolution of Global Electricity Markets. New paradigms, new challenges, new approaches*. Elsevier.

Smetanin, N. (2011). Fuzzy search in text and in a dictionary [Нечёткий поиск в тексте и словаре]. Retrieved from https://habrahabr.ru/users/ntz/topics/

Smirnova, N. S., & Dvoryanchikov, N. V. (2015). Studying manipulative impacts strategies realized by totalitarian sects via Internet network (e-resource) [Исследование манипулятивных стратегий воздействия, реализуемых тоталитарными сектами посредством сети Интернет]. In Psychology & Law [Психология и право] (2015. N° 2.). Academic Press.

Sokolova, M., Japkowicz, N., & Szpakowicz, S. (2006). Beyond accuracy, F-score and ROC: a family of discriminant measures for performance evaluation. In *Australasian Joint Conference on Artificial Intelligence* (pp. 1015-1021). Academic Press. 10.1007/11941439_114

STATISTA. (2016). *Leading global social networks 2016*. Retrieved March 11, 2016, from http://www.statista.com/statistics/272014/global-socialnetworks-ranked-by-number-of-users/

Stepashko, V. (1981). A combinatorial algorithm of the group method of data handling with optimal model scanning scheme. *Soviet Automatic Control*, *14*(3), 24–28.

Stern & Pallickara. (2013). On the role of topology in autonomously coping with failures in content dissemination systems. In *Proceedings of the 2013 ACM Cloud and Autonomic Computing Conference (CAC '13)*. ACM.

Stonebraker, M., & Çetintemel, U. (2005). "One Size Fits All": An Idea Whose Time Has Come and Gone. *21st International Conference on Data Engineering (ICDE'05)*. 10.1109/ICDE.2005.1

Sushko, V. A., Pronchev, G. B., Proncheva, N. G., & Shisharina, E. V. (2016a). Emigration in Modern Russia. *Social Sciences*, *11*, 6436–6439.

Sushko, V. A., Pronchev, G. B., Shisharina, E. V., & Zenkina, O. N. (2016b). Social and Economic Indices of Forming the Quality of Life. *International Journal of Environmental and Science Education*, *11*(18), 10839–10849.

Suvak, A. (2010). Integrated urban development strategies- comparing European and Hungarian approaches. *Review of Landscape Studies*, *3*, 139–146.

Suvorov, K. B. (2013). *Folksonomy as a method of social classifying Web resources* [Фолксономия как метод социальной классификации веб-ресурсов]. Retrieved from http://www.rusnauka.com/6_PNI_2013/Informatica/3_129815.doc.htm

Swiftbic. (2017).*A list of banks of Great Britain*. Retrieved February 20, 2017, from http://www swiftbic.com/banks-in- UNITED-KINGDOM.html

Tan, H., & Gao, Y. (2017). Patch-based principal covariance discriminative learning for image set classification. *IEEE Access: Practical Innovations, Open Solutions*, *5*, 15001–15012. doi:10.1109/ACCESS.2017.2733718

TechNavio. (2017). *Global Digital Marketing Software Market 2015-2019*. Retrieved November 9, 2017, from https://www.technavio.com/report/global-digital-marketing-software-market-2015-2019

Tumasjan, A., Sprenger, T. O., Sandner, P. G., & Welpe, I. M. (2011). Election forecasts with Twitter: How 140 characters reflect the political landscape. *Social Science Computer Review*, *29*(4), 402–418. doi:10.1177/0894439310386557

Tzeng, G. H., Chiang, C. H., & Li, C. W. (2007). Evaluating intertwined effects in e-learning programs: A novel hybrid MCDM model based on factor analysis and DEMATEL. *Expert Systems with Applications*, *32*(4), 1028–1044. doi:10.1016/j.eswa.2006.02.004

UK Government Chief Scientific Adviser. (2014). The Internet of Things: Making the most of the Second Digital Revolution. A report by the UK Government Chief Scientific Adviser.

United Nations. (2006a). *Convention on the Rights of Persons with Disabilities. Resolution 61/106 adopted by the General Assembly of the United Nations on December 13, 2006*. Retrieved March11, 2017, from http://www.un.org/Docs/journal/asp/ ws.asp?m=A/RES/61/106

United Nations. (2006b). *UN Convention on the Rights of the disabled / Adopted by Resolution 61/106 of the General Assembly on December 13, 2006*. Retrieved March11, 2017, from http://www.un.org/ru/documents/decl_conv/ conventions/disability.shtml

Ustalov, D. (2014). NLPub: A Catalogue and a Community for Russian Linguistic Resources. In *Selected Papers of XVI All-Russian Scientific Conference «Digital libraries: Advanced Methods and Technologies, Digital Collections»* (pp. 56-60). CEUR-WS.org. Retrieved from http://ceur-ws.org/Vol-1297/056-60_paper-10.pdf

Van der Veen, R. A. C., & Hakvoort, R. A. (2016). The electricity balancing market: Exploring the design challenge. *Utilities Policy*, *43*, 186–194. doi:10.1016/j.jup.2016.10.008

Vasilkova, V., & Koltsov, A. (2015). Crowd sourcing as a new socio-communicative technology. In *Discussion*. Ekaterinburg: PH Institute of Modern Government Technologies.

Vesnina, I. F., & Maruev, S. A. (2004). Analysing the life cycle of education program on a base of life cycle data for technologies under study. In State Regulating the Economics at Regional Level. Moscow: PH of the All-Russian State Tax Academy (ARSTA). (in Russian)

Voitikova, M., & Khursa, R. (2013). Linear regression modeling of blood pressure data to determine the risk of acute hypotensive episodes [in Russian]. *News of the Academy of Sciences of Belarus*, *1*, 117–122.

Voronin, A. N. (2004). Vector optimization of hierarchical structures. Problems of control and informatics, 6, 26-34. doi:10.1615/JAutomatInfScien.v36.i11.40

Voronin, A. N. (2009). A nonlinear trade-off scheme in multicriteria evaluation and optimization problems. Cybernetics and systems analysis, 4, 106-114.

Voronin, A. N., & Ziatdinov, J. K. (2013). Theory and practice of multi-criteria decision: Models, methods, implementation. Lambert Academic Publishing.

Voronin, A.N. (1999). *Vector optimization of dynamic systems*. Kiev: Tehnika.

Voronin, A. (2017). *Multi-Criteria Decision Making for the Management of Complex Systems*. IGI Global. doi:10.4018/978-1-5225-2509-7

Voronin, A. N. (1999). *Vector optimization of dynamic systems*. Kiev: Tehnika.

Voronin, A. N. (2014). *Multicriteria Decision-Making: Systemic Approach*. Lambert Academic Publishing.

VOS. (2017). *All-Russian Society for the Blind*. Retrieved March11, 2017, from http://www.vos.org.ru

Wade, M. R., & Nevo, S. (2005). Development and Validation of a Perceptual Instrument to Measure E-Commerce Performance. *International Journal of Electronic Commerce*, *10*(2), 123–146.

Wang, B., & Hobbs, B. F. (2014). A flexible ramping product: Can it help real-time dispatch markets approach the stochastic dispatch ideal? *Electric Power Systems Research*, *109*, 128–140. doi:10.1016/j.epsr.2013.12.009

Wang, L., An, H., Xia, X., Liu, X., Sun, X., & Huang, X. (2014). Generating moving average trading rules on the oil futures market with genetic algorithms. *Mathematical Problems in Engineering*.

Wang, R., Guo, H., Davis, L., & Dai, Q. (2012). Covariance discriminative learning: A natural and efficient approach to image set classification. In *Proceedings of Computer Vision and Pattern Recognition* (pp. 2496–2503). Washington, DC: IEEE.

Wang, W., Ozolek, J., Slepčev, D., Lee, A., Cheng, Ch., & Rohde, G. (2011). An optimal transportation approach for nuclear structure-based pathology. *IEEE Transactions on Medical Imaging*, *30*(3), 621–631. doi:10.1109/TMI.2010.2089693 PMID:20977984

Wang, W., Wang, R., Shan, S., & Chen, X. (2017). Discriminative covariance oriented representation learning for face recognition with image sets. In *Proceedings of IEEE Conference on Computer Vision and Pattern Recognition* (pp. 5599-5608). Honolulu, HI: IEEE. 10.1109/CVPR.2017.609

Warner, J. (2011). Next steps in e-government crowdsourcing. In *Proceedings of the 12th Annual International Digital Government Research Conference: Digital Government Innovation in Challenging Times*. ACM.

Web Technology Surveys. (2014). *Usage of traffic analysis tools for websites*. Retrieved November 9, 2017, from http://w3techs.com/technologies/overview/traffic_analysis/all

Weimer, M., & Gurevych, I. (2007). Predicting the Perceived Quality of Web Forum Posts. *Proceedings of the Conference on Recent Advances in Natural Language Processing (RANLP)*, 643-648.

Weisstein, F. L., Song, L., Andersen, P., & Zhu, Y. (2017). Examining impacts of negative reviews and purchase goals on consumer purchase decision. *Journal of Retailing and Consumer Services*, *39*, 201–207. doi:10.1016/j.jretconser.2017.08.015

WHO. (2014). *Visual impairment and blindness.* World Health Organization (WHO). Fact Sheet N 282, August 2014. Retrieved March11, 2017, from http://www.who.int/mediacentre/factsheets/fs282/en

Witten, I. H., Frank, E., & Hall, M. A. (2011). *Data Mining: Practical Machine Learning Tools and Techniques*. Amsterdam: Elsevier.

Wong, F. M. F., Liu, Z., & Chiang, M. (2014). Stock market prediction from WSJ: text mining via sparse matrix factorization. In *2014 IEEE International Conference on Data Mining* (pp. 430-439). IEEE.

World Bank. (2011). *Guide to Adapting to Climate Change in Cities.* Online at https://collaboration.worldbank.org/servlet/JiveServlet/downloadBody/3212-102-1-3497/GuideToClimateChangeAdaptationInCities_102711.pdf

World Bank. (2016). *Climate Action Plan.* Online at https://openknowledge. worldbank. org/handle/10986/24451

Wuthrich, B., Cho, V., Leung, S., Permunetilleke, D., Sankaran, K., & Zhang, J. (1998). Daily stock market forecast from textual web data. In *1998 IEEE International Conference on Systems, Man, and Cybernetics* (vol. 3, pp. 2720-2725). IEEE. 10.1109/ICSMC.1998.725072

Yanagizawa-Drott, D. (2014). Propaganda and Conflict: Evidence from the Rwandan Genocide. *The Quarterly Journal of Economics*, *129*(4), 1947–1994. doi:10.1093/qje/qju020

Ye, Q., Law, R., & Gu, B. (2009). The impact of online user reviews on hotel room sales. *International Journal of Hospitality Management*, *28*(1), 180–182. doi:10.1016/j.ijhm.2008.06.011

Zabara, S., Filimonova, N., & Zelensky, K. (2009). The method of selection signals invariant features [in Russian]. *Reports of the Ukraine's National Academy of Sciences*, *3*, 55–60.

Žižka, J., & Dařena, F. (2015b). Revealing potential changes of significant terms in streams of textual data written in natural languages using windowing and text mining. In *Artificial Intelligence and Natural Language and Information Extraction, Social Media and Web Search FRUCT Conference* (pp. 131-138). Academic Press. 10.1109/AINL-ISMW-FRUCT.2015.7382982

Žižka, J., & Dařena, F. (2015a). Automated Mining of Relevant N-grams in Relation to Predominant Topics of Text Documents. In *International Conference on Text, Speech, and Dialogue* (pp. 461-469). Springer.

About the Contributors

Alexander Troussov is Director of the International Research Laboratory for Mathematical Methods for Social Network Mining at the Russian Presidential Academy of National Economy and Public Administration. Former Chief Scientist of IBM Dublin Center for Advanced Studies (2000-2013), one of the creators of the major IBM linguistic technology LanguageWare, and leader of IBM team participation in the three-year integrated 6th framework EU project NEPOMUK (development of a social semantic desktop), he has published more than 40 peer reviewed journal and conference papers and has 6 patents. His research interests include data mining, natural language engineering, and network theory.

* * *

Stavroula Barbounaki is Lecturer in the Department of Engineering, at the Merchant Maritime Academy of Aspropyrgos, Greece. She holds a diploma in Electrical and Computer Engineering (5-year course) from the National Technical University, Athens Greece, an MSc in Applied Intelligent Engineering (Diplômes d'Etudes Approfondies – DEA, Genie Biomedical) from the Department of Biomechanics and Biomedical Engineering at the Université de Technologie de Compiègne (UTC), France and a Ph.D. in Applied Intelligent Engineering (Doctorat) from the Université Paris V - René Descartes, France, (UFR Biomédicale des Saints Pères). Dr Barbounaki has participated in many international research projects in IS/IT, biomedical engineering, telematics and e-health, intelligent systems, etc., since 1998. She has taught at undergraduate and postgraduate level IS courses at the University of Athens and the Piraeus University of Applied Sciences for over 10 years. Dr Barbounaki's main research interests include intelligent systems, services customisation and recommender systems, fuzzy logic, and business process management. Author of a book in Electromechanics of Biological Fluids, her research has been published in the proceedings of international conferences, journals and edited book chapters. She has been advisor to Greek companies in areas of Data Analytics, Information Systems, Strategic Planning, Intelligent Decisions Support, Process Management and Digital Marketing Analytics.

František Dařena, Ph.D., is a senior lecturer, researcher and head of the NLP and Text Mining group at the Faculty of Business and Economics, Mendel University in Brno, Czech Republic, and a member of International Association of Engineers (IAENG) and SoNet research center. He formerly worked as a senior analyst and developer, participating in the creation of a successful information system for universities in Europe. The research and pedagogical work are concerned with the utilization of information systems and technologies for supporting business activities, intelligent data processing, text mining, sentiment analysis, and opinion mining. He is an author of several publications in international scientific journals, conference proceedings, and monographs, member of editorial boards of international journals, and editor-in-chief of the International Journal in Foundations of Computer Science & Technology.

Oleg Dzikun is postgraduate student of the Russian Academy of National Economy and Public Administration, Russia (RANEPA). His research interests include computational linguistics, natural language processing and information retrieval.

Inna B. Goncharova was born in 1973. She graduated from the Moscow State Pedagogical University (M.S.) in 1995. Inna defended her Ph.D. thesis in pedagogy in 1999. She worked at Moscow State Pedagogical University from 1996 to 2014. Goncharova has been an Associate Professor in the Department of Sociological Research Methodology at the Faculty of Sociology at the Lomonosov Moscow State University since 2014. She is an author of more than 40 scientific publications, including 5 scientific monographs and textbooks.

Stavros D. Kaperonis is Laboratory Teaching Staff (Media, Communication and Administration) in the Department of Communication, Media and Culture at the Panteion University of Social and Political Sciences, Athens, Greece. He holds a BSc (Hons) from the School of Science and Technology, department of Natural Sciences, Hellenic Open University, an MSc in Services Management from the Department of Business Administration at Athens University of Economics and Business and a PhD in Web Design affect (aesthetics) on User behavior from the Department of Public Administration at the Panteion University of Athens-Greece. Dr. Kaperonis has participated in many research projects and he has been teaching at undergraduate and postgraduate programs of Communication, Media, Culture and Design in Greece, since 2015. He has been invited to give guests lectures in Italy and China. Main research interests of Dr. Kaperonis include web design, UX, aesthetics, Atmospherics, Communication management, Social media, new media tools in journalism, strategic information systems planning, services customization, business process modeling and management. His research work has been published in Conferences and chapter of edited book.

Bill Karakostas is the R&D Director of VLTN BBVA, a Belgian SME that develops innovative ICT solutions for the transport and logistics industry. Bill has over thirty years of IT experience in both academia and industry, in Belgium, Greece and the UK. He holds an MSc in Computer Engineering and Informatics, from Patras University, Greece and an MSc (Research) and PhD in Software Engineering, both from UMIST, UK. He has held various academic posts in City University, London, University of Manchester and University of Surrey, UK. He has a broad research track record in areas ranging from software engineering, systems requirements, service engineering and cloud computing. He has developed methodologies and applications for the transport and logistics industry, utilising simulation, AI/knowledge based approaches, Internet of things, Big Data and cloud computing techniques. He is the author/co-author of over 200 papers and of three books on requirements engineering, model-driven software development and service customisation.. He has participated, in various research roles, in over 30 EU funded R&D projects since 1994. He has generated over 1 million euros of research income. He is currently participating in an EU Horizon 2020 funded project that develops technologies to ensure safety in industrial IoT systems. He is an affiliated member of IEEE Computer Society.

Dimitris K. Kardaras is Assistant Professor in Information Systems Management in the Department of Business Administration, at the Athens University of Economics and Business (AUEB), Athens, Greece. He holds a BSc (Hons) in Informatics and a BSc (Hons) in Management both from the Athens University of Economics and Business, an MSc in Information Systems Engineering and a PhD in Information Systems from the Department of Computation at the University of Manchester Institute of Science and Technology (UMIST), England. Dr Kardaras has participated in many research projects in IS/IT since 1990 and he has been teaching at undergraduate and postgraduate level IS courses in the UK and in Greece for over 22 years. Dr Kardaras' main research interests include e-Business and Information Systems Strategic Planning, Services Customisation and Recommender Systems, Fuzzy Logic, and Business Process Management. Author of two books on Service Customization using Web Technologies (2012, Publ. IGI Global, U.S, forwarded by Prof. F. Piller, MIT, USA) with B. Karakostas and on Data management and Business Intelligence (2015 in Greek) with G. Stalidis, his research work has been published in journals (e.g. Expert Systems with applications, Information and Management, International Journal of Information Management, Internet Research, International

Journal of Web based Communities, Information and Software Technology), in chapters of edited books, handbooks of research and conference papers. He is regularly acting as a reviewer to academic journals such as IEEE Transactions on Fuzzy Systems, Information and Management, International Journal of Information Management, International Journal of Information Systems and Management. Dr Kardaras is a member to the steering and scientific committees of international conferences in the area of Information Management. He has been advisor to English and Greek companies in areas of e-Business, Information Systems and Processes Management and Digital Marketing Analytics.

Oleksandra Konoval received her MS on specialty "Informational Managing Systems and Technologies" at the National Technical University of Ukraine "Igor Sikorsky Kyiv Polytechnic Institute" at the Faculty of Biomedical Engineering in 2016. Since October 2016 she has been a PhD student at the National Technical University of Ukraine "Igor Sikorsky Kyiv Polytechnic Institute". Her researches are mostly devoted to set classification problem solution based on GMDH algorithms modifications.

Pavel Makagonov is PhD (technical sciences) from 1978. He is currently a professor researcher of the Russian Academy of National Economy and Public Administration (RANEPA); Russia. Dr. Pavel Makagonov is author of more than 140 scientific publications, including 9 monographs. His research interests include computational linguistics, natural language processing, system analysis and urban computing.

Alexander Mikhailov was born in 1947. He graduated from the secondary school in 1965. Alexander graduated from the Moscow Institute of Physics and Technology (M.S.) in 1971. He was a post-graduate at MIPT in 1971-1974. Mikhailov defended his Ph.D. thesis in physics and mathematics in 1978 and obtain a higher doctoral degree in 1987. He has been worked at Russian Academy of Sciences since 1974 and at Lomonosov State University since 1997. He is an author of more than 200 scientific publications, including 18 scientific monographs and textbooks.

Danila N. Monakhov was born in 1985. He graduated the secondary school in 2002. Danila graduated from the Moscow State Open University named M.A. Sholokhov in 2007. Monakhov defended his Ph.D. thesis in pedagogical science in 2009. Monakhov is senior lecturer of the Department of Sociological Research Methodology at the Faculty of Sociology of Lomonosov Moscow State University since 2012. He is an author of more than 200 scientific publications, including 20 scientific monographs and textbooks.

Ievgen Arnoldovich Nastenko received in 1977 Dipl. Eng., Master degree in Kiev Civil Engineering Institute. 1989 - Ph.D. of biomedical cybernetics. 2008 - D.Sc. of biophysics. 2011 - Leading Scientific Researcher, biophysics. 2011 – 2017 - Head of dept. of biomedical cybernetics of National Technical University of Ukraine "Igor Sikorsky Kyiv Polytechnic Institute". 1989 - 2017 - Head of dept. of Information Technologies and Mathematical Modeling of Physiological Processes of National M. Amosov' Institute of Cardio-Vascular Surgery of National Academy of Medical Sciences of Ukraine. Published 340 papers, including: 16 patents; 136 articles (30 – in foreign journals); 2 chapters in 2 books, 186 abstracts on topic of development and use the statistical and deterministic models in technique, biology and medicine.

Olena Nosovets received her MS in Computer Science from the National Technical University of Ukraine Igor Sikorski Kyiv Polytechnic Institute in 2009. She became the Candidate of Technical Sciences in 2015. Defended the candidate dissertation in the specialty "Models and methods of cardiovascular system condition control in various human body's operating modes". Currently an assistant professor of biomedical cybernetics department of the National Technical University of Ukraine «Igor Sikorski Kyiv Polytechnic Institute». She writes and presents widely on issues of inductive modeling, predicting modeling and causal analysis.

Volodymyr Pavlov was qualified as an engineer at the Kiev Polytechnic Institute (KPI), specializing in Automated Control Systems (1977). Defended the candidate dissertation in the specialty "Automatic control and regulation, technological processes control in the metallurgical industry". He Became the Candidate of Technical Sciences in 1981, worked as a junior researcher, senior researcher at the Kiev Institute of Automation. Currently an assistant professor of biomedical cybernetics department of the National Technical University of Ukraine «Igor Sikorski Kyiv Polytechnic Institute». His research interests and publications are in the field of inductive modeling, pattern recognition, causal analysis.

Jonáš Petrovský is a Ph.D. student at the Faculty of Business and Economics, Mendel University in Brno, Czech Republic. He graduated with a red diploma and his master's thesis has been chosen as a finalist (top 10) in IT SPY 2016 (a competition of IT-related theses in the Czech and Slovak Republic). In his research, he focuses on text mining with a connection to financial markets. He also works as a Python developer at Kiwi.com.

Jan Přichystal, Ph.D., is a senior lecturer, researcher and member of the NLP and Text Mining group at the Faculty of Business and Economics, Mendel University in Brno, Czech Republic. He also works as Business Intelligence analyst and consultant. He is a leader of team developing applications for decision support. The research and pedagogical work are concerned with the databases and technologies for supporting business activities.

Gennadi B. Pronchev was born in 1967. He graduated from the secondary school in 1984 with honors. Gennadi graduated from the Moscow Institute of Physics and Technology (M.S.) in 1990. He worked as visiting scholar at University of Delaware (DE, USA) in 1992-1994. Pronchev defended his Ph.D. thesis in physics and mathematics in 1995. He worked at Russian Academy of Sciences since 1987. Pronchev is Associate Professor, Deputy Head of the Department of Sociological Research Methodology at the Faculty of Sociology of Lomonosov Moscow State University since 2007. He is an author of more than 300 scientific publications, including 28 scientific monographs and textbooks.

Nadezhda G. Proncheva was born in 1967. She graduated from secondary school in 1984 with honors. Nadezhda graduated from the Moscow Institute of Physics and Technology (M.S.) in 1990. Proncheva defended her Ph.D. thesis in physics and mathematics in 1995. She has been worked at Russian Academy of Sciences since 1994. Proncheva is Associate Professor, Deputy Head of the Department of Mathematical modeling and applied mathematics of Moscow Institute of Physics and Technology since 2002. She is an author of more than 80 scientific publications, including 8 scientific monographs and textbooks.

Olga Proncheva was born in 1991. She graduated from the secondary school in 2008 with honors. Olga graduated from the Moscow Institute of Physics and Technology and Russian Academy of National Economy and Public Administration (B.S.) with honors in 2012 and from the same universities (M.S.) in 2014 with honors. At the present time she is postgraduate and junior research associate at Keldysh Institute of Applied Mathematics and an assistant at Moscow Institute of Physics and Technology. Olga is an author of 40 works.

Celia Bertha Reyes Espinoza received her Master of Science degree in Computational and Structural Linguistics from "Mixtec Technological University in Oaxaca; Mexico in 2008. She is currently a full professor researcher of the Mixtec Technological University, author of more than 20 scientific publications. Her research interests include computational linguistics, natural language processing and information retrieval.

Amando Alejandro Ruiz Figueroa is PhD in electronics and computing. He obtained his academic degree with the subject: Analysis of laws and models of hardware and software by the Technological University of Mixteca, Huajuapan de León, Oaxaca, Mexico in 2011. He is currently a full-time research professor at the Institute of Information Technology the University of the Sierra Sur, Miahuatlán, Oaxaca, Mexico. Author of more than 20 scientific publications. He served as Academic Vice-Rector of the Universidad de la Sierra Sur (UNSIS) in Miahuatlán, Oaxaca Mexico and Universidad de la Costa (UNCOS) in Pinotepa Nacional, Oaxaca, Mexico. His areas of research include: computational linguistics, information retrieval and the study of the development of electronics and computing.

Mikhail Simonov received the M.Sc. degree in mathematics from Moscow State University, Moscow, Russia, in 1987, and the Ph.D. degree in electrical engineering from the Politecnico di Milano, Milano, Italy, in 2011. He has multi-disciplinary and cross-sectorial experience in several European industries, service companies, and the finance sector. He has worked in management consultancy, in private industrial companies, and software houses. He was a Project Leader and a Manager for more than 15 years. He has been performing research and development activities since 1999.

Luisa Tibiletti is a Professor of Financial Mathematics at the University of Torino, Italy. Her research concerns problems at the intersection of finance, insurance and economics. Current research topics include: Quantitative Behavioral Finance, Dependence Modelling; Portfolio Selection and Asset Management and Financial markets in general. She has published more than 100 papers in academic journals, including European Journal of Operational Research, Journal of Banking and Finance, Journal of Risk and Insurance, Journal of Derivatives & Hedge Funds, Operations Research Letters, Journal Risk Finance, International Journal of Risk Assessment and Management among others.

Irina V. Vasenina was born in 1955. She has higher economic education. In 1994 she defended thesis in sociology (Ph.D). Working at Lomonosov Moscow State University since 1985 (at the faculty of Economics). Since 1990 is sociology, worked at the Center for sociological researches of Moscow State University. Since 2005 she works at the Department of Sociological Research Methodology at the Faculty of Sociology of Lomonosov Moscow State University in the post of Associate Professor. She is an author of more than 50 scientific publications, including 10 scientific monographs and textbooks.

Albert N. Voronin is a Doctor of Sciences (Eng.), Professor of Chair of Computer Information Technologies of National Aviation University of Ukraine; Member of American Mathematical Society. In 1957 he graduated from the Moscow Power Engineering Institute. His research interests include information technology of multicriteria decision-making, man-machine control systems.

Jan Žižka, CSc., works as Associate Professor at Mendel University in Brno, Czech Republic. He graduated in Computer Science (Technical University in Brno, Czech Republic). At the moment, Jan Žižka is involved in research and teaching of advanced artificial intelligence, machine learning, soft computing, and data and text mining. He has participated in introducing machine-learning/artificial intelligence areas to teaching and research at Czech universities supported by several Czech and European grants. Editor-in-Chief of International Journal of Computer Science & Information Technology, and International Journal of Information Sciences and Techniques, a member of editorial boards and program committees of several other international scientific journals and conferences. He is also an author and co-author of many journal and conference peer-reviewed articles, and co-editor of several books in the area of informatics. Jan Žižka's contemporary main research interests are in the sentiment/opinion semantic-analysis area using very large real-world unstructured textual data in different natural languages as well as in applying data/text-mining to various areas including business intelligence, health care, economy, and others. Jan Žižka worked at universities and research centers in several states/countries in the USA and EU.

Oksana G. Zubova was born in 1979. She graduated from the secondary school in 1996.Oksana graduated from the Astrakhan State University in 2001 with honors. Zubova defended her Ph.D. thesis in political science in 2005. She worked at Astrakhan State University since 2001. Zubova is Associate Professor, senior researcher of the Department of Sociological Research Methodology at the Faculty of Sociology of Lomonosov Moscow State University since 2016. She is an author of more than 50 scientific publications, including 3 scientific monographs and textbooks.

Index

A

architecture 84, 86-87, 93, 95-98, 281-282

B

Balancing and Ancillary Services Market (BASM) 290
balancing services 261-263, 286
barrier-free environment 296, 303-304, 314-315
Big Data 1, 4-5, 29, 36-39, 41-42, 44, 75, 80, 212, 215, 219, 226, 296-297
bigrams 116-117, 119-120, 123

C

Change in Demand (CiD) 265, 291
classification 2-3, 13, 22, 44-54, 62, 66, 68, 70-72, 74-76, 78-80, 83, 85-87, 95-96, 125, 134, 139-144, 150-153, 158-159
classification accuracy 87, 134, 142-144, 158
classifiers 51, 68, 70-74, 76, 80, 85, 88, 95, 98, 125, 139, 141-142, 151-153
close subject matter field 31
cluster kernel 79
COMBI 56, 58, 60, 65, 82
common structure 55-56, 70, 72-74, 80
correlation 8-9, 11, 37, 128, 133, 144, 158, 269
Customer-Centered Smart Grid (CCSG) 273, 291

D

data analytics 211-213, 215, 219, 223, 226-228, 234-236
Day-Ahead Market (DAM) 242, 245, 291
Demand Factor (DF) 253, 291
Demand for Energy (DfE) 253, 291
Demand for Power (DfP) 249, 253, 291
Demand Profile (DP) 254, 291
Demand Response (DR) 291
demand side flexibility 265, 292
Demand-Response Management System (DRMS) 291
Demand-Response Measurement Unit (DMU) 291
DEMATEL 214, 223-224, 231-234, 236
determination 51, 67-68, 79, 89, 102, 104, 107-108, 110-111, 123, 141, 267
digital marketing 211-214, 223, 225-228, 230-232, 234-236
Distribution System Operator (DSO) 291
DOD 123

E

Effective Generation Capacity (EGC) 292
Elasticity of Demand (ED) 292
Electric Consumption (ECkWh) 292
Electric Demand (ED) 292
Electricity Cost (EC$) 292
Electricity Generation (EG) 292
Electricity Generation Capacity 258, 292
Energy Management System (EMS) 249, 292

energy markets 242-245, 259-261, 284, 288, 290
external criterion 53, 56-57, 63, 71-73, 76, 80, 82-83

F

feature space 44-45, 47, 49, 51-52, 62, 69, 76, 78, 80
Flexibility (F) 292
folksonomy 18, 22, 28, 114
forum life cycle 108
forum thesaurus 100, 115, 119, 121

G

generalized variable 63, 71, 82
Generation-Centered Smart Grid (GCSG) 292
GMDH 56, 59-60, 62-63, 71-72, 74, 80, 82-83
Golden Section 112-113, 124
Group Method of Data Handling 54, 56, 83

H

holistic text 104, 111-112, 121
hypertext 6, 114, 119, 121

I

Industrial Control System (ICS) 282, 292
Intraday Market (IM) 245, 292
IoT 211-219, 221-222, 225-228, 230-232, 234-236

L

limited resources 160-161, 164-166, 168, 170, 287
linguistic analysis of texts 7, 14, 23, 42
Linking or Syntactic Word 28, 124
Load Profile (LP) 254, 292
LSMB 59-61, 65, 83

M

machine learning 3-5, 9, 14, 134, 137-139, 150, 153-154, 159, 213, 215, 223, 236
Model of the Optimal Structure 83
model parameters space 71
multicriteria optimization 88, 93, 95, 160, 162, 165, 167

N

natural language processing 137-138, 159
neural network 84-88, 93, 95-96, 98
neurons 84-88, 98
nonlinear compromises scheme 88

P

Partial Description 83
Pattern (P) 292
Pattern of Demand (PoD) 265, 293
Python 141, 148, 150

Q

Quantities Demanded (QDs) 293
Quantity Demanded (QD) 253, 293

R

RAMMA 63, 71, 83
Rate of Change (RoC) 293
Renewable Energy Source (RES) 293

S

SCLS 48-49, 83
SCMLO 48, 83
SCP 48-49, 78, 80, 83
Screening Curve (SC) 293
Service Level Agreement (SLA) 281, 293
set classification problem 44, 48, 54, 76, 80, 83
Set Clustering 78
Small-Scale Actor (SSA) 293
Smart Grid (SG) 250, 293
Smart Meter (SM) 293
social protection 298-299, 303
stemming 15, 25, 28, 117, 138
stock market 126, 128, 159
Stock Markets 128, 154
stock price movements 125, 127-129, 134, 139, 141, 153
Supervised Learning 78-79, 159
System Harmony 124

T

Testing Sample B 83
text documents 14, 137, 139
text mining 137-138, 159
Time of Use (ToU) 251, 255, 258, 293
Traditional Energy Source (TES) 294
Training Sample A 83
Transactive Energy Control (TEC) 259, 294

V

Value Being Modulated (VbM) 265, 294
Virtual Social Environments 298, 301
virtual social networks 1-2, 6, 21
visually impaired people 295, 299-300, 314

Z

Zipf law 111, 124

Premier Reference Source
Emerging GIS Applications for Emergency and Disaster Management

Premier Reference Source
Managerial Strategies and Green Solutions for Project Sustainability

Premier Reference Source
Comparative Approaches to Using R and Python for Statistical Data Analysis

Premier Reference Source
Solutions for High-Touch Communications in a High-Tech World

www.ingramcontent.com/pod-product-compliance
Lightning Source LLC
LaVergne TN
LVHW080602300926
849162LV00005B/1026